G000320279

Buying a property

FRANCE

CADOGANguides

Contents

About the authors

Mark Igoe, whose parents lived in France, has been travel writing for twenty years and been an annual visitor there for twice that. He has three children whose mother is a descendant of the Grand Condé – at least that's what his father-in-law says!

John Howell established John Howell & Co in Sheffield in 1979 and by 1997 it had become one of the largest and most respected law firms in the north of England, employing over 100 lawyers. On moving to London in 1995, John Howell has gone on to specialize in providing legal advice to clients buying property in France, Spain, Italy and Portugal.

Author's acknowledgements

Every book has many authors, they say, and this one is no exception. Apart from a plethora of source works, including those published by the French Government and Chamber of Commerce in London, I should like to thank all those people in France who shared their experience with me, particularly the case studies, most of whom wished to remain anonymous. I am also very grateful for the advice of Neville and Anne Gay, Nick Jones, Jeremy Boyce and many more happy British residents of France. Especially I must thank Sue Elliot for her painstaking and sometimes passionate contributions, some of which I have included verbatim. I owe most to Fay Franklin, my editor, whose knowledge of the subject, calm professionalism and sound advice were indispensable. And not to be forgotten is Rupert Wheeler, whose idea the whole series was in the first place.

Navigator Guides would like to thank Mark Igoe, John Howell for his legal expertise, Fay Franklin for her invaluable help as series editor, Sarah Rianhard-Gardner for design and Yvette Douglas for DTP. And finally to Linda McQueen at Cadogan Guides and Max Adam for taking the decision to publish.

Conceived and produced for Cadogan Guides by
Navigator Guides Ltd., The Old Post Office
Swanton Novers, Melton Constable,
Norfolk, NR24 2AJ
www.navigatorguides.com
postmaster@navigatorguides.com

Cadogan Guides
165 The Broadway, Wimbledon,
London SW19 1NE
info.cadogan@virgin.net
www.cadoganguides.com

The Globe Pequot Press
246 Goose Lane, PO Box 480, Guilford,
Connecticut 06437–0480

Cover and photo essay design by
Sarah Rianhard-Gardner
Cover/photo essay photographs © John Miller
Maps © Cadogan Guides, drawn by Map Creation Ltd
Series Editor: Fay Franklin
Proofreading: Michelle Clark and Jacqueline Chnéour
Indexing: Isobel McLean

Printed in Spain by Mateu Cromo
A catalogue record for this book is available from the British Library
ISBN 1-86011-877-1

Introduction

01

If you have spent a holiday paddling in Breton rock-pools or guzzling *raclette* in a winter Savoyard chalet or lying by a pool in Provence, thinking of lunch, you will have fantasized about living in France. It is a secret British passion. We have had it ever since the English lost the Hundred Years' War and the Gascon wine industry collapsed. With Boney safely marooned on St Helena, we crept back. We built villas in Pau, Biarritz, Hyères, Cannes, Nice, Deauville and Dinard in the Old Queen's time. In the new one's, we have been renovating farm houses in the *argoat* of Brittany, the *bocage* of Normandy and in the dreamy summer afternoons of the Dordogne.

This book is to help you look at the practical side of turning fantasy into stone and terracotta, granite and slate – or at least to encourage more dreams. The fact is that several hundred thousand families – it's difficult to get exact figures – have already done it. There are even some excellent books about doing it. Why do we do it? That question needs a book of its own. One commentator lists the attractions: weather, property prices, health services, transport system, dining out. Perhaps it's something more esoteric: a cocktail of sentiment, taste, scent, and envy.

Buying a property in France has never been easier and has become a huge business; sceptics should visit one of the *French Property News* exhibitions, held throughout the year in several locations, and reflect on the fact that the 80 or so estate agents, financiers and lawyers with stands there are only the tip of an iceberg. Property in France is still cheap by British standards. The reasons for this are simple. France has about the same population as the UK, but with twice the land mass. France has only two major conurbations, neither particularly large. The French do not share the British attitude to home ownership – bricks and mortar – there is no feeling that ownership is inherently more sensible than renting. The net result of all this is that house prices in France increase at very modest rates.

The British are not just buying houses, however. They are buying everything from campsites to vineyards, chalets in ski resorts to studio flats in Paris, town houses in Avignon to cottages in Brittany – we even found a boar farm and a chestnut farm on the books of one estate agent.

This book has been written with the help of a large number of British people who have actually made the move, and some of them have shared their stories and their experience in our case studies. Some of them live permanently in France and have bilingual children, some have bought a property to which they hope to retire, others have a holiday home that they let when they are not using it and some have a *pied à terre* to impress their girlfriends. They all are part of a demographic phenomenon that is becoming a fact of new European life. Thomas Jefferson said 'Every man has two countries, his own and France'; he meant it figuratively, but for many British people it is coming true.

First Steps and Reasons for Buying

02

You may have picked up this book because the idea of living in France has always appealed to you and, although you can't quite see the scenario where dreams become real, you intend to keep them flourishing (there you are in a sunny square, playing *pétanque* with M. le Maire, full of *badinage* and garlic); or your plans may have more immediacy. You may have realized that by selling your house and retiring across the Channel you can make a hefty profit, which will go a long way to plugging the impending hole in your pension. Or you might have worked out that if you invested the money that you presently spend on an expensive annual overseas holiday in a French holiday home, you would not only save money but also have an appreciating asset in France. Or perhaps you have a business idea or a marketable skill that you can transfer to France and your friends have convinced you that the lifestyle is better there. Or maybe the trains, traffic jams, hospital waiting lists, weather and work canteen have just become too much and you want to find a job in France.

In any of those cases, we hope this book will help.

Why France?

Long before Shakespeare extolled *Fair France*, her embarrassment of riches had made her the envy of her neighbours. In that sense, everyone knows 'Why France?' If you are reading this book you may already have your own reasons. Alternatively you might have been told that you have to go and work there.

There are half a million British homeowners in France, with ever-increasing numbers of Americans and other Anglophone folk in their wake. Dutch, Germans and Scandinavians are also on the move; in a demographic wave that resembles the migration from the northeast to southwest USA, Europe is looking south. Spain now has huge expatriate populations on its Mediterranean coast. Italy has had smaller ones for years. Portugal, Cyprus and Greece are in the field and Croatia is catching up fast. But France is in a different league.

It's not just that France has the most diverse geography of all these places; France is a world power and cultural giant, with one of the highest standards of living in Europe. Her greatest buildings are household names; her science and philosophy, language and art are part of the mantle of western civilization. Her tourist boom has been going on for a century already. Not that all these things are unmixed blessings from a potential house-buyer's point of view. France is, for instance, on the same latitude as Canada and Manchuria, and the weather in the north can be wet and cold. France, when compared to the destinations mentioned above, is not cheap. And tell any Frenchman what a wonderful land he lives in and he will tell you that you might disagree if you were paying his taxes.

Words From the Sharp End

One of the best ways to see what British people in France feel about their ex-pat lives is to visit the forums of the English-language French magazines, which give an interesting insight into the actual concerns of British people living in France.

In one case, the first message is from somebody who has just bought a house and land in a rural *département*; he loves it. He made so much profit on the sale of his house in England that he has a year's living expenses in hand. The schools are better, he says; the weather is better, the roads and health service are better. There must be a downside. Can somebody tell him please what it is?

He soon gets a response – the drivers, he is told; the bureaucracy; VAT at 19.6 per cent; French TV; high income tax and social security contributions; the French ignoring European laws they don't like; hunters; the French banking system; many areas being dead in winter; isolation if you are not fluent in the language; and French workmen who never come when promised but often arrive unannounced. He would rather be in the UK, he says, if it had better weather, emptier roads and affordable housing, but it hasn't.

Then a third visitor joins in and asks: since when is it bad for the French to ignore European laws? He points out that those high taxes apply only if you're self-employed. Hospitals are clean, quick and efficient, roads are empty, yearly household bills and rates are lower; there is no road tax, car insurance is less and there is great community spirit. Plus, you can watch a top division football match for ten quid!

Ah, yes, but there's another thing, answers the second respondent: its awful having to live in France because they won the European Cup, the World Cup, the Davis Cup...

There is another side to her geography, of course: the stately Loire and wide Camargue, Alpine snow and Atlantic breakers, bracing St-Malo, basking St-Tropez. And the dividend of wealth is a dazzling infrastructure: trains and roads for the 21st century and a national health service the envy of most. Of course, France has its own social problems, like anywhere else. But it does not have them in greater measure than other developed countries and they can seem very distant from the deep and ancient countryside. The French monster lies not in urban blight but in a gargantuan bureaucracy that can be the terror of native and settler alike. But that, like the direct action which often greets unpopular government policies, is part of the nature of this complex national personality.

France is not for people who want to live in a perpetual holiday resort with things familiar imported to spare them the effort of integration. She is not, like some Mediterranean destinations, a sunny confection of high-rises, olive oil and diesel fumes. France demands, and returns, much more. If you are seriously thinking of buying property there you will already know that. You will know 'Why France?'; and our task is to answer the question 'How?'. This chapter outlines some of the important issues that will be dealt with in more detail later in the book.

Getting There and Getting Around

Travelling to France is easier and cheaper now than ever before. There is a choice of two dozen ferry crossings, long and short, regular and fast. There is the Channel Tunnel, with vehicle transport by Eurotunnel or the passenger service of Eurostar to Paris, Lille or Avignon (summer) and with good connections beyond, and there is air travel from a record number of British airports to a record number of French destinations. Once in France, travelling around is also easy. French motorways are famously good, as is the high-speed TGV rail network. The ordinary trains offer a useful service as well and modern rolling stock is improving it further. French stations are efficient and user-friendly. The general road system is also a welcome change for British drivers, except during the holiday seasons. For details of all of these, *see* **Selecting a Property**, 'Travelling to France', pp.62–75, and 'Travelling Around France', pp.75–7.

Select an Area

You cannot scour the whole of France looking for a property. It is just too big. France is more than four times bigger than England. Those who do not narrow down the scope of their search fairly early on tend to go round and round in ever decreasing circles and never buy a property. No area is perfect. No area has the best climate or the finest beaches or the best food or the cheapest prices or the prettiest girls. It is all a question of personal preference. Yet there is, behind it all, a logical process of selection that, if used sensibly, can help you choose an area – or, more likely, eliminate others.

This process is explained in 'Where in France', p.17.

Make a Preliminary Selection of a Type of Property

This is not always as obvious as you might first think. Once again the application of common sense and logic can help form your decision but, mercifully, the human spirit often ignores such considerations. If you, or your spouse, falls in love with an abandoned water mill in the middle of the countryside whereas reason tells you that you ought to be looking for an apartment near an airport you will probably buy the water mill. And you will probably enjoy it.

This does not mean, however, that it isn't worth spending a little time thinking about the type of property that would suit you best *before* you travel to France to look at buildings. Buying an inappropriate type of property can prove very expensive and, worse still, can put you off the whole idea of a property abroad.

As well as helping you to focus your ideas, thinking about these issues will help you give any estate agents a clear brief as to what you are looking for. This will help them help you and avoid your time being wasted by them showing you totally inappropriate properties. Always discuss your requirements with the local agents who are helping you find a property rather than dictate those requirements to them. They may well say that what you are asking for is not obtainable in their area – but that something very similar is, and at reasonable cost.

Do not be afraid to change your mind. It is quite common for people to start off looking at cottages for restoration and to end up deciding that, for them, a new property is a better bet. Or, of course, the other way round. If you do change your mind you *must* tell the estate agents you are working with. Better still, you should be discussing your developing views with them and getting their confirmation that what you want is 'do-able'.

Fix a Budget

Fix a budget for the operation. What is the maximum that you are prepared to spend to end up with a house ready to live in? Include the cost of purchase, any essential repairs or improvements and the taxes and fees payable.

If you are buying a new property or one that does not need major repair this is simpler. The taxes and fees involved on acquisition of the property usually amount to about 9 per cent of the purchase price, so the overall cost is easy to work out.

If you are buying a house in need of repair fixing a budget is clearly more difficult. You will always under estimate the cost of the repairs. No job ever finishes exactly on budget! That is as true in France as it is in England. Buyers, however, create a rod for their own backs by their unrealistic costings. Often the extent of repairs needed goes far beyond what is obvious. It is just as expensive to repair a roof or rewire in France as it is in Dorset. *If you are buying a property that needs major work do not commit yourself until you have had a survey and builders estimates for the work shown to be necessary.* If you are told that there is no time for this and that you will lose the property if you can't sign today/this week/before Easter, walk away.

Case Study: Assess Yourself

Frank and Liz bought a property in the northern Dordogne a couple of years ago, choosing the Bussiere-Badil area because they had friends nearby, and because they liked it. The cost was £42,000 and they did not need a mortgage. Although habitable when they bought it – one of the attractions – the house needed a fair amount of renovation work, such as converting the attic into a bathroom and replacing floors that were affected by dry rot. They find they are doing most of the work themselves because of the difficulty of arranging for local artisans to visit during the short periods they are able to spend there at the moment, which amounts to about six weeks a year. They haven't yet been assessed for *taxe d'habitation* but pay about *£45 taxe foncière*.

Frank advises, 'When looking at houses, don't just assess them – assess yourself too. Be honest with yourself about you and your family's needs, what you can manage financially and what time you have available. It's simply depressing to buy a beautiful old farmhouse for holidays but never have a restful time in it because there's always pressing maintenance and repair work to be done – or to get done by someone else, which can be difficult to arrange. All this can add to the stress that you're possibly trying to escape in the UK. When looking at houses I think it's important to keep a balance between head and heart.'

Unless you are in the happy position that money is no object, do not exceed your budget. It is too easy, after a good lunch and in the company of a silver-tongued estate agent, to throw your financial plans to the wind. 'Only another £30,000' is a statement you may later come to regret.

Which Property is Right for You?

In the end, the choice of location and type of property is down to personal preference. You are probably buying a home in France because you have been reasonably successful in life. One of the rewards of such success should be the ability to do as you please. It is too easy to forget, as you become immersed in the detailed planning for the purchase, that this whole exercise is supposed to be fun. If you want to throw reason to the wind and buy the house of your dreams there is nothing wrong with doing so – provided you understand that this is what you are doing. After all, who really needs a castle or chateau? Do your research. The time spent will be fun and amply repaid.

A Second Home

A large proportion of British buyers are looking for a second home, rather than a place to live permanently. Often this turns into a retirement home in due course. You won't have to worry about a *carte de séjour* (*see* pp.25–7) until then, if ever, because the European legislation is in the process of changing.

The best place to start is with property magazines and exhibitions. *Living France*, *French Magazine* and *France* magazine are all available from major newsagents or on subscription, while *French Property News* is subscription-only. For the main property exhibition organizers, *see* p.105. Or you could, if you have the money and time, just drive around France until you see something you like.

The great thing about a holiday home as opposed to a first home is that it doesn't have to be built or renovated for immediate occupation and you can work on it over several years, especially if it's not too far away. A large proportion of British house-hunters buy and restore derelict or rundown properties, usually because the prices seem very attractive (*see* pp.83–8). This has the advantage of absorbing your investment over a period of time rather than in one lump. But the disadvantage of taking years to renovate a property is that it cannot produce any income for you, and many people like to offset their expenses by letting. You will, after all, have local taxes to pay (*see* p.182), not to mention utilities bills (*see* p.229). There is also the problem of who is going to look after it when you are not there. And, as in the UK, your insurance company may insist on mortise locks on the external doors and lockable shutters or grills. A way of dealing with the problem of long absence is to invest in a development called a *copropriété* (*see* pp.148–9), where the owners share all the services and security collectively, most commonly in an apartment block but also in holiday areas where the shared facilities may range from a swimming pool to a golf course.

This brings us to the next thing to consider – where should your holiday home be? That depends primarily how long your holidays are. If they are school holiday length, you have the whole of France to choose from. If they are long weekend length, you will need to have easy access. And that brings you straight on to cost. A flat in Nice might be very easy to get to but it could cost you as much as a mansion in Charente and you cannot always guarantee that a cheap flight will be available. Indeed, when you are looking at easy access, remember that airline schedules are subject to change – that cheap flight might be axed next year. Then again, your own motivation for buying a second home is important. If it's to escape the British weather, don't choose Brittany, go south.

Do You Want to Let the Property?

There are two types of people who decide to rent out their home in France. There are those who see the property as mainly, or even exclusively, an investment proposition and there are those who are buying what is, predominantly, a holiday home but who wish to cover all or part of the cost of ownership from rental income.

For the first group this is a business. Just as in any business, the decisions they take about where and what to buy, how to restore the property and what facilities to provide will be governed by the wish to maximise profit.

The second group will have to bear in mind most of the same considerations, but will be prepared to compromise (and so reduce potential income) in order to maximise their enjoyment of the property as a holiday home. Just where they draw the line will be determined by their need to produce income from the property. Many buyers will simply allow their family and a few close friends to use the property. They will let it for, perhaps, 10 or 12 weeks per year and will cover their basic expenses such as local taxes, water, electricity etc from the proceeds. Others will bring in outsiders and, perhaps, let for 20 weeks per year. They will perhaps produce enough to cover these expenses and the interest on a modest mortgage. Some will be prepared to rule out use of the property themselves during the prime rental months of July and August. Others, especially those with children of school age, will sacrifice a large part of their potential rental income by using the place themselves during those months.

Whichever group you fall in, you are most unlikely to cover all of your expenses and both capital and interest repayments on a large mortgage from letting your property, however efficiently you do so.

The issues arising out of renting your property and the likely returns to be obtained are covered in **Letting Your Property**. At this point I simply want to stress that the choice of the location for your property and the type of property you buy will have a huge impact on the income you will derive from it. Whichever group you fall into you will have to think of the needs and desires of those renting the property as well as your own needs and wishes.

A First Home

A first home – or a second home that may become a first home – involves a different range of criteria. Your pocket, profession (if you still have one) and family will all come into the equation. For what sort of property you can get for what price *see* 'How Much, For What and Where?', pp.83–8. And for whether it is conducive to gardening, skiing or snorkelling *see* pp.80–2. The range of places you can pick is much greater for the permanent house- rather than the holiday home-hunter because you do not have to worry about access times. But you do have to confront a wide range of other issues, such as proximity to shops, employment if you have a job or plan to, schools if you have kids, and a doctor or hospital if you are older, all of which are considered in **Settling In**.

An Investment

If you want to speculate in the property market you will probably do better in Britain than in France, which historically has a housing price rise of about 5 per cent per annum. Having said that, house prices are rising in parts of France, sometimes at a phenomenal rate, and largely because of foreign interest. The Dutch and Germans, as well as the British, have inflated the market in several well-publicized areas. The Côte d'Azur is the most famous, and still basks in a boom that started in the 1830s. Provence has benefited from this and from a migration of high-tech industries, which have come from northern Europe and brought their personnel, pushing prices up. Like a tidal wave from the Mediterranean, the hardening market has rushed westward along the coast to Languedoc and up the Rhône Valley to lap at the foothills of the Alps and the Massif Central. The trick is to get into it before the wave breaks.

British interest in the Dordogne became newsworthy in the heady 1980s, and house prices rose by 40 per cent and are still higher than the national average. Here, a medium-sized period farmhouse can fetch £250,000. The attraction, apart from pretty countryside and a big British community, is a temperate climate, without the extreme cold of the interior or the heat of the south. A spillover has affected the neighbouring departments of Lot, Lot-et-Garonne and Charente. This, of course, is the problem for the investor: what area will be affected next? Prices around ski resorts have their own micro-market. At the moment the northern and southern Alps have the main concentration but there is another crop in the Pyrenees. The Auvergne in the Massif Central, where there are also a few stations, has the cheapest property in France.

Factors that are currently motivating the market are developments in the transport infrastructure. The ever-extending TGV network and expanding budget airline destinations are putting places that were several days' drive from England within easy reach. Markets such as Burgundy have come into focus, where a habitable three-bedroom holiday home can be got for £40,000, and an entire village for under £4 million. Of course, you can get the transport prognoses wrong – many people thought that the completion of the Channel Tunnel would lead to a boom in the market in the Pas-de-Calais, but it never really materialized.

For information on Capital Gains Tax, *see* **Financial Implications**.

Investment Potential

The British view property as an investment as well as a home. We expect our house to rise in value, if not year by year, at least over time. Until recently this was not really a consideration for the French. As a result there has been a perception that property in France does not increase in value – or, at least, not to any significant extent.

That perception is false.

There is a grain of truth in relation to some very rural areas where there is still a lot of property left over after the massive depopulation of the twentieth century. In 1914, 80 per cent of the French lived in the countryside. It is now less than 20 per cent. The thousands of rural homes they abandoned in their flight to the city and large towns lay empty for many years. This depressed rural property prices. Even in these areas, especially where property has 'sold out', there have been increases in value. A cottage in Normandy bought for £10,000 in 1990 might well be worth £40,000 today.

In popular areas – and, in particular, in popular tourist areas – there have been large amounts of property inflation. Fortunately, we do not need to speculate about this. The French government keeps statistics through its Land Registry system.

Estate Agents

Any option will put you in touch with the French property market, including estate agents. The first question is, should you use estate agents at all? The French use them much less than is common in Britain. If you look at our arguments in **Selecting a Property** you will see that, for most people, we say, on balance, yes, you should. French property law is so different from that in England, Scotland and Ireland that you probably need more help than just the *notaire*. The *notaire* is a lawyer who represents both parties in a property transaction (for the details of how this works, *see* **Making the Purchase**). If you have experience of dealing in property in France, or any other country in western Europe, you might be able to manage with just the *notaire*, as most French do, but, if your purchase is a complicated one, it is a good idea to have an estate agent who understands the British market as well as the French, so that they are clear about how different the systems are and what the differences mean for you.

For more on estate agents and other ways of finding a property, *see* **Selecting a Property**.

Where in France?

Having decided to buy a house in France, the most fundamental decision to make is whereabouts you want to buy. It's twice the size of mainland Britain and offers a choice of mountains, plains, gorges, beaches, cliffs, marshes, forests and fields. And those fields may be full of mustard, olives, wheat, barley, vines, orchards, sunflowers, tobacco, maize, cows or even ostriches. The rooves of your local village may be of slate against a western gale, low-pitched to trap the alpine snow or a red terracotta armour against the southern sun. Your town may have ancient walls or a Gothic cathedral, a Roman temple or a 19th-century casino. In other words, there is quite a lot of choice. Do you want the sea and sand of the west, the winter sports of the east, the proximity of the north, the chic and sun of the south or the Dordogne because you have friends living there? Here is a quick résumé but, for a closer look, *see* **Where in France: Profiles of the Regions**.

The North

The north of France is the nearest to Britain, but what other advantages does it have? Certainly not the weather, although that is marginally better than most places in the UK. The northeast is a strategic choice, at the north European communications crossroads, within easy reach of Holland, Belgium, Germany and Luxembourg. Despite the great sprawl of Lille, there is some pretty countryside and some fine provincial towns. Even central Lille is much admired for its architecture and shopping. Normandy is famous for its coastal resorts, deep, lush green countryside and its history, which has often been entwined with Britain's. It also has some big industry. It has all the advantages of the real French landscape without being too far from either England or Paris. It offers golf, water sports and rich food. Brittany is France's Celtic fringe, with distinctive traditional music, a coastline of cliffs and beaches and a taste for seafood, cider and pancakes. Like Normandy, it has been popular with the British for generations but has a slightly less sophisticated persona. (*See also* pp.38–41.)

The East

France's eastern border starts with Flanders, gentle in topography if not history. It then rises along a series of hills and mountains, which get ever more dramatic until they culminate in Europe's highest peak. First there are the modest Ardennes, with their pine forests and trout streams, overlooking the rich rolling fields of Champagne and the Marne. Next come the Vosges, high enough to produce ski stations in winter, followed to the south by the charming Jura range with its views of the snow-capped Alps. These eastern marches have been a corridor for armies since the Roman times, but that hasn't stopped them producing some of the most creative people, finest wines, most attractive towns and prettiest countryside in France. As France faces Switzerland over Lake Geneva or Lac Leman, the border turns east and carves a mountain fief out of the ancient kingdom of Savoy, now the domain of winter sports fans, ski lifts, holiday chalets and fondues. It is here that most British people have paid attention to the east, as interest in skiing has snowballed in the UK since the 1960s. These resorts of the Northern Alps, as the French call them, are flanked by those of the Southern Alps, which spill over into Provence and, eventually, plunge into the Mediterranean at Menton. To the west of the mountains runs the Saône–Rhône river valley system, famous for its historic cities – Lyon, Valence, Orange and Avignon – for its wine, gastronomy, nougat and the Mistral. (*See also* pp.41–3.)

The South

At times the Mistral blows down the Rhône and torments Provence, even keeping some of the yachts in the fashionable harbours of the Côte d'Azur from setting out to sea. Here we reach the land of legends, Fauvist painters, chic boutiques and seafronts of expensive apartments, art galleries and casinos. But it is also Provence, the older Provence of rugged mountains, cicadas, rosemary and *bouillabaisse*, of Jean de Florette and, now, of Peter Mayle. There are British buyers in both worlds, but those seeking the coast may be paying some of the highest prices in France. Moving towards the Rhône, prices become more reasonable with the cities of Toulon and Marseille, more picaresque than picturesque. Then we cross into Languedoc, which stretches to the Pyrenees. The Rhône delta offers the famous Camargue, with its wild horses and cowboys; the high Pyrenees have sombre forests and ski resorts. In between lie in profusion vineyards, fishing villages, walled cities, art galleries, *villages perchés*, sandy beaches, Roman remains, orchards, seaside resorts and every sort of sporting facility you can imagine. This is becoming a very popular area with northern immigrants, whether in the highlands of the Cevennes or the foothills of the Pyrenees, and Hérault, the third department going west, is reckoned by a recent French newspaper survey to be the most desirable place to live in France. (*See also* pp.44–8.)

The Southwest

The British, over the last few years, have particularly selected the southwest, specifically the *départements* of Dordogne, Lot, Lot-et-Garonne and Charente (in the Poitou-Charentes region). The reasons for this are not hard to see. Dordogne has gorges, vineyards and arcaded market towns. It has a climate that does not bring with it the searing heat of the south, nor the snow of the mountains. To a greater or lesser degree the adjoining départements share its advantages, although not necessarily its property prices. There is much more to Aquitaine, as the region is called, than that. Around the biggest estuary in Europe lie some of the world's most famous vineyards and on it stands historic Bordeaux. To the south lie the Continent's finest surfing beaches, on which can be found its highest sand dune, and, behind that, its largest planted pine forest. To the east of Aquitaine lies the region of Midi-Pyrénées with its twin highlands of the Pyrenees themselves and the limestone plateau of the Massif Central. In between is a broad valley dominated by high-tech Toulouse. Around it are other pleasant and more user-friendly towns: Albi, famous for its medieval character and because it gave its name to the Albigensians; Montauban for its Place National, the original for the bastide towns of the south; Moissac for its abbey; Agen for its plums. British house-hunters are now discovering all these delights. (*See also* pp.48–52.)

The Centre

Central France, which historically has not received so much attention from British house-buyers, is now becoming more popular. Paris was always considered too expensive until, in recent years, the exchange rate moved in sterling's favour. Most Parisians themselves rent apartments, which means the property market has been a little restricted, but now there is interest. Luxuriant Burgundy, with its wines, Charolais cattle, blackcurrants and mustard fields, is widely tipped to be the next focus of attention and it does seem to have a combination of factors – weather, position and countryside – in its favour. The Loire Valley has been longer established as a second- or first-home centre for expatriates. Here stand Angers, Saumur, Tours, Blois and Orléans, august cities beside that most majestic of rivers. And the Loire means châteaux: Chenonceau, Chambord, Amboise, Azay-le-Rideau, haughty names that are only the most familiar of hundreds. It is also supposed to be the climatic dividing line between northern France and the warmer south. At the heart of France are bucolic Limousin and Auvergne. Neither is popular yet with the British market but, especially in the case of Limousin, this is changing. Both are very beautiful regions, although inclined to be cool in winter – in the case of the Auvergne, ski-station cold. (*See also* pp.52–6.)

The West

The west coast, from Brittany to Aquitaine, is married to the Atlantic and the names of its towns even sound like the breakers: St-Nazaire, Sables d'Olonne, La Rochelle, Rochefort. La Rochelle sent out the men who named St Louis,

Louisville, Baton Rouge and New Orleans, while others took their Huguenot faith south, to people South African rugby teams with names like du Toit, de Villiers, du Plessis and Marais. *Marais* means marsh, and marshes are a distinctive feature of the coast, the most famous being the fascinating Marais Poitevin in the south. The productive farmlands behind them have been a target for British home-buyers, especially in the department of Charente in Poitou-Charentes, but the coast, with its watersports and many sandy beaches, is also a great attraction. Summertime offers all the advantages of the Gulf Stream and a warmth that earns Maine-et-Loire the title of Garden of France and prompts some writers to compare the Vendée with the Spanish *costas*. (*See also* pp.56–9.)

Corsica

Napoleon's birthplace has an unspoiled interior and a coast of rugged cliffs, sandy coves and deep clear water. Mild in winter and hot in summer, it is mountainous, wild and romantic. A big favourite with Italian second home-owners, it has never attracted many British, presumably because politics are a little more volatile than the mainland and because it is a further away and with no direct air links. (*See also* pp.59–60.)

Living in France

Just as borders between countries are becoming blurred, so are those between the designations of how and where you live. Today many people can work from home, and home can be in another country from the office. It's also becoming increasingly easy for people to commute from one country to another. Despite the efforts of lawmakers and tax inspectors, traditional restrictions are becoming increasingly flexible. But, unless you are among this growing population of indefinables, if you are going to be full-time retired or planning to have a job or start a business in France, there is a range of circumstances you will have to confront, all rather different from those you may be used to in the UK.

Retirement

Retiring to France has many attractions because the downsides of French life are more associated with working life. Age, like education and food, has a higher status in France than in Britain; that children must support elderly parents by law is an indication of this. French weather isn't always warmer but in many places it is, and the winters are shorter anyway. And, if you are a householder, the difference in the value of your house and its equivalent in

Case Study: Making Retirement Work

At the age of 56, and facing redundancy, Peter and Sheila bought some French magazines and realized that the equity from the sale of their English house would be sufficient to purchase a French one and have enough left over to invest for income. The Dordogne appealed to them because it was far enough south to escape the northern winter and had a British ex-pat community. They stayed in a *gîte* while house-hunting, found a very helpful estate agent and got a temporary *carte de séjour* from their *préfecture*, where the staff spoke English. They advise:

'If either of you is retired, as soon as possible before leaving the UK, obtain and complete form POD 708 from the Department of Social Security in Newcastle-upon-Tyne. This form will enable your state pension to be paid into a French or UK bank. This will then instigate your E121 being issued – this entitles you to French state health care, but, be warned that it only pays back a percentage of what you will have had to pay in advance (private health care insurance tops up the rest). In the meantime, bring an E111 with you, obtainable from any UK post office. When you finally receive your E121 from the UK, take it (with copies) to the local CPAM (*Caisse Primaire d'Assurance Maladie*), which will then issue a temporary *Numéro de Sécurité Sociale*. This number must be written on all forms from your doctor and/or pharmacy in order to reclaim monies paid. This will eventually be replaced with a permanent number on a Green Card (*Carte Vitale*) that can take up to six months to be issued (still awaiting ours). They will also need details of your bank for reimbursement of payments.

'Finally, we have found virtually everyone to be extremely helpful and friendly. It certainly helps to be able to *parler* a little of the language and the French seem to appreciate the fact that one tries. We have found attending French lessons to be very useful, both for the language and for swapping experiences with fellow ex-pats, also for making new friends. We certainly cannot think of any reason to want to return to the turmoil and traffic of the UK.'

France probably creates an immediate profit. There is no problem in having your pension paid in France, and if you can contrive to qualify for a French pension then so much the better. The health system is more efficient and the population longer-lived. Yet sometimes ex-pat retirement doesn't work: when this is the case it is usually because of the difficulties of adapting to a strange environment in later years. These are discussed in detail in **Settling In**.

Working in France

If you want to work, there is nothing to stop you, provided, of course, that you can get a job. Casual and seasonal jobs don't even need a *carte de séjour* (the French residence permit, issued to all those living in the country for more than three months) and there is usually work to be found in the resorts, big cities and vineyards in the appropriate season – as a one-time waiter in Paris called Tony Blair will tell you. For anything more permanent you should have your *carte*; apart from anything else you can't make full use of France's very generous social services until you do. Apart from the fact that public services are very much better, the mechanics from then on are much the same as in the UK. To help you find a job there are government employment offices called ANPE, there are private recruitment agencies and there is the press, the Internet and a number of international organizations. For serious employment you will need to speak French and, if you have a *carte de séjour*, ANPE will organize free lessons. Working conditions are, on the whole, better in France; there is a 35-hour week and 72 per cent of the workforce take more than 5 weeks' holiday a year, compared with 22 per cent in Britain. Nor is there anything to stop you being self-employed in France if you register with the appropriate authority. (*See* 'Working and Employment', pp.220–4.)

Running a Business

British people do start and run successful businesses in France, but many are unprepared for the challenge they encounter. It is not sensible to consider setting up any sort of business in France unless you or your partner or associates are pretty competent French-speakers(*see* below). The whole business environment and ethos are different, too. There is a huge and unwieldy civil service, which British people are not used to dealing with, very heavy social security contributions and competitors who not only know the ropes but also are happy with profit margins much narrower than people in the UK would expect. As if by way of compensation for all that, there are tax breaks and finance available for small businesses in certain areas – especially for farmers under 40 years old, whom the French government is trying to attract to, and keep on, the land. France is a country of small businesses and the countryside holds a sort of mythic place in the French psyche. It is because of this that there are few hard feelings when British people with spare money disappear into it and renovate barns and derelict farmhouses. (*See* 'Self-employment', pp.221–4.)

Learning the Language

French is one of the Romance languages, a descendant of Latin with an astonishingly rich and ancient literature that dates back a thousand years. It is the language of northern France and has taken over from many provincial languages and dialects as the French Kingdom expanded, picking up loan words on the way. From Frankish it borrowed *marais* (a marsh), from Breton

Words From the Sharp End

The forum of one of the French property magazines' website has an entertaining and enlightening exchange between some children who are about to be taken to France and some who are already there.

'What are the schools really like?', asks one concerned 11-year-old, 'what are the school dinners like?'; (note the mature sense of priorities); and 'what are the French kids and teachers like?' In a few days the responses come in. School is fine, they say. Lunch, all agree, is good although you have to eat it all, even the cheese – yeugh – but you can give that to the French kids. French kids are fine, too, except one or two who are 'nationalistic', and the teachers are OK but they don't praise you very much. You will learn French very quickly, they say, and the younger you are the better, but it's best to have the basics before you go, so that you can ask for things like an exercise book or a new pen. They praise a sense of freedom in the French countryside that they did not experience at home. And they agree on one thing that is exactly the same in France – little sisters are still a pain.

bijou (a jewel) and, from Occitan, *bouillabaisse* (a fish soup). In the 15th century it became a European international language and held the position of international diplomatic language until the 20th century. There is a rich and flourishing literary culture – some scholars think, the most vital in Europe.

Are you going to have to learn it? The advice in 'The French Language and Learning It', (*see* pp.255–7) is the same as that in every other book that has ever been published about living in France – which is, that you try. It is better that you speak it badly than to expect others to speak English, and it is better to speak it well than speak it badly. But, having said that, it is not an absolute prerequisite to buying a property or living in France. Most British residents do not speak it that well, although some have achieved amazing virtuosity, and there is a whole generation of children of British parents who are growing up bilingual in French schools.

Education

Having your children educated in the French state system might be a reason for buying a home in France. It is hard to find British people who have put their children through French schools and not been pleased. Teachers have social status, and there is constant parent–teacher consultation. In France a father doesn't go to 'sort out' the teacher because his son got into trouble at school, a parent will cringe when the teacher sends a note in his exercise book asking why he didn't do his homework. Truancy is rare because the whole ethos of schooling is different. It is centralized, and rigid and it yields little to political correctness – and has been criticized on all these counts – but delivers one of the best-educated people in the world. Academic choices are made much later in the curriculum than in the UK, and it is fiercely secular. There are church schools, too, but these also teach the national curriculum and are subsidized by the state so much cheaper than British independent schools. There are also bilingual and international schools for those children who, for whatever reason, do not fit into the system. (*See* 'Education', pp.224–6.)

Health

From a consumer's point of view the French state health service is excellent. Hospitals are clean and efficient, there are no waiting lists and the patient has a choice of GPs and a wide range of treatments. It is a service known to foreigners for its quality, to the French for its expense and to its own doctors for underpaying them. But it differs from the British NHS, to which it is often flatteringly compared, in that it is not totally free. By means of a complicated, and now automated, system of expense reclamation, patients can get back between 50 and 100 per cent of what they spend on health care, but they do have to spend it first, although most people have insurance policies to cover the difference. For fuller details *see* pp.235–40.

Tax

You could become liable for French tax without being aware of it. The rule is that if you spend more than 183 days (6 months) of each tax year in France then you can be deemed a tax resident. If you don't spend 183 days but your main home is in France, or if you are not a tax resident of any other country but have a home in France and visit it regularly, or if your family home is in France, you might also be deemed a French tax resident (*see* pp.178–9). There is no tax restriction on moving your personal effects and furniture to France from another EU country. For more detail, *see* **Financial Implications**.

Permits and Visas

If you are a British or Irish national (or a citizen of any EU state) you do not need any special documentation to visit France for up to three months or to own property there. After that baseline, the rules and regulations begin to apply but first you should understand the context in which these rules exist.

At the time this book went to press the European Parliament was debating how to make labour in Europe more mobile. Only about one per cent of Europeans work in other countries of the Union. Present legislation, even that of the EU itself, still discourages easy movement between member states and

Where is the Mairie *or* Préfecture?

In a village or small town the *mairie* or *hotel de ville* is difficult to miss, as it's often the biggest building with its identity prominently written on it. *Préfectures* are found in the prefectural town of the *département*, where the *préfet* used to reside, and it is not always the largest town. On Michelin maps it is marked with a little square around it. These buildings will also be identified by flags, the tricolour at least, and perhaps the European and regional flags as well. If it's not perfectly obvious, look at the town maps, in the Yellow Pages under '*Préfectures, Sous-préfectures*', look for signs or simply ask. In Paris each *arrondissement* has its own.

this will have to change. Currently, the regulations governing living and working in France and other European states is being rethought. Some of the rules and regulations are virtually unenforceable. For instance, technically the privileges of free movement extended to EU members do not apply to residents of the Isle of Man or the Channel Islands. But place of residence is not now recorded on a passport, so how would anyone know? In this and other areas, legislation that exists is not always enforced at a local level and interpretation of it varies with different geographical authorities. Officialdom in Lille and the Auvergne will wear very different faces. This seems inequitable but, in practice, makes decisions possible at a local level.

Carte de Séjour

If you intend to stay longer than three months, technically you need a residence permit or *carte de séjour*. In practice this doesn't become essential until you cease to be covered by your UK health insurance. Some people remain much longer without a *carte de séjour* but, if you intend to stay in France and especially if you want to work, you cannot make use of the generous French social security and health services without one. At the time of going to press all foreigners need a *carte de séjour*. But moves are under way to abolish it for people who work in France, so you should check to see if new rules have come into effect when you are making your move – and you will no doubt be told the current situation when you apply. In fact, this will bring theory into line with practice, as most second home-owners who spend more than three months in France are not even aware that they should have one, and certainly few are ever asked about it.

To get a *carte de séjour* (*de ressortissant de l'Union Européenne*), apply to your local *mairie* if you live in the countryside or, if you live in a town, to the *service des étrangers* at the *préfecture* of your *département*. It is a good idea to go in person to avoid the countless exchanges of correspondence that may follow a misunderstanding. Also, the French prefer meeting to writing. Furthermore,

Carte de Séjour

Remember, you will need proof of some sort of income to acquire your *carte de séjour*. Entitlement to a British state pension will do. Simply approach the DSS International Section, Newcastle-upon-Tyne NE98 1YX (t 0191-218 7269) and ask them about form E121. Receiving a UK pension in the EU has the advantage of continuing the index-linked increment, while in most other destinations it gets frozen at the rate in place when you leave the UK. If you have the option of making French social security contributions for long enough to get a French pension, that is by far the best option as it is calculated on your previous earnings and linked to pay, not prices.

if you live in a small community, and especially if you have bought a house there, it is a very good idea to introduce yourself to the local mayor early on, as a matter of courtesy. Then, when your residence permit application arrives, you will not be faceless. This only applies in rural districts: the mayor of Bordeaux might not be interested in meeting you, newly arrived in his beautiful city. However, it may not be the *mairie* dealing with your application at all. In one case recently a *préfecture* decided that *mairies* were dispensing *cartes de séjours* much too readily and made all applicants traipse up to the prefectural town.

To get your *carte* you will need:

- **a valid passport**
- **proof of income sufficient to support yourself if you are not working**

If you don't have a French bank account, translations (by a French government-approved translator) of British bank documents may be required. This can get expensive. If you want a French bank account but are in Britain and can't speak French, Crédit Agricole in Calvados, Normandy, has opened a branch for UK clients called Britline (*see* p.227), and other French banks may follow. A lump sum is usually unacceptable, but has been known to suffice.

or

- **a work contract**

or

- **evidence that you have registered with the Chambre de Métiers or the Chambre de Commerce (depending on your activity)**

These are, respectively, the bodies in which trades- and businesspeople are registered. The Chambre d'Agriculture is for farmers. The French official mind is very tidy and everybody has to be in his or her correct slot. Some people have encountered a Catch 22 situation when documents required for the *carte* cannot be issued without the production of the same *carte*! In this case ask for temporary documentation – valid for three months – to be issued. The amount of income you have to show if you are not working varies from department to department, but a current general guideline is not less than £600 per month.

- **three passport photos**
- **a copy of your marriage certificate if you are married to a French citizen**

A wife or husband is included on the working partner's *carte de séjour*, even if he or she does not work. A *carte de séjour* is automatically issued to anyone married to someone working and resident in France but you may have the 'chicken and egg' scenario that they ask for proof that the applicant is already in the health system, and the health authorities say you need a *carte de séjour* before they can register you. Insist that the *préfecture* issues the *carte de séjour* and, if necessary, arrange for a top-up insurance and get written proof of this. This probably won't happen but it can, so be prepared.

- **proof of residence. A utilities (gas, electricity) statement will do for this.**
- **other documents for special cases**

If you are a student you have to get a student *carte de séjour*. If your parents live in France you have to get your own when you turn 18 anyway. To get this you will need a document from your place of study and it has to be a recognized education establishment.

You may also be asked for:

- **a birth certificate**
- **an affidavit to the effect that you have no criminal record or have ever been declared a bankrupt**
- **a marriage or divorce certificate if your passport is not in the same name as your birth certificate.**

All of these documents are important and may require translations from official, approved translators.

The *carte de séjour* experience varies immensely from place to place and from person to person. While some people report a nightmare of delay and expense, others have simply wandered down to the *mairie* and got their *carte* almost by return of post. In country districts it may well depend on what impact you have made on the local community. If you can fulfil the above criteria, nobody can stop you getting one.

Visas

If you are not a citizen of the EU, things are more complicated. Unless you are from Australia, Canada, Cyprus, the Czech Republic, Hungary, Iceland, Japan, Malta, New Zealand, Norway, Singapore, Slovakia, South Korea, Switzerland or the USA, you will need a visa to get into France. You may also be required to show proof of funds and/or a return ticket. If you intend to work, you should apply to the French consular office in your country of origin before even setting out, but your chances of success are not high. Unemployment and the pan-European refugee and asylum-seeker problem make the French even more sensitive on this topic than the British.

There is a very useful French civil service website, partially in English, at **www.service-public.fr**.

Where in France: Profiles of the Regions

03

As important as any other factor in your decision to buy in France is that universal consideration – location.

You may already have a clear idea of where you want to own a property – gleaned, perhaps, from years of happy holidays or a pragmatic consideration of maps and distance charts, transport infrastructure (the encouraging rash of new low-cost airline destinations) and weather patterns. All these are good and important reasons for choosing a location, but don't forget that it's not always summer and that proximity to, say, the Channel Tunnel may have its downside.

Alternatively you may be wondering about an area you've never visited or simply taking the first step to following up your dream 'to live in France' somewhere, but with no idea about where would be best for your needs. The following mini Tour de France looks at her regions from the point of view of the potential house-buyer, rather than just covering the usual holiday-maker's requirements, giving you the pros and cons, based on the experiences of those who have travelled this path before you.

First, a quick point about regional names. Take two editions of the same guidebook to the region we know as the Dordogne – one in English and the other in French. The French edition will probably announce itself as a guide to Périgord. Confused? The same conundrum faces those of us who remember names from our school history lessons but can't find them on the map. What has happened to Anjou and where has Artois vanished to? The answer is that, after the French Revolution, the old names were abandoned for a complete geographical make-over and the country was divided into *départements* (departments), mostly named after rivers. The French themselves often still use the old names and they frequently appear in culture and cuisine, so they do retain a real significance. In this section you will find some of the regional names most familiar to you, as well as the names of the departments that they encompass, gathered into logical geographical groupings.

You will notice that there is much more emphasis on some areas than others – for instance, little Dordogne gets as much coverage as huge Paris and mighty Lille gets only a line or two. This focus reflects the preferences of British house-hunters as far as is discernible, although exact figures are difficult to compute. Thus there is a concentration on the countryside rather than the cities – something that may change in future editions as the European labour market becomes increasingly mobile and more Britons start to work in France.

An idea of France's past is really necessary to understand her now, and it presents so many fascinating epochs that there are plenty of books about it in English.

A Little History

What follows is a thumbnail sketch of French history, a journalist's sketch rather than an historian's. Because remains and artefacts make good tourism, there is a lot of investment in the preservation of France's heritage, so you will be made constantly aware of France's pride in her past.

Prehistory

Everybody has heard of Neanderthal man, but few that the stone tools associated with him are called Mousterian, from a site at Moustier in the Dordogne. More people know that Cro-Magnon (modern) man was named after a village in the same district. In fact much of what we know about the Stone Age comes from investigations into sites in southern France. This is no coincidence. The abundance that was to bless the country in future millennia was revealed to early man by the retreating ice and he seems to have made the most of it, leaving traces of continual occupation over thousands of years. The Stone Age cultures named Perigordian, Magedelenian and Aurignacian are all called after places around south central France. The most famous cave paintings in the world were probably those at Lascaux, also in Dordogne, showing the extraordinary creativity of France's first artists, some 20,000 years ago. Then, in 1994, discoveries were made on the Ardèche River at a cave near Chauvet that pushed that creativity back to 35,000 years ago. There were further discoveries in the Dordogne in 2000; the extent and timespan of prehistoric painting gets wider and wider as our knowledge increases.

As various tribes peopled the land, were overrun by others and disappeared, one took hold in the southwest that has survived to this day: the people whom the Romans called Vascones, a word which became Basque, and whose language is the oldest in Europe. By the time the Romans were writing about France, the Greeks had already established trading centres in the south and most of the country had adopted a culture known as Celtic, Iron Age or La Tène, depending on what aspect of it you are talking about.

They were a tribal people, fragmented and with no large state structures; creative and proud, violent and passionate, and yet their civilization was a bit less primitive than you might suppose by reading *Asterix* comic books. For instance, finds made during the construction of the TGV line to the Mediterranean suggest that wine production was already established before the Greeks arrived and, if you find yourself in southern France, there are the remains of several Gallic settlements to visit. Their language survives in place names such as Lyon, named for the god Lug, and in loan words to French.

From Gaul to France

There is much more to see of the Roman occupation that started in Provence in 121BC and, in a sense, never ended for, despite its conquest by German tribes, the country was to remain Latin in culture, outlook and language. The Gallic tribes put up fierce but piecemeal resistance to Rome and a final battle under Vercingetorix at Alesia (supposedly Alise-Ste-Reine in Burgundy) settled the matter. After that they became more Roman than the Romans, and Roman remains in France, such as those at Orange, Arles, Vaison-la-Romaine and many other places, are the most impressive outside the Italian peninsula. When, in 406, the Rhine defences finally collapsed, Roman influence and the Christian religion were not swept away as they were in England, but percolated in the bubbling cauldron of peoples and cultures that was post-Roman Gaul, until settling slowly into the scattered kingdoms that would eventually become France.

The catalyst for this would be the German-speaking Franks, who settled in the north and who, over the next few centuries, saw off invasions from Germany (the Saxons) and Spain (the Moors). This period culminated with the magnificent and ruthless Charlemagne, who created Europe's first super-state by uniting France, half of Germany and northern Italy in a nominally Christian Empire. It didn't last long after his death, being initially divided between his sons, but its ghost was to haunt Europe ever after and its shadow survived in the form of the Holy Roman Empire. But little unity survived in practice. Raiding Vikings were bought off with land at the mouth of the Seine, which would become Northmandy; Britons who had fled invading Saxons became well-established in an independent Brittany. Vascones became Basques and Gascons, who lived in an independent Aquitaine, while Burgundy, Toulouse and Provence were in practice ruled by warlords.

Medieval France

But Europe was on the eve of the Middle Ages, the age of chivalry, Crusades and the emergence of France as a nation state, eventually to be the most powerful one in Western Europe. Trade and agricultural wealth combined to create towns and commercial networks that provided the building blocks of the new kingdom. The church provided a moral philosophy, learning, art and, particularly, architecture. Monasteries also contributed now-forgotten labour in clearing forests and draining marshes. War with England forged a strong centralized monarchy in northern France, which acquired the population, culture, and military strength to be without equal in the region. It also gave Europe the great Gothic cathedrals that were to be the architectural marvels of the age.

France's expansion continued. The next victim was Languedoc where a southern civilization had developed, (partially the result of influence from multicultural Spain), which was prosperous, scientifically progressive and with a propensity for heresy. This last provided the excuse for a huge northern land grab in the form of the Albigensian crusade, in 1205, with the result that French culture and language would develop from its northern form and parts of the south would remain fallow for centuries.

The Hundred Years' War is a convenient name for the sporadic struggle with the Anglo-Normans, which included elements of civil war, revolution, depression and plague. At one stage, after the battle of Agincourt (Azincourt if you are looking for it on the map) in 1415, Henry V of England controlled more of France than Charles VI of France. But eventually France recovered and, by 1453, England, which had once had possessions stretching from Normandy to the Pyrenees, had lost all her vast lands. Peace, prosperity and the canny Louis XI soon had France on her feet again and it wasn't long before she was picking fights with the Hapsburg Charles V in Italy and voraciously consuming the fruits of the Italian Renaissance. This competition with the Holy Roman Empire would set the scene for centuries to come, as the balance of power in Europe was to be France versus the Empire, France versus Austria and France versus Germany, right up to the 20th century.

Renaissance and Reformation

While Queen Catherine de'Medici was teaching the French to use forks and they were lapping up the Renaissance in all its other forms (particularly building châteaux), a horror was awaiting Europe, in that other great intellectual rebellion of the 16th century, the Reformation and ensuing religious wars. Frenchman John Calvin, a central figure of the Reformation, made Geneva the capital of the reformers in 1541. The violence started in France with the massacre of the Waldensians, a sect dating from the Middle Ages, in Provence. In 1562, full-scale civil war broke out, which tore the country apart and continued until 1593 when Protestant Henry of Navarre became a Catholic and Henry ('Paris is worth a Mass') IV of France. Once again, France had found the man to put her back together after one of her fits of self-destruction. The administration was overhauled, the infrastructure repaired, state industries started and the foundations were laid for France's most exuberant and flamboyant century and king.

France Supreme

The first half of the 17th century was to be dominated by the good governance of Cardinal Richelieu and, to a lesser extent, of Louis XIII. It was also to see the end of the Protestants as a territorial force, after the siege of La Rochelle in 1628. Louis XIV came to the throne in 1642, at the age of five, with the government in the hands of his mother and the capable Cardinal Mazarin, Richelieu's successor. This competent, if corrupt, cleric saw the young king through some difficult times, which included an invasion by the Spanish and civil war. Through the rest of his reign he was fortunate in his choice of ministers and generals, particularly Colbert, Turenne and Condé. During his extraordinary 72-year reign, France became once again the dominant power in Europe, now boasting some of the Continent's finest buildings, including its king's vast new palace at Versailles. It was an age of French paramouncy in literature, art, architecture and arms. She replaced Spain as the European super-power and was politically and culturally unrivalled in Europe.

Revolution and Republic

But then the impetus stopped again. While her own intellectuals led into the Enlightenment, and while political debate was openly discussing democratic forms of government, France froze in a time-warp of powerful aristocrats, grasping Church, corrupt public servants and stupid kings. To make things worse she stopped having military successes and suffered painfully at the hands of the British in the Seven Years' War, losing all her American colonies. The middle class was restless and the country was broke. In 1789 the king called the nearest thing that existed to a parliament, the Estates General, which hadn't met since 1610.

The original idea was to give France a constitution of the same type that the British enjoyed. When the king prevaricated, enlisted foreign aid and tried to flee the country, he was arrested and held prisoner. Invasion by Prussia followed but a hotchpotch revolutionary army defeated it. In the National Assembly (as the Estates General now called itself) the moderate Girondins were replaced by the radical Jacobins, the slaughter of real and perceived enemies, including the king, by guillotine, began, and France found herself at war on three fronts with Prussia, Austria and Britain.

What happened next was extraordinary. A young general named Bonaparte, with his sometimes barefoot soldiers, drove the British out of Toulon and the Austrians out of the whole of northern Italy. Back home, he seemed just the man to sort out the inefficient and corrupt government of the current constitutional experiment called the Directorate and was soon in charge of the country with the title of First Consul. Like Cromwell, Bonaparte made the transition from successful general to dictator in the name of a new political and social philosophy. France, in the twinkling of an eye, was transformed from the most conservative and reactionary power in Europe to being in the very vanguard of contemporary political thought. An avalanche of reforms, many of which have lasted to this day, was instituted and, once again, France became the crucible of European politics. Soon her armies were marching all over Europe as well.

'The impetus of the French Revolution had been spread by the genius of Napoleon to the four quarters of Europe,' Winston Churchill was to write. 'Ideals of liberty and nationalism, born in Paris, had been imparted to all European peoples...they were to play a notable part in changing the shape of governments in every European country, Britain not excepted.'

Searching For a Destiny

The next century was to be one of political experiment interspersed with short periods of bloodshed. Louis XVIII, who replaced Napoleon, survived and was succeeded by the reactionary Charles X, who was thrown out in favour of the more democratic Louis-Philippe. He was a casualty of the Europe-wide troubles of 1848 and abdicated in favour of another republic, whose first presidential election was won by Louis-Napoleon, Bonaparte's nephew. This so-called Second Empire was characterized by colonial expansion (in Africa and Indo-China), military adventurism (in Italy and Mexico) and political repression (at home). It all ended in tears after the Prussian invasion of 1870, the rout of the French armies, the loss of the provinces of Alsace and Lorraine and declaration of yet another republic.

This Third Republic was destined to last longer than either of its predecessors. Yet the defeat and the loss of Alsace and Lorraine deeply affected the national consciousness. How could this happen to a France that had historically always only expanded? The angst showed in a variety of strange ways. The building of the Sacré-Cœur at Montmartre, with its Romano-Byzantine architecture and statue of Charlemagne, was one – a sort of act of national penitence as though defeat was divine retribution for something. The recovery of the lost regions became a subject of national obsession and the French turned to sport, as though physical prowess would aid national resurgence. The first rugby international was held in 1872 and the Olympic movement was set up by Pierre de Fredi Baron Cobertin in 1896.

But physical fitness had little to do with France's decline from pre-eminence. She had dominated Europe when her population was larger than anyone else's and agriculture was the major wealth-creator. Now, both Germany and Britain had bigger populations and huge industrial complexes from coal and iron deposits that geography had denied France. In the political theatre, the usual left–right wrangles continued, sometimes coming to vicious climaxes in domestic confrontations and to the edge of war in colonial rivalry. Such was the Fashoda Incident of 1898, when a French officer called Marchand crossed Africa to thwart British ambitions on the Nile and brought the two countries to the brink. France blinked first, but the crisis encouraged the bullying policies of the British, which led to their humiliation in the Boer War and frightened both countries into the 1904 *Entente Cordiale*.

Pre- and Post-war France

High noon with Germany came in 1914. After four bloody years of the western front gobbling up human life, Germany collapsed. France's allies, particularly the British, suffered heavily, but it was France that sustained the most damage in material terms and in the loss of nearly 1.5 million men. The days when Louis XVI and Napoleon could squander armies were gone: the country was exhausted. Then followed the Depression. Politics, as elsewhere in Europe, took on extremist's hues with both left and right attracting large followings.

Despite the victory of 1918, it seemed as though France was in one of her periods of relapse, a feeling that took form in the defensive Maginot line and was confirmed by her collapse of 1940, when the Germans simply bypassed it. The right, on the whole, acquiesced to the new order, although few guessed how truly awful the Nazis were going to be. Resistance was slow in coming and dominated by the left. Liberation came without victory. But the illusion of victory was established by the conduct of the indomitable De Gaulle.

The immediate post-war years seemed to confirm the country's continuing malaise. Governments quickly and monotonously came and went, her army was defeated in Indo-China, her currency was weak and France received little respect abroad. While Germany and Italy worked hard at their economic miracles, France remained primarily a pre-war country with inefficient industries, pockets of intense poverty and an old-fashioned infrastructure.

There were stirrings from her hinterland: green shoots were appearing and drawing boards filling with plans. However, before anything was to change, there would be more melodrama. In 1958 the war with Algerian nationalist insurgents had come to a head and the country was profoundly divided between those who wanted to extricate France and those who supported the million French settlers and the army. De Gaulle was brought out of retirement to save the nation, which he did by drafting a new constitution that gave the presidency much greater executive power. France accepted it by referendum, and the Fifth Republic was born. A referendum also approved his move to give Algeria independence, prompting part of the army to try to kill him.

The Road to Modern France

At the time, De Gaulle's presidency did not seem to be a turning point. It was a period of apprehension, with internal threats from the rightist Secret Army (OAS) and an independent foreign policy that took France out of NATO, gave it its own nuclear weapons programme and blocked Britain's entry into the Common Market, ensuring that Europe would be dominated by a French–German partnership. At home there was a new feeling in the air; there was intrusive security and state-controlled TV and radio, but public buildings were cleaned, official uniforms smartened up and France was given a shiny new currency.

It may have been coincidence but the products of the drawing boards also started to materialize. The *autoroutes* were being completed, new French aircraft appeared in the skies, huge canal projects were built in the south and new resorts were constructed on the empty eastern Mediterranean coast. When he fell, in 1968, a victim of one of his own many referenda, the country was on a new path, although people still argue how much was due to him.

For France, once again, was reinventing herself. Technology was the watch-word, and the Grandes Écoles were churning out the technocrats that were to build the nuclear power plants, TGV, Airbus and the Ariane rocket. Her telecommunications system forged ahead with the Minitel a decade before the international domestic computer revolution. Today, France is recognizably back into one of her robust periods, irritating her allies but inviting envy instead of contempt. Her governments come and go without huge swings of policy, as in Britain. Her commerce is world-class and world-wide, her cars even fill Britain's roads, her sportsmen excel, yet her haunting and delightful landscape remains to be enjoyed by her people and ours.

And her population is rising again and has now surpassed the UK's. No need for alarm. This time, we don't have to look to the sea defences at Chatham for, whether we like it or not, the future of France, Britain and the whole of Europe is being drawn together, not so much by treaties or single currencies, but by the dictates and speed of our own technology.

Profiles of the Regions

The North

France's north contains a variety of lands and people that became attached to the French kingdom between the Middle Ages and the 16th century. Flemings, Normans and Bretons, all culturally distinct, have left their mark on this bountiful green swathe and, if they don't now differ much from one another, their influence lives on in architecture and gastronomy. The regions are climatically temperate, being milder and wetter towards the west. British buyers find the north attractive partly because of its proximity to England. This is certainly true of the eastern part, but gets less so the further west you look. Nevertheless, for those who don't mind weather not much better than her northern neighbour's and simply want to be in France, the prices are competitive and the transport communications good.

Nord-Pas de Calais and Picardy

Calais and its environs are the first things many visitors see of the Continent, which is a pity because, in the charm league of French towns, Calais ranks somewhere in the fourth division. But first impressions are misleading and there is more to the two departments of Nord and Pas-de-Calais than meets the eye. They are, in fact, a bit of a Cinderella. This Cinderella sits beside her 'opal' sea with her toes in the ash of 19th-century industrialism and 20th-century wars. Those wars destroyed many of her old towns and the industry created one of the only two great conurbations in France. But that's only half the story. Coal-mining stopped here in the 1990s and the spoil heaps are mostly grassed over. Between the small industrial towns are pleasant country villages, and at the heart of many of the larger ones is historic charm. Take Lille – a sprawling metropolis and transport hub, but its Vieille Ville is a delightful kernel of traditional architecture, shopping and fashion. Then there are the towns of historic Artois, like St-Omer and Arras, and of ancient Hainault, such as Douai and Cambrai, each with its own venerable character. Along the coast are the famous ferry and resort towns; inland, rolling chalk downs cut by winding river valleys hide little working villages; and old market towns lie along the network of roads heading south.

Into Picardy the countryside becomes less undulating and the valleys longer. The department names – Somme, Oise, and Aisne – recall the killing fields of the Great War and much of the tourism is to the many military cemeteries. Amiens, the regional capital, boasts the greatest medieval cathedral in France. Huge, productive fields alternate with large and ancient forests as the autoroute sweeps south to Paris and the Ile de France. Picardy's tiny stretch of coastline at the estuary of the Somme boasts two delightful fishing ports and the superb, marshy wildfowl reserve of the Marquenterre.

In character and history, Nord-Pas-de-Calais has been a land of transition between France and Flanders. In the north especially, the Flemish influence shows strongly in architecture and food, with stews, pâtés and pancakes making up many regional specialities. Beer is the traditional drink and a type of gin the regional spirit. This is also one of the parts of Europe that has been fought over interminably as far back as records go. Gauls, Romans, Franks, Burgundians, Walloons, English, Spanish, Germans and many others have all contested these fields and left their bones in them.

For the potential peaceful invader, the whole region has two great attractions and two drawbacks. On the downside there is the weather. As you would expect of this northerly realm, winters are cold and wet and summers not much warmer than those of England. Then there is the fact that, despite Gothic cathedrals, medieval towns and rolling fields, this is not the most attractive part of France. The good news is that property prices are not too bad when you consider that the area sits between two of the world's most famous cities, London and Paris, has all the attractions of being in France and has excellent transport links in all directions. Prices are particularly interesting away from the seaside resorts and larger towns.

The region is not particularly famous for its sporting activities, although there are all the usual seaside pursuits at the coastal towns and golf courses at Boulogne, Le Touquet, Fort-Mahon-Plage and Nampont-St-Martin. There is another little group in southern Picardy but these really cater for Paris. It is pleasant, if unchallenging, cycling country if you are lucky with the weather and the bird-watching opportunities attract aficionados.

Normandy

William the Conqueror, lace, cream, Calvados, Mont-St-Michel, the Bayeux Tapestry, cream, D-Day landings, André Gide, Monet, cream, Flaubert, Camembert, cider, cream, mussels cooked in cream, apple tart and cream, *sole dieppoise* with wine and cream... Normandy's heritage is rich and so is its food. The countryside defines the cuisine – lush, dairy and productive. Deep green grass and laden apple trees are the Normandy stereotype, perhaps with a happy cow beaming from the cover of a Camembert box. But there is some serious industry in the region, too, particularly at Rouen, Caen and Le Havre, France's second port. There are also some resort towns along the coast.

Normandy's origin lies with the Vikings who settled in the Seine estuary in 911. British people remember the date 1066 better, an invasion that was part of a Norman conquest that reached to Sicily and the Near East. Then there was that other invasion date of 1944, whose D-Day landing beaches attract many visitors.

This is a lovely region and although some of it, Caen for example, was flattened during World War II, other timeless attractions remain. The Bayeux Tapestry (which is actually an embroidery), for instance, and Mont-St-Michel, which is best appreciated out of season. Geographically the region is varied, lapping up against the rolling Ile de France and Picardy in the east and the more broken and rugged country towards Brittany in the west. The Cherbourg (or Cotentin) peninsula and the Seine estuary dominate the north. South of Caen, the area is known as La Suisse Normande, although this is a bit of an exaggeration. One of the wetter regions of France, Normandy has a climate similar to that of southern England but is a little warmer in summer. Five departments (Calvados, Eure, Manche, Orne and Seine-Maritime) are divided between Lower (western) and Upper (eastern) Normandy.

The most fashionable places to buy are around the coastal resort towns – Deauville, Honfleur and Trouville – but Parisian, and other, weekenders have tended to push prices up here. Property prices away from the coast, deep in the agricultural hinterland, or *bocage*, are still reasonable and this is probably where you should look. The regional architecture is the half-timbered *colombage* house, reminiscent of, but not identical to, those of southern England.

Normandy affords good sailing and sea fishing, windsurfing and water-skiing, pleasant cycling and half a dozen golf courses around the Côte Fleurie between Bayeux and Le Havre, as well as a course at Caen, another at nearby Clercy and another three in the Seine valley. There is also freshwater fishing to be had inland.

Brittany

At Brocéliande, near Rennes, the wizard Merlin fell in love with Viviane and built an underwater palace for her, making her the Lady of the Lake. The ethereal figures of Arthur and Guinevere, Lancelot, Tristan and Isolde appear out of the Celtic mist to remind us that the first cross-Channel house-hunters appeared on these shores well over 1,000 years ago. With post-Roman Britain becoming insupportably English, a mass of Britons settled here, bringing with them their name, Celtic tongue and a plethora of saints. For the next millennium Brittany shared a cultural tradition and a language with Cornwall and Wales, which is why Arthur and Merlin are so at home here. With a picaresque character that embraces piety, piracy and seafood, the Breton is both similar to, and different from, his Celtic cousins. In fact, the region has a history whose most startling monument dates from the Neolithic era – the 10,000 menhirs of Carnac. This and an abundance of other Stone Age sites are enough to delight any would-be Obélix – there is also plenty for the twitcher, hiker, cyclist, angler, sailor and diver. Not to mention the golfer, who is spoiled with 16 courses, mostly spread along the coast, except for a couple near Rennes. And that coast is spectacular, especially in the west and north. High cliffs and headlands alternate with bays and clean, sandy beaches, islands and rockpools. The charming custom of naming coasts for their dominant hue tells the story: emerald, rose-granite and heather. Behind the hugely popular coastline lies a patchwork of cottages, meadows, wood and heath (the *argoat*) with picturesque villages and ornate calvaries with deep estuaries running in from the sea.

The first English visitor to popularize the coast was a Mrs Faber in the 1850s, who made her home in Dinard, which subsequently became a resort. Today, property prices are higher around Dinard, Dinan and Quimper but a better bet near Roscoff, Vannes and away from the sea. As with Normandy, the best value left is probably away from the resorts in the *argoat*, where the typical granite-under-slate-roofed cottages, many in need of renovation, can be had.

The weather is windy and the wettest in France, but with a Gulf Stream mildness, and is often very pleasant in summer. Cider is the regional drink, while local dishes feature seafood, ham, mushrooms and, of course, pancakes – both savoury (*galettes*) and sweet (*crêpes*).

The East

Eastern France is a land of rolling fields and tall mountains, historic waterways and deep forests, ancient cities, famous ski resorts and the European parliament. France overlooks Belgium, Luxembourg, Switzerland and Italy here – it is a land of borders. It also incorporates the newest parts of France, for although we are inclined to think of it as a land of invasions, for the past millennia most of them came from the west.

Champagne-Ardennes

There are two parts to this region – the hilly forests of the Ardennes, whose name is so familiar to military historians, and the rolling chalk fields of Champagne, whose name is so familiar to anybody who has ever heard a cork pop. This product, invented in the 17th century, only began to dominate the region in the 19th, when it achieved international renown. Tradition tells us that a blind monk, Dom Pérignon, having accidentally stopped the fermenting process, tasted his mistake and said he had drunk the stars. Apart from its acres of vine-covered rolling hills, the region is known for one city, Reims, and for Reims' spectacular cathedral. This is not a popular area with British buyers, but for no really good reason. There are walled towns such as Laon and Langres, attractive villages and reasonable property prices. There's also easy access to much of northern Europe, with Brussels only 100km away. The departments are Ardennes, Marne, Aube and Haute-Marne.

There is trout-fishing in the Ardennes and golf courses at Villers-Agron and Cerny-en-Laonois. The cyclist finds the region a little more challenging with the appearance of some serious hills. The region touches the foothills of the Vosges to the north and the Jura to the south, where there is skiing in winter.

Alsace, Lorraine and Franche-Comté

These eastern marches have been a corridor for armies since Roman times, but that hasn't stopped them producing some of the most creative people, finest wines, most attractive towns and prettiest countryside in France. Lorraine, named after Charlemagne's son Lothair, is the most northern, containing the venerable city of Nancy with its beautiful Place Stanislas, and is famous, among other things, for its battlefields, spa towns and Art Nouveau. Alsace is defined by the Vosges Mountains and the Rhine and, for many, by the vineyards that lie between. Both regions have a distinct German flavour that is reflected in the cuisine. Both have an enviable collection of castles, abbeys and cathedrals and both were part of Germany from 1871 until 1918 when they were called Elsass-Lothringen. The departments of Lorraine are Meurthe-et-Moselle, Meuse, Moselle and Vosges, while those of Alsace are simply Bas-Rhin (lower Rhine) and Haut-Rhin (upper Rhine). Part of France since 1674, Franche-Comté borders Switzerland, and contains the departments of Haute-Saône, Doubs and Jura, as well as the Territoire-de-Belfort (not, in itself, a department). The Jura mountains are a charming mix of hills, fields and flower-decked villages that look across to the snow-capped Alps. You are also close to alpine weather patterns here; both the Vosges and the Jura mountains have roads closed by snow in winter.

These ranges support two distinct skiing areas, the Hautes Vosges in the north and the Jura to the south. The Hautes Vosges stations are all contained in a square between Metz, Strasbourg, Mulhouse and Dijon: Le Bonhomme, a traditional family resort with cross-country skiing; La Bresse Hohneck, which is similar; Ventron which only has cross-country skiing; St-Maurice-sur-Moselle, which has traditional skiing as well as being classed as a 'snowrider' resort, offering instruction in snowboarding and other non-traditional sports; and Gérardmer, with family and cross-country skiing. Bussang, Le Valtin, Xonrupt-Longmer, Frenz and Le Markstein shouldn't be overlooked. In the Jura there are three ski stations at Métabief-Mont-d'Or, Les Rousses and Monts Jura – all traditional and family resorts with some cross-country skiing. Golfers are also catered for with courses at Metz, Nancy, Colmar and Faulquemont.

All three regions are delightful in slightly different ways but share a picturesque, window-box quaintness that, together with their food, wines and history, make them very popular with tourists. Not with British home-buyers, though. This may be because they feel less French than some, it may be because property is priced above the national average or it may be because there are few deserted farms to be renovated. Bear in mind, too, that the lush greenery and many gushing rivers and cascades, so pleasant to the eye, are accounted for by heavier than average rainfall.

The Rhône-Alpes

This is a land of giants, lying between the mighty river Rhône and Mont Blanc, the highest mountain in Europe. Savoy is a rugged kingdom of mountain villages and ski resorts. Tucked up in an alpine corner between Switzerland, Italy and Provence are high forests, deep gorges and terrifying hairpin bends. Also here are the world-class winter sports resorts of Courchevel, Megève, Val d'Isère, Chamonix and Albertville where the 1992 winter Olympics were held. The region sweeps round the corner of Lac Leman, as Lake Geneva calls itself in French, and up towards the Jura. Cutting through it from north to south is the great valley of the Rhône, a major European communications artery, a huge river system and the funnel down which blows the Mistral to the Mediterranean. On the west side of the valley are the highlands of the Massif Central, cut by gorges such as the Ardèche, so beloved of the summertime kayakers. There is massive industrial development in the valley and around Lyon, which also claims to be the nation's gastronomic capital. But there is much agriculture here, too, especially market gardening and, of course, wine production. And, in the valleys, delightful towns and villages sit between swift-flowing rivers and ancient vineyards, such as those of the Drôme.

The region has a split personality as far as climate is concerned, with a warm Provençal summer and a snow-clad alpine winter. For this reason it is popular with adventure sportspeople of all seasons. To list the ski stations in the region – known to skiers as the Rhône-Alpes or Northern Alps – would turn this book into one about winter sports. There are 69 officially listed, making this one of the major ski resort areas of Europe. The principal access towns are Grenoble, Chambéry and Annecy. All the other mountain sports are present in summer, too: climbing, hill-walking and white-water kayaking and rafting. Neither is the golfer ignored: there are four courses within striking distance of Grenoble, two at Villefranche-sur-Saône and one each at Annecy, Morzine, Evian and Chamonix.

The departments are Aine, Ardèche, Drôme, Isère, Rhône, Savoie, Haute-Savoie and Loire. Because of its winter sports profile and because it lies between Lyon, France's second city, and Switzerland, it is not cheap. There is a lot of winter sports accommodation – chalets and apartments – on offer, beginning quite far west. A good tip is to check these out in the summer as snow hides an abundance of sins. Houses are still available to renovate in the villages along the valleys.

The South

'Our nights are more beautiful than your days', Dana Facaros and Michael Pauls quote Racine in the opening of their matchless *The South of France*. On the whole, that is still true. Its light, climate and history have conspired to make this region different from any other part of Europe. Provence was the first non-Italian province of the Romans, hence its name. In late Latin *hoc ille* meant 'yes'. As the languages of Gaul became those of France, northerners corrupted *ille* into *oïl* and then to *oui*, while southerners made *oc* out of *hoc*. The huge area over which the southern version was spoken came to be called Languedoc (the tongue, or language, of Oc). Historically, and still when discussing vineyards, everything to the west of the Rhône is Languedoc and everything east, Provence. In actual administrative areas though, these are divided between the regions of Provence-Côte-d'Azur (Hautes-Alpes, Alpes-de-Haute-Provence, Alpes-Maritimes, Var, Bouches-du-Rhône and Vaucluse) and Languedoc-Roussillon (Gard, Hérault, Aude, Pyrénées-Orientales and Lozère (which, in this book, falls into another region).

In the past century, France's southern regions became a byword for opulence, but, today, much of that wealth lies in high-tech industry rather than with bejewelled casino-goers. And there are huge contrasts in the character and nature of the region's environment and development and, consequently, in the cost of property. An apartment in Monte Carlo and a farmhouse in an Aude vineyard will have little in common except the sunshine. Medieval Aigues-Mortes could not be more different from the neighbouring resort of La Grande Motte. So don't write off the south simply because you don't like, or think you can't afford, its glamorous profile.

That profile is very real along the Alpes-Maritimes coast and in Monaco, but that is only one aspect of an astonishing region. Not far away across the mountains lie the gorges of the Verdon River, so deep and mysterious that they were not fully explored until the 20th century. The Rhône delta offers the famous Camargue, with its wild horses and cowboys; the high Pyrenees have sombre forests and ski resorts. In between lie in profusion vineyards, fishing villages, walled cities, art galleries, *villages perchés*, sandy beaches, Roman remains, orchards, seaside resorts, olive groves and every sort of sporting facility you can imagine. The cuisine is totally different from the classical traditions of northern France, as it eschews dairy products and is infinitely healthier. It is true that the Mediterranean is not as clean as it was, that parts of the coast are grossly over-commercialized and expensive and that organized crime is not unknown in cities like Marseille, but that does not seem to alter the affection that so many foreigners, particularly British ones, seem to feel for the South of France.

Provence-Côte-d'Azur

There are several faces of this most celebrated of regions. The best known is that fairyland of high life between Cannes and Menton, once called the Riviera, familiar through the lenses of thousands of movie cameras. The yachts, the chic boutiques, the nightlife, the art galleries, the elegant hotels and restaurants – they are all still there and all still expensive. If it is aware that there are other even more fashionable and exclusive playgrounds in the world now, it doesn't show it. Then there is the dream of rural Provence, the deafening cicadas, the scent of rosemary, thyme and lavender, gnarled vineyards and Jean de Florette somewhere over the hill. That idyll still exists, too, but shares living space with autoroutes, dams and commercial and residential development. And there is the industrial face. Cities such as Marseille and Toulon have always been manufacturing centres; what is new is the migration of high-tech companies from northern Europe in a move that parallells that in the southwestern United States.

Among all these lie the region's venerable towns and cities, with their character, charm and individual histories. Avignon, great lady of the Rhône, with her papal palace and broken bridge, Orange, with her Roman theatre and

A Taste of the South

Eric and Madeleine Vedel (*www.cusineprovencale.com*), who run an establishment for the teaching and preservation of Provencal cuisine, say:

'Provence is a region riddled with vegetable farms and fruit orchards, with the delightful result that vegetables and fruit are picked ripe only a day before they are sold at local markets. Ripened by natural sunlight, they taste better. Be it a ratatouille from Nice – a classic summer vegetable dish of tomatoes, aubergines, courgettes, bell peppers, onions, garlic, a few bay leaves and olive oil – or the Bohemienne– a bit simpler with tomatoes, aubergines, onions, garlic, olive oil and bay leaves – from the Bouches-du-Rhône, you will enjoy dense, nearly sweet flavours in your mouth.

All year long vegetables grow in this land that never freezes. In the spring enjoy fresh asparagus, peas, pea pods, the new garlic and, for dessert, strawberries and, in early June, cherries. In the summer taste sun-ripened tomatoes, a dozen varieties of aubergine and courgette, apricots, peaches, the melons of Cavaillon. Come fall, revel in the last of the tomatoes (from the field through early October!), the first squash and, towards the end of October, the wild mushrooms. From the hills come fresh apples, pears and white watermelon (known locally as the *citre*), used to make a tart jam. With the winter comes the root vegetables, cardoon (a relative of the artichoke, but resembling celery), the royal black truffle, and, late February, spinach, broccoli... '

triumphal arch, Arles with her amphitheatre and memories of Van Gogh, and Aix-en-Provence, the ancient capital of the region with its many splashing fountains and elegant tree-lined avenue Cours Mirabeau.

The Greeks traded and settled along this coast and it was thought that they introduced the vine until Neolithic finds of grape pips on the TGV Méditerranée route showed that viticulture was older in France than anyone imagined. The Romans came to stay and their imprint on the place is indelible. The Dark Ages introduced a number of uninvited guests, including Visigoths, Franks, Saracens and even Magyars, although it was the Saracens who proved the most difficult to dislodge, only finally being expelled in 979. Something of a golden age followed for Languedoc that lasted until the Albigensian crusade of the 13th century, which was augural of the expansion of the northern French.

The second home invasion began at Hyères in the early 19th century. The Empress Josephine, Victor Hugo, Tolstoy and Robert Louis Stevenson all had villas there. It was the English Lord Brougham who started the fashion for wintering in Cannes in the 1830s, and the town acknowledges it with a statue of him. In 1830 the British community subscribed for the building of the Promenade des Anglais at Nice. At that time it was still part of the Kingdom of Savoy (and known as Nizza) and it did not become French until 1860, when it was swapped by Victor Emanuel for French military help against the Austrians – enraging Garibaldi, the Italian patriot, who had been born there. The next year the Prince of Monaco sold Menton and Roquebrune to France and the coast took on the international configuration it has today. Shortly afterwards the railway arrived. By 1890 there were 20,000 British and Russians wintering in Nice and the word *anglais* came to mean tourist. By 1910 there were 150,000.

A fashionable destination for Brits for a century, the coast has enduring allure and, if you have the money, property and yachts are still to be had on this most famous Mediterranean littoral. There is a wide range of accommodation, from basic studios to a villa on Cap d'Antibes, and the price range will match – the villa out of most people's reach but the studio probably within it, especially as you get towards the less fashionable western end. Letting and charter potential are also good. But the Riviera is only a tiny part of Provence, which stretches from the salty lagoons of the Rhône delta to the precipices of the Maritime Alps and up the Rhône itself beyond Orange. There are plenty of places in this huge area where costs are much more credible than on the hedonistic Côte. Architectural styles are as varied as everything else and the predominant one might well be the modernistic apartment block. The traditional Provençal terracotta-tiled *mas* (farmhouse) or village house is still to be found, but almost equally common are modern interpretations, often developed into entire communities, such as that of Port-Grimaud.

For the active, there is a lot more to do than lie on the beach. All the pursuits usually associated with the seaside are available – the boating, sailing, water-skiing and diving – but all at a greater price than you might expect in Torquay. Indeed, for those frustrated admirals who have a pocket to match their fantasies, there are huge and glamorous yachts to be chartered and Corsica is only a day's sail away. For those with more modest aspirations there is kayaking in the mountains, especially towards the northwest of the region. And, of course, in winter you are a few hours' drive from the Southern Alps' ski resort region, offering the singular experience of both skiing in the mountains and swimming in the Mediterranean on the same day. There are 18 ski stations in the area – again, too many to detail here but they are all in the departments of Hautes-Alpes and Alpes-de-Haute-Provence. Golfers, as you might expect, are well catered for – there are four courses in the area between Grasse and Cannes, one at Antibes, another at St Raphaël, one at Ste-Maxime, an eighth near Draguignan, and another four between Toulon and Avignon.

Languedoc-Roussillon

The Roman road, the Via Domitia, which runs from the Rhône Valley to Spain, passes through the old cities of Nîmes, Montpellier, Béziers, Narbonne – where it is theatrically exposed in the main square – and Perpignan. But it is the Albigensian Crusade of the 13th century that haunts this region. Before then, Languedoc had been culturally, linguistically and religiously independent. In the centuries that followed, it became a backwater. Today there is a movement to revive the old Occitan language, and the red-and-yellow flag ('the blood and gold') of the Catalans and of Aragon is seen everywhere. So there is a certain amount of regional feeling in Languedoc and an occasional tendency to look towards Barcelona rather than Paris for cultural identity. The last 50 years have seen economic regeneration. It is also attracting lots of foreign house-buyers, some of whom have been pushed along the coast from the Côte d'Azur by property prices and some whom have been here for decades, like the late English authors Patrick O'Brian and Lawrence Durrell.

Gard guards the right bank of the Rhône then ascends towards the arid massifs, past the definitive Roman aqueduct, the Pont du Gard. Gard also boasts august Nîmes, celebrated for two square buildings, the Carré d'Art (a cultural centre) by Norman Foster, and the next-door Maison Carée (a temple) by the Romans. It is also famous for passions for rugby, bullfighting in its Roman arena, contesting the title of the Rome of France with Arles, and competing in everything else with Montpellier in Hérault, which modestly styles itself the Rome of Tomorrow. Montpellier also likes to call itself a *'technopole'* and grafts a dynamic futurist air on to an ancient university town, one that has the second-oldest medical school in Europe.

Northwest lies the Cévennes – rugged and beautiful country that has attracted many northern settlers, with some British among them. Westward, along the shoreline, is an almost unbroken series of lagoons and sandy beaches reaching nearly to the Spanish border. They are interspersed with a number of custom-built resorts, most famously La Grand Motte, which has a definite, if unidentifiable, 1960s feel to it. The hinterland is a huge vineyard, historically known only for its mediocrity but now producing some internationally familiar wines such as Minervois and Corbières. These all lie in the vast valley that stretches between the Massif Central and the Pyrenees and at whose heart sits the medieval citadel of Carcassonne and the plane-tree-lined 17th-century Canal du Midi in Aude. To the south rise the Pyrenees, which offer winter sports at their higher altitudes and charming fishing villages, such as Collioure in Pyrénées-Orientales, where they meet the Mediterranean.

This contrast affords a huge diversity in sport and leisure. The sandy coast from the Rhône delta to Spain is great for most watersports except, perhaps, diving but that gets better in Pyrénées-Orientales. There are three ski stations near the Spanish border: Font-Romeu, a family and 'snowrider' resort, Les Angles, which is similar, and Ax-les-Thermes, a family resort where you can ease your aches and pains away with thermal baths. There are some thirty-five ski stations in the Pyrenees but these are the principal ones at the eastern end. The Gardon, Hérault, Orb and Petit-Rhône rivers all have organized canoeing and kayaking and there are golf courses at Nîmes, Cap d'Agde, Perpignan, Font-Romeu and four around Montpellier. Rugby and bullfighting are two of the popular spectator sports.

Unlike in Provence-Côte-d'Azur there is no super-priced region dominating the market, although seaside resorts like Narbonne-Plage obviously demand a premium. There are some sizeable cities, too, that have an impact on property values, especially Montpellier. Buildings vary with the environment: from traditional stone-under-terracotta in the vineyards to chalet complexes in the ski resorts.

The Southwest

It's not quite the same Aquitania that the Romans knew, but water is still the dominant feature here: water surging west from the Massif Central, cascading down from the Pyrenees and pouring itself into the biggest estuary in Europe. The Romans called the locals Vascones, a word that became both Basque and Gascon in the following centuries. Probably the Vascones had occupied much more of the southwest and perhaps had done so since the Stone Age. Later the dour, seafaring Basque, with his distinctive sports and democratic ways would cut a rather different figure from swashbuckling Gascons like d'Artagnan and Cyrano de Bergerac, but they all shared one particular virtue, a passion for food. With truffles and *fois gras, confits* and *magrets, poule au pot*, pigeons and pimentos, salt pork, oysters and Bayonne ham on offer, and wine from some of the greatest vineyards in the world at the table, who can blame them?

South of Bordeaux

Grand and grandiose, twice legislative capital and birthplace of the Third Republic, Bordeaux is the provincial *city par excellence*. She lies on the largest estuary in the largest department of France – Gironde. On her southern seaboard are the departments of Landes and Pyrénées-Atlantiques. Here on the longest beach stands the highest sand dune, and the biggest lake fronts the most extensive forest in France. The other superlatives are surfing, wind-surfing and sailing. This coast is said to offer the best surfing in Europe and Australian visitors confirm that it is comparable with many Pacific venues. Like so much of France it is fine hiking and cycling country, and this is where the now-popular walking route to Compostela crosses the Pyrenees by the pass of Roncevaux. There is skiing, too, but, as it is on the border with Hautes-Pyrénées, we'll leave it till later (*see* Midi-Pyrénées p.51). Golf, as you might expect with so much pine, sand and connections with Britain, is well represented with four courses around Bordeaux and the rest along that famous coast at Lacaneau-Océan, Arcachon, Moliets-et-Maa, Seignosse, Bayonne and Biarritz.

The coast from Soulac to Biarritz is really one long beach, interrupted only by the bay of Arcachon, which became a resort for the Bordelais in 1852. This huge sweep is called the Côte d'Argent. At its far end are appealing Bayonne and faded Biarritz, once the premier resort of France and now reinventing herself. Inland is a huge pine forest, planted on the orders of Napoleon III to secure the sandy, wind-blasted landscape of the Landes. To the south lie the foothills of the Pyrenees, the department of Pyrénées-Atlantiques and the land of the Basques. Here are towns like Dax, with its mud spa for aches and pains – appropriate when you consider the fame of its rugby team. Then there is Pau, of which a Scots doctor named Taylor wrote a laudatory book in 1869 that sparked off a British residence-rush. This in turn conjured up a rash of villas, a racecourse and the first golf course in France.

Why aren't the Britons there now? Biarritz eclipsed Pau and the Riviera took over from Biarritz 70 years ago. Now the Dordogne is the place to be. When you consider this extraordinary coast, and all those superlatives, and the Pyrenees with their ancient villages and unique ornithology, the sport and the proximity of romantic Spain, it is difficult to find an answer. Property prices are low compared to the Dordogne and Lot-et-Garonne but the over-flow from those regions has started, particularly in Gironde.

The Dordogne and Lot-et-Garonne

Before the Dordogne became so attractive to second home-buyers it was known for its prehistoric sites. Many of the most famous names associated with early man come from these valleys and the discoveries keep on coming – rock engravings found near Cussac in 2000 pushed the known period of man's artistic creativity back another 8,000 years. The same environment that gave early man strategic shelter and abundant food sources gives his descendants spectacular countryside and a romantic historical heritage. Forested gorges and lively rivers running under limestone cliffs are overlooked by ruined castles and hilltop churches. Thus, here are parts of France that have been at the desirable end of the property market for 25,000 years. In recent decades, the southern architecture and weather, dramatic scenery and productive vineyards have made it such a flare path for the Brits that Eymet has over 2,000 of them in the vicinity and supports its own cricket club!

In fact, what they call the Dordogne and what the French call the Dordogne are slightly different things. The French use the historic term Périgord, subdivided into Green (its verdure) White (limestone) Black (forest) and Purple (vineyards). The British are inclined to include much of Lot-et-Garonne in their Dordogne. The area is centred on an axis from north of Périgueux to Agen. The upper part lies on a limestone plateau, cut deep by rivers mostly flowing west. The lower part slopes south towards the Garonne into that huge valley between the Atlantic and the Mediterranean. To the west, our area extends to Castillon-la-Bataille where the last battle of the Hundred Years' War was fought and, to the east, to just beyond spectacular Sarlat-la-Canéda. The climate is not so torrid in summer as Provence and the region is spread with many *bastide* towns (*bastides* are custom-built medieval market towns).

The English have been here before, of course. This was one of the much-contested areas of the Hundred Years' War and many of the *bastide* villages are of English foundation. It is possible that you may not want to be among so many ex-pats; certainly this is the view of many who want to really immerse themselves in France. Many estate agents here speak English, too, and there are British people carrying on businesses. Any resentment of this invasion is ameliorated by the knowledge that much of rural France, which has an almost mystical place in the French psyche, suffers from chronic depopulation and decline, and money, restoration and, children, can only help to arrest that.

With a large number of British householders, you might have expected a plethora of golf courses, too, but Dordogne and Lot-et-Garonne have only a few, as at at Les Vigiers near Ste-Foy and at Castlenaud-de-Gratecambe near Villeneuve-sur-Lot. Both the Dordogne and Lot are popular canoeing and kayaking rivers and the region is popular with cyclists and hikers. The nearest skiing is in the Auvergne but the Pyrenees are not much further.

Property prices are highest near the Dordogne river and lower in Lot-et-Garonne. On the whole, though, they are high for rural France. In the 1980s, when the British tide was at its height, prices rose by 40 per cent and, although they have normalized a bit since then, there is still a marked premium because of the foreign interest. For all the attractions of the area this is the corollary. If you are still keen and looking for a regional style of home, there is a *maison périgourdine*, a long, low structure under tiles, but you are more likely to come across two-storeyed half-timbered rural dwellings.

Midi-Pyrénées

This huge region is actually part of three distinct geographical areas: the Pyrenees, Massif Central and valley in between. It is divided into eight departments and this book includes another, for reasons you will see later. The three that back on to the Pyrenees are Hautes-Pyrénées and Ariège, with a little bit of Haute-Garonne squeezing in between them. This is high mountain country with ski resorts and spectacular hiking in summer. It is here, not in the Alps, that you will find the tallest waterfall in France, the Grande Cascade. Lourdes, the second most popular Christian pilgrimage site in the world, is also here. Secular tourism is not new either. The romantic movement of the 18th century attracted aristocrats to Cauterets, which maintained popularity to the end of the 19th. The foothills have their own charm, too, part of which is Armangac. This famous tipple has been produced here, they say, since 1285, which makes it the oldest brandy in Europe. Nearby is d'Artagnan country, but this high-spirited combination is a little compromised by the presence of the neighbouring town of Condom.

Toulouse stands astride the Garonne and the 17th-century Canal du Midi in unchallenged dominance of the region. Centre of both Europe's space and France's aircraft industries, and with a population of over 600,000, the city nevertheless has an attractive medieval kernel. Around it are other pleasant and more user-friendly towns: Albi, famous for its medieval character and because it gave its name to the Albigensians; Montauban for its Place National, the original for the *bastide* towns of the south; Moissac for its abbey; Agen for its plums. Indeed, the valleys falling down from the north are a veritable fruit basket with their offerings of grapes, cherries, peaches, nectarines, apples, hazelnuts and even kiwi fruit. Painting is another aspect of the local picture. Colonies of artists live in quaint villages and collections of modern art are to be found in many a town.

Lozère is not in the region of Midi-Pyrénées at all – it is in Languedoc-Roussillon – but it appears here because it contains the Parc National de Cévennes, which is typical of much of the high country of the departments of Tarn and Aveyron. Here, the rainfall of millennia has sculpted a wild, wonderful and sometimes weird mountainscape in the limestone massifs. Huge caverns have been carved beneath the high, flat and barren sheep-runs and rivers have cut impossible gorges through them. Along the banks of these rivers ancient villages perch, ruined castles cling and gin-clear streams leap to the rushing waters below. In summer, many of them are wall-to-cliff-wall with kayakers, rafters and traffic jams, but that is the story of much of France in July and August. In the department of the Lot, the roughcast east meets the gentler west and the result is a district that is proving increasingly popular with foreign home-buyers. Tarn is also coming up, with Aveyron at its heels and Ariège has a growing following.

The Pyrenees are famous among those cyclists who are very fit or masochists or (usually) both. In winter they offer a number of ski resorts in two groups – the eastern, which are covered in the Languedoc-Roussillon section, and the western, which are south of Tarbes. Unusually, three of the five stations in this district have thermal baths: St-Lary-Soulan, Luz-Ardiden and Gourette. Piau-Engaly and La Mongie are family resorts with 'snowrider' instructors. There are some thirty-five ski stations in the Pyrenees but these are the principal ones in the Midi-Pyrénées. Across the valley, the Massif Central is great country for speleologists but that is probably not a good enough reason for buying a house. It is, though, also famous for kayaking, especially on the Tarn and Lot, which is good for rentals even if you are not a paddler yourself. Golfers have three courses to choose from around Toulouse and there are others at Albi and Rodez. There are over 2,000 miles of marked paths in the region.

The great selling point of this region is that it resembles many others but is less developed and less expensive. It has mountains and ski resorts, for instance, but is cheaper than the Alps. It has the Lot, which is cheek-by-jowl with the Dordogne but without the tens of thousands of expatriates; and it has Tarn and Aveyron, which look and feel like Provence, but aren't. Having said that, prices are above the national average, especially in the Lot. But it is still worth looking for a bargain: this is an immense and diverse region. An architectural feature popular here and everywhere over southern France is the *pigeonnier* – a (usually) square tower, often at the end of a building, which was originally, and sometimes still is, a dovecote.

Central France

Although the centre of France is undoubtedly among the regions below, this area really consists of those that do not obviously conform to being North, South, East, West or Southwest. These are prosperous Burgundy, the historic Loire Valley, wild and beautiful Limousin and Auvergne and, of course, Paris, the City of Light herself, and her hinterland, the Ile de France.

Paris and the Ile de France

There is probably more to be written about in this area than any other in France of the same size, perhaps in the world. Except on the subject of buying property. There are two reasons for this: most Parisians rent, and prices are extremely high. Combined, these factors are not inclined to make Paris and its environs a popular destination for British house-buyers. You, on the other hand, may not be affected by either of these considerations. Also, the strength of sterling against the franc and now the euro in recent times has brought even Paris within the reach of buyers who would never otherwise have thought about her. Lucky them – to be near the centre of so much artistic, architectural, historical and gastronomic wealth. It is also all easily accessible, with an efficient and subsidized underground (*métro*) and suburban (*RER*) rail network. Eurostar is another influence on potential buyers, especially those in southern England, for whom the French capital is now an effortless three hours away. People who have tried to leave the city on a holiday weekend won't be so quick to praise the road system though.

If you are in Paris to work, a neat little studio to impress your friends and hide from your relations is probably not what you need. You are more likely to be looking towards the dormitory and neighbouring towns such as Créteil, Evry, Bobigny, St-Denis, Nanterre, St-Germain and Versailles. Beyond the city are six other departments: Seine-et-Marne, Essonne, Yvelines, Val-d'Oise, Hauts-de-Seine and Seine-St-Denis. The city itself is divided into 20 districts, or *arrondissements*, emanating from the centre and referred to by number: 'the Sixth' for instance, as you might say 'West One' in London.

Forget the First and Second, they are not for mere mortals. The Third to the Sixth are both central and desirable and include areas like the Latin Quarter, still an academic centre that gets its name from the medieval student ban on speaking anything else there, and the newly trendy and desirable Marais district. The Seventh (the Eiffel Tower) is very posh and very expensive. The Eighth (the Elysée Palace, the Champs-Elysées) is even more so and potential residents would rub shoulders with the President, among others. The Ninth does have some residential properties but is mostly home to the head offices of big companies. The Tenth to the Fourteenth (with the Bois de Boulogne) tend to be less glamorous and consequently less expensive. The Fifteenth is a mixture both of reasonable and expensive and of old and new, and is residential. The Sixteenth (the Arc de Triomphe) is grand, exclusive, expensive and conservative. The Seventeenth (also running from the Arc de Triomphe), is posh, too, but more trendy and lively, with some affordable pockets. The Eighteenth, which includes Montmartre and Pigalle, is the reverse – a few fashionable pockets in an otherwise mixed and rumbustious area that includes the largely immigrant Bàrbes. The Nineteenth (Gare du Nord) is a quieter continuation of the Eighteenth. The Twentieth (around Père Lachaise cemetery) is quieter, bigger and cheaper still.

Burgundy

Several important Roman towns stood here on the route between Lyon and Boulogne – then the main point of departure for Britain. But it was 1,000 years later that Burgundy came into her own. During the Middle Ages, only a small number of historical accidents prevented her from becoming the great power and France the delightful but politically insignificant backwater. At their height, the Dukes of Burgundy controlled the whole of what are now the Benelux countries and sided with the English during the Hundred Years' War. At an earlier time she held sway to the Mediterranean. What remains now is but a rump; but what a delightful rump it is!

No spectacular mountains or coastline here, but some of the most famous vineyards in the world, so that a list of the towns and villages of the Saône valley would make you think you are walking round an off-licence. Here is superabundance. Charolais cattle graze under oak trees; Gothic abbeys stand by fields of blackcurrants grown for cassis liqueur. Barges chug along hundreds of miles of avenued waterways through fields of yellow mustard, reminding us that Dijon is in the neighbourhood. But where are *les Anglais*? They are coming. Burgundy is tipped as the next target for foreign investors. At the moment there are not too many British or anyone else. But, with its food, wine and idyllic setting, it was not going to remain the private preserve of Parisian weekenders forever, and prices are already above the national average. The weather here is said to be 'Continental', that is to say colder in winter and hotter in summer than southern Britain, but drier and without the heavy snows of the mountain regions. There are plenty of châteaux and mansions around but they are not often on the market and so houses for renovation in villages and farms are where the new buyers are looking. The *galerie maçonaise*, a covered verandah, is the local architectural idiosyncrasy. The departments of Burgundy are Côte-d'Or, Nièvre, Saône-et-Loire and Yonne.

The region has no ski resorts, and just one solitary golf course near Auxerre, but there are miles of rustic roads for the cyclist and sleepy river and canals for the bargee or marine motorist. Sailing and canoeing are on offer in the lake of the Parc Régional de Morvan.

Centre

'Centre' is a lacklustre title for a stately region whose other names tell of historic and architectural grandeur. Here are ancient Anjou, Berry and Touraine. Here stand Angers, Saumur, Tours, Blois and Orléans, which are noble cities beside that most majestic of rivers, the Loire. And the Loire means châteaux – Chenonceau, Chambord, Amboise, Azay-le-Rideau, which are haughty names that are only the vanguard of hundreds of others. Even the food sounds aristocratic in this region: salmon, asparagus and artichoke; potted pork, pike and perch; veal and lamb and most of the *champignons de Paris* grown in the country. And so with the wines: Sancerre, Pouilly-Fumé, Vouvray, Montlouis...

There is a long historical connection with the British Isles here. England's Henry II was born in Angers and, by ascending the throne in 1128, started the Plantagenet dynasty. In 1429 Joan of Arc raised the English siege of Orléans, which perhaps was the watershed of the Hundred Years' War. Aubigny-sur-Nère was given to a Scotsman, John Stuart, for his help against the English, while an Irish family called Walsh, who followed James II into exile, once owned the Château de Serrant. Away from the noble piles and their formal gardens are woods, lakes and meadows, plantations of poplars and a remarkable number of subterranean dwellings, some in current use, carved out of the predominant limestone. These *maisons troglodytes* sometimes come on to the market, and many other homes in the region at least have a wine cellar, garage or a room or two hewn into the hillside.

British people tend to call the region the Loire Valley and include the department of Maine-et-Loire (confusingly in Pays de la Loire), which makes geographical sense, so this book does, too. The other departments are Eure-et-Loire, Loiret, Loir-et-Cher, Indre-et-Loire, Indre and Cher. Anecdotally, the river marks a border in weather patterns, so you should expect to see the sun on the southern side. Unfortunately this doesn't always follow. It is a popular area for holiday homes and property prices are above the national average, although the area around Tours is better-known and higher-priced than some of the more outlying areas, such as near Bourges. Chartres, with its magnificent cathedral, is a bit to the north of the valley on a wheat-carpeted plain called the Beauce. The boat and the horse are the preferred recreational accessories but there are several golf courses, too: three around Orléans, one at Sancerre, one east of Vendôme, two north west of Tours and one south of Blois.

Limousin and the Auvergne

If there is a heart of France, if the expression *La France profonde* – Deep France – has any meaning, this is where to find it. There is a difference between the two regions. Limousin is perhaps a little less extreme, a little more sociable. Guidebooks tend to ignore it and tourists drive through it, yet, for simple rural charm, it is hard to beat. It has forests and lakes as pretty as any and gorges and castle too. But the gorges and castles are perhaps not as spectacular as some others, nor the forests and lakes as large and so the whole area does not attract foreigners in the way that better-known regions do. The French know all about it, though, and, in high summer, platoons of singing school children will be found marching gaily along the shores of many of its thousand or so lakes. History connects the region with Richard Coeur de Lion and a tradition of tapestry. Limoges, famous for its porcelain, is the best-known centre, but who could forget a town called Brive-la-Gaillarde

– Brive the Strapping Wench. Summers are warm, winters cold. Property prices are well below the national average. So what is the catch? It's a mystery. It is true there is no sea, mountain range or large Anglophone community here, but why this area has not been a focus for British buyers remains obscure. The departments are Corrèze, Haute-Vienne and Creuse.

Isolated, underpopulated, vast and spectacular, Auvergne is France's Wild West, except it is almost in the dead centre, and Tolkien's Middle Earth might be more appropriate. It boasts a volcanic ancestry that has bequeathed it extinct craters, which add to its mildly fantastical persona. It has dense forests and river gorges and lies on the edge of the imposing Massif Central. As everywhere else in this area there is plenty for the antiquarian and the adventure sportsperson, and it offers two famous regional parks – the Parc Naturel Régional du Livradois Forez and the Parc Naturel Régional des Volcans d'Auvergne. Property prices are the cheapest in France and, once again, one is forced to speculate why more foreigners haven't invested in this most magnificent of regions. Perhaps the extremely cold winters and the less-than-outgoing reputation of her citizens have something to do with it. Clermont-Ferrand – child of a marriage between the Clermont of the bishops and Ferrand of the dukes (the dukes won) – is the main town, although Vichy has acquired more international, although rather dubious, celebrity. The departments are Allier, Cantal, Haute-Loire and Puy-de-Dôme.

Hiking and cycling are popular in both regions but the area is also known for skiing, with three stations southwest of Clermont-Ferrand: Le Mont-Dore, Besse-super-Besse and Le Lioran, all family resorts with 'snowrider' options, and Le Lioran offering cross-country as well. Mont Dore also offers a golf course, presumably when the piste becomes the fairway.

The West Coast

Our division of France has left the west coast rather short, as Brittany occupies the northwest and Aquitaine falls in the southwest. What is left is France's fine Atlantic coast and its hinterland. A department of Pays de la Loire, Mayenne, is actually nearer the Channel than the Atlantic, and another department, Maine-et-Loire, has been included with Centre, because it is in what is thought of as the Loire Valley. This unilateral swapping of departments may not be ideal, but it is sometimes difficult to correlate administrative regions with what foreigners perceive them to be. Pays de la Loire is often known as the Western Loire.

Pays de la Loire

Nantes doesn't look like Bristol, but they have much in common. They were both once great seaports, they are both at the head of large estuaries and became rich on the slave trade. One might also add that both are close to their countries' Celtic fringe, and Nantes was actually capital of Brittany before it married into France in 1532. Indeed, it was Brittany's regional capital until replaced by Rennes. St-Nazaire is now the seaward port and the coast is known for its beaches: it's said that neighbouring La Baule has the whitest sand in Europe. Now linked to the shore by a bridge is the island of Noirmoutier, famous for its oysters, while a little further offshore is Ile d'Yeu where Vichy France's Marshal Pétain was imprisoned for his last years. From here down to La Rochelle are several resorts, ever-popular with the French, but only beginning to increase their profile among the British – Les Sables d'Olonne, for instance, finishing point for the Vendée Round the World Yacht Race. Indeed, for most British, when Ellen McArthur sailed to fame here it was the first time they had heard of Les Sables – the Sands. Inland of many of the beaches are *marais*, or marshes, most famously the Marais Poitevin on the border of the Vendée and Charente-Maritime.

The Vendée's is a coastal cuisine: oysters from the sea; waterfowl, eels, frogs and snails from the *marais*; pork, geese and a goat's cheese called *chabichou* inland, also *mojettes*, a large white bean that is a regional speciality. Travelling south along the Atlantic coast, it is also the first region we find producing wine – we are in Muscadet country. Summertime offers all the advantages of the Gulf Stream and a warmth that earns Maine-et-Loire the title of Garden of France and prompts some writers to compare the Vendée with the Spanish Costas. 'Hot Holland' has been another label that captures the feel of this flat, marshy and sandy coast.

To historians, the name Vendée will mean a bloody war fought in 1792 between the revolutionary National Guard and the locals, largely in defence of their Catholic faith. The behaviour of the government forces was particularly vicious and, by the time it was over, between 200,000 and 300,000 people had died. The event is still remembered here, and there are several exhibitions and monuments to commemorate it.

Recreation here means the sea – sailing and other big sea sports are the main things on offer. But there are golf courses up the Loire at Angers and Saumur, then at Nantes and Punic and, after that, a further five spread down the coast to La Rochelle.

The Vendée coast is obviously of prime interest to house-hunters and prices there are steadily rising. There is also much interest in the department of Mayenne, but for completely different reasons. The town of Mayenne is much nearer Rennes than Nantes. Neither of the region's two northern departments – Sarthe, with its capital Le Mans, is the other – feels very coastal and the truth is that foreign home-hunters are often those who are really looking to buy in Normandy, Brittany or the Loire Valley. Such are the complexities of French geography. Nantes is another place to bear in mind; the decline of the shipbuilding industry has meant that prices are reasonable and, it is very convenient for the Vendée coast, the Loire and Brittany.

Poitou-Charentes

Charente, you will be told, is not as pretty as the Dordogne, but cheaper. The reason for this unflattering comparison with the cricket-playing department is that they are next door and Charente acts as an overflow for foreign house-buyers. It is, anyway, a calumny. Charentes is just different. It lies at the foot of the plateau that makes the Dordogne so scenic, and earns its keep by the sweat of its agricultural brow. But it does have some very pretty parts, such as the Charente River between Cognac and Angoulême. Slightly further west is Saintes, and it is between these three that most of the British interest has been. The idea of ending your days in Cognac is certainly appealing. Then there is Angoulême itself, an historic hilltop city in whose cathedral King John of England was married. The Dordogne can't compete with that. Grand old Poitiers is where the Black Prince beat Jean le Bon and Charles Martel, the Saracens and stopped the northward march of Islam. Poitiers also has Futuroscope, a sci-fi vision in steel and glass that rises out of Poitou's fields and and celebrates advances in, and the future of, technology. It boasts the largest collection of giant cinema screens in the world and even has its own TGV station.

Neighbouring Deux-Sèvres has two pastoral delights: the valley of the Thouet river between Parthenay and Thouars, and the Marais Poitevin. These last are marshes, set just back from the coast, which have been reclaimed over the centuries, first by monks and then by Dutch drainage engineers. There are many *marais* but these are the most famous. Here is a water-logged kingdom of river fowl, frogs and dragonflies that can be explored by punt and supports a tourist trade accessed by several villages, principally Coulon and Maillezais. The whole inland area of the region is also particularly rich in Neolithic sites and, more famously, in Romanesque churches that once ministered to the pilgrims en route for Compostela. So it is an injustice to portray the inland departments of this region simply as a poor relation of the Dordogne.

Nobody ever accused the coastal department of Charente-Maritime of being anyone's poor relation. La Rochelle sails through French history like the galleons it once sent forth; a substantial percentage of French North Americans claim ancestry of the city. Picturesque and well preserved, it has a Vieux Port, cathedral and bevy of museums on the subjects of fine arts, perfume, ceramics and slavery. Just offshore, but now reached by bridge, is Ile de Ré, which is supposed to have its own microclimate and offers several pine-backed sandy beaches. Off the coast between La Rochelle and Rochefort are several other islands, among them Fort Boyard, made famous by the TV programme. Rochefort itself is another naval town where you can visit an international sea centre and naval museum among other nautical delights. Between here and Gironde is another run of beaches, some better than others for swimming because of dangerous currents. The sea, once again, offers the principal leisure options with sailing, windsurfing and other watersports along the coast while, inland, Poitiers and Parthenay have golf courses.

As you would expect, this coastline is not the place to go looking for a bargain. However, watersports fans may feel the premium is worth paying when you consider what is on offer. The agricultural back-country is where there is still opportunity and, in many ways, it resembles the Dordogne of 20 years ago. Some of our informants told us that they preferred Poitou-Charentes *because* it had fewer British residents. Having said that, prices have doubled in the last decade, a very unusual occurrence in France. As noted above, the Cognac area is popular with foreigners, but there are surely more undiscovered places for the adventurous to find. The local architecture is supposed to be similar to Périgord, but in practice there is a bit of a mix, with modern styles predominant in the resorts.

Corsica

'I would recognize my island with my eyes closed by nothing more than the smell of the *maquis* carried on the waves,' said Napoleon. What is also striking for those approaching by sea is its clarity: you can watch the island rising to meet you through fathoms of deep blue water. For this is the least polluted, least spoilt, least developed part of France. In fact, it has only been part of France since 1769 – the year of Napoleon's birth, when Genoa sold it off. The fourth biggest island in the Mediterranean, it has the second highest mountain – indeed, it is practically all mountain and forest and, for hikers, bikers, divers and boaters, it is a paradise. It strikes one as being more Italian than French – the local language is similar to two Italian dialects – but is really very much Corsican, with its own regional government and independence movements. The summers are hot, the winters mild and one can imagine that this just how the south of France must have been 100 years ago – Italianate villages clinging to pine-cloaked hills above cliffs that drop to a coast of sandy beaches and a profound sea that hides the wrecks of antiquity's shipping.

It is not only this and the clear water that attract the divers, but the deep-shelving coastline, which makes for spectacular under-seascapes. Hiking along the ancient mule paths that run the length of the island is another uniquely Corsican experience, as is exploring the thousands of sandy coves along a generally iron-bound coast. If all this isn't enough, there is one golf course on the island at Bonifacio.

Corsica is a popular second home destination for Italians, but several factors act to put off British buyers. First, there is distance: Italy is only 50 miles away; from Britain you have to cross France, then 100 miles of sea. Plus, the independence movements haven't all been completely non-violent and some are reputed to have links with organized crime. It is said that starting a business here may involve having to pay protection money. Some second homes have been blown up, which doesn't enhance the profile of the island for investment. This may all simply be a perceived disincentive, based on a tiny amount of non-representative activity, but perceptions have an important effect on any market.

Selecting a Property

04

The first rule is, don't be easily seduced. There are a hundred and one things that may entice you to buy a property where, with a little more forbearance, you might have done better. It's much easier if you have bags of time and money, but, if you haven't, use the time sensibly and you'll save in the end. People have even been known to buy unseen; some have been lucky, others not. Don't be overwhelmed just because it's near or seems cheap or has a lovely view or a fine restaurant down the road or mild winters or an English-speaking café *patron* or was once owned by Mme de Pompadour. (Mind you, if it was *all* those things, you probably should be overwhelmed!) House-hunt sensibly – your prey might be well camouflaged, but it is plentiful.

Travelling to France

It is an interesting thought that travellers between London and Paris could use the same technology in 1850 as they might in 1950 – telegraph their hotel bookings and then catch the boat train and ferry – but, by the end of the 20th century, all forms of transport between the two cities had undergone a revolution. Flying – in 1950 the most expensive option – has become, in some cases, the cheapest. Yet, from city centre to city centre, the train is sometimes as fast. This is due not only to the realization of that old dream of a tunnel under the sea, but also to high-speed train technology, which didn't exist in 1950. While train journey times are coming down, air travel journey times are going up, thanks to congestion in the air and at airports. The Channel Tunnel, the TGV, low-cost airlines and the motorway systems of both countries have revolutionized travel to, and within, France. There had been another change that would have astonished the Englishman of 1950: on balance, the French have been responsible for the bulk of the technological innovation.

These generalizations actually represent quite a complex travel scenario. Flying is not the cheapest way to travel unless you are using a low-cost airline, and there may be good reasons for not doing so – most likely because the nearest destination is too far from where you want to go or you can't travel when they want you to. On the whole, budget flight destinations are some way from city centres, although they can be very useful if you have a country home nearby and don't have to go to the nearest city. If you are lucky in this respect, they will certainly save you travel time within France – Buzz's flight to Bergerac, for instance, saves the many British residents of the Dordogne from having to travel to the other side of Bordeaux. As for overall travel time, they can also represent a huge saving. Nice, for example, is served by both the TGV and low-cost airlines – the latter taking a couple of hours from London as against almost ten hours by rail. Don't forget, though, your journey time on the British side of the Channel – your choice of route will depend on where you are starting from. If it is Suffolk, the quickest way to central Paris could be to fly from Stansted, but if it is central London, Eurostar would be a quicker option. The complexity exists because of the many different choices available, not because of a lack of them. So, the best way to approach this subject is to examine the transport options one by one.

Car

The car is still the favourite of the house-owner and house-hunter because, first and foremost, unless you are looking for property in a town, there is rarely any real public transport option in the French countryside. Buses are infrequent and many villages have no services at all. As for the rail network, like its British counterpart it now only serves substantial towns. Second, a car can be loaded with either personal effects or merchandise from its cheapest source – at the moment this is probably France, where fuel is also usually cheaper, but this might not always be the case. If several people travel in one car, it could prove very economical per head.

Although French *autoroutes* (**www.autoroutes.fr**) are much better than British motorways, you may prefer to use the French N roads to avoid paying tolls. Your journey will be slower, but you will also see more of the country. However, if you are making a long journey, your food and accommodation bills will negate any saving on the tolls. Your choice depends on how frugal you want to be and how much time you have.

Planning your journey and navigating your way around is now easier than ever with online maps and route planners that work out routes and estimate costs, distances and times. Visit **www.mappy.com**, **www.michelin-travel.com**, **www.rac.co.uk**, **www.theaa.com** and **www.shellgeostar.com**.

The Channel Tunnel

The Channel Tunnel vehicle transport service is by far the quickest and most convenient way to get to France, but it isn't the cheapest (except sometimes with off-season deals) and not everybody wants to start his or her journey at Calais. As well as a discount scheme called Points Plus, the company operates a Property Owners' Club, which entitles its members to genuine discounts and fast-track boarding if blocks of tickets are purchased at one time, as long as they are *bona fide* owners of property in Europe.

Ferries

There are several good reasons for taking ferries. They are usually cheaper mile for mile, can cut out a lot of driving, depending where you are going, and, if you enjoy the sea, can be fun. For one English family, their holiday at their house in Périgord begins when they board the overnight ferry to Normandy. However, there is much discussion among regular cross-Channel car travellers as to how to get the best deals, which, at the time of writing, range from £15 (usually for very short stays out of season) upwards. Quotes from the various operators often seem to be erratic and illogical: booking online can be more straightforward. Each company offers its own discount schemes for regular travellers: Brittany Ferries has a Property Owners' Travel Club, Condor has a Frequent Travellers' Club, P&O has a Traveller Club, a Portsmouth Travellers' scheme and a Travellers' Residents Club for home-owners. Hoverspeed has a Frequent User scheme, Sea France a Past Passenger scheme and P&O a Voyager scheme.

Operators are Brittany Ferries (Portsmouth to Caen and St-Malo, Cork to Roscoff), P&O Ferries (Dover to Calais), Sea France (Dover to Calais), Norfolkline (Dover to Dunkirk), Condor Ferries (Poole to St-Malo), Hoverspeed (Dover to Calais, Dover to Ostend, Newhaven to Dieppe), P&O Portmouth (Portsmouth to Le Havre and Cherbourg), and Irish Ferries (Rosslare to Cherbourg and Roscoff).

Air

Received wisdom is that the national carrier airlines are a dying breed and that budget airlines will control the European skies in the future. Perhaps, and perhaps not. Low-cost airlines are not always cheaper, especially during busy periods, and you should check out the traditional carriers. On the whole, they are more expensive, but, if you can afford them, they do have a number of genuine advantages. They fly to the major airports, often have more regular flights and better baggage allowances, proper cabin service, and you can pre-book your seat. They will telephone you if your flight is cancelled. For people who find low-cost airlines a disagreeable and unreliable scrimmage, the traditional airline may well be worth the extra cost. So, consider Air France, British Airways, British Midland and, from Ireland, Aer Lingus.

The effect of the budget airlines on the shape of the European travel industry has been enormous and, although there are some pretty drastic predictions going around, nobody can be quite sure where it will all end. Early 2002 saw a whole crop of new destinations in France from a widespread raft of British airports. For people with a rural French home, these new flights have sometimes dramatically cut the distance to the nearest airport. Certainly, these operators have drawbacks that the national carriers don't, but for most people their price advantages are what count. Remember that the earlier you can book your flight, the cheaper it will be – as each plane fills up, the cost of a seat on it increases. If you are travelling regularly, it's a good idea to sign up to the carriers' website newsletters, which will give you first news of special offers. A word of caution, though: at the time of writing, the whole airline industry is in a state of unprecedented upheaval. Budget airlines are making offers that they would not in normal trading conditions. Even 18 months ago,

Profiles of the Regions

The North

<< see page 38

So close to home and yet so very French, this region appeals for a thousand reasons. Its coastlines, given names like Opal, and Emerald, are the stuff of childhood dreams. Its forests, meadows and woodlands are a joy to nature-lovers. Its food and drink encompass hearty creamy Norman cheeses and lacy Breton crêpes, northern beers, fruity cider and fiery Calvados. And its appeal to home-buyers is as varied – from low-lying Picard farmhouses to the half-timbered *colombages* of Normandy to the granite and slate cottages of Brittany's fishermen, there is something for everyone.

1 Gerberoy, Picardy
2 Bergues, French Flanders
3 Brittany, near Kerhinet
4 Beuvron-en-Auge, Normandy
5 Vernon, River Seine
6 Ile d'Ouessant, Brittany
7 Pas de Calais

The East

<< see page 41

France's eastern frontier crosses the deep forests of the Ardennes and the vine-covered hillsides of Champagne, and mounts the green and rolling Vosges and Jura ranges before reaching the pinnacle of the Alps and Mont Blanc, the highest peak in Europe. Here are picturesque wooden chalets and streamlined apartment complexes, chic boutiques and rustic restaurants serving fondues and mulled wine, for this is one of the world's great skiing regions. Summer brings hill-walking, rafting and kayaking, and the lower slopes blossom under a southern sun.

1 Hunawihr, Alsace
2 Alsace
3 Vosges, Alsace
4 Neidemorschwir, Alsace
5 Hautvilliers, Champagne
6 Briançon
7 French Alps
8 Chapel, St-Lie, Champagne

5

6

7

8

The South

<< see page 43

Everyone knows the magic of the South of France – from its lavender- and herb-scented hills, perched villages and lonely Camargue lagoons to the glitz and glamour of the Riviera and St-Tropez. Many are drawn to the same light that dazzled Matisse and Picasso. Gourmets can seek out the best bouillabaisse or buy their olives from France's finest markets. Some dream of a villa on the Côte d'Azur or an ancient stone-built *mas* straight from the pages of Marcel Pagnol or Peter Mayle, but even a tiny hill-town cottage or a simple studio-apartment is enough to be able to say 'my place in the South of France'.

3

1 Roussillon
2 Côte d'Azur
3 Vineyards
4 Provence
5 View from cactus garden, Eze
6 Luberon, Provence
7 Calanque du Sorimou

4

5

6

7

8 Menton, Côte d'Azur
9 Roussillon
10 Cêpes, Aix market
11 Olives, Nice market
12 Vineyards, Luberon
13 Provence

The Southwest

<< see page 48

Southwest France is a land of contrasts. Here are the valleys of the high Pyrenees, the Silver Coast with Europe's longest beach, and the ancient limestone cliffs of the Dordogne valley. Its rich river valleys produce not only the duck and goose foie gras, *confits* and *magrets* for which it is famous, but also Cognac and Armagnac and the great wines of Bordeaux. It was here, around Pau in 1869, that the British first began to buy houses and it is still here, in Périgord, that the present generation of cross-Channel purchasers come to find their dream home.

1 Aveyron
2 Sete
3 Arrens, Pyrenees
4 Vineyard, Dordogne

5 Dordogne
6 Ardèche gorge
7 Languedoc
8 Dordogne
9 Albi, Languedoc

8

9

1

2

Central

<< see page 52

From the stately Loire to the vineyards of Burgundy, and from the extinct volcanoes of the Auvergne to the 'City of Light', Paris herself, lies a stunning hinterland of mountains, plains, forests and ancient cities. The Loire – haughty châteaux and troglodyte dwellings, salmon and Sancerre – is perhaps, after Paris, the destination best-known to British house-hunters, but Burgundy has long been popular with Parisian week-enders who admire its rural tranquillity. To the south, historic Limousin appeals with its lakes and forests while, by its side, broods majestic Auvergne with its spectacular scenery.

1 Vineyards, Burgundy
2 Cévennes
3 Cévennes
4 Auvergne
5 Grape harvest
6 Massif Central, Auvergne
7 Vézelay

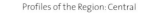

1

2

The West

<< see page 56

The Atlantic winds, and the whitest sand in Europe, define the other great French coast. Spectacular beaches and sailing boats against a blue sky, and ancient seaports with ringing names like La Rochelle and Rochefort, remind us that this is France's ocean shoreline – bracing and sportive in contrast to the hedonistic Mediterranean coast. Yet, for all its breezy Atlantic bluster, the Vendée can be surprisingly hot in summer and is a treasured secret among those British buyers who have already discovered its delights.

1 Aquitaine
2 Coulon, Aquitaine
3 Blaye, Gironde
4 Vendée market
5 Picnic

Corsica

<< see page 56

Corsica – with its maquis-covered hills, dotted with ancient perched villages, dropping to a clear blue sea – offers much of what the French Mediterranean coast did 80 years ago. French since only the 18th century, this land is the most unspoilt part of European France. It has high mountains, pine forests and a spectacular hiking trail from north to south, while its delightful coastline offers hidden sandy beaches and dramatic cliffs. Corsica has long attracted Italian house-hunters, but distance and accessibility leave it still relatively untouched by British buyers.

1 Evisa
2 Beach, Palombaggia
3 Col de Bavella

many seats on these airlines were not hugely discounted from the regular national carrier flights. For the moment, though, the offers are great so check Ryanair, easyJet and Bmibaby (British Midland's budget contender).

Rail

Finally, you could take the 1850 option – the train. The glamorous one is Eurostar, which runs through the Tunnel to Lille,Paris and Avignon (summer). The present three-hour journey time will be further cut when eventually the English end of the line is upgraded, the new terminus built and people stop making jokes about the northern end of the line. (When using Eurostar, mark your luggage with your name and seat number. It's a recent security measure that is unusual for a train and, on board, it's too late. Also, of course, remember your passport!)

The advent of the Chunnel has completely changed the old boat-train and ferry set-up. You cannot buy a through ticket from London via any English port to France and onward by rail any more. Rail Europe (**t** 0870 584 8848; **www.raileurope.co.uk**) will still book you the traditional trains, but not the ferry part. The only way you can still get a combined ticket is via Dover-Calais through the specialist Trains Europe (**t** 020 8699 3654; **www.trainseurope.co.uk**; info@trainseurope.co.uk). This is still the cheapest way.

Alternatively, you may prefer to put your car on the train. The French railways' service is called Motorail and, having crossed the Channel by your preferred method, your car is loaded on to a train in Calais, you board for your allocated sleeping compartment and you are all offloaded at Avignon, Brive, Narbonne, Nice or Toulouse. Accommodation is in two-bed sleepers (with wash basins) or four or six-berth compartments, with washing facilities at each end of the carriage, but there is no facility for dining on board and the service is quite expensive – indeed, it is the most expensive way of getting a car to southern France. *See* the Rail Europe website (**www.frenchmotorail.com**) or telephone French Motorail (**t** 0870 241 5415).

Routes to the Regions

Only the final destinations for the TGV are detailed below, but there are stops en route, so it's worth checking with Rail Europe (**t** 0870 584 8848; **www.raileurope.co.uk**) in case there is one near your destination.

Paris

Air: Paris Charles de Gaulle airport is the destination for British Airways and Air France flights from Heathrow, Gatwick and several other UK departure points. Paris is also served by easyJet flights (to Charles de Gaulle) Ryanair, BMI Baby and Aer Lingus from 17 airports in the UK and two in Ireland.

Road: The French *autoroute* nexwork marches out from Paris to all corners of the 'hexagon' with names like those of revolutionary armies (the Autoroutes of the North, of the East) or Roman legions (the Aquitainian, Occitanian and Oceanic). Just allow plenty of time getting on to them from the city if it is a public holiday. For route planning, look at **www.mappy.com**, **www. michelin-travel.com**, **www.rac.co.uk** and **www.theaa.com**.

Rail: Paris is not only the primary TGV terminus, but also the other end of the Eurostar Channel Tunnel connection from London and Ashford; a huge network of conventional railways centre on Paris too.

Nord-Pas de Calais

Sea:

From	To	Operator	Telephone	Website
Dover	Calais	P&O Ferries	0870 600 0600	www.posl.com
Dover	Calais	Sea France	0870 571 1711	www.seafrance.com
Dover	Calais	Hoverspeed	0870 524 0241	www.hoverspeed.com
Dover	Dunkirk	Norfolkline	0870 870 1020	www.norfolkline.com
Newhaven	Dieppe	Hoverspeed	0870 524 0241	www.hoverspeed.com

Air: Lille has a regional airport with links to Paris. Don't forget there are always connecting flights via Paris or other centres.

Road: The A1 Autoroute du Nord goes to Paris via Béthune and passes near to Arras; the A26 cuts off it for Calais. The A16 follows a more westerly course via Boulogne and Amiens. The conurbation south of Lille is one vast spaghetti junction. For route planning visit **www.mappy.com**, **www. michelin-travel. com**, **www.rac.co.uk** and **www.theaa.com**.

Rail: Lille is a Eurostar station, two hours from London Waterloo International, and one hour from Paris. There is also a TGV link to Paris, Gare de l'Est, which, like Eurostar, takes an hour (Rail Europe: **t** 0870 584 8848; **www.raileurope. co.uk**). Lille is also linked direct with many other French destinations from its TGV station, Lille Europe. Conventional trains run from nearby Lille Flandres. Calais is also the starting point for the seasonal Motorail service to Avignon, Brive, Narbonne, Nice and Toulouse (Motorail: **t** 0870 241 5415 or through **www.frenchmotorail.com**).

Tunnel: Eurotunnel's passenger service carries cars, vans and coaches in special trains – you stay with your car for the 35-minute journey and no foot-only passengers can travel (unlike ferries). You can't miss the terminals on either side of the Channel – the English one is just off the M20 to the east of

Folkestone and the French one is well signposted on all the *autoroute* approaches to Calais. There is a huge adjacent shopping centre called Cité Europe at the French end. Advance booking is strongly advised for peak season crossings, such as during school holidays (Eurotunnel: **t** 0870 535 3535; **www.eurotunnel.com**).

Normandy

Air: There are small airports at Deauville and Cherbourg, but services to them are not consistent, so check. Don't forget that there are always connecting flights via Paris or other centres.

From	To	Operator	Telephone	Website
Gatwick	Le Havre	British European	0870 567 6676	www.flybe.com
Gatwick and City	Le Havre	Air France/ Brit Air	0845 0845 111* 08 20 820 820	www.airfrance.co.uk www.britair.fr
Stansted	Rouen	Buzz	0870 240 7070	www.buzzaway.com
Stansted	Caen	Buzz	0870 240 7070	www.buzzaway.com

*Air France is the UK booking agent for Britair.

Sea:

From	To	Operator	Telephone	Website
Newhaven	Dieppe	Hoverspeed	0870 524 0241	www.hoverspeed.com
Newhaven	Dieppe	Transmanche	0800 917 1201	www.transmanche ferries.com
Portsmouth	Cherbourg	P&O Portsmouth	0870 242 4999	www.poportsmouth.com
Portsmouth	Le Havre	P&O Portsmouth	0870 242 4999	www.poportsmouth.com
Poole	Cherbourg	Brittany Ferries	0870 5561600	www.brittany-ferries.com
Portsmouth	Caen (Ouistreham)	Brittany Ferries	0870 5561600	www.brittany-ferries.com
Poole/ Portsmouth	Cherbourg	Condor	0845 345 2000	www.condorferries.co.uk
Rosslare	Cherbourg	Irish Ferries	0870 517 1717	www.irishferries.ie

Road: The A13, the Autoroute de Normandie, is the main road from Paris to the region and becomes the A84 west of Caen. Take the A28 if coming from Calais, via Rouen and Abbeville. For route planning, visit **www.mappy.com**, **www.michelin-travel.com**, **www.rac.co.uk** and **www.theaa.com**.

Rail: There is no TGV line to the region as yet. Trains from Paris to stations in Normandy depart from either Gare St-Lazare or Gare Montparnasse (Rail Europe: **t** 08705 848 848; **www.raileurope.co.uk**).

Brittany

Sea:

From	To	Operator	Telephone	Website
Cork	Roscoff	Brittany Ferries	0870 536 0360	www.brittany-ferries.com
Plymouth	Roscoff	Brittany Ferries	0870 536 0360	www.brittany-ferries.com
Poole	St-Malo	Condor Ferries	0845 345 2000	www.condorferries.co.uk
Portsmouth,	St-Malo	Brittany Ferries	0870 536 0360	www.brittany-ferries.com
Rosslare	Roscoff	Irish Ferries	0870 517 1717	www.irishferries.ie
Weymouth via Guernsey	St-Malo	Condor Ferries	0845 345 2000	www.condorferries.co.uk

Air: Don't forget there are always connecting flights via Paris or other centres.

From	To	Operator	Telephone	Website
Gatwick	Brest	Air France/ Brit Air	0845 0845 111* 08 20 820 820 (Fr)	www.airfrance.co.uk www.britair.fr
Gatwick	Nantes	Air France/Brit Air	As above	As above
		British Airways		
		British European	0870 567 6676	www.flybe.com
Stansted	Brest	Buzz	0870 240 7070	www.buzzaway.com
Stansted	Dinard	Ryanair	0870 156 9569	www.ryanair.com

*Air France are the UK booking agents for Britair

Road: The main route from Paris is the A11, L'Océane, via Rennes and Le Mans. Coming from Normandy, take the A84 via Caen and Rennes. For route planning, visit **www.mappy.com**, **www.michelin-travel.com** and **www.rac.co.uk**.

Rail: There is a TGV service from Paris, Gare Montparnasse, to Rennes, Lorient, Quimper and Brest. Connections from Lille are by conventional trains (Rail Europe: t 0870 584 8848; **www.raileurope.co.uk**).

Champagne-Ardennes

Air: Paris is the prime air terminus served by a raft of services, among them Air France (**t** 0845 0845 111; **www.airfrance.co.uk**) and British Airways (**t** 0845 773 3377; **www.britishairways.com**).

Road: The main route from Paris is the A4, Autoroute de l'Est, which goes to Metz. From Calais, take the A26 via St-Quentin, which continues south to Troyes. For route planning, visit **www.mappy.com**, **www.michelin-travel.com**, **www.rac.co.uk** and **www.theaa.com**.

Rail: Reims is connected to both Paris, Gare de l'Est, and Brussels by conventional services (Rail Europe: **t** 0870 584 8848; **www.raileurope.co.uk**). A TGV route is on the drawing board.

Alsace-Lorraine and Franche-Comté

Air: Air France flies from Gatwick to Strasbourg (**t** 0845 0845 111; **www.airfrance.co.uk**). Don't forget there are always connecting flights via Paris or other centres.

Road: The A5 is the main connection with Paris via Troyes. From Calais, the Alsace-Lorraine region is reached via the A4, Autoroute de l'Est, via Reims. For Besançon and Franche-Comté, take the A36, La Comtoise, from Beaune. Running via Belfort and Mulhouse, this *autoroute* connects the Rhine and the Saône valleys. The route from Luxembourg is the A31, which runs to Dijon via Toul and Nancy. For route planning, visit **www.mappy.com**, **www.michelin-travel.com**, **www.rac.co.uk** and **www.theaa.com**.

Rail: There are good rail links to all major towns and a TGV line to Besançon (Rail Europe: **t** 0870 584 8848; **www.raileurope.co.uk**).

Rhône-Alpes

Air: Don't forget, there are always connecting flights via Paris or other centres.

From	To	Operator	Telephone	Website
Birmingham	Lyon	British Airways	0845 773 3377	www.britishairways.com
Gatwick	Lyon	Air France British Airways	0845 0845 111 0845 773 3377	www.airfrance.co.uk www.britishairways.com
Stansted	Lyon	easyJet	0870 607 6543	www.easyJet.co.uk
Stansted	Chambéry	Buzz	0870 240 7070	www.buzzaway.com
Stansted	Grenoble	Buzz	0870 240 7070	www.buzzaway.com
Stansted	St-Etienne	Ryanair	0870 156 9569	www.ryanair.com

Road: The main north-south arterial and Paris route is the A6 and A7, the Autoroute du Soleil, via Lyon and Auxerre, but coming from Calais it is sensible to use the A21 and A36 via Reims and Troyes. Grenoble is reached by the A43 and A49 and the mountain region is served by a network of autoroutes around a Geneva-Grenoble axis. For route planning, visit **www.mappy.com**, **www.michelin-travel.com**, **www.rac.co.uk** and **www.theaa.com**.

Rail: Lyon is connected to both Paris, Gare de Lyon, and Lille Europe by TGV (Rail Europe: **t** 0870 584 8848; **www.raileurope.co.uk**). The rest of the region has a good conventional service.

Provence-Côte d'Azur

Air: Don't forget, there are always connecting flights via Paris or other centres.

From	To	Operator	Telephone	Website
Birmingham	Nice	British Airways	0845 773 3377	www.britishairways.com
East Midlands	Nice	Bmibaby	0870 607 0555	www.flybmi.com
Gatwick	Marseille	British Airways	0845 773 3377	www.britishairways.com
Gatwick	Nice	easyJet	0870 600 0000	www.easyJet.co.uk
Heathrow	Nice	British Airways	0845 773 3377	www.britishairways.com
Stansted	Nice	easyjet	0845 605 4321	www.easyJet.co.uk
Stansted	Toulon	Buzz	0870 240 7070	www.buzzaway.com
Stansted	Marseille	Buzz	0870 240 7070	www.buzzaway.com

Road: The A6 and then the A7, the Autoroute du Soleil, via Lyon and Auxerre, is the principal route south, and the A8, La Provençale, cuts off it at Aix to serve the region. From Calais, start out on the A26 via Reims and Troyes, then use the A5 and A31 to join the A6 at Beaune. For route planning, visit **www.mappy.com**, **www.michelin-travel.com**, **www.rac.co.uk** and **www.theaa.com**.

Rail: Rail connections are very good, but the distance from the UK makes it a long journey, now mitigated by a direct Eurostar connection from Waterloo to Avignon between July and September. The completion of the TGV link to Nice means that it is now 9¾ hours from London, though this will shrink further when the upgrade of the British line has been completed. The line to Paris Gare de Lyon serves Avignon, Aix, Marseille, Cannes and Nice. There are also services from these stations to Lille Europe (Rail Europe: **t** 0870 584 8848; **www.raileurope.co.uk**). There are Motorail services from Calais to Avignon and Nice (Motorail: **t** 0870 241 5415 or through **www.frenchmotorail.com**).

Languedoc-Roussillon

Air: Don't forget, there are always connecting flights via Paris or other centres.

From	To	Operator	Telephone	Website
Stansted	Montpellier	Ryanair Buzz	0870 156 9569 0870 240 7070	www.ryanair.com www.buzzaway.com
Stansted	Perpignan	Ryanair	0870 156 9569	www.ryanair.com
Stansted	Carcassonne	Ryanair	0870 156 9569	www.ryanair.com
Stansted	Nîmes	Ryanair	0870 156 9569	www.ryanair.com

Road: The A9, the Languedocienne, cuts off the A7 and runs down to Spain along much the same route as the Roman Via Domitia, via Nîmes and Montpellier. The A62, Deux Mers, for Toulouse, cuts off south of Narbonne. For route planning, visit **www.mappy.com**, **www.michelin-travel.com**, **www.rac.co.uk** and **www.theaa.com**.

Rail: The same comments apply here as for Provence-Côte d'Azur. It's a long way, but the connections are good. Nîmes, Arles and Montpellier are served by

TGV from Paris, Gare de Lyon, and Montpellier is also served from Lille Europe. Perpignan and the other regional centres are served by conventional trains (Rail Europe: **t** 0870 584 8848; **www.raileurope.co.uk**). There is a Motorail service to Narbonne from Calais (Motorail: **t** 0870 241 5415 or through **www.frenchmotorail.com**).

The Southwest

Sea: The nearest ferry port is Santander in Spain, to which there is a Brittany Ferries service from Plymouth (Brittany Ferries: **t** 0870 536 0360; **www.brittany-ferries.com**).

Air: Don't forget, there are always connecting flights via Paris or other centres.

From	To	Operator	Telephone	Website
Stansted	Bordeaux	Buzz	0870 240 7070	www.buzzaway.com
Stansted	Biarritz	Ryanair	0870 156 9569	www.ryanair.com

Road: The N10 runs north–south. It is an *autoroute* for the first 52km south of Bordeaux and then dualized until it become the A63, 36km north of Hossegor. When it crosses the border, it becomes the Spanish A8, but during all these personality changes it remains the E5, which is easier to remember. The A64 from Toulouse via Pau and Tarbes meets it at Bayonne. For route planning, visit **www.mappy.com**, **www.michelin-travel.com**, **www.rac.co.uk** and **www.theaa.com**.

Rail: There is a TGV service from Paris to Bordeaux and conventional connections with Biarritz, Toulouse, Lourdes and Spain (Rail Europe: **t** 0870 584 8848; **www.raileurope.co.uk**).

Dordogne, Lot-et-Garonne

Air: The nearest large airport is Bordeaux, with a wide selection of destinations, including London, and Bergerac serves many of the British residents of the Dordogne. Don't forget that there are always connecting flights via Paris or other centres.

From	To	Operator	Telephone	Website
Stansted	Bordeaux	Buzz	0870 240 7070	www.buzzaway.com
Stansted	Bergerac	Buzz	0870 240 7070	www.buzzaway.com

Road: A mixed blessing is that no *autoroutes* actually cross the area, which is served by three that form a triangle around it. The A10, L'Aquitaine, runs from Paris to Bordeaux on the west side via Saintes and Poitiers; the A20, L'Occitane, from Paris to Toulouse via Orléans and Limoges, goes down the east side; and the A62, the Deux Mers, runs along the south side between Bordeaux and Toulouse via Agen.

Rail: The nearest TGV stations are Bordeaux and Angoulême, although ordinary trains serve stations such as Bergerac and Agen (Rail Europe: **t** 0870 584 8848; **www.raileurope.co.uk**).

Midi-Pyrénées

Air: Don't forget, there are always connecting flights via Paris or other centres.

From	To	Operator	Telephone	Website
Birmingham	Toulouse	British European	0870 567 6676	www.flybe.com
East Midlands	Toulouse	Bmibaby	0870 607 0555	www.flybmi.com
Gatwick	Toulouse	British Airways	0845 773 3377	www.britishairways.com
Stansted	Toulouse	Buzz	0870 240 7070	www.buzzaway.com

Road: The direct link with Paris is the A20, L'Occitane, from Toulouse via Limoges and Orléans. It cuts off the A62, the Deux Mers, which runs from Bordeaux to the A9, 40km west of Toulouse. The A64 for Biarritz runs from Toulouse via Tarbes and Pau.

Rail: Toulouse is served by TGV from both Paris, Gare d'Austerlitz, and Lille Europe. (Rail Europe: **t** 08705 848 848; **www.raileurope.co.uk**). There is a Motorail service from Calais (Motorail: **t** 0870 241 5415 or through **www.frenchmotorail.com**).

Burgundy

Air: Buzz (**t** 0870 240 7070; **www.buzzaway.com**) flies direct to Dijon from Stansted but most other flights go via Clermont-Ferrand. Don't forget that there are always connecting flights via Paris or other centres.

Road: Dijon is at the centre of an *autoroute* hub. The A6 is the main route from southeast Paris, via Beaune and Auxerre. The A39 heads southeast and is a link road with the Alpine system via Dijon and Bourg-en-Bresse. The A36, La Comtoise, goes to Belfort from Beaune via Besançon, while the A6 runs south to Lyon as the Autoroute du Soleil via Beaune and Mâcon. The Calais connection is via Reims and Troyes on the A26 and A5 and then along the A31 to Dijon and Beaune, while the A38 from Dijon is a short link road to the A6. For route planning, visit **www.mappy.com**, **www.michelin-travel.com**, **www.rac.co.uk** and **www.theaa.com**.

Rail: Dijon has TGV connections with Lille Europe, Paris Charles de Gaulle Airport and Paris Gare de Lyon. (Rail Europe: **t** 0870 584 8848; **www.raileurope.co.uk**).

Centre

Air: There is a regional airport at Tours, served by Buzz (**t** 08702 407 070; **www.buzzaway.com**). Don't forget that there are always connecting flights via Paris or other centres.

Road: The A10, l'Aquitaine, is the main Paris connection to Orléans and Tours. The A71, l'Averne, runs to Vierzon and Bourges, and the A20, L'Occitane, goes to Châteauroux. For the Loire Valley, from Calais, the only almost entirely *autoroute* connection from the A16 or A26/A1 skirts east of Paris. For route planning, visit **www.mappy.com**, **www.michelin-travel.com**, **www.rac.co.uk** and **www.theaa.com**.

Rail: There is a TGV connection at Tours with Paris and a direct one with Lille, via nearby St-Pierre-de-Corps, which puts London 4¼ hours away (Rail Europe: **t** 0870 584 8848; **www.raileurope.co.uk**).

Limousin

Air: Limoges has an airport served by Buzz (**t** 0870 240 7070; **www.buzzaway.com**). There is a substantial airport at Clermont-Ferrand, but Bordeaux is bigger and nearly as close. Don't forget that there are always connecting flights via Paris or other centres.

Road: The A20 (L'Aquitaine) runs north-south. From Calais, the main autoroute connection takes you around the eastern fringes of Paris. For route planning, visit **www.mappy.com**, **www.michelin-travel.com**, **www.rac.co.uk** and **www.theaa.com**.

Rail: There are good conventional rail connections from Limoges to Paris or Toulouse (Rail Europe: **t** 0870 584 8848; **www.raileurope.co.uk**). There is a Motorail service to Brive from Calais (Motorail: **t** 0870 241 5415 or through **www.frenchmotorail.com**).

Auvergne

Air: Air France (**t** 0845 0845 111; **www.airfrance.co.uk**) and British European (**t** 0870 567 6676; **www.flybe.com**) both have flights to Clermont-Ferrand from City Airport in London, and regular connections with Paris and other domestic destinations. Don't forget that there are always connecting flights via Paris or other centres.

Road: The route from Paris is the A71, L'Averne, which goes to Clermont-Ferrand via Vierzon. St-Etienne is reached on the A72 and Isoire on the A75. For route planning, visit **www.mappy.com**, **www.michelin-travel.com**, **www.rac.co.uk** and **www.theaa.com**.

Rail: There are regular services from Paris to Clermont-Ferrand (Rail Europe: **t** 0870 584 8848; **www.raileurope.co.uk**).

Pays de Loire

Air: Air France (**t** 0845 0845 111; **www.airfrance.co.uk**), British Airways (**t** 0845 737 3377; **www.britishairways.com**) and British European (**t** 0870 567 6676; **www.flybe.com**) flies to Nantes from Gatwick and there are regular regional flights. Don't forget that there are always connecting flights via Paris or other centres.

Road: Nantes and the north of the region are reached from Paris on the A11 via Angers and Le Mans; Rennes on the dualized N137 via Nantes, and Niort on the A83. Les Sables-d'Olonne is better approached on the A87 via Angers (almost completed at time of writing, and opening 2002). For route planning, visit **www.mappy.com**, **www.michelin-travel.com**, **www.rac.co.uk** and **www.theaa.com**.

Rail: Nantes and Le Mans are both TGV stations from Paris, Gare Montparnasse (Rail Europe: **t** 0870 584 8848; **www.raileurope.co.uk**).

Poitou-Charentes

Air: Don't forget, there are always connecting flights via Paris or other centres.

From	To	Operator	Telephone	Website
Gatwick	Nantes	Air France	0845 0845 111	www.airfrance.co.uk
		British Airways	0845 773 3377	www.britishairways.com
		British European	0870 567 6676	www.flybe.com
Stansted	Poitiers	Buzz	0870 240 7070	www.buzzaway.com
Stansted	La Rochelle	Buzz	0870 240 7070	www.buzzaway.com

Road: The A10 (L'Aquitaine) runs right through the region. For route planning, visit **www.mappy.com**, **www.michelin-travel.com**, **www.rac.co.uk** and **www.theaa.com**.

Rail: There is a TGV line to La Rochelle via Niort from Paris, Gare Montparnasse, and also to Futuroscope (Poitiers) and Angoulême. There is also a direct connection from Lille Europe to Futuroscope (Poitiers) and Angoulême (Rail Europe: **t** 0870 584 8848; **www.raileurope.co.uk**).

Corsica

Sea:

From	To	Operator	Telephone	Website
Marseille	Bastia, Ajaccio and Calvi	SNCM	0891 702 802	www.sncm.fr
Nice	Bastia, Ajaccio	Corsica Ferries	(F) 00 33 825 095 095	www.corsica-ferries.co.uk
Nice	Bastia, Ajaccio and Calvi	SNCM	0891 702 802	www.sncm.fr
Toulon, Bastia,	Ajaccio	Corsica Ferries	(F) 00 33 825 095 095	www.corsica-ferries.co.uk
Toulon	Bastia, Ajaccio and Calvi	SNCM	0891 702 802	www.sncm.fr

Air:

From	To	Operator	Telephone	Website
Lyon	Calvi	Air France	0845 0845 111	www.airfrance.co.uk
Marseille	Ajaccio	Air France	0845 0845 111	www.airfrance.co.uk
Nice	Bastia, Ajaccio	Air France	0845 0845 111	www.airfrance.co.uk
Paris	Bastia, Ajaccio and Calvi	Air France	0845 0845 111	www.airfrance.co.uk

Travelling Around France

House-hunting without a car is not easy. While commuting to your new French property might be done happily by budget airline or TGV, to find it in the first place you are probably going to need your car or somebody else's. If it's yours, you have now got it across the Channel and the spectacular, if rather pricey, *autoroute* network is before you. If you decide to use the *autoroutes* instead of the N roads and you have already opened a French bank account, here is a suggestion. To avoid time-wasting toll queues, which are particularly inconvenient if you are travelling alone and have to stretch across the car to pay, go *télépéage*. All this requires is a visit to the *télépéage* office at the start of many *autoroute* sections and the production of your *relève d'identité bancaire*. You will receive a transponder that fits on the windscreen and you are off – whizzing through tollgates while your bank account is automatically debited with the charge. There is a one-off fee and, of course, the perennial danger of an unauthorized overdraft, which in France is no joke (*see* p.227), but that's it. You may prefer to hire a car; local car hire firms are of variable reliability and price. Otherwise, try the usual fallbacks: Avis (**www.avis.com**), Hertz (**www.hertz-europe.com**) and Budget (**www.budget.co.uk**). There are offices at all the main airports and stations. A less expensive French firm is ADA (**www.ada-location.fr**).

France's Rail Network
ENGLAND
London
Dover
Amsterdam
NETHER-
LANDS
Brussels
GERMANY
LUX.
English Channel
Channel
Is
Calais
Dunkerque
Boulogne
Lille
Lens
Arras
Cambrai
Dieppe
Amiens
St-Quentin
Charleville-
Mézières
Cherbourg
Le Havre
Rouen
Caen
Reims
Thionville
Metz
Granville
Evreux
Mantes
Epernay
Morlaix
Brest
St-Brieuc
PARIS
Nancy
Sarrebourg
Strasbourg
St-Dizier
Alençon
Chartres
Fontainebleau
Rennes
Quimper
Lorient
Vannes
Châteaudun
Le Mans
Sens
Montargis
Epinal
Colmar
Mulhouse
Vendôme
Orléans
Auxerre
Angers
Blois
Vesoul
Belfort
St-
Nazaire
NANTES
Tours
Dijon
Besançon
Bourges
Nevers
SWITZER-
LAND
La Roche-
sur-Yon
Châteauroux
Poitiers
Montceau-
les-Mines
Chalon-sur-
Saône
Mâcon
Niort
Bourg-
en-Bresse
Geneva
La Rochelle
Rochefort
Vichy
Roanne
Royan
Cognac
Gironde
Limoges
LYON
Chambéry
Angoulême
CLERMONT-
FERRAND
St-Etienne
Périgueux
Brive-la-
Gaillarde
Grenoble
ITALY
BORDEAUX
Arcachon
Valence
Villeneuve-
sur-Lot
Montélimar
Rodez
Alès
Orange
AVIGNON
Montauban
NIMES
NICE
MONTE-
CARLO
BIARRITZ
TOULOUSE
MONTPELLIER
MARSEILLE
Pau
Tarbes
Lourdes
NARBONNE
TOULON
PERPIGNAN
SPAIN
Madrid
N
TGV rail network
100 km
50 miles
Balearic Islands

To most people, French railways mean the TGVs (*trains à grande vitesse*) and certainly these have turned the system into a practical, efficient and exciting transport alternative, although they do have a reputation for being the occasional casualties of industrial disputes. The TGV network is wide but not ubiquitous, the latest addition being the Mediterranean connection with its spectacular line. It is also intelligently planned and uses Lille as a primary junction, so travellers on Eurostar can reach much of the country without the inconvenience of changing stations in Paris. Then you are off to your destination at 186 miles an hour. There is always a supplement charged for the TGV and it can make you forget that there is another part of the system. This consists of the regular services that reach like arteries into most of the country – a huge system when you consider that France is twice the size of mainland Britain. The nationalized and subsidized SNCF offers a complicated fare structure, which is worth checking for age and group discounts, and several very useful rail passes. If you are using one of those that has open day options on it, remember to fill in the date before departure. Though the system itself is now large, as in Britain, you will see telltale cuttings and tunnels that speak of an even wider network in bygone days. The older rolling stock can be a little grubby but the newer air-conditioned trains are startlingly 21st century, with electronic signing on the side so that you can't get on the wrong train, and with comfortable seat configurations inside. For current details, contact Rail Europe (**t** 0870 241 5415; **www.raileurope.co.uk**).

French stations are, on the whole, a welcome centre of logic and good planning. Get off a train with 10 minutes to spare before your next connection and you will find a monitor on your platform giving you the time, platform and status of all other departing trains, so you can descend into the underpass and emerge on the correct platform without having to scurry to the far-off main concourse to get the information. Different from the UK, though, is the system of ticket validation. Before using your ticket, you must get it validated by an orange machine as you access the platform. Gardeners will be interested to note that the verb describing this procedure is *composter*.

Faster even than the TGV are aircraft, and France has a very effective internal air service run by Air France Europe, a subsidiary of the state airline. There are several other airlines operating – Buzz, easyJet and British European all operate internal flights too. The internal fares are not high and offer a viable alternative to both the road and the rail systems, with 27 domestic destinations served from Paris Orly and 17 from Paris Charles de Gaulle. The second domestic airline is called Corsair and can be booked through Nouvelle Frontiers (**t** 0122 774 5851). Otherwise, contact Air France (**t** 0845 0845 111; **www.airfrance.co.uk**). There are other ways of travelling around France – coach, bus, taxi, etc. – but they are too slow for house-hunting.

France's Road Network

Case Study: Keeping Warm

David and Shirley bought a house in need of renovation in Charente-Maritime – chosen for its warm summers and mild winters – two years ago for £26,000. Since then, they have completely rebuilt it and probably spent another £20,000 on it. They gutted the building and put it back together themselves, working ferociously with only local materials, until they had a charming retreat in France that they hope will double as a retirement home. They put in a large wood-burner, as is common in rural France, and, with an electric storage heater and the occasional help of a portable gas fire, have no heating problems, despite cold winter temperatures. They pay £178 *taxe – foncière* and *habitation* – far less than they'd pay in the UK. They spend three and a half months a year there and will keep that up until it becomes a permanent home. David says the quality of life is better than they could enjoy in Britain, which is why they are making the move. His advice to anybody considering it is to go ahead and, once there, do your best to integrate with the local community. David and Shirley got over initial reticence among their neighbours by showing their commitment to their project and a willingness to join in the activities of the community. They now feel they are among friends.

Climate

France has four climatic zones – Mediterranean, Atlantic, Mountain, Continental. Mediterranean is what it sounds like in summer – hot, fine and perfect for the beach – but if you don't like it too hot, be careful where you go because you might get more than you bargained for. Winters can be colder than you would expect, too, and houses in the south, often with no or ineffective heating, can be very uncomfortable in mid-winter. Happily, the winters are short and any rain mostly falls in autumn or spring. Mediterranean France blows hot and cold. The notorious mistral – a cold wind that blows from the Alps down the Rhône valley – affects much of the Mediterranean area that stretches from the Midi to the Côte d'Azur. The sirocco – a hot wind in spring – blows from North Africa, and the tramontana – cold and from the Pyrenees – is the last of a trio that can make the weather unseasonable.

Atlantic is also what it sounds like, and is influenced by the Gulf Stream. This is the climate of the west and northwest, which have mild summers and winters but get hotter as you go south, and have rain spread through the year. Naturally, Biarritz will be a lot warmer than Brest. Mountain climate refers to the Alps and the Pyrenees, with cool summers and very cold, snowy winters. The Massif Central and the Vosges are a cross between mountain and Continental – not quite mountain in summer, but with enough snow in winter to support ski resorts. Continental is everything that the other three aren't and reflects the influence of the Continental land mass – warm, dry summers and cold winters, such as in Burgundy.

There are some other seasonal considerations apart from the weather to note when house-hunting. August is a bad time because it's when France goes on holiday, and July is the height of the tourist season. Try not to do it in late December either, because the French also celebrate Christmas! Winter is a good time to look at ski resorts, but snow can hide a lot of shortcomings in a property. Also, if you are driving, mountain roads are subject to snow and ice problems and many may be closed. For weather forecasts, *see* **www.meteo.fr**.

For a regional temperature and rainfall chart, *see* p.315.

Location, Location, Location

Well, you have read **Where in France: Profiles of the Regions**, and you have a general idea of the French regions. Your own personal situation must dictate the next decision. If you are looking for a weekend hideaway and can't leave the shop until Friday night, don't look at a hamlet lost in the Auvergne because, by the time you have got there, it will be time to come back. Also, remember that, although there is a flight to a certain city or a fast train connection, it may be only once a day. So, if you are thinking of a holiday home, your own disposable time is a factor to take into account. Then there are your personal interest requirements and phobias. Languedoc is no good if you are allergic to sun, there is no skiing in Charente, there is only one golf course in Corsica and Normandy is not low-fat-diet-friendly. This all seems pretty obvious, but can sometimes gets lost in the light of some other attraction, like the presence of friends or a good deal on a property. One can also forget the extended family. Will your children spend their holidays with you if they are fanatical divers and you live in Limousin, or grandchildren if there is nothing for them to do?

Another factor that affects most people, but often for different reasons, is the presence of a British community. Many people choose an area because they have friends or relations who have a property nearby. Also, if you don't speak French, the presence of English-speaking people in the vicinity is reassuring and probably means that some of the locals speak English (they have even been found being helpful in *préfectures*!). Some spots in France are truly international – a cauldron of languages, a *bouillabaisse* of cultures – and what or who you are means nothing if you have enough money. The Côte d'Azur is one, fashionable Paris is another and the upmarket ski resorts are, too. In most of the countryside, however, you really need French, though you might get by with Welsh in parts of Brittany (and I did once meet a Gaelic-speaking monk in the Alpes-de-Haute-Provence, but don't expect too many of them). 'English-speaking enclaves' is too strong a designation, but there are heavy sprinklings of English speakers in the Dordogne and adjoining departments, Provence and the Côte d'Azur, Normandy, Brittany and the Alps. These are the places to avoid, of course, if you don't want to be with other ex-pats. Many who go to France do so to get away from the British mindset, and the thought of a French version of the Costas is, for them, a horror.

Having sorted out the area, you will need to decide on the situation – town, country or suburb. Some French towns are works of art in themselves and living in them does not bear the same connotations as in the UK. To live in a town, even Paris, has the attraction of being near the centres of culture, which is what you may have come to France for in the first place. Being in a town offers proximity to art exhibitions, music, ballet, cinema, theatre – if you can understand it – restaurants, nightlife, shops and all the other things you would normally find in towns. Schools and colleges are generally found in towns and may be relevant to your circumstances. You may only be able to afford the suburbs, but French metropolitan transport systems are usually good. If you are working, the suburbs will probably be where you will be living anyway and you may not have much choice. Alternatively, France has some really deep countryside, parts of which are still idyllic but the downside is that even electricity may still be a thing of the future. If you want to take up the challenge of an old ruin down a dirt track 10km away from the nearest hamlet, good luck: you are joining a band of British pioneers that has pumped new life into many a rural backwater. However, have you thought about getting an ambulance to you in a hurry or children to school or fresh bread in the morning?

The medical aspect is a factor that people give differing amounts of consideration to in proportion to their age. Mountaintop chalets are very romantic when you are young, but, after retirement, you want to know that there is a good clinic down in the valley and that the road is not too winding. The same goes for shopping. There is a great attraction to being able to trot down to pick up something you forgot in the weekly shop, to buy a newspaper or have a cup – or glass – of something and exchange banalities with the patron. Take all these things into account. Another serious consideration, if it is a holiday home, is its rental value, which will be dictated by many of the factors that affect your own choice. Is it in an area that visitors come to on holiday? Are there things for them to do? What is the weather like in the holiday season? Can the property be easily found? Can it be furnished to a suitable standard? Most people prefer a property within about an hour's drive of a city or substantial town. All these things are part of the complicated equation that will decide whether your purchase is a success or not and they all have to be considered carefully.

Think about travel once you or your visitors have arrived by air or train. Most people either hire a car or own their own French car, which they leave at the house or (better) in the airport car park waiting for their next visit. It is worth doing a careful price comparison. Surprisingly, often the cost of insuring and maintaining your local car, plus airport parking and the depreciation of its value, can amount to nearly as much as – or more than – the cost of renting a new, clean car on each visit, which requires no 'management' on your part. Renting also means that you can choose the type of car you need for that particular visit. For example, if granny is coming, you can rent an upmarket car with lots of legroom and easy rear seat access. Look to cheap, local car hire companies as well as the big names, which sometimes have surprisingly good deals available. Finally, how will your family or visitors travel when they arrive in the area? Will they have to rent a car? Is there any public transport? Will you be an unpaid taxi service for the duration?

House-hunting in France

Most people know within a few minutes of arriving in a town whether or not it is somewhere that they would like to live. A two-week self-drive holiday, using some of France's attractive small hotels (especially those in the Logis de France chain), can therefore cover a lot of ground. Take a large-scale map or motoring atlas. Be a vandal: write your comments about the places you visit on the page. Otherwise you will never remember which was which. Buy some postcards to remind you of the scenery or, if you are a gadget person, take a video camera. Pick up a copy of the local paper for each area. Even if you do not speak French, it will give you some idea of what goes on in the area and also supply details of local estate agents. Visit the local tourist office, if there is one, for more information about the place and an idea of events and so on throughout the year. Look in estate agents' windows and make a note – again on the map – of the sorts of prices you will have to pay for property of the type that interests you. However, and most importantly, don't go inside. Make it an absolute rule that you will not look at any properties on your first research trip. If you do, you will be caught in the classic trap of focusing on bricks and mortar rather than the area. What matters most is the area where you are going to live – there are nice houses in every area. Provided the initial look at prices doesn't make you faint, if you like the town, mark it with a big ✔ (and move on to the next place. If it is not for you, mark the map with an ✘ (and, likewise, move on. Once you have shortlisted your two or three most likely places, visit them in both summer and winter, spend a little time there, make contact with estate agents and finally allow yourself look at properties to your heart's content.

Generally, when you go to see a property, the estate agent will accompany you. If you are dealing with a private seller (that is, someone who is not using an agent), when you do finally go looking at property, take a mobile phone and their number with you. If you don't have a mobile phone, buy one. Property in rural France can be nearly impossible to find and it can save much

Case Study: Cash is King

Nick and Nic bought a dilapidated 20-room farmhouse in three acres of orchards and woodland in a stunning location in northern Provence three years ago for £140,000. The house is L-shaped and they have converted one leg of the L into a comfortable living area for themselves and the other into a two-bedroom *gîte* and three-bedroom *chambres-d'hôtes* accommodation. They run this from April through to October and, combined with a small pension income, they find that they can live comfortably all year around. They chose France because property is such good value for money, Nic is French and Nick speaks the language well. They chose Provence because they wanted to go into the hospitality business and the season is longest in the south, with the guaranteed sun attracting visitors to the region. There is also easy access: the TGV from Waterloo; the Motorail service to Avignon; by car there are good, if expensive, *autoroutes* from the ferry ports joining the A7, the Autoroute du Soleil, leading into Provence; and by air there are currently three budget airlines flying to the South of France from Stansted: Ryanair to Nîmes and Montpellier, easyJet to Nice (also from Luton) and Buzz to Marseille. British Airways and Air France also fly into Marseille but the cost is significantly higher.

The major problem in their decision was that property tends to be more expensive in Provence than elsewhere in the south and southwest of France, so one effectively gets less for one's budget. Nick's principal piece of advice to anybody thinking about making the move to set up in their type of business is to make sure that the financial side is all sorted out right from the start. It's the old business maxim, 'Cash is King', and to run out of money for a project of any description is financial suicide. Work out your budgets for purchasing, repairing and setting-up costs and then stick to them. Failure to do so leads into the black hole of financial ruin. One other important piece of advice he gives is to learn the language as quickly as possible, as it makes the transition period much more agreeable.

gnashing of teeth if you can phone and ask for directions. It is also courteous to telephone if you are delayed en route.

For a comprehensive checklist of what to notice, watch out for and ask about when viewing a property, *see* **Appendix 1**, pp.318–22.

How Much, For What and Where?

As is the case anywhere else, there is a choice of ways of investing in property in France. There is a **direct purchase**, pure and simple, either with a mortgage or without. There is ***copropriété***, an arrangement usually applying to blocks of flats, but also sometimes on private estates, such as the type of development that surrounds a golf course. Here, the owner not only owns their property but also has shares in the development as a whole. This means that they have to pay their share of the cost of the facilities, from a simple foyer to a swimming pool. Then there are **leasebacks** in which, for a substantial discount, the buyer contracts to let a developer rent out their property for most of the year while the owner has its use for a certain period, usually for their own holiday. These schemes have a finite period and can only work well in a resort area and only apply to new or totally rebuilt properties. Then there is **co-ownership**, where a number of people share the ownership of the house and share the use of it, too, by having occupancy every year in proportion to their share. The advantage is that you can afford a much more expensive property than you could as a sole buyer. Then there is **timeshare**, a development of this, where the investor buys shares in a company in exchange for a certain amount of time a year in a property. Finally, there is the **holiday property bond**, a development of timeshare, where properties are available to swap in many alternative places and countries. (*See also* 'Other Types of Ownership', pp. 111–2.)

There is a large disparity of prices over the whole of France. A few examples below, taken from the pages of property magazines and estate agents' books, will give an idea of the huge range available from an unrestored farmhouse in Brittany at £10,000 to a four-bedroom apartment on the Côte d'Azur for half a million. A sum of £120,000 will buy you a habitable farmhouse with farmland and barns in Dordogne or Lot-et-Garonne, or a one-bedroom flat at Antibes on the Côte d'Azur.

The problems of property description and categorization are probably even more difficult in France than in the UK because the range is wider. You don't get wild boar or cobnuts farms, alpine chalets or AOC vineyards in Britain. Also – useful given the British propensity for restoration – the number of rundown or ruined properties on the market in France is very high.

The term *gîte* means self-catering accommodation, so a property that includes, or has the potential for, one or more of them implies an opportunity for income. A property that is being sold as a *chambre d'hôte* means that it has been offering bed-and-breakfast accommodation – another potential source of income, bearing in mind France's huge tourist trade. A studio is a bedsit, but without its UK connotations as they are to be found in the most fashionable places in the country. Architectural types are too numerous to list, although we have made some mention of them in **Where in France: Profiles of the Regions**. They range from the *colombage*, or half-timbered building, that is popular all the down the west and southwest and particularly on the eastern border, the granite-and-slate of the northwest, the dovecote towers and mountain villages of the south, to a host of modern interpretations of traditional buildings that would require a book of their own. The following examples have been gleaned from estate agents' books and advertisements in the property magazines, at the time of writing.

€20,000

- Unrestored farmhouse in Limousin.
- Building plot of one hectare in Lot-et-Garonne.
- Apartment in a chalet in Savoy.
- Unrestored cottage in Brittany.

€25,000

- Unrestored farmhouse in Charente-Maritime.

€35,000

- Unrestored stone cottage in Finistère.

€40,000

- Unrestored three-storey village house in Ariège.
- Two-bedroom village house and one-acre garden in the western Loire.
- Breton farmhouse with €95,000 restoration estimate.

€50,000

- Building plot with one hectare in the Dordogne.
- Three-bedroom house in a medieval town in Limousin.
- Three-bedroom furnished cottage in Brittany.
- One-bedroom furnished seaside flat in Brittany.
- Norman *colombage* two-room cottage with €50,000 restoration estimate.

€60,000

- Unrestored house/barn in the Dordogne or Lot-et-Garonne.
- Two-bedroom bungalow in Finistère.
- One-bedroom flat in a chalet in Haute-Savoie.

€80,000

- Small house for modernization in Lot-et-Garonne.
- Village house with a garden in the Dordogne.
- Small bungalow in Lot-et-Garonne.
- Farmland with planning permission in the Dordogne or Lot-et-Garonne.
- Two-bedroom beach apartment in Pyrénées-Orientales.
- Three-bedroom detached country house in Brittany.

€100,000

- Detached village property in Lot-et-Garonne.
- Country property for modernization in the Dordogne.
- Watermill and one hectare in Limousin.
- Rural house with barn in Charente.
- Village bar/shop needing upgrading with limited land in Lot-et-Garonne.

€120,000

- Country property for modernization in Lot-et-Garonne.
- One-bedroom flat near Antibes.
- Village bar/shop needing upgrading with limited land in the Dordogne.
- Double-fronted village house in Brittany.
- Stone cottage and barn in a regional park in Burgundy.
- Detached village property in Lot-et-Garonne.

€135,000

- Small stone property, but not a lot of land, or modern bungalow.
- Stone property, semi-modernized, with barn and garden or bar/restaurant needing upgrading in Lot-et-Garonne.
- Three-bedroom stone country house in Brittany.

€150,000

- Five-bedroom restored farmhouse in Cher.
- Modernized stone house with garden in the Dordogne.
- Stone property and unrestored barns with one hectare in Lot-et-Garonne.
- Four-bedroom stone 18th-century house in Pyrénées-Orientales.
- Partially renovated farmhouse and land in Gers.

€170,000

- Modernized stone house, with garden, in the Dordogne.
- New house with garden in Lot-et-Garonne.
- Farm for modernization, with outbuildings, in Lot-et-Garonne.
- One-bedroom flat in Juan-les-Pins, Côte d'Azur.
- Two-bedroom renovated farmhouse on 2.5 acres in Brittany.

€200,000

- Habitable farmhouse with farmland and barns in the Dordogne.
- One-bedroom flat at Antibes, Côte d'Azur.

€250,000

- Three-bedroom renovated *colombage* farm in Normandy.
- Restored farmhouse and holiday cottage used as *gîte* on one hectare in Poitou-Charentes.
- Renovated stone house with barns and land in a good situation in the Dordogne or Lot-et-Garonne.
- New four-bedroom house in the Vendée, with pool.
- Farmhouse with outhouses and barns, 15 hectares of wood and river in Limousin.
- Farmhouse with four *chambres d'hôtes* in the Somme.
- Two-bedroom apartment in Paris, 16th *arrondissement*.

€350,000

- Stone house with a basic *gîte* in the Dordogne.
- Luxury modern house in a superb situation in Lot-et-Garonne.
- Four-bedroom house in the old port of Antibes, Côte d'Azur.

€420,000

- House with *gîtes* with rental income in the Dordogne.
- Hotel with low registered turnover in Lot-et-Garonne.
- Three-bedroom chalet in Savoy.
- Six-bedroom mansion in Charente.

€500,000

- Fine old house with *gîtes* in an excellent situation in the Dordogne.
- Large property, ideal for B&B, in Lot-et-Garonne.
- 18th-century five-bedroom manor with three acres and pool in Garonne.

€540,000

- Four-bedroom house and two *gîtes* in Brittany.

€555,000

- **18th-century house, stable and barns on 2.5 hectares in Gers.**

€625,000

- **Vineyard in Aude.**
- **Five-house *gîte* complex in Haute-Vienne.**
- **Three-bedroom flat in Juan-les-Pins, Côte d'Azur.**

€670,000

- **16th-century château in Rhône.**

€750,000

- **Four-bedroom renovated farmhouse in Var, Provence.**
- **Six-bedroom mansion and cottage in Charente-Maritimes.**
- **Seven-bedroom manor house and 20 acres in Garonne.**

€835,000

- **Château with original features, *gîtes*, etc.**
- **Hotels with excellent registered turnover in most of France.**
- **Four-bedroom renovated farmhouse in Var, Provence.**

€915,000

- **Three-storey, ten-bedroom mansion in 1.5 hectares in Haute-Garonne.**
- **Four-bedroom apartment in Var, Provence.**

€1,000,000

- **Vineyards, equestrian properties, château with keeps.**
- **Six-bedroom inn with licence in Charente.**

€1,600,000 upwards

- **AOC vineyards , château with excellent rental income.**

There are, obviously, huge variations in price depending on location, aspect, quality, state of repair and desirability. The specialist property press will give you more and up-to-date information.

Your Choice of Property

In Britain, when we think about buying a home in France, we think about a house. In France, as in so many things, it is different. If you live in a town of any size, you are likely to live in a flat. Many British buyers are reluctant to contemplate this, yet there can be many advantages to flat living, particularly if you do not have young children and are looking for a holiday home. The purchase price will probably be cheaper, it will cost less to run, you will not be responsible for organizing the maintenance and repair of the outside of the property, you may have shared facilitie, such as tennis courts or a pool and, at the end of your holiday, you can simply turn off the water and electricity and leave. Flats also often provide you with a ready-made community of neighbours who can look after your property in your absence and leave a loaf and milk in the fridge for your arrival. Of course, there are drawbacks. For the majority of us, the most obvious is the lack of a private garden. There will also, usually, be less space – particularly storage space – than in a house. If you are not ready for such a revolutionary change to your lifestyle, there is a wide variety of house types available – from small workers' cottages to luxury villas, so something will take your fancy and suit your pocket.

Bear in mind, though, that if you are buying a holiday home for use, say, two weekends per month and twice per year for longer periods, you will need to ask yourself who is going to look after your land. Who is going to maintain your glistening pool – and at what cost?

Think about your current and future requirements. In Britain, we are used to moving frequently. We buy a house to suit our present needs and, as they change, we sell it and buy another. This is a very expensive thing to do in France. The move could cost you about 13 per cent of the price of your new home. As a result, most French people still live in homes that have been owned for many years, sometimes generations.

There are some factors you may not have considered that will confront you when you are making your choice of property – some that you may never even have considered in the UK.

- **Space**. Most people underestimate the space that they will need in their home overseas. This is because they underestimate how popular they will become once they have a villa in Cap d'Antibes! The combination of your own accommodation needs, those of visitors and storage space means that, if the budget permits, it is worth thinking of buying one more bedroom than you first contemplated.

  Especially if you are buying a property for retirement, you will also need to think about adequate space for 'stuff'. Most of us are very bad at throwing things away, particularly items of sentimental value, and this is even more the case when we have taken the major decision to move away from our roots. Many of us move into a smaller property in France than we occupied in Britain. This is a recipe for rooms full of packing cases and a lot of matrimonial ill feeling. Fortunately, in France space is still fairly cheap. It doesn't cost that much more to buy a house with four bedrooms than one with three. It is certainly much cheaper to do so now rather than move later.

• **Heating**. In the north and west of France, it can be as cold and wet as it is in Britain – or worse. Even in the warmest parts of the south of France, you need a decent heating system because there are numerous days each year when warmth will be needed. It may be a lot warmer than it would have been in Manchester, but if you have been used to daily temperatures of 21°C, then a drop of 10°C will make you feel cold.

Piped gas is rare in rural areas. Bottled gas is too fiddly to be genuinely convenient. Installing large tanks for gas can be problematic from a town planning point of view. Solid fuel has all the drawbacks of 30 years ago that we have forgotten. Solar heating – particularly solar water heating – works well in sunnier areas, but cannot be relied on as the sole form of heating. For many people, this leaves oil and electricity as candidates. Whichever you choose, installing a good, centrally controlled heating system will be money well spent. This is particularly worth considering when you are building a new house, where the extra cost can be very small, *see also* 'Utilities', pp.229–32.

• **Air-conditioning**. Air-conditioning still has the reputation of being a luxury item. Some people think that giving in to the heat and turning on the air-conditioning is 'cheating'. We recommend that everyone buying a home in southern France should install at least some minimal air-conditioning. With predicted global warming, summer temperatures are likely to rise. However macho you may be, if the 2am temperature is 35°C and you cannot sleep, it is hard to deny the value of air-conditioning. You may not need it often, but when you do, you really need it. For people buying a home for retirement or with elderly relatives who will visit, it is worth remembering, too, that, as we get older, we gradually lose our ability to adjust to extremes of temperature. A period that is unpleasantly hot for a 55-year-old can be life-threatening for a 90-year-old.

Whether to install full air-conditioning, possibly combined with a heating system using some of the efficient modern technologies such as heat pumps, or a stand-alone portable system, will depend on the location of your property, preferences and wallet.

• **Septic Tanks**. The septic tank figures much more in the French property scene than the British one because such a large portion of the housing market is rural. For city-dwellers this is a strange concept, but there is nothing wrong with it. A septic tank is, essentially, a device that treats and filters sewage by breaking it down bacteriologically before discharging relatively harmless water into the ground. There are two types of septic tank commonly found in France. The older type dealt only with the waste from toilets, leaving the waste from sinks and baths to be deposited in a gravel soakaway and, thus, dispersed, without treatment, into the surrounding ground. More modern septic tanks deal with all waste water. It is all treated and ultimately dispersed. If you are buying a house with a septic tank, have it checked by your surveyor.

Septic tanks have a natural lifespan, which can be lengthened by careful treatment but cannot be extended indefinitely. If you need to replace an old-fashioned tank, you will have to do so with a new-style tank and you will need planning permission. If you are replacing the tank, make sure that the size is adequate for your requirements. It should be based on the maximum use of the house and the amount of water that would be generated by people having baths, showers or doing washing. If you install a tank that is too small, you will simply have to have it emptied with monotonous frequency and considerable cost. If you install a large tank, emptying will be a rare event and, more important, will be beneficial in terms of its maintenance and longevity.

• **Swimming Pools**. Swimming pools are expensive. There is not just the capital cost of building the pool (typically about £10,000 for a modest pool), but also the annual cost of maintaining it. That can rise to several thousands of pounds if you are often absent from the property and require a professional maintenance company to come in and treat it – as often as twice a week in the summer months. Maintenance costs vary from place to place, so, if you are thinking of buying a property with a pool, do get an estimate for the maintenance liability before committing yourself to the purchase. If you wish to install a pool at an existing property, you will need permission to do so. This will involve an application for what we would call planning permission (*certificat d'urbanisme/permit de construire*) from your local town hall. The process is swifter if entrusted to a local builder/pool specialist.

• **Wells**. Wells and boreholes are a definite advantage. Even though you may not use them for drinking water, they will be an excellent and cheap way of watering your garden or filling your swimming pool. Beware, however, some wells dry up in the summer. If your property has a well and you think that it is going to be important to you, make sure that your rights to it and its water are protected in your contract of purchase. If you want to use your well for drinking water, you should get it checked by the health department or by your local water company, which will issue a certificate if it is fit for human consumption.

• **Parking**. If you have a nice car and want to keep it secure, parking is an asset in any country. Much property in France is sold without any dedicated parking spaces. These can cost a surprising amount if bought separately.

• **Broadband**. A final influence may be that you want to work on the Internet and so need broadband in France. Whether France Telecom can provide it or not depends on the area you want to be in so, before making a final decision, check with them at France Telecom's International Sales Support Unit (**t** 00 33 492 93 42 08; **f** 00 33 492 93 44 60; activite.issu@francetelecom.com).

New or Old?

There is no right answer!

Traditionally the French, except for the wealthy, have scorned older, restored properties in favour of newly built ones. This left the market open to the British to buy up the older homes for a pittance, love them, restore them and live happily ever after. Things have changed. In many areas, the French have developed an interest in older, 'character' property. A visit to a French DIY store will show you that it is not just the British who spend money on home improvements. Also, the seemingly inexhaustible supply of houses and cottages abandoned as a result of rural depopulation after World War II has, in areas such as Brittany and Normandy, almost run out. They have been bought up not just by thousands of British and other foreigners, but also by local people, and prices are rising. The habitable £10,000 cottage is, in most areas, a thing of the past – soon to be followed by its cousin the habitable £20,000 cottage.

The decision between new and old is, in France, essentially the same decision as in Britain. It involves considering the features of each type of property in the light of your own personal preferences. Most people are clear from the outset which they prefer.

New and Old Property in France – Advantages

New Property	Older Property
The technical specification and design will be better than in an older property. This is particularly so in areas such as insulation and energy efficiency.	The property has 'character'. Its architecture may be beautiful, and the detailed workmanship will probably be superior to today's product.
It will have been inspected and built to known standards.	The garden will be mature.
Most people prefer new kitchens, which get more sophisticated each year.	It may occupy a better site than a newer property – on the basis that the best were often built on first.
It will probably have a reasonable heating system.	It may be a more attractive rental proposition than a new property, especially in rural areas.
Electrical and plumbing installations will be to a superior standard.	You will feel that you are living in a truly French property.

New Property	Older Property
Few people will have used the bathrooms!	What you see is what you get. You turn on the taps, there is water. You can see the room sizes and how the sun falls on the terraces. You can see the views and the distances to adjacent properties.
Provision will probably have been made for car parking.	It may be cheaper than a comparable new property.
You may share common resources such as pools or tennis courts with other people.	It will probably have more land than a comparable new property.
The building will require less maintenance than an older property, certainly for the first few years.	
It should be cheaper to run	
You can design your own property or, at least, often fine tune the existing design to your special requirements.	
The fabric will be guaranteed.	
If you bought 'off plan' you may see some pre-completion growth in value.	

New and Old Property in France – Disadvantages

New Property	Older Property
The building will be new and brash, not mellow.	Older properties can need a lot of maintenance and loving care.
It can be hard to envisage what you are going to get from a plan and specification.	It will be more expensive to heat and run.
You will have to sort out all the small snags inevitable in any new building. You may spend all your holidays chasing the builder or doing the work yourself.	You may need to spend significant sums on, say, the kitchen and bathrooms to bring the property up to modern standards.
You will have to sort out the garden.	You may have to sort out an overgrown garden.
You may have to decorate.	You may have to decorate.
Although technical design has improved, the aesthetic appeal may be less than that of an older property, and the detailed workmanship less rewarding.	
As a rental property most people prefer a tradional cottage to a new house.	

Case Study: Doing the Paperwork

Richard and Mavis retired to Spain, but had one of those unfortunate property experiences for which the costas are famous. Undeterred, but with the war chest depleted, they settled in the department of Lot-et-Garonne in August 2000. They brought a very rundown farmhouse for £20,000 and then subsequently some land and outbuildings for another £35,000. Richard has done all the renovation himself, a magnificent achievement, although there is some way to go yet. Despite being far from fluent in French, they have joined in all the local activities and feel part of their rural and isolated community. He says, 'We love it here and are extremely happy.' His advice to house-hunters:

'We bought a dilapidated house far in the country in the Lot-et-Garonne region that needed renovating. We found that everyone living in France who has come from the UK offered all the advice one needed and more. Some of it was useful and some not so. Some was hearsay. The best thing we found was to see for ourselves and find out from the source, not necessarily to follow what others said. Knowing some French is most helpful. The first thing we did was to get the insurance arranged on the outbuildings, house and contents. We exported our car from the UK, so the next thing was to get the importing of our car into France done. This was a long and frustrating task. The local mayor was most helpful in helping us with this and other tasks. It meant having an MOT, paying the fee and then filling in forms with details of the car and obtaining other documents from the manufacturer, then going to Agen to have everything checked and passed by the registration department. We also had to find the local DIY store, usually 'Bricomarché'. The local builders' merchants are normally on the outskirts of the town, with the most popular being 'Point P', as well as other 'out of town' stores and supermarkets. Deliveries of building materials cost about £25 to £50 each, depending how far you are from the source. Obtaining the *carte de séjour* is relatively easy if you go to the *mairie* and ask for their help. Getting the tax situation sorted is also easy, provided you fill in the necessary forms from the UK and take them to the *Hotel des Impôts* yourself and wait for the duplicate form to be stamped. You then pay only French tax. One must also obtain the *carte vitale*, your health card. Finding a doctor is essential. Many speak or understand English. As in the UK, it is essential to get permission from the *mairie* for alterations and additions to the property. The taxes are in two parts for the property. If you are over 70, you do not pay the 'habitation tax' (or for a TV licence either). The *taxe foncière* is due on all land to do with the property and, in our case, was about £77 per annum. Everything is an adventure in itself and fun, provided you treat it as such. Homesickness is the most common cause of unhappiness in France among the ex-pats. In most cases the only remedy is to return to the UK. How sad!'

Estate Agents and Other Ways of Buying

The vast majority of British people buying a property in France will use an estate agent. A good estate agent can make the process smoother and less perplexing. A bad or uncooperative agent can make it much more complicated.

Whichever agent you use and wherever they are based please remember that they are being paid by the seller to sell the property. They are not being paid by you to look after your interests. However helpful and professional they may be, if you do not sign a contract to buy then they do not receive their commission and their children starve. They therefore have their own interests to look after, which broadly coincide with those of the sellers but which might not coincide with yours.

Despite this the estate agent can be a mine of useful information, knowledge about the area and practical help. The large majority is genuinely enthusiastic about property in France and about you joining their community. Take advantage of what they have to offer, form a rapport with them, buy a property through them... but get everything checked by your legal adviser just as you would in Britain.

Some agents will tell you that you do not need to use a lawyer. That the services of the local Notary Public (*notaire*) will suffice. Ignore that advice. It is quite true that the average French person would not use the services of an independent lawyer when buying a house unless there was something complex about the transaction or about their own circumstances. For a foreigner, however, this is generally not good enough. There are many issues on which you will need guidance that it is no part of the notary's duty to provide. Furthermore, your French notary will almost certainly know nothing about British law and so will be unable to give you any help as far as such vital issues as who should own the property in order to make the most of UK *and* French tax and inheritance rules. As to the function of the notary, *see* 'Notaries as Selling Agents', p.99 and 'The Notary', pp.143–4.

French-based Agents

The role of the French estate agent (*agent immobilier*) is similar to the role of the British estate agent. Their job is to find buyers for properties entrusted to them by a seller. But there the similarity ends.

In England a person can be a plumber today and, without any qualifications or experience, set up an estate agency tomorrow. They cannot do this in France. In France in order to practice as an estate agent you must be professionally qualified and hold a licence to practice (*carte professionelle*) and, in most cases, indemnity insurance and a fidelity bond (*pièce de garantie*). The latter guarantees that if you run off with a buyer's deposit he will get his money back. All this is partly an example of the generally greater paperwork and red tape prevalent in France and partly a useful consumer protection measure.

There are quite large numbers of agents operating in France without a licence. That is, they are operating illegally. Many are foreigners servicing the foreign buyer. British selling to British, Germans to Germans, etc. Some of these 'illegals' are excellent, skilled people who offer a service at least as good as many of the legal agents. Despite this, you are better dealing with a 'proper' agent or his genuine employee as you will then be covered by the legislation and the codes of conduct to which the agents must adhere as well as by the insurance and bond.

You can tell whether the agent is licensed because he must display details of his licence (and, if he has one, his insurance and bond) in his offices and he must give details of his licence and any insurance and bond in all correspondence and contracts. If you are dealing with the agent by telephone, fax or email he will not take offence if you ask to see proof of these documents.

Do not worry if your agent does not have a bond. Some have chosen not to. This saves them not only the cost of obtaining the bond but also having to comply with a lot of accountancy regulations. If your agent does not have a bond it simply means that you cannot pay him the deposit cheque. Instead it must be paid to the notary whole will be dealing with signing over the title. All notaries are bonded.

Many estate agents join the French equivalent of the British National Association of Estate Agents, known as FNAIM (*Fédération Nationale des Agents Immobiliers et Mandataires*) or a competing professional body known as SNPI (*Syndicat Nationales Professionnels Immobilier*). This is worth looking out for as it gives yet more in the way of redress in the case of under-performance or dispute.

In order to sell a property for its owner not only must the estate agent be licensed but he must hold a written authority from the owner permitting him to do so. There are several types of authority or 'mandate' (*mandat*). The two main ones are the ordinary authority (*mandat simple*) and the exclusive authority (*mandat exclusif*). As the names suggest, the first gives the agent the authority to sell the property, but similar authorities may have been given to other agents and the owner will have also reserved the right to sell the property in person – i.e. without the intervention of any agent. The second gives the agent the exclusive right to sell the property. Depending on its precise wording the exclusive authority may or may not permit the owner to sell the property in person. Both types of mandate will be time limited. They must state the amount of the estate agents fees and who is expected to pay those fees. These forms of authority are therefore important. If the agent is offering to take the property off the market under a reservation contract (see below) then he will probably not be able to do so without an exclusive authority as other agents could, at that minute, be negotiating with other possible buyers. If the agent has an exclusive mandate that does not permit the seller to deal directly with any buyers then you could, part way through a transaction, be faced by an agent claiming commission. If the authority has been given on the basis that the buyer pays all or part of the commission then you need to know this and the amounts involved. Before you part with any money you and your lawyer ought to ask to see the *mandat*.

As you will have gathered from the preceding paragraph, in France it is not always the seller who pays the estate agents commission. This is still the normal practice, but there are local variations in the normal. In some places the buyer could be expected to pay all the commission. In other places the buyer might be expected to contribute half the commission. Be clear when you are looking at property whether the price mentioned includes or excludes these fees.

In order to protect his substantial commission the agent may ask you to sign a document – generally called a *bon de visite* – before he takes you to see the property. This is a statement that it is he who has introduced you to the property, so avoiding later arguments about who should be paid the commission due.

There are other significant differences from English practice. Generally agents are rather less proactive than they are in England. This is particularly true in rural areas, especially non-tourist rural areas. You will seldom find printed property particulars or be supplied with photographs. Still less will you find plans or room dimensions in most estate agents' offices. They see their role as capturing property to sell and then showing buyers around that property. Many agents are either 'one man bands' or in small firms with a limited range of property on their books. This is, again, especially true in rural areas but if you walk down any street in Nice or Paris you will see evidence of the large numbers of small agents offering services to the public. This can make it difficult to get a comprehensive view of what is on the market in a locality. In addition, there are few local or national groupings of agents. To make matters worse, only about half the property in France is sold through estate agents. The rest is sold in a number of other ways. In rural areas – where there are only a small number of transactions in the year – a common method is by word of mouth. Everyone knows that Mme Dupont had died and that her house is for sale. No one from outside the areas is likely to be interested. Why do you need an estate agent? In such areas your best way of finding out what is available could be to ask at the local bar or bakers. A lot of property is sold via notaries (*see* p.99) or privately via the specialist property press (*see* p.101).

One of the reasons that a lot of property bypasses estate agents could be the fees that they charge. By UK (but not US) standards they are high. Until a few years ago there was an official tariff that could not be broken. This no longer exists, but it is still a good indication of the likely level of fees that the agent will be asking for. Generally estate agents fees vary from four to 10 per cent of the purchase price. The amount will depend on the value of the property and the area it is located. Cheaper properties generally pay more commission than more expensive properties and properties in main tourist areas tend to pay more commission than in less sought after (and generally poorer) areas. Remember that you may end up paying all or part of this commission, so the level of charges is important to you! Agents must display their commission tariff in their premises and the rate agreed in respect of any property you might be interested in is, as already mentioned, specified in the agent's *mandat*.

You are probably best off starting to look for property by using an estate agent in the immediate vicinity of the place where you are looking. Many rural agents will only cover an area about 20km in diameter. If you are still uncertain where precisely you intend to buy, try several adjoining agents or, if there is one in your area, one of the big chains such as Domus. Local newspapers will give you an indication of which agents are advertising, and so active, in your area. You can also get names out of the French Yellow Pages (under *immobiliers*). The Yellow Pages for popular areas are kept in many city libraries in the UK. Many agents also advertise in both the French and UK specialist property press. An excellent and simple way of obtaining a comprehensive list of agents is to write to both FNAIM and SNPI. The list, though comprehensive, will probably contain details of specialist agents who do not deal with ordinary residential property as well as those who do.

Estate agents also often operate as property management companies and as property letting agents. In order to do this they need a separate licence and mandate from the person letting the property.

Developers (*Promoteurs Immobiliers*)

The developer is the person or company building and selling new property. They do not need to be licensed as estate agents (provided they are only selling their own property). Many developers sell via third party estate agents. Others sell direct. Some carry out marketing and sales in Britain.

Marchands de Biens

These are people whose business is to trade in property. They are entitles to sell property without holding a license as an estate agent but can only sell property that they have owned for a minimum of three months. There are also rules as to the maximum period for which such people can hold property 'in stock' without tax penalties. It is important to understand the status of a *marchand de biens* if you are buying from one. Seek advice from your lawyer.

Notaries as Selling Agents

In France just under 20 per cent of all property is sold by a notary acting as property selling agent. There are some differences to the position when dealing with an estate agent.

It may seem odd to an English mind that the property selling agent is also the person who deals with the transfer of ownership on behalf of both parties. We are just about getting used to the idea that firms of English solicitors can sell properties. We are a long way away from being ready for the solicitor selling the property (and acting for the seller in connection with the legal work) to do the legal work for the buyer as well.

This is not uncommon in France, particularly in rural areas. It is, however, one of the occasions when it is probably sensible to exercise your right – which exists in all property purchases – to appoint a second notary specifically to look after your interests. This is not the expensive disaster that it sounds. Such is the generosity of the statutory fee levels paid to French notaries for their work that the second notary simply splits the fee with the original notary and charges you nothing!

Another curiosity when dealing with a notary as property seller is that his fee for dealing with the sale will be paid by the buyer, not the seller – irrespective of the local custom as far as estate agents fees are concerned. Again, this is perhaps not as bad as it sounds. The notary normally charges less than the estate agent would charge – typically two per cent of the price of the property and, even if the estate agent's fee is payable by the seller, it is usually calculated and added to the asking price for the property. The buyer thus ends up paying the seller who, in turn, pays the agent.

UK-based Estate Agents

There are growing numbers of people based in the UK who sell property in France. Most popular areas are covered. Although, under English law, they are entitled to call themselves estate agents it is important to note that, in the vast majority of cases, they are not licensed French estate agents.

They very often work in association with one or more French agents, generally covering a wider area than a single French agent would cover. They tend to choose properties from the 'book' of those French agents that they think will be of particular interest to the British buyer. They then either obtain the descriptions and photographs necessary to sell those properties (if none exist) or translate the existing materials. They advertise or market the properties through exhibitions etc and then act as an intermediary between the potential buyer and the French estate agent – who may not speak English. Because they deal with British buyers all the time they should be able to anticipate some of the common problems that can arise and smooth the progress of the transaction.

Generally they should share the commission of the French agent – who is very pleased that they can expand his potential buyer base by introducing foreign buyers. Thus their services should cost you nothing extra.

These people can be very useful, particularly if you have little experience of dealing with France and don't speak French.

Unfortunately, it is not as simple as that. Some charge substantial amounts of extra commission for their services. Often they do not disclose that commission to the buyer. There is nothing wrong with paying someone who is doing a useful job some commission, but you should be told that you are expected to do so. You can then decide whether the convenience of dealing with someone in Britain is worth the extra cost. Always ask for confirmation that the price you will be paying is exactly the same as you would have paid in France or, if there is an extra charge, the amount of the charge.

Some UK based agents advertise their prices as a global price including the price of the property, tax, notary's fees and all commissions. This can be very useful for the British buyer unused to these transactions but it can also, in the hands of the unscrupulous, be a way of hiding a large element of hidden commission. Mme Dupont has agreed to sell her cottage for €50,000 (about £30,000). Commission has been agreed at five per cent (€2,500). Notaries fees and taxes will amount to about seven per cent (€4,000). An all-inclusive price of €60,000 therefore gives a hidden charge of €3,500. If you are offered property on this basis check what the price includes.

Many of these UK based sellers are highly experienced and very reputable. Before deciding which to use ask about their level of experience. It is more difficult to assess whether they are reputable. A good starting point is to see whether they are members of FOPDAC (the Federation of Overseas Property Developers, Agents and Consultants – **t** 020 8744 2362). This is a non-profit organisation that agents and developers can join if they are experienced in the field, are prepared to be scrutinised and abide by its code of conduct.

DIY Sales

In France far more property is sold person to person than in the UK. Depending on area this can be between 15 and 30 per cent. There are a variety of different sources of information about such properties for sale.

A Vendre (For Sale) Signs

As you drive around you will see a number of DIY for sale signs. They normally give a contact telephone number. To take advantage of property offered in this way you, obviously, have to be in the area and you will probably need to speak French. If you do not speak French it is worth a trial phone call. You never know your luck! If the person who answers doesn't speak English there may be a local English speaking person – perhaps in your hotel – who would make contact on your behalf. As a last resort phone your lawyer. He should be able to find out the necessary details for you and, if you wish, make arrangements to view. He will, of course, charge for this work but the saving of estate agents fees will make his charges look cheap.

Local Newspapers

Individuals place advertisements in the 'For Sale' section of the local paper. Once again, the ability to speak French is an advantage.

'Freesheets'

In some towns and in popular tourist areas in the countryside there are free local news sheets, similar to those in the UK. In some places there are specialist free property papers. All are likely to have adverts from private sellers.

National Newspapers

These, as in Britain, tend to carry advertisements mainly for more expensive properties

Specialist Local Property Press

In most areas there are specialist magazines which exist primarily to carry advertisements from private individuals selling their property. Some have just a local coverage, others a regional or even national coverage. Go and browse through a couple of newspaper kiosks (*presse*) and see what is on offer. Buy them all. They will give you a good general guide to prices.

There are also several more glossy lifestyle publications, covering property (particular more expensive property) in main tourist areas such as the Côte d'Azur. Again, buy the lot. They will be full of useful information.

Specialist British Property Press

Private individuals advertise in the main specialist British property press such as *Focus on France*, *French Property News*, *Living France* and *Homes Overseas*. Also try more general publications such as *Daltons Weekly* and *Exchange & Mart*, especially for cheaper property. You may also find advertisements from private sellers in the *Sunday Times*, *Weekend Telegraph* and *Mail on Sunday*. Generally speaking people advertising in the British press are British.

Internet

There is a huge amount of property available for private sale on the internet. Finding it can sometimes be tricky. Remember that you should search in French as well as in English. The following combinations in the search box have been proved to work:

+property+"for sale"+France

+house+"for sale"+France

+apartment+"for sale"+France

+maison+vendre

+apartement+vendre

You can further limit the geographical area where the property is located by typing in the name of the place where the property is located, but this has very mixed results because of the vary different ways people enter the details of the property the are selling. The best bet is probably to use the province or, if you are looking in a city, the city as the limiter:

+apartment+"for sale"+Paris

+apartement+vendre+Paris

+house+"for sale"+Var

+maison+vendre+Var

Auctions (*Ventes aux Enchères*)

Property in France can be bought at auction, just as in England.

Some auctions are voluntary, others run by court order. The voluntary auctions are run by notaries (*Marché Immobilier des Notaires*). Only notaries are permitted to run voluntary auctions. There are relatively few such auctions. There you will find a combination of properties that the sellers have decided to sell in this way. Properties that have 'stuck' in the market, properties that the sellers think will sell best at auction and properties which have been inherited which the heirs wish to dispose of quickly. An attraction of such auctions for the seller is that his share of the auctioneers fees (usually one per cent of the price) is lower that the normal level of estate agents fees (say, five per cent).

Other auctions are judicial auctions (*ventes judiciares*). In theory there are several circumstances where the law requires a sale by auction but increasingly, in practice and by consent, these sales take place as ordinary sales by private agreement in order to save the considerable cost of an auction. In a judicial auction you will find properties sold, for example, as a result of mortgage repossession, unpaid debts, disputes between joint owners, in connection with the administration of the estate of someone who has died or by virtue of some other court order.

Prices can be very attractive. A few years ago, at the height of the last recession, there were incredible bargains with prices, perhaps, 30 per cent of 'value'. Now auctions usually offer less spectacular bargains but still offer the possibility of good bargains. This is because, particularly in many judicial auctions, the process is intended first and foremost to recover someone's debt. Once that and the considerable costs have been covered there is little reason to press for a higher price, even though the owner will ultimately receive the excess.

Buying a property at auction is not simple for someone who does not live in the area and it is vitally important that you have taken all the normal preparatory steps – including seeing a lawyer – before you embark on the process.

The procedure leading up to the auction is basically the same whether the auction is a judicial auction or a notarial auction.

First, you must know that the auction is taking place. They are usually advertised six to eight weeks in advance. Auctions ordered by the court will be advertised by order of the court in the local press. Notices will also be posted in the area.

Second, you must find out what is in the auction. Brief details of the property to be sold including the commune's land/rating registry (*cadastre*) reference, the arrangements for viewing, the notary dealing with the sale, the reserve price and the deposit that must be lodged in order that you can be allowed to bid. These details of the property will mean nothing to you. The place could be derelict or next door to a nuclear power station. You will need to inspect the property and decide whether it is of interest. This is a time consuming and potentially costly process. Remember that you could have to inspect twenty properties to find three you might like and then you might be outbid on all three. An alternative to personal inspection is to get someone to do it for you. This is not as satisfactory but a local estate agent will, for a fee, go to look at the property and give to a description of it. If you're luckly he might post or email you some photographs. His fee, about £200 if the property is close to his office, will probably be less than the cost of travel. Some people buy blind. This is for real poker players.

Thirdly, you will need to check out the legal situation of the property before the date of the auction. Most of the steps needed in an ordinary purchase will be required (*see* below).

Fourthly, many properties on sale by auction are not in the best of condition. You will therefore need to get estimates as to the likely cost of repairs or improvements so as to make sure that the price you bid is not so high as to make the project non-viable.

Fifthly, you will have to appoint a notary or local lawyer (*avocat*) to act on your behalf at the auction. At a judicial auction individuals cannot turn up and bid as they can in England. Only notaries and *avocats* are entitled to bid. Even at an ordinary notarial auction you would be brave or foolish not to be represented. The lawyer will explain precisely what will need to be done for this particular auction. You will have to tell him the maximum price you want to offer and pay him the bidding depost – a refundable deposit levied by the auctioneer in order to allow you to enter a bid. You will also have to give your personal details (marital status, occupation, nationality, passport number, etc.) a deposit of 10 per cent of the price you are offering, less the bidding deposit. The full deposit is paid across at the time your bid is accepted.

You do not need to attend the auction – the lawyer will be able to do so for you. He will probably require a power of attorney for that purpose. He will, of course, charge you for this work. The fee can be substantial, so get an estimate.

Even though you do not need to be present, an auction (especially a judicial auction) is a most interesting event, so you might want to go along. The traditional auction, gradually disappearing, is the 'candle' auction (*vente à la chandelle*). The sale is *à la bougie* or *aux trois feux*. This picturesque, if confusing and often noisy, affair sells the property on the extinction of a candle flame. Once the last bid has been received a 20-second taper is lit. Once it burns out a second is lit. If no further bides are received a third – the knock down candle (*feu d'adjudication*) is lit. Once that splutters out the sale is made!

If you are successful your deposit will be taken. You will then have to wait 10 days to know whether you have actually got the property as the results of the auction can be attacked during that period by anyone who is prepared to bid 10 per cent more than the sale price (*surenchère*). This might, for example, be the dispossessed owner of the property that has been sold for a pittance by the bank that repossessed it. If the auction is challenged it will be repeated. It can only be challenged once and it is a rare event.

Although the prices at auction can be very attractive you must bear in mind that you will face additional costs over and above those on a normal purchase. These are likely to raise the overall costs of buying from the normal 8–9 per cent of the price to perhaps 17–20 per cent of the price paid. The extra costs include the fees paid to your lawyers for dealing with the auction, extra land registry fees for publishing the result and the fees and charges related to the auction itself.

On the other hand, many people will be entitled to automatic mortgage finance of 60 per cent of the price paid if they by at a notarial auction. Check with your lawyer if this will apply to you.

It is also possible to buy a French property at auction in Britain. This is very rare. The auction acts simply as a preliminary sale of the property. The sale will need to be formalised in France in the usual way.

Exhibitions

An easy way to go house-hunting is to attend property exhibitions in the UK – that way you don't even have to cross the Channel until you are sure of what you want, where and how much. These can offer the whole range of services to do with buying property – estate agents, lawyers, financiers and banks. The *French Property News* exhibition at Olympia is run in conjunction with the annual 'Vive La France!' promotion, so it's worth a visit on both counts. *French Property News* runs four other exhibitions, too – an autumn one in London and others at Harrogate, Taunton and Birmingham. Blendon Communications also organizes a range of 'Homes Overseas' exhibitions throughout Britain and Northern Ireland, with coverage of properties in France and other countries. They take place throughout the year in London, Edinburgh, Manchester, Glasgow, Somerset and Birmingham. London's *Evening Standard* newspaper also runs a 'Home-buyer Show'.

Property Shows

Some of the international property shows have a section where private individuals can post details of property for sale. French Property News shows have traditionally provided this facility. Others may also do so. Contact the show organizers for details.

Building and Renovation

Throughout this book there is a theme that keeps recurring. The demography of France creates many of its differences with Britain. In other words, with a population of similar size and a land mass that is double that of Britain, France has a lot of characteristics that don't occur in Britain. One is the large number of derelict, rundown or ruined houses in the countryside (and in some villages). With a much larger proportion of its land under agriculture and a shift away from farming in the last few generations, inevitably there are abandoned buildings at low prices to be had. Add to this the fact that rural poverty is a recent memory in much of France, so a lot of people have been occupying buildings that many British would consider dilapidated or at least in need of renovation. Hence, the number of unrestored buildings on the market in our list on pp.85–8.

Renovation

The main attraction of these buildings is often their charm, position and price. Sometimes this is sufficient to overcome much more practical considerations. Then there is the erroneous assumption that, as a ruin is, by definition, partially built, it should cost less to restore than to build something completely from scratch. This is untrue: costs of renovation and of new building are the same – about €800 per square metre – so you might as well build your own property, if that's what you would prefer. A renovated house may have much

Case Study: A Plum Restoration Job

In the olden days in France, plums were made into prunes in a house on the farm where a large drying oven was situated. Once upon a time, in one little village in Périgord, one of these ovens set fire to such a house and it was virtually destroyed. For many years it was left as a ruin until George and Shirley and their builder friend Richard decided to renovate it. They worked at it with their two sons and local artisans, rebuilding it in traditional style with traditional materials. They worked at it over a number of years, gradually extending both house and property and eventually adding a swimming pool. The result was a charming three-bedroom home that blends remarkably well with its environment and is appreciated by the locals as well as the many British visitors to whom it is rented every year, when George, Shirley and family are not there. They initially paid £40,000 for it, but, over the years, have invested a lot more. Their *taxe foncière* and *d'habitation* (local taxes) come to £300 a year. Naturally the house is called Le Prunier. Shirley says, 'We have never regretted it and would advise anyone else to do the same thing. We would urge people to use local artisans, if you are renovating, and to restore your property with the local architecture in mind.'

more charm than a new one and be easier to let, but it can actually cost more to maintain. A barn was built as a barn, so is likely to be a nightmare to heat. It will certainly not have a damp course – indeed, neither will most farm buildings. On the other hand, a farm granny may have lived in your unrestored property for the last 50 years and it may just need electricity, mains water and a septic tank. Even these can be expensive, so consider the costs, especially if you are a long way from the nearest power source.

DIY

Many British people do some, or even all, the renovation themselves – a move seen as a bit eccentric by the locals, among whom DIY has not yet become so common. Because of this, the distribution of DIY suppliers is lighter than in the UK and enthusiasts complain about the cost, especially of paint, which some import from Britain. Most people who can afford to employ local artisans for at least part of the work. They are best found by word of mouth or from the local *chambre de métiers*.

Building from Scratch

A new build obviously requires more than just the help of the odd artisan and, whether you are doing this or simply renovating, planning permission has to be obtained from the local town hall, too. Make sure that you put a get-out clause in your *compromise de vente, see* pp.141–68, should this be withheld. In France, the main variable building cost is the price of the land because the building costs themselves are standard, so only the costs of the materials should alter.

Builders

A contractor should be able to offer an accurate estimate; be sure to ask for it in writing. A properly qualified and registered French builder will also offer a ten-year guarantee, which is covered by his professional insurance policy, even if he goes out of business. Plumbers and electricians should offer a

Case Study: Choosing Your Conversion

John (a retired engineer) and Joan moved to the Dordogne 13 years ago to escape the rat race and bought an attractive manor house at the edge of a small village. They chose the area because the climate is conducive to gardening and they enjoy the countryside. They initially spent about £100,000, but a contemporary valuation puts it nearer to £250,000. John says:

'Unless a barn conversion has been exceptionally well done and the building has been fully lined, with interior walls, it is best to avoid buying anything that hasn't always been a dwelling, even if it is for restoration. The construction is totally different.

'Only if you are on the Mediterranean coast could you possibly do without central heating. Even there, some form of background heating is considered necessary for a limited period of the year. No matter what any salesman will tell you, electric central heating will prove expensive to run, even if the capital cost is lower. Winters inland can be quite cold, especially if the property is positioned in a hollow. Check on the orientation of the property and that at least the living areas look south. Winters can be very long if you don't see the sun between September and March, which could well be the case in a property looking north. A frost hollow can be at least 5°C colder than the rest of the area. Select your property in the rain, during the winter – if you like it then, you are sure to be happy there in the spring and summer.

'Get the property checked over by an expert (a well-respected artisan or a surveyor) who will see problems if there are any. The heaviest cost in the repair line is roofing, which will come fairly high on the list of priorities for an old property if it has not been attended to for some years. Make sure that the electricity installation is totally safe – 25 years ago, the French were not too well disciplined about their electrical work, although they are now.

'Get a good idea of property prices and values before setting out on the search for a suitable property. There are lots of folks who come here looking at property and see it as a bargain when the truth is that they will never get their money back if they try to sell again, except to other Brits.'

two-year guarantee. Hire a British builder if you like – there are plenty advertised in the French property magazines – but they should be properly registered in France. You may find that it is unpopular with your neighbours, though, if you don't use local artisans.

For building work under 170 square metres in extent and where no change in the use of the property is involved, planning permission can be got by the *notaire* at the time of purchase. If there is a change of use, a *certificat d'urbanisme* is required and this has to be applied for by a *notaire* or surveyor. If you are in a protected building or, as is more common, a protected village, there may be grants available to help with your conversion (and conservation), but, if it affects another seriously historic building, clearance may have to be obtained from the *Architecte des Bâtiments de France* in Paris. For buildings over 170 square metres, an architect will be needed to produce a full set of drawings and photographs, which have to be delivered in person and a receipt obtained or else sent by registered post to the town hall. Here it should be displayed and the applicant advised as to how long the approval process will take. If nothing is heard after this period, then it is understood that permission has been granted.

Renting Before You Buy

If you are in a position to do so, it is quite a good idea to rent for some time in France before you take the plunge and buy, to get some useful experience. By renting, I mean long-term renting, not staying in somebody's *gîte* for a few weeks during the off-season. You could consider letting out your property at home and renting a property in France with the income. There should be a surplus. Finding a French property to rent can be done in the usual ways – publications, word-of-mouth, the Internet and estate agents. In French adverts, the number of rooms is what is mentioned. The 'T code' that you often see means that the accommodation has a kitchen, bathroom and then that number of other rooms – thus, 'T2' is kitchen, bathroom and two other rooms. Sometimes the number of bedrooms (*chambres*) is mentioned as well. Check the maintenance costs, particularly in flats, many of which have their own *concierge*. When it comes to signing the contract, you could have to produce a *dossier*, or set of documents, proving to the owner or estate agent that you are able to pay the rent for the period of the let. They may want you to show that your monthly income is at least three times the cost of the rental. This is a provision to protect you from getting into debt and them from losing their money. They can also demand to see your payslips for the last year and, possibly, evidence of other income. On top of all this, a statement from your bank that you are solvent may be required. You may not be asked for all of this, but the law requires you to be prepared and, like so many French laws, it is there if it is needed. You may be asked to take out third-party insurance as well, which you do have to do, but not necessarily with the company the landlord suggests.

There is a standard legal rental agreement form that is much too detailed to go into here, but should be looked at carefully – get a translation if you have to. One way to avoid all of this is to rent from British owners, best found either on the Internet or in the French property magazines, although, on the whole, this may be a more expensive option.

If you are looking for an apartment, types on offer are very varied, from privately owned subdivided houses to multistorey blocks owned by large property companies, old blocks in cities with large rooms, and beach properties and there are even short-stay furnished lets in the middle of Paris from about £100 a night! It is with an apartment that you may encounter a *copropriété* (*see* pp.148–9) whereby the owner – and the tenant – has an agreement to share the maintenance of a property, including facilities such as the garden or pool, which, in a normal situation, would be the responsibility of the landlord. This means that you have an additional charge to pay, but it also means the rent is going to be less.

Keeping 'A Foot in Both Camps'

There is no doubt that living in France, whether part-time or permanently, seems to have many attractions for British people, especially those who live in the overcrowded and stressed southeast of England. However, there are reasons when it might not work out and we come to them in other parts of this book. It may be nothing to do with you personally – it may be a financial or family matter quite beyond your control – but, if you do need to move back and you have sold your house in the UK and perhaps used up the surplus on living expenses in France, you may have gone straight to the bottom of the UK property ladder. Getting on to the French one will not have helped because the chances of French values ever matching British ones are minimal. There are ways around this. If you can let your UK property and take out a second mortgage on it to finance your French project or if you don't have a mortgage – in which case you will probably be able finance it out of rental income – you will keep your place on the British escalator. Remember, however, that if your house in the UK is rented out and not permanently available to you, you are immediately deemed to be a French resident for tax purposes, *see* 'The Rules that Determine Residence', pp.178–9.

If you are really confident that your move is final or you can realize enough cash from the sale of your French property to get back to where you were, or if you don't have a property in Britain to start with, that's fine. However, if you have spent a fortune doing up a ruined farm in the back of beyond, you may be waiting a long time to sell again.

Case Study: A Listed Property

Jeremy and Hélène bought a three-storey house and yard in a small town in the Cévennes for £60,000 nearly two years ago. Hélène is French and works locally, while Jeremy is a journalist working mainly for UK publications and they have a little girl. Their house was in need of some renovation, all of which Jeremy has done himself. Because the whole street is *classé* (listed), he has had some financial help with doing this from the local authority. He remarks that any alterations affecting the street side of their building have to have planning permission, but he has a pretty free hand with anything that can't be seen from the outside.

Jeremy advises: 'Be ready for endless form-filling (in triplicate with a photo and a copy of your birth certificate) and never getting the same answer twice when you ask for official advice. They drive you mad at the time, but you'll love them for it in the end – otherwise, why did we all come here?'

So, when it comes to the point of converting your British property – via the medium of sterling and euros – into a French property, think of that and don't be led astray by the fact that those euros are going much further. The average price of a house in England will buy you a renovated farmhouse and a few acres in much of France, but you may find the reverse won't work. So, do you really want a farmhouse and land? In other words, don't decide based on what seems cheap but on what you need. If you are in a rush because the bargain looks good by UK standards, you will probably pay too much anyway. Lower prices do not mean that the seller won't try to squeeze every last penny out of you.

Temporary Accommodation

Where do you stay while you are house-hunting or renovating or building your house? This will depend on how much money you have to spare. If you can afford hotels every night, that is the most comfortable option. The budget hotels that have sprung up all over France may be an answer, too, although their lack of soul does not endear them to most guidebook writers. From £15 a night, bed only, for up to three people, they are good value. Their disadvantages are that there may not be a nearby restaurant and they are often situated in light industrial parks. Some of them have high-tech gizmos that can be beyond some people. The main feature of these is automated booking. This means that you can book a room via a computerized console on the outside wall with a credit or debit card, which gives you a code to enter the hotel and your room (you can do this by phone or online, too). Once in, you have to keep your code number handy because, if your bedroom door shuts behind you, you can end up stuck in a passage at night, locked out of your room. One group has automatically self-cleaning toilets and showers. There is even a hot-air body-dryer in the shower, situated high on a wall so drying your nether regions presents an interesting challenge. By far the biggest of the budget hotel chains is Accor's Formule 1 (**www.hotelformule1.com**), but there are also Premier Classe, Nuit d'Hotel, Mister Bed, Bonsai, Fasthotel, B&B, Villages Hotel, Balladins, Best Hotel, Etap, Quick Palace, Akena and Noctuel, all of which you can access via the **www.eurapart.com** website. Formule 1 is the cheapest, but most of the others have en suite shower and WC.

Alternatively, you could stay in a *gîte*. If it is it out of season, you may get some good deals, too. Make sure there is some heating, even if you have to pay for it, because some *gîtes* – paradoxically, usually in the south – can be very cold out of season. Alternatively, you could look into renting a proper flat if it is going to take some time, *see* 'Renting Before You Buy', pp.108–9. It is a good idea to ask your estate agent, if you have one, if they know of anywhere. If you are doing a conversion or restoration, you might decide, as most people do, to camp out in a corner of it as it takes shape, but, if you do this, try to plan to do the work in the summer. Bringing a caravan or mobile home to park on your land is another popular variation on this theme. Another option is to look in the pages of the property magazines or their websites to see if there are any other British people who might have empty accommodation and be able to help. It is not a problem with an easy solution, unless you have a reasonable budget.

Other Types of Ownership

Timeshare

Timeshare is a great product too often sold by crooks.

The accommodation is almost always first class and, often, the annual usage charges are reasonable. The problem is that the purchase price is usually out of all proportion to the value of the property. But, if you buy second hand you can pick up timeshare weeks for £750 that will enable you to swap in and out of resorts all over the world. It is not like owning your own property. It won't go up in value. But if you only have three or four weeks overseas holiday per year it is very flexible and worth a thought. Be *very careful* whom you buy from. Where possible deal directly with a private seller. If you are going to deal with a company *only* deal with a resale company that is a member of OTE (The Organisation for Timeshare in Europe) and, if in any doubt, despite the low cost of the second-hand purchase, use a lawyer to protect your interests.

Good sources of resale timeshare direct from the owner include your supermarket notice board (WANTED: Timeshare week in one bedroom apartment in France), Exchange & Mart and Daltons Weekly.

We would strongly advise you not to deal with so called 'Holiday Clubs'.

Part-ownership Schemes

This is not timeshare. It is a scheme whereby several people buy a home for their joint use. Those people could be you and your children, you and your neighbours or friends or complete strangers. The property is normally owned through a company. You own a percentage of the shares of the company proportionate to your agreed usage of the property.

For example, you may buy the right to use an apartment in Nice for two months per year. The apartment may be worth £200,000. You may have paid £40,000 for the right to use it for August and £10,000 for the right to use it for November. You would own two out of 12 shares in the company. You would pay 2/12ths (16.66 per cent) of the annual running costs of the property. You would either appoint a professional manager or, if you were friends, get together every year to decide about furnishing, repairs etc. You can (subject to the rules of the group) either use the property yourself during your period of entitlement, allow friends to use it or rent it out.

It can work very well. You get all the holiday you need. You don't have to worry about finding tenants or the property being empty. You only pay for what you use. You should see a long-term growth in the value of your investment as you own the house that lies below the company structure. With luck, you become friends and therefore can leave property in the house and furnish it to a better standard than you would find in rental property because you trust each other.

If you are thinking about going into such a scheme you *must* take advice from a lawyer familiar with French law *and* the law of the country where the scheme has been constituted.

Seminars

However magnificently and clearly a book of this kind may be written, there is no substitute for an explanation given by a human being whom you can question about the bits you don't understand. Fortunately, throughout the year there are various seminars – generally run by experienced lawyers or financial advisers – that will cover the various topics included in this guide, often in more detail.

These are sometimes run in conjunction with the major property shows – such as 'Homes Overseas' and 'World of Property' (*see* 'Exhibitions', p.104). On other occasions, the lawyers or financial advisers run them themselves, and *Living France* magazine hosts an annual two-day seminar in Northampton.

Making the Purchase

John Howell
Solicitor and International Lawyer
John Howell & Co.

05

Buying a property in France is as safe as buying a property in the UK. On reading a book such as this – which must explain the potential pitfalls if it is to serve any useful purpose – it can seem a frightening or dangerous experience. If you go about the purchase in the right way it is not dangerous and should not be frightening. The same or similar dangers arise when buying a house in the UK. If you are in any doubt, look briefly at a textbook on English conveyancing and all of the horrible things that have happened to people and which have led to our current system of enquiries and paperwork. You do not worry about those dangers because you are familiar with them and, more importantly, because you are shielded against contact with most of them by your solicitor. The same should be true when buying in France. Read this book to understand the background and why some of the problems exist. Ask your lawyer to advise you about any issues that worry you and leave him to avoid the landmines!

Law

This book is intended primarily for people from England and Wales. For this reason I have drawn comparisons with English law. Scots law is somewhat different. Where the points apply also to Scots law I have tried, depending on the context, to refer to either UK or British law. The law is intended to be up to date as at 1 January 2002.

Disclaimer

Although we have done our best to cover most topics of interest to the buyer of a property in France, a guide of this kind cannot take into account every individual's personal circumstances, and the size of the book means that the advice cannot be comprehensive. The book is intended as a starting point that will enable people who are thinking of buying property to understand some of the issues involved and to ask the necessary questions of their professional advisers. **IT IS NO SUBSTITUTE FOR PROFESSIONAL ADVICE**. Neither the author nor the publishers can accept any liability for any action taken or not taken as a result of this book.

Finding a Property in France

At the moment we are in a property 'boom'. It is, in most popular areas, a seller's market. Property – and, in particular, attractive, well-located and well-priced property – sells very quickly. A few years ago it was fairly simple to go to France, look around, see a few properties and then come back to the UK to ponder which to buy. Today someone doing this would be likely to find that the house they wanted to make an offer on had sold to someone else in the few days since they saw it.

As a result of this people who are serious about buying property in France should do some research and make some preparations *before* they go on a visit to look at property. When they go on a visit they should do so with the intention that, if they see something that they really like, they will make an offer and commit themselves (at least in principle) to the purchase whilst they are still in the area.

This does not mean to say that you can never take your time over buying property in France. There are some areas, particularly the lesser-known rural areas and the industrial cities, where property still moves slowly. If you want to buy a ruin for restoration there is likely to be little immediate or pressing competition for the property and so you will have time to make a proper study of the project before making a formal offer or signing a contract. If the seller won't grant you that time, walk away. Better to lose the property than take on a restoration project that cannot be completed or, at least, cannot be completed at reasonable cost. But in most cases you must be prepared to take action. It cannot be overemphasized that in most of the popular parts of France there will be a real risk that, if you do not make a formal offer or sign a reservation contract soon after you see the property, you will lose your dream home to another buyer.

In France, once you find a property, things tend to move quite quickly. This is so even in the areas where you are not under great pressure to commit yourself to the purchase immediately. Once the decision to buy has been made a preliminary contract is signed very early in the process. As a result, if you have not thought through the process and made the important decisions about, for example, who should own the property in advance, you will be forced to make them under pressure. As we all know, decisions made under pressure are often not the best decisions. The cost of making the wrong decision can be substantial, amounting in many cases to five or 10 per cent of the price of the property bought. For this reason too it is sensible to be clear about your basic plan before you go looking at property.

What Preparation Should You Make?

Understand the System

The system of buying and selling property in France is, not surprisingly, different from the system of buying property in England or Scotland. On balance, neither better nor worse – just different. It has many superficial similarities, which can lull you into a false sense of familiarity and over-confidence.

The most important thing to remember is that buying a home in France is just as safe as buying a home in Cardiff – providing that you take the right professional advice and precautions when doing so. If you do not take such advice there are many expensive traps for the unwary.

It will help you to avoid the problems and to ask the necessary questions of those advising you if you have a broad general understanding of the processes involved.

That is what this guide sets out to do. Because of its limited length and intended audience it is general in nature. It cannot cover everybody's situation, particularly in the complex areas of international taxation and property law. There are a number of topics which, because they apply to small numbers of people, are not dealt with at all. It is certainly no subject for specific advice relating to your own personal situation and circumstances.

See a Lawyer

It will save you a lot of time and trouble if you see your lawyer *before* you find a property. There are a number of preliminary issues that can best be discussed in the relative calm before you find the house of your dreams rather than once you are under pressure to sign some document to commit yourself to the purchase. These issues will include:

- **who should own the property, bearing in mind the French inheritance. rules and the French and British tax consequences of ownership.**
- **whether to consider mortgage finance and if so in which country.**
- **what to do about converting the purchase price into euros.**
- **if you are going to be living in France, sorting out the tax and investment issues that will need to be dealt with before your move if you are to get the best out of both systems.**

Only UK lawyers who specialize in dealing with France will be able to help you fully. Your normal English solicitor will know little or nothing of the issues of French law and a French lawyer is likely to know little or nothing about the British tax system or the issues of English or Scots law that will affect the way the transaction should be arranged.

The lawyer may also be able to recommend estate agents, architects, surveyors and other contacts in the area you are looking.

A physical meeting is still the best way to start an important relationship. It has a number of advantages. It allows you to show and be shown documents, and wander off more easily into related topics. Most importantly, it is usually easier to make certain that you have each understood the other in a face-to-face meeting. But, these days, 'seeing' your lawyer does not need to involve an actual meeting. If it is more convenient to you it could be done by telephone conference call or videoconference over the internet.

Decide on Ownership

Who should be the owner of your new home? This is the most important decision you will have to make when buying a property. Because of the combination of the French inheritance rules – which do not allow you to leave your property as you please – and the French and British tax systems, getting the ownership wrong can be a very expensive mistake indeed. It can lead to the wrong people being entitled to inherit the property from you (a particular problem for people with children from more than one relationship) and it can lead to totally unnecessary tax during your lifetime and on your death. Even on a modest property this unnecessary tax can amount to tens of thousands of pounds. *See further* 'Who Should Own the Property?', p.136 and 'The French Inheritance Rules', p.207.

Get an Offer of Mortgage/Finance

These days, with very low interest rates, more and more people borrow at least part of the money needed to buy their home in France. Even if they don't need to do so, for many it makes good business or investment sense.

If you want to borrow money to part-finance your purchase it makes sense to get clearance before you start looking at property. Whether you want to borrow on your UK property or on the overseas property your lawyers should be able to put you in touch with suitable lenders. They will process your application and give you a preliminary clearance to borrow up to a certain amount. This, of course, is subject to the property and its title later proving satisfactory. Doing this removes the need for an embarrassing call to the agent a week after you have bought the property to tell him that you can't raise the finance. Getting a preliminary clearance in this way does not restrict your freedom to take up a better offer if one comes to light whilst you are looking at properties. *See* 'Raising Finance to Purchase a Property in France', pp.124–36.

Think about How You Will Pay a Deposit

If you are going shopping for property you will need to have access to some money to pay for it and you will normally need to put down a preliminary deposit of five or 10 per cent of the price of the property. How should you make this payment?

Some estate agencies, particularly those operating from Britain, will ask you to take a banker's draft for the likely amount of any deposit. Fortunately there are few of these. This is not a good idea. It is ideal for the estate agent and the seller but, puts the buyer under subtle but unnecessary pressure to spend the money on something. Happily, the usual way of paying the deposit is still via a British cheque for the sterling equivalent of the euros needed. This is a simple and effective method of payment. There is, however, a further option that people are increasingly using. This is to leave the amount likely to be needed as a deposit with their specialist lawyer in the UK. Then, when you have found the right property and the estate agent is asking you to sign some form of contract, you can tell him that it is your lawyer who has the money. You will sign the contract as soon as he has approved it and that he will then transfer the funds into the estate agent's bank account by electronic transfer. The lawyer should be able to check a contract faxed to him whilst you wait and be able to tell you that its terms appear reasonable, and that any necessary special clauses have been included. He will also be able to tell you the nature of the contract you are signing (formal offer, reservation, option or full contract) and explain, briefly, its legal effects. This has a number of advantages. It can take a lot of pressure off you. It makes it very hard for the agent to persuade you to sign a document, which has – in every case – far-reaching consequences without getting it checked. From the agent's point of view it means that he will receive the cleared funds within a couple of days rather than the two or three weeks it can take for your British cheque to pass through the banking system and be cleared into his account. This preliminary check by the lawyer, though useful, is limited. He will not have seen proof of title or planning consents. He will not have inspected the detailed documentation relating to the construction of a new building. He will not have been able to carry out any checks on the property. But it is a great deal better than nothing.

This really only works well if you have made contact with your lawyer before you go to look at properties as he will need to understand something about your circumstances before being able to give sensible advice about, for example, the special clauses needed in the contract.

Capital Growth

One of the great attractions of owning a property is the potential for the asset growing in value whilst, at the same time, you enjoy the use of it. Few would say that you get as much fun out of 10,000 Abbey National shares as you do out of a flat in Antibes! The flat in Antibes is also less likely to go bust, or to be taken over and lose half its value overnight.

For some people the choice of place to buy a property – or the selection of which of several places to choose – is governed by likely capital growth.

In popular areas – and, in particular, in popular tourist areas – there have been large amounts of property inflation. Fortunately, we do not need to speculate about this. The French government keeps statistics through its land registry system.

The Alternatives to Buying

Rental

If you are retiring, there is a lot to be said for temporarily renting a place in the area where you are thinking of living. It is best to do this for a full year before deciding whether to live there. Allowing for time thereafter to find and buy a property probably means an 18-month rental. Try to rent something similar to what you are thinking of buying and do not rent unseen – take a short holiday to find your rental property.

If you rent you are less likely to commit yourself to a purchase in an area you turn out not to like. It also avoids the expensive process of having to sell the property and buy another, either in France or back in England. The overall cost of moving in France is likely to be about 13 per cent of the price of your new property, eight to nine per cent being the fees on the purchase of the new property and five per cent being the estate agents' fee for selling the old one. A move back to the UK would (depending on the value of the property bought) be likely to cost about eight per cent – five per cent sales expenses in France and three per cent purchase expenses in the UK.

There are drawbacks to this course of action:

1. In the recent past property prices in many areas have risen rapidly. For example, two years ago, if you had been buying in Nice then delaying 18 months would probably have cost you about 15–20 per cent in increased property cost. This is a lot more than your money would have made if invested, so the delay would have cost you money.
2. The rent you paid out is dead money. This would probably be about 5–6 per cent of the value of a property per annum for a property let on an 18-month let.
3. You want to get on with your life, especially if you have just retired.
4. Moving is stressful. You will have to do it twice rather than once.
5. Moving into temporary accommodation can produce a lack of attachment to the area, which can mean that you don't commit to it and give it a fair try. You are always looking back over your shoulder at the UK rather than forward to France.
6. It can be hard to find good accommodation available on an 18-month let.

If you are thinking of a holiday home it can also make sense to rent rather than buy. The biggest drawback to owning a property overseas is that you feel compelled to take all your holidays there. You are paying for it so you should use it. If you invested the money spent on the home it would generate a good income, which would pay for a holiday anywhere in the world. Of course, renting is never as good as owning your own home. You do not know the quality of what you will find on arrival. You won't be able to leave your clothes there and so travel light. You won't have friends there and so feel part of the community. You won't be able to offer the use of the property to family and friends. You may find that your investment of the cash saved has performed less well than the house would.

Exchanges

Why not spend your holidays in someone else's home – free of charge?

If you have an attractive property in the UK you may well find a French family who are only too pleased to leave their house in Provence for August to stay in your place in London, whilst you do the reverse. Not only do you change houses but cars and possibly dogs too.

Property Inspection

Whatever property you are thinking of buying you should think about having it inspected before you commit yourself to the purchase.

In fact – foolishly – very few buyers of property in France do this. There is no tradition of doing so. It costs just as much and causes just as much disruption to repair property in France as in the UK, so you don't want any surprises.

A new property will be covered by a two-year guarantee (*responsabilité garantie biennale*), running from the date of handover (*reception des travaux*), covering defects to equipment in the a new property. The property will also benefit from a guarantee in respect of major structural defects that will last for 10 years (*garantie décennale*). As a subsequent purchaser you assume the benefit of these guarantees. After 10 years you are on your own! For property more than 10 years old (and, arguably, for younger property too) you should consider a survey.

If you decide on a survey there are a number of options available to you.

Do-it-yourself

There are several things that you can do yourself. These will help you decide when to instruct a surveyor to do a proper survey and help direct him to any specific points of interest (*see* Checklist in **Appendix 1**, pp.318–22).

Estate Agent's Valuation and 'Survey'

It may be possible to arrange for another local estate agent to give the property a quick 'once over' to comment on the price asked and any obvious problem areas. This is far short of a survey. It is likely to cost about £200.

Mortgage Lender's Survey

This is no substitute for a proper survey. Many lenders do not ask for one and, where they do, it is normally fairly peremptory, limited to a check on whether it is imminently about to fall over and whether it is worth the money the bank is lending you.

French Builder

If you are going to do a virtual demolition and rebuild then it might make more sense to get a builder to do a report on the property. A reputable and experienced qualified builder (*maître d'œuvres*) will also be able to comment on whether the price is reasonable for the property in its existing state. Make sure you ask for a binding written quotation (*devis*) for any building work proposed. These are excellent documents that set out clearly the work required and the charge for doing it. As in any country it is as well to get several quotes, though in rural areas this can be tricky.

French Surveyor

There are a number of options here. There is no single profession of surveyor in France as we have it in England. Instead, different professionals carry out surveys that are different from each other and appropriate in different circumstances. Seek advice about which to use in your case. The local notary or estate agents can put you in touch with the right people. In most rural areas there will be limited choice but, for obvious reasons, it is perhaps better not to seek a recommendation from the estate agent selling the property. Alternatively, if you are using UK lawyers, they will probably have a recommendation. If you prefer you can select 'blind' from a list of local members supplied by the surveyors' professional body.

Architect (*Architecte*)

An architect's survey will, as you might expect, tend to focus on issues of design and construction although it should cover all of the basic subjects needed in a survey. The people to contact for a list of local architects are the College of Architects. This is not a training establishment but the architects' professional body, as in the Royal College of Surgeons. Costs vary depending on the size and complexity of the house and the distance from the architect's base. Allow £500–£1500 for an average house.

Valuer/Surveyor (*Expert Immobilier*)

The survey from an expert will focus on measurement and valuation, but will also cover the essential issues relating to the structure of the property. For a list of experts contact the *Chambre des Experts Immobiliers*. Experts produce two types of report. The more common is the *expertise*, a report of limited scope – really the initial observations of a trained eye. Such a report will contain little in the way of testing. The less common is the fuller structural report (*bilan de santé*). Not all surveyors produce the latter reports.

As with architects, costs vary depending on the size and complexity of the house and the distance from the surveyor's base. They will also vary to reflect the depth of report required. Allow £200–£500 for a basic report on an average house and £500–£1,500 for a more complex report.

Whichever type of report and whether it is from an architect or a surveyor you will find that it is different from the sort of report you would get from an English surveyor. Many people find it a little 'thin', with too much focus on issues that are not their primary concern. It will, hardly surprisingly, be in French. You will need to have it translated unless you speak very good French and have access to a technical dictionary. Translation costs amount to about £60–£100 per thousand words, depending on where you are located and the complexity of the document. Always use an English person to translate documents from French into English. An alternative to translation of the full report would be to ask your lawyer to summarize the report in a letter to you and translate any areas of particular concern.

A few French surveyors and architects, mainly in the popular areas, have geared themselves to the non-French market and will produce a report rather more like a British or German survey. They will, probably, also prepare it in bilingual form or at least supply a translation of the original French document.

UK-qualified Surveyor Based in France

A number of UK surveyors – usually those with a love of France – have seen a gap in the market and have set themselves up in France to provide British-style structural surveys. As in this country they usually offer the brief 'Homebuyers' Report' or the fuller 'Full Structural Survey'. This is not as simple as it would first appear. To do the job well they must learn about French building techniques and regulations, which are different from those in Britain. Without this knowledge the report will be of limited value. Prices are generally slightly more expensive than a French report, but it will be in English and so avoid the need for translation costs. Your UK lawyer should be able to recommend a surveyor able to do a survey in your area. Alternatively, look for advertisers in the main French property magazines.

Check they have indemnity insurance covering the provision of reports in France. Check also on the person's qualifications and experience in providing reports on French property and get an estimate. The estimate will only be an estimate because they will not know for sure the scope of the task until they visit the property and because travelling time means that visits to give estimates are not usually feasible.

UK-based Surveyor

Some UK surveyors provide reports from a base in the UK. These can be very good but travelling time often makes them impractical – especially in remote areas – and expensive. Make the same checks as for a UK surveyor based in France.

Timescale

Most surveys can be done in seven to ten days.

Contracts 'Subject to Survey'

This is most unusual in France. Legally there is nothing to stop a French preliminary contract (*compromis de vente*) containing a get-out clause (*clause suspensive*) stating that the sale is conditional upon a satisfactory survey being obtained. It is unlikely to meet with the approval of the seller, his agent or notary unless the transaction is unusual – for example, the purchase of a castle where the cost of a survey could be huge. In an ordinary case the seller is likely to tell you to do your survey and then sign a contract. This does expose you to some risk. The seller could sell to someone else before you get the results of the survey. You may be able to enter into a reservation contract (*see* p.154) to take the property off the market for a couple of weeks and so avoid this risk. Alternatively, you may make a (probably) unenforceable 'Gentleman's Agreement' that the seller will not sell to anyone else for the next two weeks and so allow you to have your survey done. It helps if you have established a good relationship with the seller or his agent and have shown you are a serious player, perhaps by having already placed the deposit money with your lawyer, *see* 'Think About How You Will Pay a Deposit' p.117. The seller is reluctant to place a *clause suspensive* in the contract because of the difficulty of deciding what is a satisfactory survey. The problem exists in England too. If you try to pull out because the surveyor says the paint is peeling in the kitchen (and your wife has decided she doesn't like the house after all) the property can remain frozen until your dispute is resolved, possibly through the courts.

General

Whichever report you opt for its quality will depend in part on your input. Agree clearly and in writing the things you expect to be covered in the report. If you do not speak French (and the surveyor doesn't speak good English) you may have to ask someone to write on your behalf. Your UK lawyer would probably be the best bet. Some of the matters you may wish to think about are set out below. Some of these will involve you in additional cost. Ask what will be covered as part of the standard fee and get an estimate for the extras.

Checklist – Things You May Ask Your Surveyor to Do

- **Electrical condition and continuity check**
- **Drains check including assessment of drain to point where they join mains sewers or septic tank**
- **Septic tank check**
- **Rot check**
- **Check on cement in property constructed out of cement**
- **Check of underfloor areas, where access cannot easily be obtained**
- **Check on heating and air-conditioning**
- **Check on pool and all pool-related equipment and heating**
- **Wood-boring insect check. Roughly half of France is infested with termites, so this is important**

Raising Finance to Buy a Property in France

In these days of low interest rates many more people are taking out a mortgage in order to buy property abroad.

For many people their own money will be better employed in their business, or even in other investments, than in a home in France.

If the property is viewed simply as an investment, a mortgage allows you to increase your benefit from the capital growth of the property by 'leveraging' the investment. If you buy a house for £200,000 and it increases in value by £50,000 that is a 25 per cent return on your investment. If you had only put in £50,000 of your own money and borrowed the other £150,000 then the increase in value represents a return of 100 per cent on your investment. If the rate of increase in the value of the property is more than the mortgage rate you have won. In recent years property in most popular areas has gone up in value by much more than the mortgage rate. The key questions are whether that will continue and, if so, for how long.

If you decide to take out a mortgage you can, in most cases, either mortgage your existing UK property or you can take out a mortgage on your new French property. There are advantages and disadvantages both ways.

Many people buying property in France will look closely at fixed-rate mortgages so they know their commitment over, say, the next 5, 10 or 15 years. Again there are advantages and disadvantages.

Mortgaging your UK Property

At the moment there is fierce competition to lend money and there are some excellent deals to be done, whether you choose to borrow at a variable rate, at a fixed rate or in one of the hybrid schemes now on offer. Read the Sunday papers or the specialist mortgage press to see what is on offer, or consult a mortgage broker. Perhaps most useful are mortgage brokers who can discuss the possibilities in both the UK and France.

It is outside the scope of this book to go into detail about the procedures for obtaining a UK mortgage.

A number of people have found that, in today's climate of falling interest rates, re-mortgaging their property in the UK has reduced the cost of their existing borrowing so significantly that their new mortgage – including a loan to buy a modest French property – has cost no more, in monthly payments, than their old loan.

Advantages

- **The loan will probably be very cheap to set up.**

  You will probably already have a mortgage. If you stay with the same lender there will be no legal fees or land registry fees for the additional loan. There may not even be an arrangement fee.

  If you go to a new lender, many special deals mean that the lender will pay all fees involved.

- **The loan repayments will be in sterling.**

  If the funds to repay the mortgage are coming from your sterling earnings then the amount you have to pay will not be affected by fluctuations in exchange rates between the pound and the euro. At the time of writing (January 2002) most experts are predicting that the pound will fall sharply in value against the new euro.

  Equally, if sterling falls in value then your debt as a percentage of the value of the property decreases. Your property will be worth more in sterling terms but your mortgage will remain the same.

- **You will be familiar with dealing with British mortgages and all correspondence and documentation will be in English.**

- **You can take out an endowment or PEP mortgage or pension mortgage or interest-only mortgage, none of which is available in France.**
  Normally only repayment mortgages are available in France.
- **You will probably need no extra life insurance cover.**
  This can add considerably to the cost of the mortgage, especially if you are getting older.

Disadvantages

- **You will pay UK interest rates which, at the time of writing (January 2002), are higher than French rates.**
  British rates are about 5.5 per cent variable. French rates vary from about 3.8 per cent variable.
  Make sure you compare the overall cost of the two mortgages. Crude rates (which, in any case, may not be comparable as they are calculated differently in the two countries) do not tell the whole tale. What is the total monthly cost of each mortgage, including life insurance and all extras? What is the total amount required to repay the loan, including all fees and charges?
- **If sterling increases in value against the euro a mortgage in euros would become cheaper to pay off.**
  Your loan of €60,000 (now worth about £37,000 at €1 = £0.62p) would only cost about £30,000 to pay off if the euro rose 20 per cent to about £0.50.
- **If you are going to let the property it will be difficult or impossible to get French tax relief on the mortgage interest.**
- **Many people do not like the idea of mortgaging their main home – which they may only just have cleared after 25 years of paying a mortgage!**
- **Some academics argue that, in economic terms, debts incurred to buy assets should be secured against the asset bought and assets in one country should be funded by borrowings in that country.**

All in all, a UK mortgage is generally the better option for people who need to borrow relatively small sums and who will be repaying it out of UK income.

French Mortgages

A French mortgage is one taken out over your French property. This will either be from a French bank (or other lending institution) or from a British bank that is registered and does business in France. You cannot take a mortgage on your new French property from your local branch of a building society or high street bank.

The basic concept of a mortgage is the same in France as it is in England or Scotland. It is (usually) a loan secured against land or buildings. Just as in England, if you don't keep up the payments the bank will repossess your property. In France, if they do this they will sell it by judicial auction (*see* p.102) and you are likely to see it sold for a pittance and recover little if anything for the equity you built up in the property. Mortgages in France are, however, different in many respects from their English counterparts. It is important to understand the differences, which are explained below.

French mortgages are governed by, amongst other rules, the *Loi Scrivener* (so called because Mme Scrivener was the minister responsible for the law). This creates a complex, and typically French, administrative regime for the granting of mortgages and gives some significant elements of consumer protection.

Key elements of the *Loi Scrivener* (which applies only to commercial mortgages of residential property) include:

- **Every purchase contract must contain either a statement that the sale is subject to a mortgage and give details of the loan, or a statement in the buyer's own handwriting that the buyer has been informed of the law and that the purchase does not depend upon a mortgage.**
- **If the purchase is subject to a mortgage the contract is automatically subject to a get-out condition (*clause suspensive*) for at least one month to the effect that if the loan is refused the contract is null and void and your deposit will be returned. The buyer must make every effort to obtain a mortgage and, if he does not do so, will lose the protection of the law. This clause needs to be drafted most carefully to ensure your protection. If you are offered a contract containing such a clause, always get it checked by your lawyer before you sign it.**
- **Every offer of a mortgage must be in writing and contain full details of the loan including its total cost, interest charges, mechanisms for varying the interest rate and what ancillary steps the borrower must take to get the loan (such as taking out a life policy). It must also state any penalties for early repayment of the loan and that it is valid for acceptance for 30 days.**
- **The loan offer cannot be accepted for a period of 10 days from receipt and no money can be paid to the lender until that time. This is a 'cooling off period' that can cause some difficulty if the mortgage offer takes some time to appear and the buyer is anxious to proceed.**
- **The loan must be subject to a condition that the contract is completed within four months of acceptance of the loan.**
- **There are restrictions on the ability to impose penalties for early payment of the loan.**

The Main Differences Between an English and a French Mortgage

- **French mortgages are almost always created on a repayment basis. That is to say, the loan and the interest on it are both gradually repaid by equal instalments over the period of the mortgage. Endowment, PEP, pension and interest-only mortgages are not known in France.**
- **The formalities involved in making the application, signing the contract subject to a mortgage and completing the transaction are more complex and stricter than in the UK.**
- **Most French mortgages are granted for 15 years, not 25 as in England. In fact the period can be anything from two to (in a few cases) 25 years. Normally the mortgage must have been repaid by your 70th (sometimes 65th) birthday.**
- **The maximum loan is generally 80 per cent of the value of the property and 75 or 66 per cent is more common. Valuations by banks tend to be conservative – they are thinking about what they might get for the property on a forced sale if they had to repossess it. As a planning guide, you should think of borrowing no more than two-thirds of the price you are paying. The rate of interest you pay is likely to be less if you borrow a lower percentage of value and for a shorter period.**
- **Fixed-rate loans – with the rate fixed for the whole duration of the loan – are more common than in the UK. They are very competitively priced.**
- **The way of calculating the amount the bank will lend you is different from in the UK. As you would expect, there are detailed differences from bank to bank but the bank is not allowed to lend you more than an amount the monthly payments on which amount to 30 per cent of your net disposable income. *See* calculating your disposable income, p.129.**
- **There will usually be a minimum loan (say £20,000) and some banks will not lend at all on property less than a certain value.**
- **The way of dealing with stage payments on new property and property where money is needed for restoration is different from in England.**
- **The paperwork on completion of the mortgage is different. There is (usually) no separate mortgage deed. Instead the existence of the mortgage is mentioned in your purchase deed (*Acte de Vente*).**

How Much Can I Borrow?

Different banks have slightly different rules and slightly different ways of interpreting the rules.

Generally they will lend you an amount that will give rise to monthly payments of up to 30 per cent of your net available monthly income.

The starting point is your net monthly salary after deduction of tax and and National Insurance contributions but before deduction of voluntary pay-ments such as to savings schemes. If there are two applicants the two salaries are taken into account. If you have investment income or a pension this will be taken into account. If you are buying a property with a track record of letting income this *may* be taken into account. If you are buying a Leaseback then the leaseback rental income will usually be taken into account. If you are over 65 your earnings will not be taken into account, but your pension and investment income will be. If your circumstances are at all unusual seek advice as approaching a different bank may produce a different result.

e.g.	Mr Smith – net salary	£3,000
	Mrs Smith – net salary	£2,000
	Investment income	£1,000
	Total income taken into account	£6,000

The maximum loan repayments permitted will be 30 per cent of this sum, less your existing fixed commitments

i.e. Maximum permitted loan repayment £6,000 x 30% = £1,800

Regular monthly commitments would include mortgage payments on your main and other properties, any rent paid, HP commitments and maintenance (family financial provision) payments. Repayments on credit cards do not count. If there are two applicants both of their commitments are taken into account.

e.g.	Mr & Mrs Smith – mortgage on main home	£750
	Mr & Mrs Smith – mortgage on house in Spain	£400
	Mrs Smith – HP on car	£200
	Total pre existing outgoings	£1,350

Maximum loan repayment permitted = £1,800 – £1,350 = £450 per month. This would, at today's rates, equate to a mortgage of about £60,000 over 15 years.

If you are buying a property for investment (rental) the bank may treat this as commercial lending and apply different criteria.

Payment Table

Rough guide to repayments – £s per month per £1,000 borrowed – UK or France – Repayment Mortgage

Period of Repayment	2%	3%	4%	5%	6%	7%	8%
5 years	17.50	17.92	18.36	18.79	19.24	19.69	20.14
10 years	9.19	9.63	10.09	10.56	11.05	11.54	12.05
15 years	6.42	6.89	7.37	7.88	8.40	8.94	9.49
20 years*	5.05	5.53	6.04	6.57	7.13	7.71	8.31
25 years*	4.23	4.73	5.26	5.82	6.41	7.03	7.67

Rates will vary somewhat depending on formula used by the bank
*Not usually available in France

Applications for a French Mortgage

Once again the information needed will vary from bank to bank. It will also depend on whether you are employed or self-employed.

Applications can receive preliminary approval (subject to survey of the property, confirmation of good title and confirmation of the information supplied by you) within a few days. A formal letter of offer will take a couple of weeks from the time the bank has received all the necessary information from you. The documents you will are likely to need are:

Documents Needed to Apply for a French Mortgage

Employed	Self-employed
Copy passports of all applicants	
Application fee	
Completed application aorm	
Proof of outgoings such as rent or mortgage	
Copy last 3 months' bank statements	
Cash flow forecast in respect of any anticipated rental income	
Proof of income (usually three months' pay slips or a letter from your employer on official paper)	Audited accounts for last three years
	Last year's tax return and proof of payment of tax

Not all banks will need all of these, but having them ready will save time

The Mortgage Offer

Allow four weeks altogether from the date of your application to receiving a written mortgage offer as getting the information to them sometimes takes a while. It can take longer.

Once you receive the offer you will generally have 30 days from receipt of the offer in which to accept the offer, after which time it will lapse. You cannot accept it for 10 days from the date of receipt so as to give you a period of reflection This is very frustrating if the offer has taken ages to arrive and you are in a hurry!

Have the mortgage explained in detail by your lawyer.

Payments for New Property

In France when buying a new property one normally takes title to the land at an early stage and then makes payments as the development progresses.

You will need to tell your bank that you want to draw down the mortgage to make the stage payments. Usually you will pay off the amount you are providing yourself and then take the further money from the bank as and when it is due. During this period (the *période d'anticipation*) before the completion of the house you will only be borrowing part of the agreed loan and so you will usually pay only interest on the amount paid by the bank thus far. Once the property has been delivered to you (and thus the full loan has been taken) the normal monthly payments will begin.

Property Needing Restoration

Not all banks will finance such property.

If you have enough money to buy a property but need a mortgage to renovate it, you *must* apply for the mortgage before buying the property as it can otherwise be difficult to find a lender.

The Cost of Taking Out a Mortgage

This will normally involve an arrangement fee of one per cent of the amount borrowed, a 'valuation' fee of about £150–£200 and notaries'/land registry fees of 2.5 per cent of the amount borrowed. Occasionally there will be extra charges. Therefore taking out a French mortgage is not cheap. These charges are in addition to the normal expenses incurred when buying a property, which normally amount to about eight to nine per cent of the price of the property.

You will probably be required to take out life insurance for the amount of the loan, though you may be allowed to use a suitable existing policy. You may be required to have a medical. You will be required to insure the property and produce proof of insurance – but you would probably have done this anyway.

The offer may be subject to early payment penalties. These must be explained in the offer and cannot exceed the penalties laid down by law. The details of these rules vary from time to time.

Early payment penalties are of particular concern in the case of a fixed-rate mortgage.

The Exchange Rate Risk

If the funds to repay the mortgage are coming from your sterling earnings then the amount you have to pay will be affected by fluctuations in exchange rates between sterling and the euro. Do not underestimate these variations. Over the last 15 years – a typical period for a mortgage – the French franc has been as high as FF6.5 = £1 and as low as FF11 = £1. The same will almost certainly happen with the euro. Indeed, in the brief period since its launch it has varied from €1 = £0.57 and €1 = £0.65. This can make a tremendous difference to your monthly mortgage repayments. A monthly mortgage repayment of FF5,000 (about £500 at today's value) would on some occasions during the last 15 years have meant paying £454 and on other occasions £769. At the time of writing (January 2002) most experts are predicting that the pound will fall sharply in value against the new euro.

Equally, if sterling falls in value then your debt as a percentage of the value of the property increases in sterling terms. Your property will be worth more in sterling terms but your mortgage will also have increased in value. This is probably not of too much concern to most people.

Of course, if sterling rises in value against the euro then the situation is reversed.

Mortgaging Your French Property: Summary

Advantages

- **You will pay French interest rates which, at the time of writing (January 2002), are lower than UK rates.** British rates are about 5.5 per cent variable. French rates vary from about 3.8 per cent variable.

  Make sure you compare the overall cost of the two mortgages. Crude rates (which, in any case, may not be comparable as they are calculated differently in the two countries) do not tell the whole tale. What is the total monthly cost of each mortgage, including life insurance and all extras? What is the total amount required to repay the loan, including all fees and charges?
- **If you are going to let the property you will usually be able to get French tax relief on the mortgage interest.**
- **The loan repayments will usually be in euros.**

  If the funds to repay the mortgage are coming from rental income paid to you in euros this will give you something to spend them on!
- **Many people do not like the idea of mortgaging their main home – a debt which they may only just have cleared after 25 years of paying a mortgage!**
- **Some academics argue that, in economic terms, debts incurred to buy assets should be secured against the asset bought and assets in one country should be funded by borrowings in that country.**

Disadvantages

- **The loan will probably be expensive to set up.**

  Arrangement fees, inspection fees, notaries' fees and land registry fees will come to about four per cent of the amount borrowed.
- **You will incur further fees to pay to clear the record of the mortgage off your title once it has been paid off.**

  This will usually only be a problem if you want to sell the property during the two years following paying off the mortgage.
- **The loan repayments will usually be in euros.**

  If the funds to repay the mortgage are coming from your sterling earnings then the amount you have to pay will be affected by fluctuations in exchange rates between sterling and the euro. At the time of writing (January 2002) most experts are predicting that the pound will fall sharply in value against the new euro.

  Equally, if sterling falls in value then your debt as a percentage of the value of the property increases in sterling terms. Your property will be worth more in sterling terms but your mortgage will also have increased in value.
- **You will be unfamiliar with dealing with French mortgages and all correspondence and documentation will be usually be in French.**
- **Normally only repayment mortgages are available – i.e. mortgages where you pay off the capital and interest over the period of the mortgage.**
- **You will probably need extra life insurance cover.**

  This can add considerably to the cost of the mortgage, especially if you are getting older.

Generally speaking, French euro mortgages will suit people letting their property on a regular basis.

Saving Money on Your Euro Repayments

Your mortgage will usually be paid directly from your French bank account. Unless you have lots of rental or other euro income going into that account you will need to send money from the UK in order to meet the payments.

Every time you send a payment to France you will face two costs. The first is the price of the euros. This, of course, depends on the exchange rate used to convert your sterling. The second cost is the charges that will be made by your UK and French banks to transfer the funds – which can be substantial.

There are steps that you can take to control both of these charges.

As far as the exchange rate is concerned you should be receiving the so-called 'commercial rate', not the tourist rate published in the papers. The good news is that it is a much better rate. The bad news is that rates vary from second to second and so it is difficult to get alternative quotes. By the time you phone the second the first has changed! In any case, you will probably want to set up a standing order for payment and not shop around every month.

There are various organizations that can convert your sterling into euros. Your bank is unlikely to give you the best exchange rate. Specialist currency dealers will normally better the bank's rate, perhaps significantly. If you decide to use a currency dealer you must deal with one that is reputable. They will be handling your money and, if they go bust with it in their possession, you could lose it. Ask your lawyer for a recommendation.

As far as the bank charges are concerned, differing banks make differing charges. This applies both to your UK bank and to your French bank. Discuss their charges with them. In the case of your UK bank there is usually room for some kind of deal to be done. In the case of the French bank the level of these charges will probably – after their ability to speak English – be the most important reason for choosing one bank over another. Some French lenders may offer you a facility to pay the monthly payments into their UK branch and transfer the funds free of charge. The deals available change quickly. If this is offered it is a valuable feature. If it is not, ask for it. Who knows what the response might be. If you are using a currency dealer to convert your sterling into euros it is usually most economical to get them to send the money to France as this saves an additional set of bank charges. Some dealers have negotiated special rates with French banks to reflect the high volumes of business they do. Again, if you are using a UK lawyer, ask for a recommendation.

Another possibility for saving money arises if you 'forward buy' the euros that you are going to need for the year. It is possible to agree with a currency dealer that you will buy all of your euros for the next 12 months at a price that is, essentially, today's price. You normally pay 10 per cent down and the balance on delivery. If the euro rises in value you will gain, perhaps substantially. If the euro falls in value – *c'est la vie*! The main attraction of forward buying is not so much the possibility for gaining on the exchange rate – though at the moment this seems highly likely – but the certainty that the deal gives you. You will know precisely what your costs are going to be and, therefore, will not be constantly worried about the effect of a collapse in the value of sterling. Only enter into these agreements with a reputable and, if possible, bonded broker.

Bearing in mind the cost of conversion and transmission of currency it is better to make fewer rather than more payments. You will have to work out whether, taking into account loss of interest on the funds transferred but bank charges saved, you are best sending money monthly, quarterly or every six months.

Foreign Currency Mortgages

It is possible to mortgage your home in France but to borrow not in euros but in sterling – or US dollars or Swiss francs or Japanese yen.

There may be some attractions in borrowing in sterling if you are repaying out of sterling income. The rates of interest will be sterling rates, not euro rates. This will currently mean paying more. Usually the rates are not as competitive as you could obtain if you were remortgaging your property in the UK as the market is less cut-throat. You will have all the same administrative and legal costs as you would if you borrowed in euros – i.e. about four per cent of the amount borrowed.

This option is mainly of interest to people who either do not have sufficient equity in their UK home or who, for whatever reason, do not wish to mortgage the property in which they live.

Contracts 'Subject to Mortgage'

Any contract where it is stated that the purchase is dependant upon a mortgage automatically contains a 'get-out clause' (*clause suspensive*) to the effect that if the mortgage is not forthcoming – despite your best endeavours – the contract will be cancelled.

This is a very important clause that must be drafted so as to cover your situation precisely. The *law* is very precise in its requirements. Ask your lawyer for advice.

Other Loans

Many people may not need to incur the expense of mortgaging their property in France. Very often a buyer intends to move to France permanently. They have already paid off their UK mortgage and their UK home is on sale. They have found the perfect place in France and have, say £180,000 of the £200,000 available from savings and pension lump sums. The balance will be paid from the sale of their UK home, but they are not sure whether that will take place before they are committed to the purchase of the house in France in a few weeks' time.

It is probably unnecessarily complicated to mortgage the UK home for such a short period, and indeed, it could be difficult to do so if the bank knows you are selling and if you are, say 65 years old and not working.

In this case it is often simplest to approach your bank for a short-term loan or overdraft. This might be for the £20,000 shortfall or it could be that you don't really want to sell some of your investments at this stage and so you might ask for a facility of, say, £50,000.

Some people choose to take out formal two- or three-year UK loans for, say, £15,000 each whilst still resident in the UK prior to leaving for France to cover a gap such as waiting to receive a pension lump sum. Despite the high interest rates on such loans the overall cost can be a lot less than taking a short-term mortgage on the French property and paying all the fees relating to that mortgage.

Who Should Own the Property?

There are many ways of structuring the purchase of a home in France. Each has significant advantages and disadvantages. The choice of the right structure will save you thousands of pounds of tax and expenses during your lifetime and on your death. Because, in France, you do not have the total freedom that we have in the UK to deal with your assets as you please on your death, the wrong choice of owner can also result in the wrong people being entitled to inherit from you when you die. This is a particular problem for people in second marriages and unmarried couples.

The Options

Sole Ownership

In some cases it could be sensible to put the property in the name of one person only. If your husband runs a high-risk business, or if he is 90 and you are 22 this could make sense. If you intend to let the property and want all the income to be yours for tax purposes it might be worth considering. It is seldom a good idea from the point of view of tax or inheritance planning.

Joint Ownership

If two people are buying together they will normally buy in both their names. There are two ways of doing this: separate ownership (*en indivision*) or in a loose equivalent to an English 'joint tenancy' called *en tontine*. The choice you make is of great importance.

If you buy *en indivision* then your half is yours and your fellow owner's is theirs. On your death, and subject to the owners' matrimonial regime (*see* 'Your Civil State (*Etat Civil*) and Other Personal Details', pp.147–8), your half will be disposed of in accordance with the fixed rules laid down by French law (*see* 'The French Inheritance Rules', p.207). You may not be able to give it to the people you want to. If you buy *en tontine* then your half will pass to your fellow owner automatically on your death. The fixed French succession rules are bypassed. There are other differences. A person who owns *en indivision* (even if they own by virtue of inheritance) can usually insist on the sale of the property. So if your stepchildren inherit from your husband (as is likely under French law) they could insist on the sale of your home. A person who owns *en tontine* cannot usually insist on the sale of the property during the lifetime of the other joint owners. Creditors of other joint owners cannot claim the asset. But ownership *en tontine* can lead to more being paid overall by way of inheritance tax.

If you decide to buy *en indivision* then, in certain cases, it can make sense to split the ownership other than 50/50. If, for example, you have three children and your wife has two then to secure each of those children an equal share on your death you might think about buying 60 per cent in your name and 40 per cent in your wife's name. You might also think of giving the property to your children (or other preferred beneficiaries on your death) but reserving for you and your co-owner a life interest over the property (*usufruit*). This is the right to use the property for their lifetime. So, on your death, your rights would be extinguished but your second wife or partner, who still has a life interest, would still be able to use the property. Only on their death would the property pass in full to the people to whom you gave it years earlier. This device can not only protect your right to use the property but also save large amounts of inheritance tax, particularly if you are young, the property is valuable and you survive for many years. As ever there are also drawbacks, not least being the fact that after the gift you no longer own the property. If you wish to sell you need the agreement of the 'owners', who will be entitled to the proceeds of sale and who would have to agree to buy you a new house.

It is very important to seek clear advice from your lawyer about the form of ownership that will suit you best, both with regard to the consequences in France and the consequences in the UK.

Adding Your Children to the Title

If you give your children the money to buy part of the property and so put them on the title now you may save quite a lot of inheritance tax. On your death you will only own (say) one fifth of the property rather than one half. Only that part will be taxable. It may be such a small value as to result in a tax-free inheritance. This only works if your children are over 18. Of course, there are drawbacks. For example, if they fall out with you they can insist on the sale of the property and receiving their share.

Putting the Property in the Name of Your Children Only

If you put the property only in the name of your children (possibly reserving for yourself a life interest as explained above) then the property is theirs. On your death there will be little or no inheritance tax and there will be no need to incur the legal expenses involved in dealing with an inheritance. This sounds attractive. Remember, however, that you have lost control. It is no longer your property. If your children divorce their husband/wife will be able to claim a share. If they die before you without children of their own, you will end up inheriting the property back from them and having to pay inheritance tax for the privilege of doing so.

Limited Company

For some people owning a property via a limited company can be a very attractive option. You own the shares in a company, not a house in France. If you sell the house you can do so by selling the shares in the company rather than transferring the ownership of the property itself. This can save the roughly nine per cent acquisition costs that the new owner would otherwise have to pay and so, arguably, allow you to charge a bit more for the property. When you die you do not own 'immovables' (*immeubles*) – land and buildings – in France and so you will not run into the difficulties that can arise as a result of the French inheritance laws, which (as far as foreigners are concerned) usually only apply to land and buildings.

There are drawbacks as well as advantages.

French *SCI*

One of the ways of buying through a limited company is to buy in the name of a special type of French civil company called a *société civile immobilière (SCI)*. This type of company exists in French law only for the purpose of owning what is known as immovable property – loosely equivalent to our concept of real estate, namely flats, houses, land, etc. It is a strange type of company in that it is (usually) what is known as fiscally transparent. That is to say it is not taxed as a company but its assets and benefits are treated and taxed as those of its owners. Yet, despite this it still enjoys the advantages of a corporate identity – but not full limited liability. This is important because shares in a company are classed in France as 'moveable property' and, as such, are not covered by the rigid French inheritance rules if you do not live in France. So if you own in the name of an *SCI* you can leave your shares in the company – and thus the house itself – to whomever you like. This advantage disappears if you become domiciled in France, *see* p.179.

There are also some tax advantages to ownership in this way. If the company does not trade or let out the house no tax is paid. You get the benefit of the capital gains tax allowances that the French give to individual property owners (*see* pp.186–7 and 199–200).

The downside is that the company will cost, perhaps, £1,500 to set up and there will be an ongoing cost each year to keep it going. If the UK tax man sees you as a director or a shadow director of the company (someone who is not listed as a director but 'pulls the strings') and you use the property as a holiday home he can argue that you have received a 'benefit in kind' from your directorship of the company, which will be taxable under UK law – probably at 40 per cent of the rental value of the property. Despite all this, if you follow the right procedures the *SCI* can be a very useful tool – especially for the unmarried couple who do not intend to live in France or where several friends are buying a house together.

French Commercial Company

This, too, has its place, albeit fairly rare. It can be more flexible and sophisticated than an *SCI* in both management and financing. This can be useful if you are going to use the property primarily as an income-generator, especially if it is one of several properties owned. You will be taxed as a company and the overall taxes paid can be higher than would be the case for an individual . Setup costs can be high and there will be annual management/maintenance costs. In some cases, however, the management and funding issues and the savings in later inheritance taxes can outweigh these disadvantages.

Buying through a company gives rise to a host of potential problems as well as benefits. The plan needs to be studied closely by your advisers so that you can decide whether it makes sense in the short, medium and long term.

UK Company

It is rare for a purchase through a UK company to make sense for a holiday home or single investment property. This is despite the fact that the ability to pay for the property with the company's money without drawing it out of the company and so paying UK tax on the dividend is attractive. There are still times when it can be the right answer. Once again you need expert advice from someone familiar with the law of both countries.

Offshore (Tax Haven) Company

This has most of the same advantages and disadvantages as ownership by other types of company, with the added disincentive that you will have to pay a special tax of three per cent of the value of the property *every year*. This is to compensate the French for all the inheritance and transfer taxes that they will not receive when the owners of these companies sell them or die. For a person who is (or intends to be) resident in France for tax purposes there are additional disadvantages. If he owns more than 10 per cent of an offshore company he will have to pay tax in France on his share of its income and assets. This tax treatment has more or less killed off ownership via such companies, yet they still have a limited role to play. A 93-year-old buying a £10,000,000 property, or someone who wishes to be discreet about the ownership of the property, might think three per cent per year is a small price to pay for the avoidance of inheritance tax or privacy respectively. Needless to say, anyone thinking of buying through an offshore company should take detailed advice from a lawyer familiar with the law of both countries.

The Use of Trusts

Trusts can be a very useful way of reducing taxation in many countries, especially in continental Europe where there is generally no concept of trusts and, as a result, little in the way of legislation to limit their potential for tax saving. These advantages are less in France than elsewhere. *See* 'Trusts', pp.213–14.

As a vehicle for owning a property trusts are of little direct use. The law does not recognize the trust and so the trustees who are be named on the title as the owners of the property would be treated as private individual owners, having to pay all of the income, wealth and inheritance taxes applicable in their case. In a few cases this could still give some benefit but there are probably better ways of getting the same result.

This does not mean that trusts have no place for the owner of property in France. A trust could still, for example, own the property via a limited company if this fitted the 'owner's' overall tax- and inheritance-planning objectives.

Again, careful specialist advice is essential.

Which Is Right For You?

The choice is of fundamental importance. If you get it wrong you will pay massively more tax than you need to, both during your lifetime and on your death. The tax consequences arise not only in France but also in your own country.

Equally, because of the restrictions on the freedom to dispose of assets you own in France in your will, the wrong choice of owner now will mean that the wrong people will inherit it on your death.

For each buyer of a home in France one of the options set out above will suit him perfectly. Another might just about make sense. The rest would be an expensive waste of money.

The trouble is, it is not obvious which is the right choice! You need in every case to take advice. If your case is simple so will be the advice. If it is complex the time and money spent will be repaid many times over.

The Process of Buying a Property in France

The Law

As you would expect, this is complicated. A basic textbook on French property law might extend to 500 pages. There are certain basic principles that it is helpful to understand.

1. The main legal provisions relating to property law are found in the civil code, which was introduced in 1804 but modified since. The analysis of rights reflects the essentially agrarian society of late 18th-century France and pays limited attention to some of the issues that, today, would seem more pressing. That has only partly been remedied by the later additions to the code, such as the 1967 additions relating to the sale of property in the course of development.
2. The civil code declares that foreigners are to be treated in the same way as French people as far as the law is concerned.
3. French law divides property into two classes – moveable property (*meubles*) and immovable property (*immeubles*). The whole basis of ownership and transfer of ownership depends on which classification property belongs to. The distinction is similar to the English concept of real and personal property *but it is not exactly the same*. Immovable property includes land and buildings, but not the shares in a company that owns land and buildings.
4. The sale purchase of *immeubles* located in France must always be governed by French law.
5. The form of ownership of land is always absolute ownership. This is similar to what we would call freehold ownership.
6. It is possible to own the buildings – or even parts of a building – on a piece of land separately from the land itself. This is of particular relevance in the case of flats, which are owned 'freehold'.
7. Where two or more people own a piece of land or other property together they will generally own it in undivided shares (*indivision*). That is to say the piece of land is not physically divided between them. Each owner may, in theory, mortgage or sell his share without the consent of the others – though the others might have certain rights of pre-emption – that is the right to buy the property in preference to any outsider.
8. Where a building or piece of land is physically divided between a number of people a condominium (*copropriété*) is created. The land is divided into privately owned parts (*lots*) – such as an individual flat – and communally owned areas. The management of the communally held areas is up to the owners of the privately held areas, but can be delegated to someone else.

9. In the case of a sale of land certain people may have a right of pre-emption. One is the co-owner mentioned above. Others are (in each case only in certain circumstances) the municipality, a sitting tenant, an agricultural tenant and certain statutory bodies, the most noticeable of which is *safer* (*see* 'Full Contract', p.152).

10. Transfer of ownership of *immeubles* is usually by simple agreement. This need not be in writing, but usually is. That agreement binds both the parties to it but is not effective as far as the rest of the world is concerned, who are entitled to rely upon the content of the land register (*bureau de conservation des hypothèques*). Thus between buyer and seller ownership of land is transferred, for example, by signing a sale contract (*compromis de vente*) even if the seller remains in possession and some of the price remains unpaid. But that ownership would not damage the interests of someone other than the buyer or seller (such as someone owed money by the seller) who is entitled to take action against the person named as owner in the Land Registry. Ownership can also be acquired by possession, usually for 30 years.

11. Other rights – short of ownership – can exist over land. These include rights of way, tenancies, life interests, mortgages and option contracts. Most require some sort of formality in order that they be valid against third parties but are always binding as between the people who made the agreements.

12. There are two land registers. Each *commune* maintains a tax register (*cadastre*). In this all the land in the district is mapped, divided into plots (*lots*) and assessed for tax purposes. The register is also used as a place to record such things as tenancies and option contracts that might affect the property. The second register is the deed and mortgage register (*bureau des hypothèques*). This uses the plot numbers allocated in the *cadastre* to record deeds and mortgages relating to land, the ownership of the land.

General Procedure

The general procedure when buying a property in France seems, at first glance, similar to the purchase of a property in England: sign a contract; do some checks; sign a Deed of Title. This is deceptive. The procedure is very different and even the use of the familiar English vocabulary to describe the very different steps in France can produce an undesirable sense of familiarity with the procedure. This can lead to assumptions that things that have not been discussed will be the same as they would in England. This would be a wrong and dangerous assumption. *Work on the basis that the system is totally different.*

Choosing a Lawyer

The Notary Public (*Notaire*)

The notary is a special type of lawyer. He is in part a public official but he is also in business, making his living from the fees he charges for his services. There are about 8,000 notaries in France. Notaries also exist in England but they are seldom used in day-to-day transactions.

Under French law only deeds of sale (*actes de vente*) approved and witnessed by a notary can be registered at the land registry (*bureau des hypothèques*). Although it is possible to transfer legal ownership of property such as a house or apartment by a private agreement not witnessed by the notary and although that agreement will be fully binding on the people who made it, it will not be binding on third parties. Third parties – including people who want to make a claim against the property and banks wanting to lend money on the strength of the property – are entitled to rely upon the details of ownership recorded at the land registry. So if you are not registered as the owner of the property you are at risk. Thus, practically speaking, all sales of real estate in France must be witnessed by a notary.

The notary also carries out certain checks on property sold and has some duties as tax collector and validator of documents to be presented for registration.

His fee is fixed by law, normally 1–1.5 per cent of the price, though there can sometimes be 'extras' (*see* 'Notary's Fees', pp.165 and 166).

The notary is appointed by the seller but, if the buyer wishes, he can insist on appointing his own notary, in which case, such is the generosity of the fees that the law allows him to charge, the two notaries share the same fee! In simple transactions this is seldom a necessary or even desirable step as it can cause unnecessary delay and complication, but it can be useful in certain cases. It is particularly worth thinking about if the notary is also acting for the seller as estate agent, in which case you may be more comfortable with independent scrutiny.

The notary is strictly neutral. He is more a referee than someone fighting on your behalf. He is, in the usual case, someone who checks the papers to make sure that they comply with the strict rules as to content and so will be accepted by the land registry for registration.

Many French notaries, particularly in rural areas, do not speak English – or, at least, do not speak it well enough to give advice on complex issues. Very few will know anything about English law and so will be unable to tell you about the tax and other consequences in the UK of your plans to buy a house in France. In any case, the buyer will seldom meet the notary before the signing ceremony and so there is little scope for seeking detailed advice. It is, in any case, rare for notaries to offer any comprehensive advice or explanation, least of all in writing, to the buyer.

For the English buyer the notary is no substitute for also using the services of a specialist UK lawyer familiar with French law and international property transactions. This is the clear advice of every guidebook, the French and British governments and the Federation of Overseas Property Developers, Agents and Consultants (FOPDAC). It is therefore baffling why so many people buying a property in France do not take this necessary step.

French Lawyers (*Avocats*)

Most French people buying a home in France will not use the services of a lawyer (as opposed to the *notaire*) unless there is something unusual or contentious about the transaction.

English Lawyers (Solicitors)

For English people the services of the notary are unlikely to give them all the information or help they need to buy a home in France. They will often require advice about inheritance rights, the UK tax implications of their purchase, how to save taxes, surveys, mortgages, currency exchange, etc. which is outside the scope of the service of the notary. They should retain the services of a specialist UK lawyer familiar with dealing with these issues. The buyer's usual solicitor is unlikely to be able to help as there are only a handful of English law firms with the necessary expertise. The Federation of Overseas Property Developers, Agents and Consultants makes it a condition of membership that their members *must* recommend the services of an independent lawyer for such transactions.

The Price

This can be freely agreed between the parties. Depending on the economic climate there may be ample or very little room for negotiating a reduction in the asking price. At the moment (2002) the scope is limited for popularly priced properties in the main cities and tourist areas, which are in short supply. There is still some scope if buying in undiscovered France, especially if the property needs repair. There is also scope in the case of more expensive properties. In every area there are properties that have stuck on the market, usually because they are overpriced and/or in a poor location. Find out when the property was placed on the market. Ask to see the agent's sale authority (*mandat*). Of course, negotiating a reduction is always worth a try, but if your advances are rejected do bear in mind the probability that it is not mere posturing but a genuine confidence that the price asked is achievable. Also remember that once a formal offer is accepted it is binding upon both of you, so the price cannot be reduced. Better, if unsure, to start a little low and test the water. You can always increase the offer if the first is rejected.

If you are unsure of the value of the property – and you may well be, especially if you are buying during a short trip to France – it is often possible to obtain a valuation (*see* p.120). This is unusual in France, but useful in the case of properties, especially in rural areas, where there may be few obvious similar properties on the market to use for price comparisons. The estate agent may also be able to give you some guidance, but he is being paid by the seller to sell the property, and receiving a commission based on the amount he receives, so treat his input with caution.

Above all, don't get carried away. There is always another property. Fix a maximum budget before you set off on your visit – and stick to it. Make ample allowance for the likely costs of repair/refurbishment. They are always 25 per cent higher than you think! If necessary get estimates before committing yourself. If you are buying as a rental investment do some research into the likely rent achievable (in high and low season), the number of weeks you will potentially be able to let the property, likely returns, expenses and management costs before committing yourself.

Which Currency?

The price of the property will be recorded in the deed of sale (*acte de vente*) in euros. Until recently, of course, it would have been expressed in the late lamented French franc. Usually the euro will also be used in the reservation agreement and contract (*compromis*). In France you have the right to enter into a contract on whatever terms you please and so some people may choose to agree a price in sterling, US dollars or whatever. This would involve the buyer paying and the seller receiving the currency of their choice, which might be useful if, for example, both were British and living in the UK as it would remove the risk of exchange rate fluctuations for both parties. It would also avoid the expense of the buyer converting sterling to euros and the seller then incurring the similar expense of converting them back again. It will be necessary for an agreed figure in euros, representing the approximate value of the foreign currency, to be inserted in the *acte de vente* and land register and for the taxes due to be paid on the basis of this figure. This can prove a problem with the notary, who will almost certainly not have access to a sterling or US dollar bank account and so will not be able to perform his normal task of receiving and paying over the funds. Because he does not do this, the protection afforded to the buyer is less than would otherwise be the case. If you are paying direct to the seller, try to use a 'stakeholder', typically your solicitor, who will receive the money and keep it safe until the deed of sale is signed and then release it to the seller. Generally, unless you are very worried amount movements in exchange rates, it is better to do the deal in euros. If you are worried about exchange rates it might be more beneficial to enter into a 'forward contract' to buy or sell the euros. *See* p.134.

How Much Should Be Declared in the Deed of Sale?

For many years there was a tradition in France (and other Latin countries) of under-declaring the price actually paid for a property when signing the deed of sale (*acte de vente*). This was because the taxes and notaries' fees due were calculated on the basis of the price declared. Lower price, less taxes for the buyer and, for a holiday home (*résidence secondaire*) less capital gains tax for the seller. Magic! Those days have now largely gone. In rural areas you can still sometimes come under pressure to underdeclare, but it is now rare. Under-declaration is foolish. There are severe penalties. In the worst case the state can buy the property for the price declared plus 10 per cent. In the best case there are fines and penalties for late payment. Don't do it!

Nevertheless, there is scope for quite legitimately reducing the price declared and so reducing tax. For example, if your purchase of a holiday home includes some furniture, a boat or a car there is no need to declare the value of those items and pay stamp duty on the price paid. You can enter into a separate contract for the 'extras' and save some money.

Where Must the Money Be Paid?

The price, together with the taxes and fees payable, is usually paid by the buyer into the notary's bank account and then passed on by him to the seller, the tax man, etc. as applicable. This is the best and safest way. Any money paid to the notary is bonded, and so safe.

Try to avoid arrangements, usually as part of an under-declaration, where part of the money is handed over in cash in brown-paper parcels. Apart from being illegal it is dangerous at a practical level. Buyers have lost the bundle, or been robbed on the way to the notary's office. Sometimes there is a suspicion that the seller, who knew where you were going to be and when, could be involved.

General Enquiries and Special Enquiries

Certain enquiries are made routinely in the course of the purchase of a property.

These include a check on the planning situation of the property. This *note de renseignement d'urbanisme* will reveal the position of the property itself but it will not, at least directly, tell you about its neighbours and it will not reveal general plans for the area. If you want to know whether the authorities are going to put a prison in the village or run a new TGV line through your back garden (both, presumably, bad things) or build a motorway access point or TGV station 3km away (both, presumably, good things) you will need to ask. There are various organizations you can approach but, just as in England, there is no single point of contact for such enquiries. If you are concerned about what might happen in the area then you will need to discuss the position with your lawyers at an early stage. There may be a considerable amount of work (and therefore cost) involved in making full enquiries, the results of which can never be guaranteed.

Normal enquiries also include a check that the seller is the registered owner of the property and that it is sold (if this has been agreed) free of mortgages or other charges.

In order to advise you what other enquiries might be appropriate your lawyer will need to be told your proposals for the property. Do you intend to rent it out? If so is it on a commercial basis? Do you intend to use it for business purposes? Do you want to extend or modify the exterior of the property? Do you intend to make interior structural alterations?

Agree in advance the additional enquiries you would like to make and get an estimate of the cost of those enquiries.

Your Civil State (*Etat Civil*) and Other Personal Details

This is something you will not have thought about. For most of the time it is a matter of unimportance in England. It is something the French get very worked up about.

When preparing documents in France you will be asked to specify your civil state (*état civil*). This comprises a full set of information about you. They will not only ask for your full name and address but also, potentially, for your occupation, nationality, passport number, maiden name and sometimes the names of your parents, your date and place of birth, date and place of marriage and, most importantly, your matrimonial regime (*régime matrimonial*). What is a *régime matrimonial*? It is something we do not have in the UK. In France when you marry you will specify the *régime matrimonial* that will apply to your relationship. There are two main options for a French person, a regime of common ownership of assets (*communauté de biens*) or a regime of separate ownership of assets (*séparation de biens*). Under the first all assets acquired after the marriage, even if put into just one party's name, belong to both. Under the second, each spouse in entitled to own assets in his own name, upon which the other spouse has no automatic claim. The effect of marriage under English law is closer to the second than the first. If possible the notary, when specifying your matrimonial regime, should state that you are married under English law and, in the absence of a marriage contract, do not have a regime but your situation is similar to a regime of *séparation de biens* – '*mariés sous le régime anglais équivalent au régime français de la séparation de biens à defaut de contrat de marriage préalable à leur union célébrée le* [DATE] *à* [PLACE]'.

This is no idle point. The declaration in your *acte de vente* is a public declaration. It is treated in France with great reverence and as being of great importance. It will be hard in later years to go against what you have declared. If you say that you are married in *communauté de biens* even if the money came from only one of you the asset will be treated as belonging to both. This, in turn, can have highly undesirable tax and inheritance consequences.

If appropriate you will declare that you are single, separated, divorced, widowed, etc. at this point.

The authorities are entitled to ask for proof of all of these points by birth certificates, marriage certificates, etc. If the documents are needed the official translations into French may be needed. Often the notary will take a slightly more relaxed view and ask you for only the key elements of your *état civil*. It is worth checking in advance as to what is required, as it is embarrassing to turn up to sign the *acte* only to find the ceremony cannot go ahead because you do not have one of the documents required. In the worst case that could put you in breach of contract and you could lose your deposit!

The Community of Owners (*Copropriété*)

This is a device familiar in continental Europe but most unusual in the UK.

The basic idea is than when a number of people own land or buildings in such a way that they have exclusive use of part of the property but shared use of the rest then a *copropriété* is created.

Houses on their own plots with no shared facilities will not be a member of a *copropriété*. Most other property will be.

In a *copropriété* the buyer of a house which shares a pool with its neighbours or of an apartment owns his own house or apartment outright – as the English would say, 'freehold' – and shares the use of the remaining areas as part of a community of owners (*en copropriété*). It is not only the shared pool that is jointly owned but (in an apartment) the lift shafts, corridors, roof, foundations, entrance areas, parking zones, etc.

The members of the *copropriété* are each responsible for their own home. They, collectively, agree the works needed on the common areas and a budget for those works. They then become responsible for paying their share of those common expenses, as stipulated in their title.

There are detailed rules as to how a *copropriété* should be run. These are set out in the *règlements de copropriété*. The rules deal not only with technical matters about how the *copropriété* is to be governed and managed, procedures for meetings, etc. but also with the rules of conduct that must be followed by owners. They also set out how your share of the expenses is to be calculated.

The supreme ruling body of any *copropriété* is the general meeting of members (*syndicat des copropriétaires*). The general meeting must meet at least once per year to approve the budget and deal with other business. You must be given at least two weeks' notice of the meeting and the opportunity of putting items on the agenda. Voting is, for most issues, by simple majority vote. If you can't attend you can appoint a proxy to vote on your behalf. Your *règlements* may make additional rules but not take away your basic rights.

Day-to-day management is usually delegated to an administrator (*syndic*).

The charges of the *copropriété* are divided in the proportions stipulated in the deed creating the *copropriété*. This is usually by reference to the size of each apartment, with (probably) a larger fraction going to any commercial area included in the *copropriété*. You will pay the same *copropriété* fees whether you use the place all year round or only for two weeks' holiday. Of course your other bills (water, electricity, etc.) will vary with usage. Fees for a two-bedroom apartment are typically in the range of £300–£750, depending largely on the size of any pool and gardens and the number of lifts in the development – all of which are expensive to maintain.

The *copropriété* should provide not only for routine work but, through its fees, set aside money for periodic major repairs. If they do not – or if the amount set aside is inadequate – the general meeting can authorise a supplemental levy to raise the sums needed.

The rules set by the *copropriété* are intended to improve the quality of life of residents. They could, for example deal with concerns over noise (no radios by the pool), prohibit the use of the pool after 10pm, ban the hanging of washing on balconies, etc. More importantly they could ban pets or any commercial activity in the building or short-term holiday letting. Check them.

The *règlements de copropriété* are an important document. Every buyer of a property in a *copropriété* receives a copy of the rules. If you do not speak French you should have them translated or, at least, summarized in English.

Check the rules, the level of fees and the pending items of expenditure before you buy.

Initial Contracts

In France most sales start with a preliminary contract. The type of contract will depend upon whether you are buying a finished or an unfinished property.

Signing any of these documents has far-reaching legal consequences, which are sometimes different from the consequences of signing in similar document in the UK. *Whichever type of contract you are asked to sign, always seek legal advice before signing.*

All contracts to buy property are now subject, by law, to the right to cancel the agreement within seven days of receiving the copy signed by the seller. Do this by recorded delivery (AR) post. Strict compliance with the rules and timetable for cancellation is essential. Any money paid should be refunded.

Generally the preliminary contract is prepared, in simple cases, by the estate agent – who is professionally qualified in France – or by the notary.

Estate agent's contracts are often based on a pre-printed document in a standard format. It is very important that these contracts are not just accepted as final. In every case they will need to be modified. In some cases they will need to be modified extensively.

Some contracts coming from estate agents who are not familiar with dealing with foreign buyers can contain extra clauses into the contract that are potentially harmful to the foreign buyer. More likely, they will leave out one or more of the 'get-out clauses' (*clauses suspensives*) needed to protect your position by cancelling the contract if all turns out not to be well.

If You are Buying a Finished Property

You will be invited to sign one of three different documents. Each has different features. Each has different legal consequences. Each is appropriate in certain circumstances and inappropriate in others. Seek legal advice as to which will be best in your case.

Offer to Buy (*Offre d'Achat*)

This is, technically, not a contract at all. It is a formal written offer from the potential buyer to the potential seller. It will state that you wish to buy the stated property for a stated price and that you will complete the transaction within a stated period. The offer will normally be accompanied by the payment of a deposit to the estate agent (if he is licensed to hold the seller's money) or to a local notary who will be dealing with the transaction. The deposit is not fixed but will usually range from two to five per cent of the price offered.

This document binds you. It is not a mere enquiry as to whether the seller might be interested in selling. If he says that he accepts the offer then you (and he) become legally bound to proceed with the transaction. Until then, of course, the document has no effect on the seller and it is certainly not a guarantee that the seller will sell you the house.

Its main use is in situations where the property is perhaps offered through a variety of estate agents and the seller wants to wait for a week or two to see what offers come in before making up his mind to whom to sell.

Generally we do not like *offres*. We prefer the idea of making a verbal enquiry as to whether the seller would accept a certain price and, once he says yes, for a binding bilateral contract of sale (*compromis de vente*) to be signed.

Promise to Sell (*Promesse de Vente*)

This is a written document in which the seller offers to sell a stated property at a stated price to a stated person at any time within a stated period, up to a maximum of six months.

It is the mirror image of the *offre d'achat*.

The seller will usually require that any person taking up his offer pays him a deposit (*indemnité d'immobilisation*). This amount of the deposit is not fixed by law but is usually five or 10 per cent of the price of the property. Once he has received this deposit the seller must reserve the property for you until the end of the period specified in the contract.

This is similar to an English option contract. If you want to go ahead and buy the property you can but you are not obliged to do so. If you do not go ahead you lose your deposit.

The *promesse* should contain special 'get-out clauses' (*clauses suspensives*) stipulating the circumstances in which the buyer will be entitled to the refund of his deposit if he decides not to go ahead. These might include not being able to obtain a mortgage, finding the property was infested with termites, finding the property could not be used for a certain purpose, etc. The drafting of these clauses is of vital importance. See your lawyer.

If you do want to go ahead you can exercise the option (*lever l'option*) at any point up to the end of the agreed period.

If the seller refuses to go ahead the buyer is entitled to claim compensation.

This agreement requires certain formalities for it to be valid. It does not need to be signed in front of a notary but must be recorded at the local tax registry (*cadastre*).

This type of agreement has its place but, in general, the full binding bilateral contract of sale (*compromis de vente*) to be signed wherever possible is preferable. The *promesse de vente* can give rise to substantial problems if either the seller dies before completion of the sale or if he refuses to complete. This structure is, however, still common in several parts of France and, in those areas, it may be difficult to persuade the sellers, estate agents and notaries to use the *compromis*. If this is the case then the *promesse* should be drafted with particular care, especially as far as the consequences of non-completion are concerned.

Full Contract (*Compromis de Vente*)

This is also known as a joint promise of sale (*promesse synallagmatique de vente*) and, in most parts of France, is the most common type of document.

It is an agreement that commits both parties. The seller must sell a stated property at a stated price to a stated person on the terms set out in the contract. The buyer must buy.

This is the most far-reaching of the three documents and so it is particularly important that you are satisfied that it contains all of the terms necessary to protect your position. Take legal advice. Remember that under French law by signing this contract you become the owner of the property (though you will need to sign a deed of sale (*acte de vente*) and register your ownership to be safe as far as third parties are concerned).

The contract must therefore contain all of the safety clauses to make sure that, for example, if all is not well with the title to the property you will be released from your obligations and get your money back. These will include clauses about any mortgage you are applying for (the *Loi Scrivener* clauses), clauses requiring proof of various planning matters, clauses as to what should happen if a right of pre-emption is exercised.

The contract will contain a variety of 'routine' clauses.

- **The names of the seller and buyer should both be stated fully.**
- **The property should be described fully, both in an everyday sense and by reference to its land registry details.**
- **A statement is usually made that full details of the title will be included in the final deed of sale (*acte de vente*).**
- **A date for the signing of the *acte* will be fixed. This is usually 60 days after signing the contract. The delay is because there are various documents that must be obtained from the French authorities (particularly a confirmation that SAFER does not intend to exercise its right of pre-emption and a planning certificate (*certificat d'urbanisme*) and these typically take eight weeks to obtain. SAFER is the French Rural Development Agency (*Fédération Nationale des Sociétés d'Aménagement Foncier et d'Etablissement Rural*).**
- **A statement will be made as to when possession will take place – normally, on the date of signing the title.**
- **The price is fixed.**
- **A receipt for any deposit is given.**
- **A statement is made that the property is sold subject to any rights that exist over it (which, incidentally, you will not have checked at that stage) but that the seller has not himself created any.**
- **The property should be sold with vacant possession.**

- **It will state the notary who is to prepare the *acte*.**
- **It will provide for who is to pay the costs of the purchase.**
- **It will confirm the details of any agent involved and who is to pay his commission.**
- **It will set out what is to happen if one or both of the parties breaks the contract.**
- **It will establish the law to cover the contract and the address of the parties for legal purposes.**
- **Finally it will contain the all-important special clauses.**

If the buyer or seller drops out of the contract or otherwise breaks it, various arrangements may be made.

A deposit (*les arrhes*) might be payable by the buyer. If he fails to complete he will lose the deposit. If the seller fails to complete he will have to return double the deposit paid.

Alternatively the contract may provide for a sum of agreed compensation to be paid (*un dédit*). The *dédit* for the buyer could be the loss of his deposit. The *dédit* for the seller could be fixed in the contract. If either party is in breach of the contract the other can serve notice requiring him to sign the *acte* and complete or pay the *dédit*.

There can be a penalty clause. This was a large penalty, designed to frighten both parties into complying with the contract. Its popularity has reduced since the courts were granted the power to decrease such penalties if they thought it reasonable to do so.

If the parties fail to comply with their obligations there is the ultimate remedy of seeking a court order. As in any country this is very much a last resort as it is costly, time-consuming and (as in any country) there is no guarantee of the outcome of a court case. If a court order is made in your favour this order can be registered at the land registry.

If You Are Buying an Unfinished Property

Full Contract

There are two types of contract in this case. The first is a sale *à terme*. The second is *en l'état futur d'achèvement*, more commonly known as 'on plan'.

Contract *à terme*: You agree to buy a plot of land and building. You agree to pay once it has been built. Simple! You take title and pay the money at the same time. This type of contract is little used.

Contract *en l'état futur d'achèvement*: Here the seller transfers his interest in the land and anything he has so far built on it to the buyer at once. As the building continues it automatically becomes the property of the buyer.

In return the buyer pays an initial sum representing the value of the asset as it now exists and further payments, by stages, during the construction process.

The contract must give details of a guarantee to secure completion of the construction in the event, for example, that the seller goes bust.

Reservation Contract (*Contrat de Réservation*)

Usually in these cases there is a preliminary contract. This is the reservation contract.

There are various very detailed statutory rules governing how such contracts must be drafted and carried through in order to avoid the obvious risks that arise in such circumstances.

- **The contract must be in writing.**
- **A copy must be given to the seller before any money changes hands.**
- **It must contain a full description of the property to be built, its size and number of rooms.**
- **It must set out any central facilities or services to be provided.**
- **The price must be specified as must any arrangements to charge for extras or to vary the price such as, for example, its increasing in line with the official cost of construction index.**
- **The scheme for stage payments must be stipulated.**
- **The deposit or reservation fee (*réservation*) must be agreed. This cannot exceed five per cent of the price if completion of the work will take place within one year of signing the reservation contract or two per cent if it will take place more than one year but less than two years from the date of signing. If it will be more than two years until completion of the work, no deposit may be taken.**
- **The contract must state the circumstances in which the reservation fee is to be repaid, if requested. These include where the *acte de vente* is not signed on the date agreed because of the seller's default, the final price (even if calculated in accordance with the variation terms agreed) is more than five per cent above the initial price agreed, any stipulated loan is not obtained or the property is reduced in size or quality or some of the services are not supplied.**
- **It must provide for the buyer's receiving a draft title deed (*acte de vente*) at least one month before the date for signing.**
- **It must contain details of the guarantees in place to secure the monies paid by the buyer if the seller cannot complete the building.**

The stage payments are made on receipt of architect's certificates confirming that progress has reached a certain point. There is a maximum level of stage payments permitted at any point.

- **foundations – 35 per cent of total price**
- **building watertight – 75 per cent of total price**
- **completion of building – 95 per cent of total price**

The building is 'complete' when your part of it and all the common parts indispensable to your use of the building are finished. Minor deficiencies or small outstanding jobs are not a failure to complete and therefore not an excuse for delaying the final payment.

If there are outstanding jobs or defects they are normally listed at completion and a timetable is agreed for rectifying them. Any noticed by the buyer within one month of taking possession must be fixed by the seller.

This is your strongest guarantee. You should seriously consider having the property inspected by a surveyor or architect before you accept it as being built to specification.

The remaining five per cent of the price is held back until all of those issues have been cleared. If the defects will cost more than five per cent to rectify, the seller's liability is not limited to that five per cent.

Once that has been done the buyer will, of course, remain entitled to the seller's compulsory two-year and 10-year guarantees referred to elsewhere in this book.

Other Documentation

You will be given a full specification for the property, a copy of the community rules (*règlements de copropriété*) if the property shares common facilities, and a copy of any agreements you have entered into regarding ongoing management or letting of the property. All are important documents. Pay particular attention to the specification. It is not unknown for the show flat to have marble floors and high quality wooded kitchens but for the specification to show concrete tiles and MDF.

Renegotiating the Terms of the Contract

If you have signed a contract before seeking legal advice and it turns out that it has deficiencies that, though not legally sufficient to cancel the contract, cause you concern it may be possible to renegotiate the contract.

The sooner you attempt to do this, the better.

Checklist – Signing a Contract

Property in the Course of Construction		Existing Property
	Are you clear about what you are buying?	
	Have you taken legal advice about who should be the owner of the property?	
	Have you taken legal advice about inheritance issues?	
	Are you clear about boundaries?	
	Are you clear about access?	
		Are you sure you can change the property as you want?
		Are you sure you can use the property for what you want?
		Is the property connected to water, electricity, gas, etc?
		Have you had a survey done?
	Have you made all necessary checks OR arranged for them to be made?	
	Have you included 'get-out' clauses for all important checks not yet made?	
	Is your mortgage finance arranged OR a 'get-out' clause inserted in the contract?	
	Is the seller clearly described?	
	If the seller is not signing in person, have you seen a power of attorney/mandate to authorize the sale?	
	Are you fully described?	
	Is the property fully described? Identification? Land registry details?	
	Is the price correct?	
	Are any possible circumstances in which it can be increased or extras described fully?	
Are the stage payments fully described?		Does contract say when possession will be given?
Do stage payments meet the legal restrictions?		Is there a receipt for the deposit paid?
Is the date for completion of the work agreed?		In what capacity is the deposit paid?
	Is the date for signing the *acte* agreed?	
	Does the contract provide for the sale to be free of charges and debts?	
	Does the contract provide for vacant possession?	
	Which notary is to act?	
	Is the estate agent's commission dealt with?	
	What happens if there is a breach of contract?	
	Are all the necessary special 'get-out' clauses included?	
Mortgage?		Mortgage?
Increase in price?		Pre-emption by SAFER?
		Other pre-emption
		Survey?
		Planning certificate?
		Other?

Steps Between Signing the Contract and Signing the Deed of Sale (*Acte de Vente*)

Power of Attorney (*Procuration; Pouvoir; Mandat*)

Very often it will not be convenient for you to go to France to sign the *acte de vente* in person. Sometimes there may be other things that, in the normal course of events, would require your personal intervention but where it would be inconvenient for you to have to deal with them yourself.

Just as often you will not know whether you will be available to sign in person. Completion dates on French property are notoriously fluid and so you could plan to be there but suffer a last-minute delay to the signing that makes it impossible.

The solution to this problem is the power of attorney. This document authorizes the person appointed (the *mandataire*) to do whatever the document authorizes on behalf of the person granting the power (the *mandant*). The most sensible type of power to use will be the French style of power that is appropriate to the situation. In theory an English-style power should be sufficient, but in practice the cost and delay associated with getting it recognized will be unacceptable.

The type of French power of attorney that you will need depends on what you want to use it for. Your specialist English lawyer can discuss your requirements with you and prepare the necessary document. Alternatively you can deal directly with the French notary who will ultimately need the power.

If you want to permit someone to take out a mortgage for you, or to buy a property in the course of construction, then that must be by way of a power of attorney that is an *acte authentique* – that is, signed in front of a notary public – the French Consulate. It can be signed in England or France.

If you wish someone simply to sign the title of a property you are buying for cash, that can be authorized in writing – using the French form of words – or even verbally. Few notaries will be happy with a verbal mandate and it has other problems that make it unattractive.

The power must be drafted in express terms clear enough to leave no doubt that the person appointed has the authority to do what he is going to do. This is not always simple. For example, the purchase of a property could also involve the person drawing a cheque on your French bank account. The power will in that case have to authorize both activities. In the case of a power to buy or sell property it must contain a description of the property, the price agreed and method of payment. If payment is to be made to the person appointed that must be authorized expressly.

A power of attorney can specifically state that it cannot be revoked for a certain period. If it is not stated that this is the case the power can be revoked in a number of ways. It can, specifically, be time-limited. That is, you could grant it in such a way as it was only valid for six months from the date of signing it. Alternatively it can be cancelled by giving written notice to the person appointed. Recorded delivery (AR) post is the best way of doing this. The power ceases to be valid on the death or mental incapacity of the person granting it. It cannot, therefore, be used in the same way as an English enduring power of attorney to look after the affairs of an elderly person who has lost his mental capacity.

The power of attorney is a powerful tool. It gives the person appointed great power to do things on your behalf that could prove very costly. So it should only be given to people you trust implicitly. Generally this should only be given to a close member of your family such as your husband or child or your lawyer. In the case of an English lawyer, if he misused the power he would be struck off and you would receive full compensation. It is common for a power to be granted in favour of one of the clerks in the notary's office. This has attractions for the buyer as it doesn't add to the bill! Some notaries will not permit this. If the others stopped to think about the potential liability they were assuming they might think twice! It is only sensible in the simplest of cases.

A power executed in front of a notary in England has (unless the notary is a French consul) to go to the British Foreign and Commonwealth Office for a stamp to be attached to it so that it can be used internationally. This typically only takes a day and, at present, costs £12.

Even if you intend to go to France to sign it is sensible to think about granting a power 'just in case'. It is not something that can be done at the last moment. From decision to getting the document to France will take at least seven and more likely 10 days. If you are able to go, the power will not be used.

Even if you have granted a power of attorney, if you get the opportunity to go to France at the time of the signing it is worth doing so. It is quite interesting but, more importantly, you will be able to check the house to make sure that everything is in order before the *acte* is signed.

Getting the Money to France

There are a number of ways of getting the money to France.

Electronic Transfer

The most practical is to have it sent electronically by SWIFT transfer from a UK bank directly to the recipient's bank in France. This costs about £20–£35 depending on your bank. It is safer to allow two or three days for the money to arrive in a rural bank, despite everyone's protestations that it will be there the same day.

Europe has now (2002) introduced unique account numbers for all bank accounts. These incorporate a code for the identity of the bank and branch involved as well as the account number of the individual customer. These are known as IBANK numbers. They should be quoted, if possible, on all international currency transfers.

You can send the money from your own bank, via your lawyers or via a specialist currency dealer.

For the sums you are likely to be sending you should receive an exchange rate much better than the 'tourist rate' you see in the press. There is no such thing as a fixed exchange rate in these transactions. The bank's official inter-bank rate changes by the second and the job of the bank's currency dealers is to make a profit by selling to you at the lowest rate they can get away with. Thus if you do a lot of business with a bank and they know you are on the ball you are likely to be offered a better rate than a one-off customer. For this reason it is often better to send it via your specialist UK lawyers, who will be dealing with large numbers of such transactions. This also has the advantage that their bank, which deals with international payments all the time, is less likely to make a mistake causing delay to the payment than your bank, for which such a payment might be a rarity.

You or your lawyers might use a specialist currency dealer to make the transfer of funds instead of a main UK bank. Such dealers often give a better exchange rate than an ordinary bank. Sometimes the difference can be significant, especially compared to your local branch of a high street bank. Although these dealers use major banks actually to transfer the funds, you need to make sure that the dealer you are using is reputable. Your money is paid to them, not to the major bank, and so could be at risk if the dealer is not bonded or otherwise protected.

However you make the payment, ensure that you understand whether it is you or the recipient who is going to pick up the receiving bank's charges. If you need a clear amount in France you will have to make allowances for these, either by sending a bit extra or by asking your UK bank to pay all the charges. Make sure you have got the details of the recipient bank, its customer's name, the account codes and the recipient's reference precisely right. Any error and the payment is likely to come bank to you undeliverable – and may involve you in bearing the cost of its being converted back into sterling.

Banker's Drafts

You can arrange for your UK bank to issue you with a banker's draft (bank certified cheque) which you can take to France and pay into your bank account. Make sure that the bank knows that the draft is to be used overseas and issues you with an international draft.

Generally this is not a good way to transfer the money. It can take a considerable time – sometimes weeks – for the funds deposited to be made available for your use. The recipient bank's charges can be surprisingly high. The exchange rate offered against a sterling draft may be uncompetitive as you are a captive customer.

If the draft is lost it can, at best, take months to obtain a replacement and, at worst, be impossible to do so.

Cash

This is not recommended. You will need to declare the money on departure from the UK and on arrival in France. You must by law do this if the sum involved is over €8,000. You are well advised to do so for smaller amounts. Even then, if you declare £200,000 or so they will think you are a terrorist or drugs dealer! That suspicion can have far-reaching consequences in terms of listings in police 'dodgy person' files and even surveillance. To add insult to injury the exchange rate you will be offered for cash (whether you take sterling and convert there or buy the euros here) is usually very uncompetitive and the notary may well refuse to accept the money in his account. Don't do it.

Exchange Control and Other Restrictions on Moving Money

For EU nationals there is no longer any exchange control when taking money to or from France. There are some statistical records kept showing the flow of funds and the purpose of the transfers.

When you sell your property in France you will be able to bring the money back to the UK if you wish to do so.

Final Checks about the Property

All of the points outstanding as *clauses suspensives* must be resolved to your satisfaction, as must any other points of importance to you.

Fixing the Completion Date

The date stated in the contract for signing the *acte* could, most charitably, be described as flexible or aspirational. More often than not it will move, if only by a day or so. Sometimes the *certificat d'urbanisme* may not have arrived. On other occasions the seller's dispensation from paying French capital gains tax may be delayed. Occasionally your money to buy the house will get stuck in the banking system for a few days. For this reason it is not sensible to book your travel to France until you are almost sure that matters will proceed on a certain day. That may mean a week or two before signing.

Checklist – Steps Before Completion

<table>
<tr><th>Property in the Course of Construction</th><th>Existing Property</th></tr>
<tr><td colspan="2">Prepare power of attorney</td></tr>
<tr><td colspan="2">Check what documents must be produced on signing the acte</td></tr>
<tr><td colspan="2">Confirm all clauses suspensives have been complied with</td></tr>
<tr><td colspan="2">Confirm all other important enquiries are clear</td></tr>
<tr><td colspan="2">Receive draft of proposed acte de vente – one month in advance if possible</td></tr>
<tr><td colspan="2">Check seller applied for exemption from CGT</td></tr>
<tr><td colspan="2">Confirm arrangements (date, time, place) for completion with your lender if you have a mortgage</td></tr>
<tr><td colspan="2">Confirm arrangements (date, time, place) for completion with notary</td></tr>
<tr><td colspan="2">Send necessary funds to France</td></tr>
<tr><td colspan="2">Receive rules of community (règlements de copropriété)</td></tr>
<tr><td colspan="2">Insurance cover arranged?</td></tr>
<tr><td>Sign off work or list defects</td><td>Proof of payment of community fees</td></tr>
<tr><td></td><td>Proof of payment of other bills</td></tr>
</table>

The Deed of Sale (*Acte de Vente*)

This must be signed in front of a French notary either by the parties in person or someone holding power of attorney for them.

The document itself is, largely, a repeat of the contents of the preliminary contract with some additional elements. Because it is such an important document it is worth looking at in some detail. A typical *acte* might contain the following sections:

Name and Address of Notary (*Nom et Adresse du Notaire*)

Identification of the Parties (*Identification des Parties*)

This will set out the full details of both buyer and seller (their *états civils*) and the same details of any persons apperaring on their behalf under a power of attorney together with details of the power.

Designation (*Désignation*)

This sets out a full description of the property, its land registry details and plot numbers together with details of any restrictions affecting the property.

If it is an apartment it will also give details of the common parts – i.e. community property – from which you will benefit.

Ownership and Possession (*Propriété – Jouissance*)

This justifies the current claim to ownership of the property and states the date on which the buyer will take over possession of the property (normally that day). It will also confirm that the property is free of tenants (or not, as the case may be) and confirm liability on the part of the seller for all bills up to that date.

Price (*Prix*)

The price is stated. Methods of payment are stated. A receipt for payment is given.

Administrative Declaration (*Déclaration pour l'Administration*)

This stipulates the nature of the sale and thus the nature of the taxes payable in respect of the sale.

Capital Gains Tax (*Plus-value*)

This states the vendor's situation regarding any possible capital gains tax liability on the sale.

Calculation of Taxes (*Calcul des Droits*)

This section, if present, will calculate all of the duties payable on the sale.

Persons Present or Represented (*Présences ou Représentations*)

Details of all people present at the sale are set out.

Sale (*Vente*)

The sale is confirmed to have taken place.

Planning and Roads (*Urbanisme – Voirie*)

Details of the town planning situation and reference to the *certificat d'urbanisme* are attached.

Rights of Pre-emption (*Droits de Préemption*)

Confirmation that the various (named) people and organizations who might have pre-emptive rights have renounced them.

History of the Property (*Origine de la Propriété*)

How the present owner came to own the property – e.g. by inheritance from X or by purchase from Y on [*date*]. Details of the penultimate owner might also be given.

Ownership and Occupation (*Propriété – Occupation*)

The date on which the buyer becomes owner of the property and confirmation of vacant possession.

Charges and General Conditions (*Charges – Condition Générales*)

Any charges or burdens registered against the property together with the seller's warranties and guarantees.

Loans (*Prêt*)

Details of any mortgage finance used to buy the property. This will only refer to any French mortgage. It is of no concern to the French if you mortgaged your UK home for this purpose.

Statement of Sincerity (*Affirmation de Sincérité*)

A statement that both parties confirm the truth of all statements in the *acte*, that the price has been fully stated and (usually untrue) that the notary has warned the parties of the sanctions that may flow from false declaration.

Because it is rare for notaries to perform this important part of their duty it is worth setting out some of these sanctions.

1. The right to raise a supplemental demand for tax not paid + interest + penalty.
2. If there is a clear and intentional understatement, the right to buy the property at the price stated plus 10 per cent. This right must generally be exercised within six months.

There are other consequences of underdeclaration, *see* 'How Much Should be Declared in the Deed of Sale', p.146.

Formalities

Certain procedures are followed at the signing of the *acte*.

The parties are identified by their passports or identity cards. This will normally be done, at least initially, by the notary's clerk. The notary should also ask to see the proof of identity. The notary's clerk will also go through the content of the *acte* with the parties. This tends to be very superficial and often the person concerned will have limited English.

The parties will then be ushered into the presence of the notary. In addition to the buyer and seller it would be possible for the group to comprise also the notary's clerk, the other notary if a second has been appointed, your lawyer, a translator, a representative of the *copropriété*, a representative of your mortgage lender, the estate agent and any sub-agent appointed by the estate agent. Most of these people are there to receive money. Needless to say, if they all turn up it can get a little loud and confusing!

After the *Acte* Has Been Signed

The signing of the *acte* is not the end of the matter. Aterwards, the notary will, from the money you have sent him, pay your taxes to the state and settle his fees. From the money due to the seller he will pay off any sums due to the estate agent and the *copropriété* (if it has been agreed he is responsible for these), any debts on the property that are not being taken over by the buyer and any other agreed sums. Eventually the balance is sent to the seller. The notary is allowed one month to pay the taxes, but should do so much sooner.

Once the taxes are paid, your title and any mortgage should be presented for registration at the land registry. This must, by law, be done within two months, but again should be done more quickly as there is a potential danger of someone registering another transaction (such as a debt or judgement) against the property. He who registers first gets priority.

After several months the land registry will issue a certificate (*expédition*) to the effect that the title has been registered. This is sent to the notary who dealt with the transaction.

The notary will then send you the certificate and other paperwork related to the purchase together with his final bill and a statement showing how he has used the money you sent him. Some notaries are very slow at sending out this final paperwork, possibly because they usually ask at the outset for a little bit more than they are actually likely to need and so will have to make you a small refund!

The Cost of Buying a Property in France

These are the fees and taxes payable by a buyer when acquiring a property in France. They are sometimes known as completion expenses or completion or closing costs. They are impossible to predict with total accuracy at the outset of a transaction. This is because there are a number of variable factors that will not become clear until later. We can, however, give a general guide.

These costs are calculated on the basis of the price that you declared as the price paid for the property in the *acte de vente*. The size of these expenses, coupled with the French dislike for paying tax, has led to the habit of accidentally under declaring the price in the acte. These days are now largely over and we can only suggest that the full price of the property is declared. *See* 'How Much Should be Declared in the Deed of Sale', p.146.

The notary will ask for payment of these sums (plus his fees and a small margin in case of the unexpected, surprise or error) before the signing of the *acte*. It is normal to send them at the same time as the price of the property.

New Property

In this context a 'new' property is one that is less than five years old *and* being sold for the first time.

Notary's Fees

These are fixed by law, so are not negotiable. They will depend on the type of property being bought and its price.

Basic Notary's Fees – as a percentage of declared price

Portion of the price	Group 1	Group 2	Group 3
Fees on that part of the price below €3,049	5.000	2.20	2.50
Fees on that part of the price above €3,049 and below €6,098	3.300	1.65	1.65
Fees on that part of the price above €6,098 and below €16,769	1.650	1.10	1.10
Fees on that part of the price above €16,769	0.825	0.55	0.55
Fees on that part of the price above €12,1959			0.30

The odd sums result from the change to the euro. They are the equivalents of the old French franc values.

Most property bought by foreigners will fall into Group 1. The notary's fees for a €160,000 property (£100,000 approx) will therefore be €1611.44 – or about £1,000.

As a general guide, if you wish to avoid the detailed calculation, allow 1.3 per cent for properties less than £50,000 and one per cent for properties over £50,000.

If you have asked the notary to do any additional work over and above the transfer of title to the property, or for any advice, there will be additional charges. All of the notary's charges will be subject to VAT (*TVA*) of 19.6 per cent.

VAT (*TVA*) and Land Registration Fees

VAT (*TVA*)

This is 19.6 per cent of the declared purchase price of the property. This is normally included in the price of the property quoted to you. Check to see whether it is in your case.

Land Registry Fee

Usually 0.615 per cent.

The total of the taxes and land registry fees usually amounts to about 20 per cent of the declared price of the property.

Mortgage Costs (if applicable)

If you are taking out a mortgage there will be additional costs. *See* 'Raising Finance to Buy a Property in France', pp.124–36. These typically amount to three per cent of the amount borrowed. Most of these charges will be subject to *TVA* at 19.6 per cent.

Estate Agent's Charges (if payable by the buyer)

If an estate agent has sold the property his fees, usually between three and five per cent depending on the location and value of the property, are usually be paid by the seller. This can be varied by agreement.

If a notary has sold the property his fee will be paid by the buyer.

These will be subject to *TVA* at 19.6 per cent.

Miscellaneous Other Charges

Architect's fees, surveyor's fees, UK legal fees (typically one per cent), first connection to water, electricity, etc. Most of these will be subject to French *TVA* at 19.6 per cent, but your English lawyer's fees will be outside the scope of English VAT.

Resale Property

Notary's Fees

These are fixed by law, so are not negotiable. They will depend on the type of property being bought and its price.

Basic Notary's Fees – as a percentage of declared price

Portion of the price	Group 1	Group 2	Group 3
Fees on that part of the price below €3,049	5.000	2.20	2.50
Fees on that part of the price above €3,049 and below €6,098	3.300	1.65	1.65
Fees on that part of the price above €6,098 and below €16,769	1.650	1.10	1.10
Fees on that part of the price above €16,769	0.825	0.55	0.55
Fees on that part of the price above €12,1959			0.30

The odd sums result from the change to the euro. They are the equivalents of the old French franc values.

Most resale property bought by foreigners will fall into Group 1. The notary's fees for a €160,000 property (£100,000 approx) will therefore be €1611.44 – or about £1,000.

As a general guide, if you wish to avoid the detailed calculation, allow 1.3 per cent for properties less than £50,000 and one per cent for properties over £50,000.

If you have asked the notary to do any additional work over and above the transfer of title to the property, or for any advice, there will be additional charges. All of the notary's charges will be subject to VAT (*TVA*) of 19.6 per cent.

Taxes and Land Registration Fees

Departmental Tax (*Taxe Départementale*)

Communal Tax (*Taxe Communale*)

Always 1.2 per cent, whichever *commune* you live in.

Levy for Expenses(*Prélèvement pour Frais*)

This is based on 2.5 per cent of the *taxe départementale*.

Land Registry Fee

The total of the taxes and land registry fees amounts to 4.89 per cent of the declared price of the property.

Mortgage Costs (if applicable)

If you are taking out a mortgage there will be additional costs. *See* 'Raising Finance to Buy a Property in France', pp.124-36. These typically amount to three per cent of the amount borrowed. Most of these charges will be subject to TVA at 19.6 per cent.

Estate Agent's Charges (if payable by the buyer)

If an estate agent has sold the property his fees, usually between three and five per cent depending on the location and value of the property, are usually be paid by the seller. This can be varied by agreement. These fees will be subject to TVA at 19.6 per cent.

If a notary has sold the property his fee will be paid by the buyer. This fee will be subject to TVA at 19.6 per cent.

Miscellaneous Other Charges

Architect's fees, surveyor's fees, UK legal fees (typically one per cent), reconnection to water, electricity, etc. Most of these will be subject to French TVA at 19.6 per cent, but your English lawyers fees will be outside the scope of English VAT.

Additional Costs Following the Purchase of a Property in France

Property Insurance

Most owners of property in France take out a multi-risk household policy. This covers the fabric of the building, its contents and any civil responsibility landing upon the owner of the property other than in certain specified circumstances such as liability incurred in connection with the use of a motor car.

Premiums are comparatively cheap in rural areas, expensive in Paris and on the Côte d'Azur.

There are three important points to bear in mind when choosing a suitable policy.

1. Make sure that the level of cover is adequate.

   Just as in the UK, if you under-insure the building and the worst happens the company will not pay you out for the full extent of your loss.

   The amount for which you should be covered as far as civil liability is concerned should be a minimum of one million euros and preferably higher. Because the risk of a claim under this category is small, the premiums for this part of the insurance are low and so high levels of cover can be provided at low cost.

   The amount of cover you should have for the building itself should be the full cost of reconstruction of the building. If you own an apartment then the cost of the building insurance for the whole block of apartments should be included in your service charge. You will then only need contents and public liability insurance. Once this insurance value has been established, it should be increased each year in line with the official index of inflation of building costs.

   As far as contents are concerned, you should make a detailed estimate of the value of your furnishings and possessions likely to be in the property at any time. Remember to allow for items such as cameras that you may take with you on holiday. Pay particular attention to the details of this policy and study the small print about what you have to specify when taking out the insurance and any limitations on claims that can be made against it. Notice in particular whether there is a requirement to stipulate items of high value. If you have any items of high value it is worth having them photographed and, possibly, valued. The insurance company might specify security measures that must be in place in your home. If you do not use them you may find that you are not covered.

2. If you are using the property as holiday accommodation you must specify a policy which is a holiday policy. If you do not you are likely to find that one of the conditions of the policy is that cover will lapse if the property is empty

for 30 or 60 days. Premiums will be higher for holiday homes because the risk is higher.

3. If you intend to let your property you must notify the insurance company and comply with any requirements of the insurance company with regard to the lettings. Otherwise your cover could be void. Your premiums will be higher.

Under French law the buyer can, if he wishes, take over the existing policy of the seller of a property. Indeed, if he does nothing and the seller does nothing to cancel that policy it will be assumed that he intends to do so. For the reasons stated above this is not likely to be a good idea in the case of someone buying a holiday home in France. This is particularly so if the person they are buying the property from was a full-time resident in France. In most cases the buyer of a property in France should make his own arrangements for insurance to take effect from the purchase of the property and should require the seller of the property to cancel the insurance arrangements that they had put in place.

There are some UK insurance companies who offer cover for properties in France. The main advantage in dealing with a UK company is that the documentation is likely to be in English and if you have to make a claim it will be processed in English. There are some French companies that also have the facility for dealing with claims in English. This should not be underestimated as an advantage. Unless your French is fluent you would otherwise have to employ somebody to deal with the claim on your behalf or to translate what you have said into French – something that is never entirely satisfactory.

If you have to make a claim, note that there are usually time limits for doing so. If the claim involves a theft or break-in you will usually have to report the matter to the police. This should normally be done immediately after discovery of the incident and in any case within 24 hours. The claim should be notified to the insurance company without delay. Check the maximum period allowed in your policy, which could be as little as 48 hours. As with all important documents in France, the claim should be notified by recorded delivery (AR) post.

Local Taxes

As the owner of a property in France you will face local taxes. Two of these are the *taxe foncière* and the *taxe d'habitation*. The first is payable by the owner of the property, and the second by the person who occupies it. In the case of most holiday home owners and retired people the two will be the same.

The *taxe foncière* is payable whether the land or building is inhabited or not. If the property is sold during the tax year 1 January to 31 December, the notary will split the tax between the incoming and outgoing owners. Fixed each September by the local council, the *taxe d'habitation* is payable by anyone who lives in a property in France and is paid by the person who is resident on 1 January. It is not customary to apportion the liability between the incoming and outgoing owners of properties, with the person who was the resident on 1 January paying for the full year.

These taxes pay for local services, schools, etc. although you may (depending on the way you live) also receive a separate bill for the collection of rubbish/garbage (*ordures*).

More information on these local taxes, payable by both residents and non-residents, can be found under 'Local French Taxes', pp.182–3.

The *Copropriété* Bill

You will be responsible for payment of your community bill. This is the bill for the services that you enjoy jointly with other people living in your block of apartments or complex of houses sharing common facilities. See the explanation below as to the way in which that bill is calculated.

These charges are usually billed either quarterly or monthly. The rules of your community will specify the arrangements for billing.

Other Expenses

The other taxation that you will have to pay will depend upon whether you are resident in France or not. *See* 'Are You Resident or Non-resident for Tax Purposes?', pp.177–80 for more details.

There will, inevitably, be other expenses involved with owning property. These will include routine repairs, maintenance and so forth. *See* **Settling In**, 'Utilities', pp.229–32 for guidance on your budget for gas, water, electricity and others. As a very general guide, the basic annual cost of owning a holiday home in France is about two per cent of the value of the property if it is a self-contained property and about three per cent if it is a property in a community sharing common facilities. As with any average the figure can conceal wide variations.

This basic cost includes routine repairs and maintenance, insurance, local taxes, standing charges for water, electricity, etc. It does not include major repairs or renovations, consumables such as electricity and water or your personal taxation on income derived from the property. It will be higher if the property has its own pool.

Key Points

Property under Construction

When buying a new property the key points to look out for are:

- **Make sure you understand exactly what you are buying. How big is the property? What will it look like? How will it be finished? What appliances are included? What facilities will it enjoy?**
- **Think about who should own the property so as to minimize tax and inheritance problems.**
- **Make sure the contract has all of the necessary 'get-out clauses' (*clauses suspensives*) required to protect your position.**
- **Be clear about the timetable for making payments.**
- **Think about whether you should forward-buy currency.**
- **When you take delivery of the property, consider carefully whether it is worth incurring the expense of an independent survey to confirm that all is in order with the construction and to help draft any 'snagging list'.**

Resale Properties

When buying a resale property the key points to look out for are:

- **Make sure you understand exactly what you are buying. Are the boundaries clear? What furniture or fittings are included?**
- **Think about whether to have the property surveyed, especially if it is nearly 10 years old and your statutory guarantee will soon be expiring.**
- **Think about who should own the property so as to minimize tax and inheritance problems.**
- **Make sure the contract has all of the necessary 'get-out' clauses (*clauses suspensives*) required to protect your position.**
- **Think about whether you should forward-buy currency.**
- **When you take delivery of the property, make sure that everything agreed is present.**

Special Points – Old Properties

When buying an old property – by which is meant a property built more than, say, 50 years ago, there are one or two additional special points to look out for:

- **Are you having a survey? Not to do so can be an expensive mistake.**

• Are you clear about any restoration costs to be incurred? Do you have estimates for those charges?

• Are there any planning problems associated with any alterations or improvements you want to make to the property?

• When you take delivery of the property make sure that everything agreed is present.

Special Points – Rural Properties

• Such properties have often acquired a number of rights and obligations over the years. Are you clear about any obligations you might be taking on?

• You are probably buying for peace and quiet and the rural idyll. Are you sure that nothing is happening in the vicinity of your property that will be detrimental?

• If you have any plans to change the property or to use it for other purposes, will this be permitted?

Special Points – City Properties

• City properties will usually be apartments, *see* over.

• Unless you are used to living in a city – and, in particular, a continental city – do not underestimate the noise that will be generated nearby. If you are in a busy area (and you are likely to be) this will go on until late at night. How good is the sound insulation?

• Are your neighbouring properties occupied by full-time residents, are they weekday only *pieds à terre* or are they holiday homes? Think about security issues.

• If you intend to use a car, where will you park?

Special Points – Apartments and Houses Sharing Facilities

• Have you thought about a survey of the property? Will it include the common parts?

• Make sure you understand the rules of the community (*règlements de copropriété*) – *see* below.

• Make sure you understand the charges that will be raised by the community.

• Make contact with its administrator. Ask about any issues affecting the community. Are there any major works approved but not yet carried out?

Make sure that the contract is clear about who is responsible for paying for these.

- **Make contact with owners. Are they happy with the community and the way it is run? Remember that no one is ever fully happy!**
- **Understand how the community is run. Once you are an owner, try to attend the general meetings of the community.**

Special Points – Buying through an *SCI*

The *SCI* is a special type of French limited company. It exists only as a vehicle to own and manage a property in France. It is used both by French people and foreigners.

- **Are you clear why you are buying through an *SCI*? Too many people buy because they have heard it is the thing to do. For some it is a good idea, for many it is an expensive waste of time.**
- **Is this a commercial or a non-commercial *SCI*? An *SCI* that does not let out the property or engage in any of the other trading activities permitted (very few) will not be treated as a commercial SCI. It will be treated as totally fiscally transparent. It will then not be subject to French taxation – though its owners will be taxed on their share of any benefits. If it does trade it will pay French corporation tax on its income.**
- **How do you want the shares held? Most people choose to own them in equal shares. There may be better ways. For some people, particularly unmarried couples with children, it could be beneficial to hold the shares in unequal proportions. There may be other inheritance tax reasons for doing this. Some people may choose to own the shares *en tontine*.**
- **Make sure you make your initial tax declaration as required by French law. Do it as soon as you buy the property. Otherwise you will forget. This will absolve you of the need to pay the three per cent special tax raised against foreign companies owning property in France.**
- **Make sure you go through the annual formalities such as the AGM and make sure that you keep proper accounts of the income and expenditure of the SCI. This will make it less likely that the SCI will be challenged as a bogus device for tax evasion.**
- **Try to pay all bills through a bank account in the name of the *SCI* rather than in your own name. This, too, will make it less likely that the SCI will be challenged as bogus.**
- **If you are transferring an existing property that you own into the name of an *SCI*, check out the tax position carefully. The transfer will attract transfer tax of 4.89 per cent plus the usual notary's fee.**

- By transferring a property owned by one or more people into an *SCI* you can bring in additional owners more cheaply than by simple sale and purchase. Transferring property in this way can be very beneficial, particularly in the case an of unmarried couples who bought a property in their joint names. Under the French inheritance rules (*see* 'The French Inheritance Rules', pp.207–10) they may not be allowed to inherit the property from their 'partner'. If the inheritance is allowed it will carry tax at up to 60 per cent (sic) of the amount inherited. Transfer of shares in an *SCI* are taxed by the French Inland Revenue at the usual rate.
- If you are thinking of buying through an *SCI* or of transferring an existing property into the name of an *SCI*, you *must* take advice from a lawyer familiar with both French and English law.

Financial Implications

John Howell
Solicitor and International Lawyer
John Howell & Co.

06

Taxation

Introduction

All tax systems are complicated. The French system must be one of the most Byzantine, complex and subtle in the world. The French would say that it is nearly as complex as ours! Fortunately, most people will only have limited contact with the more intricate parts of the system. For many owners of holiday homes in France their contact with the system will be minimal.

It is helpful to have some sort of understanding about the way in which the system works and the taxes that you might face. Be warned: getting even a basic understanding will make your head hurt. You also need to be particularly careful about words and concepts that seem familiar to you but which have a fundamentally different meaning in France than they do in England. Of course, just to confuse you, the rules change every year.

Books (and lengthy ones at that) have been written about the subject of French taxation. This general introduction does little more than scratch the surface of an immensely complex subject. It is intended to allow you to have a sensible discussion with your professional advisers and, perhaps, to help you work out the questions that you need to be asking them. It is *not* intended as a substitute for proper professional advice.

Your situation when you have a foot in two countries – and, in particular, when you are moving from one country to another – involves the consideration of the tax systems in both countries with a view to minimizing your tax obligations in both. It is not just a question of paying the lowest amount of tax in, say, France. The best choice in France could be very damaging to your position in the UK. Similarly the most tax-efficient way of dealing with your affairs in the UK could be problematic in France. The task of the international adviser and his client is to find a path of compromise which allows you to enjoy the major advantages available in both countries without incurring any of the worst drawbacks. In other words, there is an issue of compromise. There is no perfect solution to most tax questions. That is not to say that there are not a great many bad solutions into which you can all too easily stumble.

What should guide you when making a decision as to which course to pursue? Each individual will have a different set of priorities. Some are keen to screw the last halfpenny of advantage out of their situation. Others recognize that they will have to pay some tax but simply wish to moderate their tax bill. For many the main concern is a simple structure which they understand and can continue to manage without further assistance in the years ahead. Just as different clients have different requirements so different advisers have differing views as to the function of the adviser when dealing with a client's tax affairs. One of your first tasks when speaking to your financial adviser should be to discuss your basic philosophy concerning the payment of tax and management of your affairs, to make sure that you are both operating with the same objective in mind and that you are comfortable with his approach to solving your problem.

Are You Resident or Non-resident for Tax Purposes?

The biggest single factor in determining how you will be treated by the tax authorities in any country is whether you are resident in that country for tax purposes. This concept of tax residence causes a great deal of confusion.

Tax residence can have different meanings in different countries. In France tax residence is known as *domicile fiscal*.

Let us first look at what it does not mean. It is nothing to do with whether you have registered as resident in a country or with whether you have obtained a residence permit or residence card (though a person who has a card will usually be tax resident). Nor does it have anything to do with whether you have a home (residence) in that country – although a person who is tax resident will normally have a home there. Nor is it much to do with your intentions.

Tax residence is a question of fact. The law lays down certain tests that will be used to decide whether you are tax resident or not. If you fall into the categories stipulated in the tests then you will be considered tax resident whether you want to be or not and whether it was your intention to be tax resident or not.

It is your responsibility to make your tax declarations each year. The decision as to whether you fall into the category of resident is, in the first instance, made by the tax office. If you disagree with the decision you can appeal through the courts.

Because people normally change their tax residence when they move from one country to another the basis upon which decisions are made tends to be regulated by international law and to be fairly but not totally consistent from country to country.

This does not mean that the situation cannot arise where, for example, the British taxman still considers you to be resident in England whereas the French taxman considers that you are resident in France. This could lead to the situation where you are expected to pay tax in two countries. Worse still, it could lead to the situation where you are expected to pay the same tax on the same income in two countries. This would clearly be unsatisfactory and unfair. Partly because of this risk there are international tax treaties, including a treaty between France and the UK. These provide for a series of rules which, in each set of circumstances, will apply a tie-breaking test to decide which country has first call on any tax due in respect of any particular category of income or asset.

The Rules that Determine Residence

You will have to consider two different questions concerning tax residence. The first is whether you will be treated as tax resident in the UK and the second is whether you will be treated as tax resident in France.

UK

It is outside the scope of this book to go into any details about UK taxation but some basic points will have to be dealt with for the explanation of French taxation makes any sense.

In England there are two tests that will help determine where you pay tax. These assess your domicile and your residence.

Domicile

Your domicile is the place that is your real home. It is the place where you have your roots. For most people it is the place where they were born. You can change your domicile but it is often not easy to do so. Changes in domicile can have far-reaching tax consequences and can be a useful tax reduction tool.

Residence

Residence falls into two categories. Under English law there is a test of simple residence – actually living here other than on a purely temporary basis – and of ordinary residence.

A person will generally be treated as **resident** in the UK if he spends 183 or more days per year in the UK. A visitor will also be treated as resident if he comes to the UK regularly and spends significant time here. If he spends, on average over a period of four or more years, more than three months here he will be treated as tax resident.

A person can continue to be **ordinarily resident** in the UK even after he has stopped actually being resident here. A person is ordinarily resident in the UK if his presence is a little more settled. The residence is an important part of his life. It will normally have gone on for some time.

The most important thing to understand is that, once you have been ordinarily resident in this country, the simple fact of going overseas will not automatically bring that residence to an end. If you leave this country in order to take up permanent residence elsewhere then, by concession, the Inland Revenue will treat you as ceasing to the resident on the day following your departure. But they will not treat you as ceasing to be ordinarily resident if, after leaving, you spend an average of 91 or more days per year in this country over any four-year period.

In other words, they don't want you to escape too easily!

Until 1993 you were also classified as ordinarily resident in the UK if you have accommodation available for your use in the UK even though you may spend 364 days of the year living abroad. This very unfair rule was cancelled but many people still worry about it. It is not necessary to do so provided you limit your visits to the UK to less than the 91 days referred to above.

France

Tax residence in France – *domicile fiscal* – is tested by a number of rules, the main ones of which are as follows:

- **If your home (*foyer fiscal*) is in France you will be classed as tax resident there. This 'home' is your main home, your long-term home, your family base.**
- **If you spend more than 183 days in France in any tax year, even if you do not have your *foyer fiscal* in France, you are tax resident in France if you do not have a *foyer fiscal* elsewhere. This time can be in one block or in bits and pieces through the year. The tax year runs from 1 January to 31 December.**
- **If you spend less than 184 days in France but do not have a home elsewhere or your principal residence is in France you will be treated as tax resident in France.**
- **If your centre of economic interests is in France you are tax resident in France. Your centre of economic interests is where you have your main investments or business or other sources of income and, usually, where you spend much of your money.**
- **If you work in France, except where that work in ancillary to work elsewhere, you will be tax resident in France.**
- **If you have a French resident's card (*carte de séjour*) you will be assumed to be resident in France unless you show the contrary.**
- **If your family is resident in France you will be assumed to be tax resident in France (under the *foyer fiscal* test) unless you show the contrary. If you satisfy the taxman that you are not resident in France then you will pay tax on your income and assets as a non-resident but your husband/wife will pay taxes on their income and assets as a resident. *See* below for details.**

Tax Residence in More Than One Country

Remember that you can be tax resident in more than one country under the respective rules of those countries. For example, you might spend 230 days in the year in France and 135 days in the UK. In this case you could end up, under the rules of each country, being responsible for paying the same tax in two or more countries. This would be unfair so many countries have signed reciprocal 'Double Taxation Treaties'. The UK and France have such a treaty. It contains 'tie breakers' and other provisions to decide, where there is the possibility of being required to pay tax twice, in which country any particular category of tax should be paid. *See* 'Double Taxation Treaty', p.205.

Decisions You Must Make

The most basic decisions that you will have to make when planning your tax affairs is whether to cease to be resident in this country, whether to cease to be ordinarily resident in this country and whether to change your domicile to another country. Each of the use has many consequences, many of which are not obvious.

The second consideration is when to make these changes. Once again, that decision has many consequences.

For many ordinary people getting these decisions wrong can cost them tens or hundreds of thousands of pounds in totally unnecessary taxation and a great deal of irritation and inconvenience. It is vital that you seek proper professional advice before making these decisions. You will need advice from specialist lawyers, accountants or financial advisers all of whom should be able to help you.

Taxes Payable in the UK

The significance of these residence rules is that you will continue to be liable for some British taxes for as long as you are either ordinarily resident or domiciled in the UK. Put far too simply, once you have left the UK to live in France:

- **you will continue to have to pay tax in the UK on any capital gains you make anywhere in the world for as long as you are ordinarily resident and domiciled in the UK.**
- **you will continue to be liable to British inheritance tax on all of your assets located anywhere in the world for as long as you remain domiciled here. This will be subject to double taxation relief (*see* p.205). Other, more complex, rules apply in certain circumstances.**
- **you will always pay UK income tax (Schedule A) on income arising from land and buildings in the UK – wherever your domicile, residence or ordinary residence.**
- **you will pay UK income tax (Schedule D) on the following basis:**

  income from 'self-employed' trade or profession carried out in the UK (Cases I & II) – normally taxed in the UK in all cases if income arises in the UK

income from interest, annuities or other annual payments from the UK (Case III) – normally taxed in the UK if income arises in the UK and you are ordinarily resident in the UK

income from investments and businesses outside the UK (Cases IV & V) – normally only taxed in the UK if you are UK domiciled and resident or ordinarily resident in the UK

income from government pensions (fire, police, army, civil servant, etc.) in all cases

sundry profits not otherwise taxable (Case VI) arising out of land or building in the UK are always taxed in the UK

- **you will pay income tax on any income earned from salaried employment in the UK (Schedule E) only in respect of any earnings from duties performed in the UK unless you are resident and ordinarily resident in the UK – in which case you will usually pay tax in the UK on your world-wide earnings.**

If you are only buying a holiday home and will remain primarily resident in the UK, your tax position in the UK will not change very much. You will have to declare any income you make from your French property as part of your UK tax declaration. The calculation of tax due on that income will be made in accordance with UK rules, which will result in a different taxable sum than is used by the French authorities. *See* **Letting Your Property**. The UK taxman will give you full credit for the taxes already paid in France. On the disposal of the property you should disclose the profit made to the UK taxman. He will again give full credit for French tax paid. Similarly on your death the assets in France must be disclosed on the UK probate tax declaration but, once again, you will be given full credit for sums paid in France.

Should You Pay Tax in France?

Under French law it is your responsibility to fill in a tax return in each year when you have any taxable income.

There are three key points to remember:

- **lots of French people don't pay the taxes they owe – and view with mild derision the fact that the British do so!**
- **the rules are applied more strictly every year.**
- **if you are caught not paying the taxes you owe the penalties are substantial.**

If you are a French resident you may also have to fill in a tax return if you possess any 'obvious signs of wealth'. This is to get round the practice of people turning up at their tax hearing in their Ferrari or speedboat and claiming to have no income. These 'obvious signs of wealth' include your main and holiday homes, your cars, yachts, aeroplanes and domestic staff. Each of these is given a notional income value by the tax inspector who will then assess you to tax on the resulting total (*revenu forfaitaire*) even if you declare you have no income at all.

Local French Taxes

Both residents and non-residents pay these taxes. The taxes payable fall into various categories.

Taxe d'Habitation

The *taxe d'habitation* is paid if you own a residential property and use it yourself (or have it available for your use). It is paid by the tenant if you let the property. It is paid by the person who occupied the property on 1 January in any year. It is not usually apportioned if they later move.

The tax is raised and spent by the *mairie* of the area where you live.

It is calculated on the basis of the notional rental value of your property. This is assessed by the land registry (*cadastre*) to whom you must send notification of any improvements or changes to the property within 90 days. You can appeal against their decision, but the sums involved are usually so small it is not worthwhile.

The amount you will be charged will be the rental value multiplied by the tax rate fixed in your locality.

Various deductions are available to those on very low incomes or with dependants.

Taxe Foncière

The *taxe foncière* is paid by the owner of the property, irrespective of who occupies it. If you sell the property part-way through the year the tax will be apportioned by the notary dealing with the sale.

The tax is divided into two parts: tax on the buildings (*taxe foncière bâtie*) and tax on the land (*taxe foncière non bâtie*).

The tax on the buildings is paid on any property that is habitable whether or not it is actually occupied. It does not apply to barns or other buildings actually used for agricultural purposes.

New houses used as your home are spared *taxe foncière* for the first two years after construction. In some cases this is extended to 10 or 15 years. You must apply for the exemption within 90 days of completion.

Tax on the land is always payable unless it is used for agricultural purposes.

Ordures

Rubbish collection charges are, in some areas, raised separately.

Local Property Taxes

The first owner of a property applies for it to be registered for these taxes. The notary will notify subsequent changes of ownership. If the home is a second home you should say so. Your tax bill will be reduced as, logically, you are not using as many services.

A demand for payment is sent each year. The sum claimed must be paid by the specified date (which varies from place to place). Failure to do so incurs a 10 per cent penalty. It is probably simplest to arrange for payment from your bank by direct debit.

The combined total of these taxes is low, perhaps £100 for a small cottage or £400 for a larger house.

Taxe Professionelle

This is a tax on business activity levied and spent locally. The revenue from this tax accounts for about 50 per cent of departmental and regional spending.

The tax is paid by most businesses and self-employed people. There is a long list of exceptions, the most significant of which are probably artisans, taxi drivers, artists, authors, teachers, people letting part of their home as holiday accommodation and, in some cases, people letting *gîtes*.

The tax is calculated by taking the *cadastral* (rateable) value of the premises owned by the business, 16 per cent of the value of its equipment and other fixed assets as shown in its accounts, the amount the business pays for leasing equipment and, depending on the size of the business, a percentage of the business's payroll costs or turnover. There are certain allowances to set against this sum, leaving a net taxable amount, which is taxed at the rate applicable in that area. The tax cannot amount to more than four per cent of the profit of the business.

Other Taxes Payable in France – Non-residents

In general a person who is non-resident for tax purposes has few contacts with the French tax system and they are fairly painless.

Please bear in mind the complexity of the French tax system. What follows can only be a very brief summary of the position.

Income Tax – *Impôt sur le Revenu*

For a married couple income tax is generally assessed by reference to the income of your household, rather than on your sole income. Unmarried couples are assessed as two households – which is, generally, a disadvantage.

As a non-resident you will generally only pay tax on:

1. Income generated from land and buildings located in France. If you own a building in France and rent it out, the French government collects the first wedge of tax from you.
2. Income from French securities and capital invested in France.
3. Income from business activities in France.
4. Earned income if you are employed or self-employed in France.
5. Some non-residents have to pay a tax based on a purely notional or theoretical income based on three times the rental value of any property they own or rent in France. Income tax is calculated on this amount at the rate applicable to them. This tax will not apply to British people living in France or to people of other nationalities where there is a double taxation treaty overriding this rule.

For each category of income there are various deductible allowances. *See* 'Taxes Payable in France – Residents', p.190.

The detailed system of calculating the tax due on your income is described in the section on taxes for residents (below) but for most non-residents tax is at a minimum rate of 25 per cent of their taxable income. Any tax of less than €300 is not collected.

Tax returns must be submitted by 30 April each year. Tax on your income for the year 1 January 2001 to 31 December 2001 is declared and paid in 2002.

Corporation Tax – *Impôt sur les Sociétés*

Non-resident companies will pay tax on basically the same classes of income as are listed above.

A company, whether French or incorporated elsewhere, will pay tax on the profits it makes from activities in France but not its activities elsewhere.

The tests of company residence and taxes are not considered further here.

Taxes on Wealth – *Impôt de Solidarité sur la Fortune*

You will pay French wealth tax on your assets in France. These include:

- **real estate (land and buildings)**
- **furniture**
- **cars, boats and other personal property in France**

Wealth Tax Rates – 2002

Assets from (€)	Up to (€)	Rate (%)
0	720,000	0
720,000	1,160.000	0.55
1,160.000	2,300.00	0.75
2,300.000	3,600.000	1.00
3,600.000	6,900.000	1.30
6,900.000	15,000.000	1.65
15,000.000	No upper limit	1.80

- **shares in French companies**
- **debts due to you in France**
- **any shares in a non-French company owning mainly real estate in France.**

You can deduct from your taxable assets any debts you owe in France or secured against the asset.

There is a long list of items exempt from wealth tax, including antiques and works of art and shares in companies of which you own less than 10 per cent.

The market value of your home may be discounted 20 per cent for wealth tax purposes.

Tax is applied at the rates shown in the table above.

Your tax return must be filed (if you are British) by 16 July. Tax must accompany the declaration. Assets are valued as at 1 January.

Tax on Real Estate Owned by Companies in France – *Taxe sur les Immeubles ... Personnes Morales*

This tax – three per cent of the value of the real estate held without deductions for mortgages or other debts – applies to all companies except property developers and dealers.

The tax is based on the market value of the property (not the lower *cadastral* value) and is payable unless one of the following applies:

1. The real estate is less than 50 per cent of the company's assets in France.
2. The company's registered office is in a country with which France has a taxation treaty for the suppression of tax evasion and the company makes an annual declaration of its real estate holdings and the identity of its shareholders.
3. Their effective seat of management is in France or in a country with which France has a double taxation treaty and the company agrees to disclose its land holdings and the identity of its shareholders upon request or make such a declaration every year.

4. They are a publicly quoted company.
5. They are a state or international organization (such as the Red Cross).
6. They are a non-profit-making company and can justify their ownership of the property on the basis of their social, charitable, educational or cultural activities.

If the real estate is owned by a chain of companies, the test is applied all the way up the chain.

British companies do not have to pay this tax but 'tax haven' companies, including the Channel Islands and Isle of Man companies, do.

Taxes on Capital Gains – *Plus-values*

You will pay tax on the capital gain you make on the sale of real estate in France. This is taxed at 33.33 per cent of the gain, after various small allowances, the costs of acquisition and sale, the cost of repairs and improvements, the cost of tax advice and an indexation allowance to increase the notional purchase price to eliminate the effects of inflation. The resultant taxable gain is reduced by five per cent for each year that you have owned the property except for the first two years.

The gain is collected by a withholding tax of 33.33 per cent taken at the time of the sale. To recover any balance due to you, you will need to submit a tax return. This will usually require a little tax advice.

Simple Example

Mr and Mrs Francophile bought a holiday home in Nice in 1990. In 1993 they carried our major improvements to the property. In 2001 they sold the property. They are UK tax resident and have never been tax resident in France.

	€
Sale Price	**500,000**
Cost of property, converted to euros	200,000
Allowance for expenses of purchase. Standard sum. If higher costs were incurred they can be claimed.	20,000
Sub total	220,000
Adjusted for inflation allowance on scale published annually, say factor of 1.22	268,400
Cost of improvements. If no receipts available, 15 per cent allowance	60,000
Cost of improvements adjusted for inflation, factor say 1.13	67,800
Project cost (adjusted price + adjusted cost of improvements)	**336,200**
Expenses of sale, possibly deductable	40,000
Taxable gain	**123,800**
Reduction for period of ownership (5 per cent for each year after the 2nd) 11 – 2 = 9 years = 45 per cent	55,710
Cost of tax advice	500
General reduction	6,000
Taxable amount	62,090
Tax payable (33.33 per cent)	**20,195**

You may be exempt from this tax if you have been tax resident in France at some stage for more than one year. If this applies to you, seek advice.

You will also pay capital gains tax on:

- **shares in unquoted companies over 50 per cent of whose assets comprise land and buildings in France**
- **holdings in French companies where you and your family have owned over 25 per cent of the shares**
- **holdings in any fiscally transparent professional companies of which you are an active member**

These are not considered further here.

Gift Tax – *Droits de Donations*

Gift tax is payable on the transfer by gift of any asset located in France.

Certain assets are exempt. These are the same as on inheritance.

Certain gifts are exempt from tax. These are gifts made informally by delivery of the asset into the hands of the recipient, unless the recipient chooses to disclose the gift to the taxman.

Certain gifts are partly exempt. These are set out in the table below.

Any sum received tax-free by way of gift within 10 years of the death of the donor will reduce any tax-free entitlement on that death.

The taxable value is stated by the parties but subject to intervention from the tax authorities.

The tax rates are as for inheritance tax.

The tax rate can be reduced in certain circumstances for gifts made by people under 75.

1. Gifts by parents to children (or children of deceased children) in equal shares or gifts by parents to an only child – tax payable reduced by 35 per cent if parent less than 65 or 25 per cent if aged 65–75.
2. Other gifts – tax payable reduced by 25 per cent if donor less than 65 or 15 per cent if aged 65–75.

The tax is payable by the recipient of the gift at the time the gift is received.

Partially Exempt Gifts – Allowances – 2002

To wife/husband	**€76,000**
To children/grandchildren or parents	**€46,000**
To a disabled person – additional to above	**€46,000**
To children on your divorce (up to age 18)	**€2,748 per year per child up to age 18**
To your employees in shares in your company	**€15,267**

If you are thinking of buying a French home in the name of your children this can, potentially, create a gift tax problem. This might be eliminated by making the gift of the cash to buy the property in England. This would then be subject to the UK 'seven-year rule' whereby, if the donor survives for seven years, the gift will be tax-free.

Taxes on Death – *Droits de Succession*

Inheritance tax is paid in France on the value of any assets in France as at the date of your death. In theory these include:

- **real estate (land and buildings)**
- **shares in French companies**
- **any shares in a non-French company owning mainly real estate in France.**

Depending on your tax residence this potential liability may be modified by the double taxation treaty with France. So, for example, in the case of people resident in the UK only the real estate located in France will be taxable in France.

All of the assets will have to be declared for the purposes of UK taxation. Again double taxation relief will apply so you will not pay the same tax twice. UK tax is not further considered in this book.

Certain assets are exempt. Few of the exemptions are likely to apply to the non-resident owner of a holiday home.

There are certain people who can leave all or part of their estate tax-free. These concessions are unlikely to apply in the case of non-residents.

If you leave your estate in France to the government, various educational institutions or charities, the gift will be tax free.

Otherwise, some gifts on inheritance are partly tax-exempt.

Partially Exempt Gifts on Inheritance – Allowances – 2002

To wife/husband	**€76,000**
To children/grandchildren or parents	**€46,000**
To unmarried brother/sister over 50 or invalid and who has lived with deceased for at least the last five years	**€15,267**
To a disabled person – additional to above	**€45,800**
To any other person	**€1,526**
To children on your divorce (up to age 18)	**€2,748 per year per child up to age 18**
To your employees in shares in your company	**€15,267**

Inheritance Tax Rates – 2002

Amount of Gift		Person Inheriting				
Gifts from (€)	Up to (€)	1	2	3	4	5
0	7,600	5%	5%	35%	55%	60%
7,600	15,000	10%	10%	35%	55%	60%
15,000	30,000	15%	15%	35%	55%	60%
30,000	520,000	20%	20%	45%	55%	60%
520,000	850,000	30%	30%	45%	55%	60%
850,000	1,700,000	35%	35%	45%	55%	60%
1,700,000	No upper limit	40%	40%	45%	55%	60%

If the recipient has enjoyed a lifetime gift in the 10 years preceding your death then any tax allowance given at that time will be deducted from the allowance due on your death.

Tax is paid on the value of the gift at the date of death. This is declared by the person who inherits but is subject to challenge by the tax authorities.

The tax rates are shown in the table above.

The rates of tax payable depend upon the relationship between the deceased and the person inheriting.

1. Your parents or children (including adopted children but not step-children)
2. Your husband/wife
3. Your brother or sister
4. Relatives up to the fourth degree – includes cousins, uncles, nephews
5. Any other person

The tax is calculated in tranches. A gift of €10,000 to your son will therefore be taxed at five per cent for the first €7,633 and 10 per cent on the balance.

Certain people are entitled to reductions on the tax payable.

- **If the person inheriting has three or more children alive at the time of the inheritance (or who have died leaving children of their own alive at that time) then there is a deduction from the tax otherwise payable. If the donor was a parent or grandparent it is €610 in respect of the third and each extra child. If the gift is from anyone else the amount is €305.**
- **War invalids are entitled to a reduction of 50 per cent of the tax up to a maximum of €305.**

The tax is paid by the person who inherits, not as in England by the estate as a whole.

The tax is due at the time of registering the inheritance but can, in most cases, be paid over five years. If you delay payment, interest is payable at the current statutory rate.

Social Security Contributions

These are, technically, not a tax but they account for a very large part of the income generated by the French government. Fortunately, they are only paid by people who are tax resident in France.

Other Taxes Payable in France – Residents

Taxes on Income

The French tax system is very complex. What follows can only be a very brief summary of the position. The detail is immensely complicated and is made worse because it is so different from what you are used to. This section is written with reference to the person retiring to France. Issues arising out of employment or self-employment are not considered in detail.

Income Tax – *Impôt sur le Revenu*

In France income tax comprises only a very small part of the state's revenue. This is because, over the years, they have introduced more and more 'social contributions' which, though effectively a type of income tax, are conveniently not classified as such for political purposes. *See* 'Social Security Contributions', pp.203–4.

If your **gross income** (before the deductions mentioned below) is less than €7,175 you pay no tax. If you are over 65 the level rises to €7,780.

Types of Income Tax

Income is divided, as in the UK, into various categories. Some are taxed at source. Of this income taxed at source, some is taxed in such a way as the tax paid is in full payment of the tax due. That income is then ignored for all other tax purposes. It is not included in your tax return and, if that is your only income, you normally need not file a tax return. Tax paid at source on other income is simply a payment on account of whatever might ultimately be due in the light of your personal tax rate. Some types of income bear tax at a flat rate, unrelated to your normal tax rate. Some income is not taxed at source and will bear tax at whatever rate when declared to the tax authorities in your tax return.

For a married couple income tax is generally assessed by reference to the income of your household, rather than on your sole income. Unmarried couples are assessed as two households – which is, generally, a disadvantage.

When assessing the income of the household the income of any dependent children is included.

As a tax resident you will generally pay tax in France on your world-wide income.

Remember that France is (taken overall, not just in relation to income tax) a high tax society. Whether for this reason or out of an independence of spirit many people suffer from selective amnesia as far as the tax man is concerned and significantly under-declare their income. Probably 30 per cent of French people and 50 per cent of foreign residents do this. This is dangerous. The penalties are severe. There are, however, quite legitimate tax-saving devices that you can use to reduce your liabilities. These issues are best addressed *before* you move to France as there are then many more possibilities open to you.

Income Taxed at Fixed Rates

Bank interest, interest from various types of savings accounts and income from French life assurance policies is either tax-free or taxed at source at fixed rates. The rates vary. The detailed rules are often complex.

If you wish, you can opt out of these tax schemes and have your income taxed on your normal tax scale. For most people this would not be a good idea as the fixed rates are generally low.

Income Taxed at Variable Rates

Income is divided into categories by the *Code Général des Impôts (CGI)*, as amended or added to by specific tax legislation. The good news is that anything not specifically mentioned is tax free. The bad news is that an awful lot is covered.

Each category of income is subject to different rules and allowances.

Property Income (*Revenus Fonciers*)

This is basically any income from land or buildings except for furnished lettings, which are treated as commercial income. The main examples of such income relevant to the retired person in France are income from unfurnished lettings and income from letting off your unwanted land to a neighbour.

From your income you can deduct most normal expenses relating to the management of the property including:

- **repairs**
- **maintenance**
- **improvement costs – but not rebuilding or enlargement**
- **management costs**
- **insurance**
- **property tax**
- **mortgage Interest**
- **an allowance for depreciation**

If your income from letting is less than about £3,000 per year you can choose to pay tax on the full amount received less 33 per cent as a general allowance for expenses. This will save you having to keep full records and can be worth looking at if you do not have any mortgage interest to set against income.

If you have UK rental income then, under the double taxation treaty, despite the general rule explained above that income will be taxed in the UK rather than in France.

Industrial and Commercial Income (*Bénéfices Industriels et Commerciaux*)

Any income from a profession or business not subject to company tax, including income from letting furnished property, is taxed under this heading.

There are various ways in which you can be assessed for tax.

If your business has a turnover of less than about £10,000 per year you normally pay tax on a simplified scheme whereby you are taxed on 50 per cent of your turnover without further deductions. This scheme, called the *micro-bic*, greatly simplifies your book keeping and administration. You can choose to be taxed on one of the other bases mentioned below if you prefer.

If you have a turnover of less than about £50,000 per year, you and your tax inspector can discuss your business every two years and agree a sum to be paid by way of tax for each of the next two years. This scheme, known as the *régime du forfait*, will generally reflect the amount such a business would be expected to earn. You can choose to be taxed on one of the other bases mentioned below if you prefer.

Businesses with a turnover of less than about £500,000 per year (if selling goods or providing accommodation) or £150,000 (if engaged in any other activity) usually pay their tax on a simplified version of the normal tax regime. Under this scheme (*régime du réel simplifié*) accounting and reporting requirements are relaxed. The taxpayer can elect to be taxed on the full basis if he prefers.

Larger businesses pay on the full normal tax basis.

It is beyond the scope of this book to look in detail at these schemes.

Company Directors' Pay (*Rémuneration des Dirigeants de Sociétés*)

Yet again there are several schemes for calculating and paying this tax. Generally directors of fiscally transparent companies will pay tax in their own right as partners in the business whereas directors of companies that are assessed for company tax are taxed as employees of that company.

Agricultural Income (*Bénéfices Agricoles*)

Again there are several different schemes, depending on the turnover of the farm. All are generous.

Salaries, Pensions and Life Assurance Income (*Traitements, Salaires, Pensions et Rentes Viagères*)

Tax is not the most important deduction for most employees in France. The various social security costs can be more significant. These are deducted from the figure for gross income before tax is calculated.

Also deducted from your gross income before tax is calculated are:

- **any legitimate expenses. These are usually formalized at 10 per cent of salary. In the past certain professions and occupations have enjoyed the ability to deduct much higher levels of expenses but this right was abolished in 2001**
- **20 per cent of salary (after expenses) up to a maximum of €22,000**
- **interest on certain loans used to buy into a business**
- **pension contributions up to about €38,000**
- **the income from profit-sharing schemes is generally exempt from income tax – but not social contributions**
- **luncheon vouchers and holiday vouchers – up to fairly low limits**

If you have pension income then the *French* state pension is tax-exempt.

Only part of an annuity pension (*rente viagère*) is taxed. The rest is tax-free. The percentage taxable depends upon your age. Under 50 – 70 per cent, 50–59 – 50 per cent, 60–69 – 40 per cent, over 69 – 30 per cent. This offers considerable scope for tax planning.

Other pension income is subject to an initial reduction of 10 per cent before the allowances mentioned above are calculated and taken into account.

Non-commercial Profits (*Bénéfices Non-commerciaux*)

This is where the profits of lawyers, doctors, architects, etc. are taxed.

There are several regimes under which tax can be imposed, as in the case of other businesses.

Investment Income (*Revenus des Capitaux*)

This covers shares, bonds, etc. Some such income – such as bank interest – is usually taxed at source, subject to the taxpayer's right to elect ordinary taxation.

Dividends from French companies are accompanied by a tax credit (*avoir fiscal*) which is added to the actual dividend for the purposes of calculating tax due.

Dividends from overseas companies are added to other income to assess the overall level of tax payable.

Short-term Capital Gains

Short-term gains on both real and personal property are added to the overall income for the year in question and thus assessed for tax. Short-term gains are usually gains made over less than two years.

Income Not Subject to Income Tax

There is a long list of bits and pieces of income that are not subject to income tax.

The most important, from the point of view of the retired person in France, are:

- **income from various French savings schemes, provided the money is left in them, typically for four to eight years**
- **a reasonable amount of rent from letting part of your own home to a permanent tenant.**
- **rent (up to about €1,000 per year) from using your home as a 'bed and breakfast'**

Deductions from Gross Income Before Calculating Tax Due

In addition to the specific deductions referred to in the various sections above, there are some general deductions from your gross income before tax is calculated. These are:

- **maintenance payments (in cash or kind)**
- **to a parent**
- **to a needy adult child**
- **to an adult child who benefits from payments under a court order**
- **under a court order to a minor child of a divorced parent where the child lives with the other parent**
- **reasonable voluntary payments to such a child**
- **maintenance payments under a court order to your wife/husband**
- **losses under certain tax incentive schemes**
- **certain investments in French cinema**

Deductions from Net Income Before Calculating Tax Due

From the net income of the household, calculated as above, there are various possible deductions.

- **If you are an invalid (as defined in France = 80 per cent disabled), an allowance of about £1,000.**
- **If you are over 65, an allowance of between £500 and £1,000. This is doubled if husband and wife are both over 65.**
- **If you have a child who is married and either under 21, under 25 and still a student or in military service, they can be brought back into your family for tax purposes. You can then claim an allowance of about £350 for each of them and their children.**

Taxable Income

The total of the sums taxable under the various headings set out above, calculated for each member of the household, less the various deductions from gross and net income also set out above, produce the household's taxable income.

This is where it starts getting a bit complicated!

Personal Allowances

There are no personal allowances.

Adjustment of Household Income to Reflect Number of People in the Household

The total taxable income is the total income of the household. To avoid large families with working children paying too much tax the French have introduced the concepts of the *quotient familial* and '*parts*'.

The '*part*' is the adjusted family unit. That is to say, each independent person in a household is a *part* but some are treated as having more weight (for tax purposes) than others.

The total income is divided by the number of *parts* and the tax due per *part* is calculated. The tax thus calculated is multiplied by the number of *parts* to work out the actual tax payable. Easy really. The effect of this is usually to reduce the rates of tax payable.

Each non-dependant in the household is normally entitled to one *part*.

Dependants are children under 21, student children under 25, invalid children of any age and children performing their military service provided in each case that they live (or are based) at home and are accepted as the responsibility of the household.

A non-dependent single person who is part of the household is normally entitled to one *part*, as is a separated, divorced or widowed person.

However in a whole range of circumstances that person could become entitled to 1.5 *parts*. These include:

- **people who have an adult child**
- **certain invalids**
- **certain people who have ever adopted children**
- **people with at least one dependent who are also invalids**

If the single person has dependants they will become entitled to an even bigger allocation of *parts*.

- **one dependant – 1 extra *part***
- **two dependants – 1.5 extra *parts***
- **three dependants – 2.5 extra *parts***
- **each extra dependant gives you one extra *part***

A married couple start off, logically, with two *parts*. As with single people, there is a range of circumstances that give rise to an additional entitlement.

- **if either spouse is an invalid they are entitled to 2.5 *parts***
- **if both are invalids they are entitled to three *parts***

If they have dependants there will be an additional allocation.

- **one dependant – 0.5 extra *part***
- **two dependants – one extra *parts***
- **three dependants – two extra *parts***
- **each extra dependant gives you one extra *part***

There is more.

If you have unmarried children who are not technically dependant but who are under 21, students under 25 or performing their military service, they may be re-attached to the household for tax purposes. In this case you will benefit from an extra 0.5 *parts* for each of them.

Finally, if any of your dependants has an invalidity card you get an extra 0.5 *parts* for each of them.

This is a simplified version of the rules. If you want to claim additional *parts* for dependants or invalidity you need specific tax advice.

Limit of Permitted Adjustment to Household Income

If the effect of calculating your *parts*, dividing your income by the number of *parts*, calculating the tax due per *part* and then multiplying the result by the number of *parts* produces a tax bill which has been reduced by more than €2,500 per half *part* compared to what it would have been without reference to the *parts* the deal is off and you are not allowed to use this system. In this event a slightly more complex calculation is used! I will not trouble you with it. You need tax advice.

There are also other statutory limitations to the maximum savings to be effected under this scheme.

Tax Rates

The tax per *part* is calculated using the following table. The tax is calculated in tranches. That is, you calculate the tax payable on each complete slice and then the tax at the highest applicable rate on any excess.

Remember, you calculate your tax per *part*, then multiply by the number of *parts* to get the total payable.

Remember also that, in addition to the tax due, you will have to pay social security costs, averaging about 10 per cent, on certain types of income. *See* pp.203–4.

Income Tax Rates – 2002

Tranche or Portion	Net Income Subject to Tax from (€)	To (€)	Rate (%)
1	0	4,121	0
2	4,121	8,104	7.5
3	8,104	14,264	21.00
4	14,264	23,096	31.00
5	23,096	37,579	41.00
6	37,579	46,343	46.75
7	46,343	No upper limit	52.75

Tax Credits

Various tax credits are available. These are deducted from the tax otherwise payable as calculated above.

The rules are complex. They include credits for:

- **mortgage interest in a small number of cases where mortgages were taken out before 1 January 1998**
- **renovation of your main home**
- **life assurance premiums – in a small number of cases**
- **charitable donations**
- **certain child-minding expenses**
- **50 per cent of sum paid to employ of a home help – to a maximum of €3,435**
- **if you are over 70, 25 per cent of the cost of residential care – to a maximum of €572**
- **allowances for children in school – amounts vary between €60–€180 per child**

Tax Rebate

If the tax due, calculated as above, is less than €500 you will receive a payment from the tax office of the difference between your tax liability and the rebate level. This is the *décote*.

Payment of Tax Due

Tax is paid at your election either in three equal instalments (31 January, 30 April and 30 September) or by monthly instalments over 10 months from 8 January to 8 October. In both cases the tax paid on account is paid on the basis of the tax paid in the previous year, with a final adjustment to reflect your liability this year.

Simple Example

Mr Francophile is employed in France. He earns €80,000. He and his family have no other source of income. He is married with two children aged 14 and 16. There are no disabilities.

	€	€
Income		80,000
– social security charges		8,000
Net		72,000
– expenses of employment		7,200
abatement of salary		14,400
Taxable sum		50,400
Tax based on three *parts*		
– Income per *part*		16,800
Tax on that income		
– First €3,813 @ 0 per cent	0	
– €3,814 to €8,271 @ 10.5 per cent	468	
– €8,272 to €14,558 @ 24 per cent	1,508	
– €14,559 to €16,800 @ 33 per cent	739	
Total tax per *part*		2,715
Multiply by three *parts*		8,145
– Tax credits		
school children		160
Tax actually payable		7,985
Plus social contributions		

Corporation Tax – *Impôt sur les Sociétés*

These taxes are not considered further here.

Equalization Tax – *Précompte Mobilier*

This tax, payable by companies, is not considered further here.

Taxes on Wealth – *Impôt de Solidarité sur la Fortune*

You will be taxed on your world-wide wealth. That includes any sums hidden in tax havens. Wealth includes:

- **real estate (land and buildings)**
- **furniture**
- **cars, boats and other personal property in France**
- **shares in French companies**

Wealth Tax Rates – 2002

Gross Worldwide Assets from (€)	Up to (€)	Rate (%)
0	720,000	0
720,000	1,160,000	0.55
1,160,000	2,300,000	0.75
2,300,000	3,600,000	1.00
3,600,000	6,900,000	1.30
6,900,000	15,000,000	1.65
15,000,000	No upper limit	1.80

- **debts due to you in France**
- **any shares in a non-French company owning mainly property in France.**

You can deduct from your taxable assets any debts you owe in France or secured against the asset.

There is a long list of items exempt from wealth tax, including antiques and works of art and shares in companies of which you own less than 10 per cent.

The market value of your home may be discounted 20 per cent for wealth tax purposes.

Tax is applied at the rates shown in the table above.

Your tax return must be filed (if you are British) by 16 July. Tax must accompany the declaration. Assets are valued as at 1 January.

Taxes on Capital Gains – *Plus-values*

You will pay *plus-values* on your world-wide gains.

There are two types of capital gains: business gains and gains made by private individuals.

Short-term gains are treated differently from long-term gains, being usually taxed as income in the year they are made. Short-term gains are normally defined as gains made over less than two years.

Long-term gains are taxed in various ways, depending on the type of gain and whether it has been made by an individual or a business.

Gains are generally only taxed when the gain is crystallized – e.g on the sale of the asset.

Gains by Private Individuals

Gains on Land and Buildings

Several gains are exempt, including – most importantly – the gain on your main residence or any other residential property held for over 22 years.

The gain is taxed by calculating the difference between sale price and cost, less various allowances.

See the example in the section on taxes for non-residents, p.186.

If the gain is a long-term gain (made over more than two years) the price, purchase costs and additional expenses mentioned are indexed to eliminate the effect of inflation. You will also benefit from a tax-free allowance of five per cent of the gain made for each full year you have owned the property after the first two years.

If you are selling a second home that you have owned for more than five years, a part of the gain may be tax-free. The amount will depend on your circumstances.

Companies whose assets are at least 50 per cent real estate are taxed under this section when they sell the property.

If you make a loss selling your real estate you cannot set this off against other gains or claim a tax refund.

Bonds, Securities and Shares Where You Own Less than 25 per cent of the Company

These are taxed on the difference between purchase and sale price.

Losses can be set against other gains under this category.

Shareholdings of Over 25 per cent in a Company

This heading applies to both French and foreign companies. The rules can be complex. Seek advice.

Moveable Assets

Gains on cars and furniture are not taxed. The first €3,200 of gains under this category are also not taxed.

If you have owned any taxable assets for less than one year, the gain is taxed as income in the year it arises. Longer-term gains are granted a tax-free allowance of five per cent of the gain for each year the asset has been held after the first year.

There is no relief for losses.

Gold, Jewellery, Works of Art, Antiques

These are exempt if the sale price is less than €3,200. Above this level the tax varies from 4.5 to 7.5 per cent depending on the price achieved. This tax is payable within one month of the gain being made.

Gains on the French or Overseas Futures Markets

These are outside the scope of this book.

Calculation of Tax Due

For long-term gains on real estate, 20 per cent of the amount of the gain is added to the taxpayer's income for income tax purposes in the year of the gain. The tax payable is five times the increase of tax resulting from this step.

Other gains are taxed at the rates stipulated.

Payment of Tax

Tax on short-term gains is paid as part of your income tax.

Tax on long-term gains can be paid by instalments over five years.

Business Gains

These are not considered in this book.

Gift Tax – *Droits de Donations*

This is paid on gifts made of any assets anywhere in the world.

Certain assets are exempt. These are the same as on inheritance.

Certain gifts are exempt from tax. These are gifts made informally by delivery of the asset into the hands of the recipient, unless the recipient chooses to disclose the gift to the taxman.

Certain gifts are partly exempt. These are set out below.

Any sum received tax-free by way of gift within 10 years of the death of the donor will reduce any tax-free entitlement on that death.

The taxable value is stated by the parties but subject to intervention from the tax authorities.

The tax rates are as for inheritance tax.

The tax rate can be reduced in certain circumstances for gifts made by people under 75.

1. Gifts by parents to children (or children of deceased children) in equal shares or gifts by parents to an only child – tax payable reduced by 35 per cent if parent is less than 65 or 25 per cent if aged 65–75.
2. Other gifts – tax payable reduced by 25 per cent if donor is less than 65 or 15 per cent if aged 65–75.

The tax is payable by the recipient of the gift at the time the gift is received.

If you are thinking of buying a French home in the name of your children, this can, potentially, create a gift tax problem. This might be eliminated by making the gift of the cash to buy the property in England. This would then be subject to the UK 'seven-year rule' whereby, if the donor survives for seven years, the gift will be tax-free.

Partially Exempt Gifts – Allowances – 2002

To wife/husband	**€76,000**
To children/grandchildren or parents	**€46,000**
To a disabled person – additional to above	**€45,800**
To children on your divorce (up to age 18)	**€2,748 per year per child up to age 18**
To your employees in shares in your company	**€15,267**

Partially Exempt Gifts on Inheritance – Allowances – 2002

To wife/husband	**€76,00**
To children/grandchildren or parents	**€46,000**
To unmarried brother/sister over 50 or invalid and who has lived with deceased for at least the last five years	**€15,267**
To a disabled person – additional to above	**€45,800**
To any other person	**€1,526**
To children on your divorce (up to age 18)	**€2,748 per year per child up to age 18**
To your employees in shares in your company	**€15,267**

Taxes on Death – *Droits de Succession*

Subject to the provisions of double taxation treaties, tax is paid on your world-wide assets as at the date of your death.

This potential liability may be modified by your double taxation treaty with France.

All of the assets may have to be declared for the purposes of UK taxation. If this is so double taxation relief will apply so you will not pay the same tax twice. UK tax is not further considered in this book.

Certain assets are exempt. The list is long and includes:

- **proceeds of most life policies**
- **certain items given to the state**
- **some rented housing**

If you leave your estate in France to the government, various educational institutions or charities the gift will be tax free.

Otherwise, some gifts on inheritance are partly tax-exempt (*see* table above).

If the recipient has enjoyed a lifetime gift in the 10 years preceding your death then any tax allowance given at that time will be deducted from the allowance due on your death.

Tax is paid on the value of the gift at the date of death. This is declared by the person who inherits but is subject to challenge by the tax authorities.

The tax rates are shown on the table on the next page.

The rates of tax payable depend upon the relationship between the deceased and the person inheriting.

1. Your parents or children (including adopted children but not step-children)
2. Your husband/wife
3. Your brother or sister

Inheritance Tax Rates – 2002

Amount of Gift		Person Inheriting				
Gifts from (€)	Up to (€)	1	2	3	4	5
0	7,600	5%	5%	35%	55%	60%
7,600	15,000	10%	10%	35%	55%	60%
15,000	30,000	15%	15%	35%	55%	60%
30,000	520,000	20%	20%	45%	55%	60%
520,000	850,000	30%	30%	45%	55%	60%
850,000	1,700,000	35%	35%	45%	55%	60%
1,700,000	No upper limit	40%	40%	45%	55%	60%

4. Relatives up to the fourth degree – includes cousins, uncles, nephews
5. Any other person

The tax is calculated in tranches. A gift of €10,000 to your son will therefore be taxed at five per cent for the first €7,633 and 10 per cent on the balance.

Certain people are entitled to reductions on the tax payable.

- **If the person inheriting has three or more children alive at the time of the inheritance (or who have died leaving children of their own alive at that time) then there is a deduction from the tax otherwise payable. If the donor was a parent or grandparent it is €610 in respect of the third and each extra child. If the gift is from anyone else the amount is €305.**
- **War invalids are entitled to a reduction of 50 per cent of the tax up to a maximum of €305.**

The tax is paid by the person who inherits, not as in England by the estate as a whole.

The tax is due at the time of registering the inheritance but can, in most cases, be paid over five years. If you delay payment interest is payable at the current statutory rate.

Companies' Real Estate Tax – *Taxe sur les Immeubles ... Personnes Morales*

This is explained in the section on taxes for non-residents, *see* p.185

Social Security Contributions

These are, technically, not a tax but they account for a very large part of the income generated by the French government. They are only paid by people who are tax-resident in France.

There is a **General Social Contribution** (*contribution sociale généralisée – CSG*) payable on most types of income. It is generally charged at 7.5 per cent on

95 per cent of earned and 100 per cent of unearned income including rental income, annuities and capital gains (except for certain savings accounts at French Post Office and Savings Banks) *or* 6.2 per cent on pension income, unemployment and social security benefits. There is also the **CRDS** (*Contribution au Reimboursement de la Dette Sociale*) which is 0.5 per cent of all income subject to *CSG*. There is also the **PS** (*Prélèvement Social*) of two per cent.

CSG and CRDS are not payable on salaries, self-employed earnings or on foreign pensions as long as you are over retirement age.

If you are tax resident you also have to pay eight per cent of your net income as a **CMU** (Health Care) contribution on income above €6,585 (€9,878 if married). If you are in receipt of a UK state retirement pension you are exempt regardless of income.

These contributions should not be underestimated. They apply in many circumstances where you would not think you would be liable for social security payments and can easily add 10 per cent to your tax rate on investment income – e.g. increasing the rate from, say, 42 to 52 per cent.

VAT

VAT is a major generator of tax for the French. The standard rate is currently 19.6 per cent. Detailed consideration of VAT is beyond the scope of this book.

Other Taxes

There is a miscellany of other taxes and levies on various aspects of life in France from alcohol to pornography. Some are national and others local. Individually they are usually not a great burden. They are beyond the scope of this book.

New Residents

New residents will be liable to tax on their world-wide income and gains from the date they arrive in France. Until that day they will only have to pay French tax on their income if it is derived from assets in France.

The most important thing to understand about taking up residence in France (and abandoning UK tax residence) is that it gives you superb opportunities for tax planning and, in particular, for restructuring your affairs to minimise what can otherwise be penal rates of taxation in France. To do this you need good advice at an early stage – preferably several months before you intend to move.

Double Taxation Treaty

The detailed effect of double taxation treaties depends on the two counries involved. Whilst treaties may be similar in concept they can differ in detail. Only the effect of the France/UK treaty is considered here.

The main points of relevance to residents are:

- **Any income from letting property in the UK will normally be outside the scope of French taxation and, instead, will be taxed in the UK.**
- **Pension received from the UK – except for government pensions – will be taxed in France but not in the UK.**
- **Government pensions will continue to be taxed in the UK but are neither taxed in France nor do they count in assessing the level of your income when calculating the rate of tax payable on your income.**
- **You will normally not be required to pay UK capital gains tax on gains made after you settle in France except in relation to real estate located in the UK.**
- **If you are taxed on a gift made outside France then the tax paid will usually be offset against the gift tax due in France.**
- **If you pay tax on an inheritance outside France the same will apply.**

Double taxation treaties are detailed and need to be read in the light of your personal circumstances.

Tax Planning Generally

Do it and do it as soon as possible. Every day you delay will make it more difficult to get the results you are looking for.

There are many possibilities for tax planning for someone moving to France. Some points worth considering are:

- **Time your departure from the UK to get the best out of the UK tax system.**
- **Think, in particular, about when to make any capital gain if you are selling your business or other assets in the UK.**
- **Arrange your affairs so that there is a gap between leaving the UK (for tax purposes) and becoming resident in France. That gap can be used to make all sorts of beneficial changes to the structure of your finances.**
- **Think about trusts. Although the French system has more restrictions on their effective use than many continental systems they can still be very effective tax-planning vehicles.**

- **Think about giving away some of your assets. You will not have to pay wealth tax on the value given away and the recipients will generally not have to pay either gift or inheritance tax on the gift.**

Residence Permits

A French person living in France needs paperwork in order to do so. So does a foreigner. Any foreigner staying in France for more than 90 days at a time needs the appropriate paperwork to justify their stay in France.

If you have children under the age of 18 they are entitled to be included on your residence paper work unless they are working.

Which paperwork you require depends on what you are doing in France. For more details on how to obtain a residence permit, *see* 'Permits and Visas', p.24.

Many clients confuse the issue of residence permits with the issue of citizenship. As an British person or, come to that, any other nationality, you are entitled to retain your nationality for as long as you like even though you are living in France. Most British people, who have settled in France will, 40 years later, still have their British passport and British nationality.

The granting of a residence permit of whatever type makes no difference whatsoever to your nationality. Nor does it generally make any difference to your tax residence, which will be calculated in accordance with the rules set out in 'The Rules That Determine Residence', p.178.

Finally a word about 'illegals'. Many British people went to live in France many years ago and never quite got round to applying for a residence permit. Sometimes this was in the quaint belief that they would somehow not have to pay taxes in France if they never applied for a permit. Other times the paperwork seemed too much trouble. Many of them have never been challenged and, indeed, have never paid any tax in France. This is illegal. There are severe penalties for living in France without a permit and there are also severe penalties for non-payment of tax. It cannot be recommended. Times have changed greatly in the last 20 years and the odds of being able to get away with all of this in the future are slender.

For a British person seeking a residence permit in France the procedure is generally simple and the authorities are generally very helpful. It is simply not worth trying to cheat the system.

Inheritance

The French Inheritance Rules

The French inheritance rules apply – at least in part – to anyone either owning property or living in France.

These rules are much more restrictive than the rules under English law. Certain groups of people have (almost) automatic rights to inherit a part of your property.

A distinction is drawn between moveable and immovable property. Immovable property is, basically, land and buildings. Movable property is anything else.

Whether you are domiciled in France or not, **immovable property** in France must be disposed of in accordance with the requirements of French law.

The way in which **moveable** property is disposed of depends on where you are *domiciled*. Be careful. This is not 'domiciled' in the UK sense (as explained on p.178) but it implies a sense of being in settled residence in France. This status is quite easily achieved. Whether it has been achieved in your case is a question of fact. This is one of those cases where you can look at the consequences of what would happen if you were domiciled in France – and French law applied to your whole estate – and then decide whether to argue the domicile point or not.

If you are *not* domiciled in France you can dispose of your immovable property in whatever way your national law allows. For British people this is, basically, as they please.

If you are domiciled in France then French law will apply to your whole estate, except for any immovable property *outside* France, which is usually 'captured' and disposed of in accordance with the law of the country where it is located.

Who Gets What under French Law?

Any assets captured for disposal in accordance with French law are divided into two parts: the freely disposable part (*quotité disponible*) and the protected or reserved part (*réserve héréditaire*).

The reserved part *must* be given to the persons established under French law. Who these are depends upon your family situation.

The Protected Part

If you have:

one child (of any age, legitimate or illegitimate, adopted or your own but not including step-children) or a dead child who left children of his own
50 per cent of the total estate must be given to these people

two children (of any age, legitimate or illegitimate, adopted or your own but not including step-children) or a combination of living and dead children who left children of their own
66 per cent of the total estate must be given to these people

three or more children (of any age, legitimate or illegitimate, adopted or your own but not including step-children) or a combination of living and dead children who left children of their own
75 per cent of the total estate must be given to these people

No children but a living parent or grandparent on *either* your father's or your mother's side
25 per cent of the total estate must be given to these people *but* the gift can be reduced to a life interest (rather than a full gift) if you have a surviving spouse and the arrangements are made by will

No children but a living parent or grandparent on *both* your father's or your mother's side
25 per cent of the total estate must be given to *each branch* of the family *but* the gift can be reduced to a life interest (rather than a full gift) if you have a surviving spouse and the arrangements are made by will

The protected part is, in each case, divided equally amongst the persons entitled.

The Freely Disposable Part

This can be given to whomsoever you wish, including your wife or one or more of your children or other protected heirs.

The Position of Your Husband or Wife

In this section, just to confuse you, 'wife' means either husband or wife and 'she' means either the surviving wife or the surviving husband.

Your wife's affairs are regulated by the 'matrimonial regime' you chose on marriage or which you chose to adopt subsequent to marriage. *See* 'Your Civil State (*Etat Civile*) and Other Personal Details', pp.147–8', for details of this. This means that she probably already has a claim to the ownership of part of the matrimonial property.

If you are treated as married under the regime of separate ownership of goods (*séparation de biens*) and the property in France was owned by you in your joint names, then, on your death, your wife will remain the owner of her part of it. Only your part will be disposed of in accordance with the rules set out above. Most British couples will be treated as married in this way unless they specify the contrary.

If, on the other hand, you are married under the regime of community of ownership (*communauté universelle*) and you have made a notarial contract that on your death the property is to pass automatically to your wife (*clause d'attribution*) then, on your death, your wife will become the owner of the property. This will be free of both French and UK inheritance tax.It also bypasses the rights of your protected heirs.

This will work only if you have no children by previous relationships.

It also has a number of tax and practical consequences that need to be considered before deciding whether to make this declaration of change of matrimonial regime.

- **More tax will be paid on the death of your wife than would otherwise be the case**
- **Your wife has full control of the assets. This can 'rob' your children of their inheritance if she chooses to spend the money. On the other hand it gives her great protection and flexibility**
- **All of the couple's property can be attacked by either person's creditors – including business creditors**

There are limitations on this option if you have children by a previous marriage. Take advice as to whether this option is right for you. The consequences of getting it wrong are expensive.

The contract is made in such a way as to have it apply only to your assets in France, so preserving the regime of separate ownership of goods for your UK or other assets.

Despite making this declaration you should still make a French will, if only to take account of the fact that you could be the surviving spouse who inherits the lot. On your death as surviving spouse your estate will be dealt with in the 'normal' way set out above.

Apart from these general rights the French civil code grants few specific rights to your wife on your death.

If you do not make a will dealing with the issue specifically – which you should do – she may choose:

- **to take 25 per cent of your estate 'absolutely' in full ownership**
- ***or* take a life interest over the whole of the estate**

The life interest means not only that she can live in the house but that she enjoys the use of all of the income from your investments until she dies, at which point the protected heirs take up their rights to the property. If you have children by more than one marriage, you cannot take the option of the life interest. This is to prevent a new 'young' wife outliving the older children of the first wife.

Which choice is best will depend on your family's personal circumstances and tax position. You should take advice on this point because the choice, once made, cannot be undone. It is usually better to make a will setting out which course of action you wish to apply on your death.

What If You Are Not Married?

Until recently French law was a disaster for people living together but not married to each other. The *PACS* (*Pacte civile de solidarité*) has helped a little – but only a little. Under a *PACS* agreement, registered with the court, each member of the couple is treated as owning half of the assets. This will not change the way French inheritance law will apply to those assets but, by concession, the tax rate applied to a gift on death by one of the couple to the other is reduced from the standard 60 per cent applicable to gifts between non blood relatives to a sliding scale of zero, 40 and 50 per cent.

PACS agreements are only of help if you are resident in France.

Getting Round the Rules

There are various devices, either individually or used in combination, that can help get round the basic French inheritance rules. Which is the best depends entirely on your circumstances. Their effects are cumulative and sometimes subtle, so you need specialist advice from lawyers experienced in dealing with affairs in both France and the UK.

- **declaration of community as matrimonial regime**
- ***PACS***
- ***tontine* clause in title**
- **company ownership**
- **borrowing to diminish (or eliminate) asset value for tax purposes**

Making a Will

It is always best to make a French will. If you do not, your English will should be treated as valid in France and will be used to distribute the freely disposable part of your estate. This is false economy as the cost of implementing the English will is much higher than the cost of implementing a French will and the disposal of your estate set out in your English will is often a tax disaster in France.

Your will – whether English or French – is always read in the light of the compulsory requirements of French law set out above. If the will does not respect those arrangements it will be interpreted as only disposing of the freely disposable part of your estate.

If you are not a resident in France your French will should state that it only applies to immovable property in France. The rest of your property – including moveable property in France – will be disposed of in accordance with English law and the provisions of your English will. If you are domiciled in France you should make a French will disposing of all of your assets wherever they are located. If you make a French will covering only immovable property in France you should modify your English will so as to exclude any immovable property located in France.

What if I Don't Make a Will of Any Kind?

A person who dies without a will dies intestate.

In France the part of your property to be disposed of in accordance with French law (*see* above) is dealt with as laid down in the civil code. These rules seem simple but are, in fact, quite complicated. Basically your assets are distributed:

- **If you have children, to them equally**
- **If you do not have children but have surviving parents, each takes 25 per cent of your estate**
- **If you have neither children nor parents but do have brothers or sisters they share it equally**
- **Failing all this, more distant relatives can inherit**

If you were married your husband or wife will also have certain rights.

- **If you had no children or surviving parents or brothers or sisters, your wife receives everything**
- **If you had no children and only *either* your mother or her parents *or* your father or his parent are still alive your wife inherits 25 per cent**
- **In any other case your wife will only be entitled to a life interest in a part of your property. If you left children the life interest will be in 25 per cent of your estate. Otherwise it will be in 50 per cent**

In each case if the person entitled died before you leaving children of their own those children take their parent's share.

Investments

The Need to Do Something

Most of us don't like making investment decisions. They make our head hurt. They make us face up to unpleasant things – like taxes and death. We don't really understand what we are doing, what the options are or what is best. We don't know who we should trust to give us advice. We know we ought to do something, but it will wait until next week – or maybe the week after. Until then our present arrangements will have to do.

If you are moving to live overseas you must review your investments. Your current arrangements are likely to be financially disastrous – and may even be illegal.

What Are You Worth?

Most of us are, in financial terms, worth more than we think. When we come to move abroad and have to think about these things it can come as a shock.

Take a piece of paper and list your actual and potential assets. A suggested checklist can be found in **Appendix 2**, p.323.

This will give you an idea as to the amount you are worth now and, just as importantly, what you are likely to be worth in the future. Your investment plans should take into account both figures.

Who Should Look After Your Investments?

You may already have an investment adviser. You may be very happy with their quality and the service you have received. They are unlikely to be able to help you once you have gone to live in France. They will almost certainly not have the knowledge to do so. They will know about neither the French investment that might be of interest to you or, probably, of many of the 'off shore' products that might be of interest to someone no longer resident in the UK. Even if they have some knowledge of these things they are likely to be thousands of miles from where you will be living.

Nor is it a simple question of selecting a new local (French) adviser once you have moved. They will usually know little about the UK aspects of your case or about the UK tax and inheritance rules that could still have some importance for you.

Choosing an investment adviser competent to deal with you once you are in France is not easy. By all means seek guidance from your existing adviser. Ask for guidance from others who have already made the move. Do some research. Meet the potential candidates. Are you comfortable with them? Do they share your approach to life? Do they have the necessary experience? Is their performance record good? How are they regulated? What security/ bonding/guarantees can they offer you? How will they be paid for their work? Fees or commission? If commission, what will that formula mean they are making from you in 'real money' rather than percentages?

Above all be careful. There are lots of very dubious 'financial advisers' operating in the popular tourist areas of France. Some are totally incompetent.

Some are crooks, seeking simply to separate you from your money as cleanly as possible.

Fortunately there are also some excellent and highly professional advisers with good track records. Make sure you choose one.

Where Should You Invest?

For British people the big issue is whether they should keep their sterling investments.

Most British people will have investments that are largely sterling-based. Even if they are, for example, a Far Eastern fund they will probably be denominated in sterling and they will pay out dividends, etc. in sterling.

You will be spending euros.

As the value of the euro fluctuates against sterling the value of your investments will go up and down. That, of itself, isn't too important because the value won't crystallize unless you sell. What does matter is that the revenue you generate from those investments (rent, interest, dividends, etc.) will fluctuate in value. Take, for example, an investment that generated you £10,000 per annum. Rock steady. Then think of that income in spending power. I will use French francs as an example because the euro does not yet have a sufficient track record to show the point. In the last few years the French franc has varied in value from £1 = 11.25FF to £1 = 6.5FF. Sometimes, therefore, your income in French francs would have been 65,000FF per year and at others it would have been 112,500FF per year. This is a huge difference in your standard of living *based solely on exchange rate fluctuations*.

To my way of thinking this is unacceptable, particularly as you will inevitably have to accept this problem in so far as your pension is concerned.

In general terms investments paying out in euros are preferable if you live in a euro country.

Trusts

Trusts are an important weapon in the hands of the person going to live in France.

Legislation has been introduced in France to limit the abuse of trusts as devices to conceal income and assets but it is still limited in scope and effectiveness.

Trusts offer the potential benefits of:

1. Allowing you to put part of your assets in the hands of trustees so that they no longer belong to you for wealth tax or inheritance tax purposes.

2. Allowing you to receive only the income you need (rather than all the income generated by those assets) so keeping the extra income out of sight for income tax purposes.
3. Allowing a very flexible vehicle for investment purposes.

So how do these little wonders work?

After leaving the UK (and before moving to France) you reorganize your affairs by giving a large part of your assets to 'trustees'. These are normally a professional trust company located in a low tax regime. The choice of a reliable trustee is critical.

Those trustees hold the asset not for their own benefit but 'in trust' for whatever purposes you established when you made the gift. It could, for example, be to benefit a local hospital or school or it could be to benefit you and your family. If the trust is set up properly in the light of the requirements of French law then those assets will no longer be treated as yours for tax purposes.

On your death the assets are not yours to leave to your children (or whoever), and so do not (subject to any local anti avoidance legislation) carry inheritance tax.

Similarly the income from those assets is not your income. If some of it is given to you it may be taxed as your income, but the income that is not given to you will not be taxed in France and, because the trust will be located in a nil/low tax regime, it will not be taxed elsewhere either.

The detail of the arrangements is vitally important. They must be set up precisely to comply with French tax law. If you do not do this they will not work as intended.

Trustees can manage your investments in (virtually) whatever way you stipulate when you set up the trust. You can give the trustees full discretion to do as they please or you can specify precisely how your money is to be used. There are particular types of trusts and special types of investments that trusts can make that can be especially beneficial in France.

Trusts can be beneficial even to French resident people of modest means – say £350,000. It is certainly worth investing a little money to see if they can be of use to you as the tax savings can run to many thousands of pounds. If you are thinking of trusts as an investment vehicle and tax planning measure you must take advice early – months before you are thinking of moving to France. Otherwise it will be too late.

Keeping Track of Your Investments

Whatever you decide to do about investments – put them in a trust, appoint investment managers to manage them in your own name or manage them yourself – you should always keep an up-to-date list of your assets and investments *and tell you family where to find it*. Make a file. By all means have a computer file but print off a good old-fashioned paper copy. Keep it in an obvious place known to your family. Keep it with your will and the deeds to your house. Also keep in it either the originals of bank account books, share certificates, etc. or a note of where they are to be found.

As a lawyer it is very frustrating – and expensive for the client – when, after the parents' death, the children come in with a suitcase full of correspondence and old chequebooks. It all has to be gone through and all those old banks contacted lest there should be £1,000,000 lurking in a forgotten account. There never is, and it wastes a lot of time and money.

Conclusion

Buying a home in France – whether to use as a holiday home, as an investment or to live in permanently – is as safe as buying one in the UK.

The rules may appear complicated. Our rules would if you were a French person coming to this country. That apparent complexity is often no more than lack of familiarity.

There are tens of thousands of British people who have bought homes in France. Most have had no real problems. Most have enjoyed years of holidays in France. Many have seen their property rise substantially in value. Many are now thinking of retiring to France.

For a trouble-free time you simply need to keep your head and to seek advice from experts who can help you make the four basic decisions:

- **Who should own the property?**
- **What am I going to do about inheritance?**
- **What am I going to do about controlling my potential tax liabilities?**
- **If I am going to live in France, what am I going to do about my investments?**

Cost of Living

Many people report that the cost of living in France is about 25 per cent cheaper than in England. Much, of course, depends on where you live and what you do.

Coming Back to England

You are, of course, free to return to England at any stage.

Very few people do.

Many people wonder whether they should preserve an escape route by, for example, keeping their old house and renting it out until they are sue of their intentions. Generally I feel this is a bad idea. The house will be a worry and a distraction. How do you manage it? Are the tenants ruining your lovely home? The house will probably not be ideal for investment purposes and may generate you less than you could get by putting the value elsewhere. It may not be in an area with good capital growth. The income (and capital value in euro terms) will be at the mercy of exchange rate fluctuations. The house might not even suit your requirements if you do return to England. It also encourages you to look backwards instead of forwards. I believe you are usually better selling up and investing the proceeds elsewhere.

Retirement to France

Pensions

Your State pension will be paid in the way described in 'Social Services and Welfare Benefits', pp.240–7.

If you have a company pension it will be paid wherever the pension scheme rules dictate. Some permit the administrators to pay the money into any bank anywhere and others, ostensibly for security reasons, insist on the money being paid into a UK bank account.

If yours does this you can, of course, simply ask the bank to send it on to you in France. Bank transfer costs mean that it is probable best to do this only three or four times per year. You can also make an annual arrangement with some currency dealers whereby they will send the money at an exchange rate that will apply for the whole year. This provides certainty of income. Whether you will do better or worse than you would have done by waiting is in the lap of the gods.

If you have a government pension (army, civil service, police, etc.) your pension will still be taxed in the UK. Otherwise the pension should be paid gross (i.e. tax free) and it will be taxed in France. *See* 'Taxation', pp.176–206 for more information.

Settling In

07

The key to your happy stay in France will be a matter of attitude. Yours. Some people don't make it in France because they have genuine family problems, some because of money problems or for professional reasons, but, sad to say, others simply don't want to make the adjustments needed to feel at home in this lovely country. Of course there are people who stay in France, never learn French, make no French friends, talk disparagingly of their hosts and survive in little pockets in parts of the country that support a British community. They are despised by the British who have made the effort and ignored by the French. (The exceptions are the truly international communities, as in parts of the Côte d'Azur and the Alps, but these are so multinational as hardly to be considered France.) Others come back because they have not realized that a certain mental adjustment is required on their part.

Speaking French is, of course, very important, but attitude is even more so. Some people genuinely have enormous difficulty with languages and, if you have never learned French before, it takes time. French people will accept this if you at least make an effort. Some people have so much personality that they can communicate quite well without knowing a foreign language. That's OK, too, so long as the message is that you want to be part of the community, not a lordly parasite. One English lady who has just arrived and speaks good French hopes to give free English lessons in order to, as she puts it, give something back. Another Englishman who had been in the country for 11 years says that if he gives anything to his neighbours, it is returned twofold. He is talking of personal relationships, by the way, not commercial ones!

This is not just a question of good manners; it is one of self-interest. You are, after all, going to be immersed in one of the most influential and interesting cultures on earth. You won't enjoy the swimming if you sit on the beach. The advice of everyone who has made a success of living in France is 'get involved.' One elderly couple has been there for a few years, living deep in the countryside. They attend all the local fundraising dinners and picnics – speaking little French and without an idea what they are for, but enjoying them – and are accepted by their community as a result. The spirit of hospitality that has been shown to so many British people has brought forth a fierce Francophile response. If ever you got a dressing-down for being rude about France it would probably be from a British person living there.

I don't suggest all is sweetness and light. A high-pressure job in a big city will be stressful wherever you are. Business will always be competitive and create rivals. The good relationships that exist between locals and British expatriates in many areas do so because of a symbiotic relationship and, should that ever become a competitive one, it will become strained. There are areas of the country where a surfeit of foreigners has caused resentment. In the country areas and small towns that make up most of France, though, you will, on the whole, find French people helpful, friendly and hospitable, so long as you don't think you are Henry V. *Entente cordiale* will work for you.

Removals

As there is no customs restriction in transporting some or all of your worldly goods to other EU countries from the UK, in that respect you might just as well be moving to another part of Britain. However, numerous specialist removal firms exist to tackle the special problems of transporting your belongings across the Channel and their advertisements can be found in the Francophile magazines. As with any removal firm, it pays to shop around and go by personal recommendation if possible. If you are only transporting a small load, small ads in the same magazines often offer space to share in large vans heading for a specific area on a specific date. Also *see* p.304.

Retirement

It makes sense, doesn't it? To look forward to one's 'third age', as the French call it, in a country with good weather, inexpensive accommodation, efficient health services, cheaper motoring costs and notorious longevity? All these things are true. Many of the drawbacks connected with life in France are attached to work. Unless you are going to the Côte d'Azur or the most fashionable addresses in major cities, you could sell your UK home and move into something similar with a handsome surplus. Moving away from family and friends? You may actually find that you see more of them than you did before!

Yet, of all those who fail to settle, people who go at retirement age have the highest casualty rate. Why? It doesn't have to be so. Here are some of the reasons for it happening. Without being morbid, the fact is that some people like the thought of dying in their own country. If you don't want to exchange this for the possibility of a few more years on earth, at some stage you will go back. Another thing to consider is that, if a partner dies and he or she was the only French-speaking one, it will make the survivor feel even lonelier than they would expect at such a time. If you have only been to France on holidays previously, there may come a time when the holidays are over, the crowds have gone, the evenings are drawing in and you find you don't know charming Madame in the *boulangerie* or the garrulous patron of the café as well as you thought. Unless you are happy enough with both your French language and *milieu*, you may get a panic attack and find yourself wistfully thinking of a stroll down to the King's Head for a pint of bitter. This is actually a serious hurdle – people are often set in their ways by retirement and a sudden, complete absence of familiar things may just be a step too far.

These things aside, we now know that keeping the mind active with advancing years is one of the important ways of keeping well. The challenge of learning a new language, making new friends and fitting into a new society may be just the stimulus we need. The most serious danger we have to face is French inheritance law, which is so vastly different from what we are used to, so draconian, that it requires special attention, especially if you have much capital tied up in your house, *see* **Financial Implications**.

In principle, there is no problem in having income from investments or a UK private or state pension paid to you in France. In practice, while the UK remains outside the EMU, there is a theoretical vulnerability to exchange loss – that is, if sterling weakens dramatically or the euro hardens a lot, your pension will be worth less in France than in the UK. Most people we have talked to felt that the benefits outweighed the risks, especially when you consider the savings in road and council tax. Be mindful of the possibility, however, and don't overexpose yourself. Exchange rate fluctuations have spoiled the dreams of more than one family. This, of course, does not apply if your pension is French or if you are drawing income from assets brought to France or anywhere else in Euroland. To localize your investments is a way to avoid this risk. Apart from all that, majority opinion in the UK at the time of writing is that it will enter Euroland in the next decade, however reluctantly. Then, all currency risk factors will evaporate.

As a retired person (over 65 for a man and, currently, 60 for a woman) you are entitled to the full use of the French health care system on the same basis as a French person. In practice, because in France retirement is at 60, you will often receive treatment as a retired person at 60 – whether a man or a woman. *See* 'Health and Emergencies', pp.235–40.

Working and Employment

Finding a Job

This is not a book about employment or business in France, but here are some observations. One: if you want a job to go with that house, anything above the menial will require adequate French (*see* p.255). Two: as a resident of the EU there are no official impediments to you getting a job in France, even before your *carte de séjour*. In fact your *carte de séjour* application will need to show that you have a job (or other source of income) and a place to live. If you find you can't get one without the other, a not uncommon situation, get a temporary *carte de séjour*. Three: if you are a professional, make sure your qualification is valid in France. French CVs are quite short – usually no more than a page – and your academic qualifications are as important as your experience. Include a passport photo and write the covering letter by hand.

Apart from the fact that social services are very much better, the mechanics from then on are more or less the same as in the UK. There are government employment offices called ANPE (Agence National Pour l'Emploi), private recruitment agencies, the press, the internet and a number of international organizations that recruit dual-language staff. In some situations – such as ski resorts at the height of the season, on the coast in the summer and vineyards at harvest-time – temporary work can be found without much need of French, but, on the whole, a settled job requires a good working knowledge of the language. In most professions being foreign is a definite competitive disadvantage, but in others it isn't and it becomes less of a problem in proportion to your language skills. This is because of the vast number of English-speaking visitors and, if you are competent in your own profession and reasonably confident in your new language, openings in a host of areas from banking to hairdressing may occur. Always keep a weather eye on the general economic climate though, as in a downturn it will always be foreigners who find the opportunity windows narrowing first.

Both Britain and France have gone through some traumatic changes from the average employee's point of view over the last 30 years, although they have been very different in character. In France, working conditions were poor by western European standards, pay low, job security bad and strikes common. Now, productivity and pay have improved dramatically, there is a 35-hour week and 72 per cent of the workforce takes more than 5 weeks' holiday a year, compared with 22 per cent in Britain.

If you are employed in France permanently, by a French company, and are insured under French social security laws, you are entitled to local benefits and will not be paying UK contributions. However, in the many other in-between situations that are actually more likely – such as needing your UK benefit or pension while house- or job-hunting in France – you may be able to access UK benefits, assuming that you are entitled to them there. Even the Jobseeker's Allowance – the contribution-based element – anyway, is available. It is all quite complex, though, and you will have to get the DSS form SA29 to see what your entitlement is and how to get it. Contact the DSS International Section, Newcastle-upon-Tyne NE98 1YX (**t** 0191 218 7269).

We couldn't recommend working illegally even if we agreed with it. The attraction is that you escape all the costs associated with being 'legal', but the disadvantages are also substantial. Finding employment is the first and, unless you have a very specialized skill, this will probably be limited to the English-speaking communities, who will be doing themselves no favours by employing other than local labour. Then, if you have an accident at work, you have no legal insurance cover. In some trades where there is a shortage of qualified French people, as there is in some regions with building, this is less of a problem, but unofficial, especially foreign, tradespeople have got themselves a cowboy reputation even among British ex-pats. Also, you can't really expect a big welcome for cheating a system that is costing your hosts so much.

Self-employment

You may be too young to have a pension, too independent to work for somebody else and have some spare capital. If so, your mind will turn towards the entrepreneurial option and you may see yourself running a business. It is being done and sometimes with much success. In that most French of industries, in the town of Cognac, a couple of names were made, after all, by an Englishman and an Irishman called Hine and Hennessey a couple of centuries ago! For most modern punters, though, something lucrative enough to support them and integrate them into French society is the limit of their ambitions.

Much of what you need to know about setting up a business in France is common sense. There is a saying among British residents in France that newcomers 'leave their brains on the other side of the Channel'. Would you, for instance, come to Britain without the first idea of the language, law or customs and set yourself up in a business at which you had little experience even in your home country? Probably not. Yet some people think that this is possible in France. So, before launching a new career, ask yourself whether or not you would be likely to succeed at your chosen enterprise in Britain. If the answer is yes, ask if your language skills are good enough or you are prepared to make them good enough to perform as well in a foreign tongue. If the answer is again yes, you are ready to confront the problems that will face you in France.

These consist of social service contributions at intimidating levels, a labyrinthine and vast bureaucracy and competition from people who seem to survive on profit margins as thin as a leaf of *millefeuille*. If you intend to set up a business when you apply for your *carte de séjour*, you will be expected to register it, which has to be done anyway before you go any further. This is achieved at the Chambre de Commerce (for businesses), Chambre des Métiers (artisans) or Chambre d'Agriculture, (farmers, agriculture, horticulture, etc.), depending on which is relevant. Be prepared to have at least £50,000 available for establishing any sort of meaningful enterprise. Most French banks will not be prepared to lend more than you are going to invest yourself, nor are you likely to get more than a seven-year term, even though profit margins are slim and up to 65 per cent can be eaten up by social security payments. A simple way to approach this whole matter is through London business branches of the principal French banking houses.

Yet, as with so much in French life, there is a paradox here. This is a country of small businesses and there is a raft of incentives to help take the sting out of some of the red tape. Both start-up finance and tax breaks are available from the industrial development authority DATAR (Délégations à l'Aménagement du Territoire et à l'Action Régionale; London Office, 21–24 Grosvenor Place, London SW1X 7HU), which will be helpful even if you are not targeting a specifically depressed area (although that would be an advantage). There are also branches of the Agence Régional de Développement that may be of assistance with launching your enterprise. These can be found, as their name implies, scattered throughout the country. There are also organizations called Centres de Gestions, a collection of professionals whose function it is to assist with start-ups. Representatives of the amorphous bureaucracy may even be helpful in dealing with it. There's another paradox: for every obstructive official there will be somebody else who will try to help you beat the system. Business licences are waived for the first year of operation and these can be extended with the approval of the local authorities. There is a status for the self-employed called EURL (Entreprise Unipersonelle à Responsabilité Limitée) that gives you some protection against creditors.

For all the mechanics of start-up, approach your *mairie* and *chambre de commerce*. If you want to set yourself up as a one-person business you can't just get the cards printed and start work. This is illegal and can result in very heavy fines or even deportation. The French don't like untidiness and everything has to have a proper, identifiable slot. You may be sent on a week-long business start-up course, for which you will be expected to pay. If you can't speak French yet, nobody translates this, but don't worry – you will still get your certificate. Theories as to why you should get a certificate for a course of which you may have not understood one word range from one that suggests they are checking that you are really serious to another that states that they simply want your money, but it is most likely because the mammoth of French bureaucracy says so. Going it alone requires a lot of commitment and the acceptance that you will have to deal with the notorious French civil service. Unless you are completely fluent and streetwise, it is a good idea to have a French partner to help unravel the red tape or at least engage the services of local accountants or other professionals. If your business is a bit bigger, of course, your own British bank, legal practice or accountants will probably have a French branch or correspondents who, for a price, will give you the help you need.

A better bet than starting your own business might be to buy someone else's. It is said that money goes further in this market and, with a favourable exchange rate, it should go further still. There are two drawbacks, the first of which is finding a suitable business in the first place. Many smaller businesses in France are family-run and therefore tend to be inherited, while others change ownership by word of mouth. The second disadvantage may only affect you if you are an aspiring Richard Branson instead of someone looking for a way to live in France, which is that many small businesses operate at profit margins that would be unacceptable in the UK and don't have the potential for very much increased profitability or expansion.

You may find that there is a business attached to the property you want to buy – a *gîte*, some vines or an orchard, for instance – and you get into business because of that. Perhaps it's the other way round and you like the idea of the business that has a house coming with it. A wild boar farm? A hazelnut farm? Both properties are on the books of a Périgord estate agent at the time of writing. More likely, you are just looking for a business as a business. If this is the case, you should be aware that, whatever type it is, it involves at least two

Jeune Agriculteur

A note for those under the age of 40. If you set up as a *jeune agriculteur* (young farmer) and have a property with sufficient land (this varies depending on what you intend to do), you qualify for reduced social security contributions, the right to various grants for diversifying and free advice on what to grow or how to do it. Application should be made to the Chambre d'Agriculture. This can be done by the *notaire* at the same time as the purchase contract for the property and can be put in as a *clause suspensive* – that is, if you are not issued with the licence to farm, then you don't continue with the purchase and you get your deposit back.

distinct negotiations. The actual property, machinery (if there is any), buildings, fixtures and fittings are sold separately from the goodwill, trade name and customers. The stock is often negotiated separately again. The property is called *murs* (walls) the goodwill *fonds* (literally, funds) or *fonds de commerce*. Renting is usually more economically sensible than buying industrial property.

Much of what is written about setting up or buying a business in France applies equally in Feltham, Fife or Fermanagh. The cardinal points are the same: know what you are doing, be thorough in your research and take competent professional advice. Don't leave your brains on the other side of the Channel.

Education

Apart from job concerns, the most common reasons given for people not feeling able to live abroad centre on the education of their children. However good the education might be, the notion of sending a child to a school where he or she can't understand a word that is said is enough to send a shiver up any parent's spine. In fact, it needn't. Children under ten adapt amazingly quickly and well. Children under six don't so much adapt as grow into it. Toddlers can learn two languages simultaneously with the panache of a circus performer. For older children, it is a challenge, but not an insuperable one. Few people can fail to learn a language in an environment of total immersion, which is what a school is. Very much older children are probably too involved in their academic careers for the switch to be beneficial, but beneficial it will be for the others because they will enjoy one of the best educational systems in the world. Even if they learn nothing but French, at least as bilingual adults they need never be unemployed. In fact, having your children educated in the French state school system may be an argument for going to France, not the reverse.

Compared to the British system, the French one is rigid, uniform and centralized. There was a time when kids at different ends of the country would be doing the same lesson at the same time on the same day, but they have loosened up a bit since then. In France, education is not simply a problem for the finance minister (although it is that, too), it is a national obsession. Teachers have social status, truancy is rare and there is constant parent–teacher consultation. In France, fathers don't go to sort out a teacher because their child got into trouble at school, they cringe when teacher sends a note in the child's exercise book asking why they didn't do their homework. British people can find the level of discipline usual in France strange, but it is because the status of education is different. It makes few concessions to political correctness and the result seems to be one of the best-educated populations in Europe. Critics of the French system will say it does not encourage individual self-expression and creativity, is too rigid and old-fashioned and doesn't include a hefty sports curriculum. They would, however, be hard put to it to describe the French as an inexpressive, uncreative people who could never win the soccer European or World Cup or a Rugby Six Nations Grand Slam! A more serious criticism is that French teachers are slow to recognize learning difficulties, such as dyslexia and that the schools are unsympathetic in dealing with them. This has certainly been true in the past, although efforts to improve are in train.

This is how it works: education is obligatory and free between the ages of six and 16. To assist working mothers, state help is given earlier. The *écoles maternelles* are nursery schools that take children from the age of three – and sometimes before – and you can sometimes spot them nestling around the local *mairie*. There are even pre-nursery schools on offer, called *jardins d'enfants*. These earliest stages are followed by junior school, or *écoles primaire* or *élémentaire*, when, at the age of six, the children join an 11-year class system during which the years are counted backwards, not starting with year 11 age 6 when they enter but at *sixième* (year 6, age 11), from which they may aspire to the first, or what in the UK would be the sixth, form. Subjects taught include French, history, geography and civic studies, mathematics, science and technology, PE, arts, crafts and music. From the age of nine, they are offered a foreign language; most choose English. At 11 (*sixième* or *cycle d'adaptation*), children go on to a *collège*, or, to give it its full title, a *collège d'enseignement secondaire*. The first three years there are spent with a uniform curriculum and, during this time, students have a chance to consider what they are going to specialize in. During the *troisième*, by means of the *cycle d'orientation* they are able to add more subjects. At 15, the further direction of their career is decided by exams, with the more academic going to the *lycée* while others have options of technical and vocational courses. At the end of every year after that, the results of more exams can switch the students from the academic to the more vocational education stream and vice versa.

If the education offered by the state is so good, why is there a flourishing private sector in French education? Not, most people agree, because of the

On Course

So – as a pupil in France, you are on course for the academic stars at the *lycée* and your family is well pleased. The trouble is, you start having nightmares about something called the *baccalauréat*, which may be the terrible and final culmination of this gruelling process. In fact, it's not one specific exam, but a raft of them that varies in orientation, difficulty and use. With it you can get into university or technical college. Alternatively, you can go to preparatory school for one of the *Grandes Écoles*, the last word in tertiary and élitist education. Entrance here is by competitive exam and the purpose is to turn out super-specialists in engineering, science, administration and management studies. Napoleon dreamt them up to keep his army and empire ticking over efficiently. There are now 250 of them and they represent the very pinnacle of a vast, tiered educational system.

quality of the academic courses. Because of its uniformity, there is little scope for subjects such as religion in the system. So strict is the secularism that items reflecting faith, such as headscarves or crucifixes, may not be worn. Christians, especially Catholics, have therefore set up their own private, fee-paying schools, although these receive a state subsidy if they follow the national curriculum. There are also international schools, some bilingual and some multilingual, but they are generally confined to the big cities and Provence-Alpes-Côte d'Azur. It is in one of these that children too old, or too briefly in the country to slot into the French state system, can be happily accommodated. However, even private education does not carry the cost burden that it does in the UK as there are varying degrees of state subsidy. For example, a private secondary school in Bergerac in the Dordogne will cost approximately £200 a term, while a recently established bilingual school for the children of aircraft industry children in Toulouse costs £8,000 a year – and that is expensive by French private school standards.

Unfortunately, the system does not function perfectly everywhere. As elsewhere in the Western world, inner-city and ghetto areas have their depressingly familiar problems of crime, violence and drug abuse. However, as you are zoned for your school, you would have to be living in a substantially disadvantaged area for this to affect you. This does not mean that you won't find drugs in most of the more upmarket areas, but they do not have such an impact on society as in the UK. Perhaps the kids are too busy comparing binomial distribution of random variables in the playground?

Money and Banks

The euro is the national currency of France and, while most French people still think in francs, by the time you read this book they may have got out of the habit. Most regular British visitors are likely to do the same initially, especially as the old calculation of ten francs to the pound was such an easy one to manage. If you are into architecture or history, the euro notes are attractive, their arches and bridges following technology through the centuries as the denominations increase through notes of 5, 10, 20, 50, 100, 200 to 500. The coinage varies in design from country to country but is usable Euroland-wide with coins of 2, 5, 10, 20 and 50 cents (which the French are referring to as *centimes*) and 1 and 2 euros. The smaller denominations are confusingly similar and have to be handled with caution until you are used to them. While the UK remains outside the EMU, people with fixed incomes in sterling have to be aware of the dangers of fluctuations in exchange rates (*see* p.132).

You will probably already know from experience that visiting France presents little trouble from a banking point of view – most tourists now use a credit or debit card, or euros purchased before or on arrival, and travellers' cheques are waning in popularity as a result. Cards bearing Cirrus and Visa emblems are generally welcomed and credit cards as a whole are accepted almost as widely as in the UK and considerably more so than in Germany or Italy. However, if you are going to live in France, you will not want to incur the charges they entail, so you should open an account with a French bank. There are British banks with branches in France, but these are found only in the bigger cities and it makes more sense to sign up with a local French one. Crédit Agricole – which pays us nothing for saying this! – saw this gap in the market and has opened a division targeting British customers. It is called Britline and is based at its branch in Calvados, Normandy. It offers such things as an English-speaking telephone banking service and Internet banking. If you have invested in a property in France that you rent out or visit your second home only occasionally, this may suit you. However, if you are living permanently in France, it makes sense to use a bank with a branch convenient to where you live, work or shop.

Although the British and the French will argue about which country has the more inefficient banking system, there are some serious differences in how French banks operate. The most alarming thing to the new British client of a French bank is the overdraft rule: sign a cheque for money that isn't there and that is the end of your account! You will be given 30 days to sort things out, then not only will your account be closed but also your name will go on the Bank of France's computer and you won't be able to open one anywhere else for five years. Even the police are informed. It may seem an overreaction. but it does concentrate the mind. Another surprise is that stopping a cheque is by no means as simple in France as it is in Britain, and cheques are used for daily transactions more often in France than the UK. Once you have opened your account, you will receive, with your chequebook, a *relevé d'identité bancaire* (known as a RIB – pronounced *reeb*), a useful document that will let you open accounts or set up direct debits. Ask your bank for several of these as soon as you open your account – they are supplied free of charge and you will need one each for services such as gas and electricity.

Most French banks issue debit cards, or charge cards, that are debited to your account more or less immediately, just like a British debit card. Credit cards are not really compatible with the overdraft regulations mentioned above and so are not issued by banks, but by the credit card companies themselves. The most commonly accepted cards in France are Carte Bleue and Carte Bleue/Visa. The main difference in their use is that a PIN number is required for all transactions, not simply for using ATMs. The card works on the chip (*puce*) in the card, not the magnetic strip that the techno-conscious French think outdated. This arrangement means that you have a safety mechanism if your card is stolen, but you are not usually asked for a bank guarantee card with your cheque, so your chequebook is what you have to watch!

Bank Accounts

Who Can Open a Bank Account?

Anybody. You will need to prove that you are over 18 and provide the bank with proof of your identity, your civil status (*état civil*), your address in France and the various other bits and pieces of information that will vary from bank to bank. The French have always been a trifle bureaucratic when it comes to opening bank accounts but in these days of international terrorism anything to do with the movement of money from one country to another gives rise to enquiry.

The type of bank account that you will open will depend upon whether you are resident or non-resident in France (*see* .pp.178–80). For most practical purposes there is little difference between the two types of account.

Which type of account?

Most people will operate a simple current account (*compte de chèques*) and will ask the bank to make payments of the electricity, water and other bills by direct payment (*virements*) from that account. There are no cheque guarantee cards in France, yet cheques are still widely accepted because of the severe penalties that result from abuse of a cheque. Ask for a Carte Bleue (French SWITCH card). You will be allocated a PIN number for use with it. This will be required for any purchases using the card.

Banking Tips

Whichever bank you use and whichever account you open the two most important messages are:

- **Learn to write the date in French and use the French crossed 7 rather than the English 7 when writing cheques.**
- **Keep a close eye on your bank statements and reconcile them to the payments you sent to France and the items you paid out in France.**
- **Make sure that you do not write cheques when there are insufficient funds in the account to cover those cheques.**

French banks pay no interest on current accounts. It is therefore sensible also to have a deposit account. Most banks will arrange for the balance on the current account over a certain to be transferred automatically into an interest pay account. Interest rates in the Euroland are low.

If your needs are more sophisticated study carefully the various types of account available to you. These, and the terms of conditions of use, deferred substantially from the accounts you may be familiar with in England.

Your Existing UK Account

There is no reason why you should not retain this account. It will probably be convenient to do so.

'Offshore' Accounts

These are the subject of considerable mystique. Many people resident in France think that by having an offshore bank account they do not have to pay tax in France. This is not true. They only do not pay the tax if they illegally hide the existence of the bank account from the French taxman. This is dealt with more fully in the section on taxation below. There is no reason why you should not have an offshore bank account either as the owner of a holiday home in France or as a person resident in France but you should only do so for good reason. If you are thinking of taking up residence in France you should take detailed financial advice. This would include advice on the issue about the location of bank accounts.

Utilities

Domestic power supply in France is characterized by a reliance on nuclear generating stations, less use of mains gas and the continuance of wood-burning fires, especially in the countryside. This difference of emphasis from that of the UK is partly because the population is much more thinly spread and, in the case of nuclear power, the result of decisive and ruthless central long-term planning.

Electricity

Electricity in France is cheaper than in the UK, thanks to the mixed blessing of a regiment of nuclear power stations. It is run by a state-owned body called Electricité de France (EDF–GDF, a duel body with Gaz de France), which has a good reputation with its customers and a bad one with environmentalists. It supplies technicians as well as power if you have an electricity problem. As a new householder you may be asked for a deposit and, when you open your account, your *relevé d'identité bancaire* will be needed.

EDF will suggest which tariff is suitable for your circumstances. At the moment, there are three options. The first is *Tarif de Base*, which is only for people who don't have any true electrical consumption and so is probably not for you. *Heures Creuses, Heures Pleines* is the most widespread system, with which you get 8 hours of cheap-rate electricity during a 24-hour period (the hours are always marked on the back of the bill). Finally, there is *Tempo*, which breaks down into three periods – 'blue days' (300 per year and very cheap); 'white days' (43 per year, during which you get eight hours of cheaper electricity); and 'red days' (22 days per year, falling between 1 November and 31 March, when the price is horribly expensive). For the latter, a red light comes on (wherever you have chosen to have it installed) the night before, to warn you for the following day. You can only install this system if you have a form of heating other than electricity, such as an open fire (they don't want the responsibility of you freezing to death on a 'red day'). There is speculation that new EU legislation may put an end to this system.

If you are considering buying a property that does not have mains electricity, check the installation charge, as it can be prohibitive if you are any distance from a source. If you buy a ruin or somewhere previously lived in by an elderly person, the electricity will need not only rewiring, but you will also need to change the input kilowatts. Many older properties only had a 3-kW supply (you can now have anything from 9kW to 36kW) because their owners used few or no electrical appliances and cooked on wood-burning stoves or used bottled gas. Contact the EDF–GDF (Electricité de France–Gaz de France) and they will send a technician to assess what you intend to use. You can use a number of domestic appliances on the lower wattage, for example, but if you plan to use electric radiators or power tools, then you should make this clear as EDF has to supply you with sufficient power for your usage. If you intend to use power tools or live in the deepest countryside where the power has to travel a long distance, it is recommended that you ask for the incoming supply to be in '3-Phase', which means there is less risk of overloading the system. The average cost for a family of three living in an old house of about

150sq m is €1,800 per annum. This includes all standard appliances, but if you have a wood fire or use gas as well, then obviously you will need to add these costs in order to work out your total annual energy expenditure.

As every tourist knows, French plugs have two or three round pins, depending on whether the plug is earthed or not, and the system is 220 volts, so most UK appliances will work, if not at 100 per cent efficacy, if you use an adaptor. This doesn't apply to TV sets because the UK system is different from that of the rest of Europe. A television purchased for use in the UK will not receive the terrestrial transmissions from French transmitters. France uses Sécam L, the UK uses PAL I and the rest of Europe uses PAL B/G.

Gas

There are many aspects of French life that differ from the British system and many, when you look for the cause, come down to the relative size of the country. In a land of huge distances between towns and with a great part of the population living in the country, mains gas does not figure as prominently as it does in Britain. Gaz de France – the other half of EDF–GDF – operates the gas supply in towns and cities and offers similar discount systems to those of their electricity service. In the countryside, gas is bought in bottles at the supermarket or delivered in tankers to domestic tanks. There are four tariffs for this, depending on your consumption, and an expert will visit to advise you on which is best for your needs if, say, you are installing central heating or gas water heating. If you buy an old house, you will probably spend about three times as much on heating it as you would if you bought a newly built house that complies with the insulation norms introduced in 2001. Average consumption for a family of three in an older house of approx 150sq m is €1,000 per annum. Again, you have to add the cost of the use of your electrical appliances to this to assess your annual energy consumption. Butane bottles can only be used indoors, and there are French gas cookers designed to use with them, with a panel behind which the bottle stands. Propane bottles (which are larger) can be stood outdoors, however, so, if your gas cooker is against an outside wall, you could consider drilling through in order that the longer-lasting bottle and its changeover valve can remain outside. This makes it possible for a supplier to deliver and install replacement bottles for you – gas bottles are heavy and not everyone likes hauling them back from the petrol station in the boot of the car.

Water

There are still people who ask if the tap water in France is safe to drink. It is, although in some areas there is talk of pollution from agricultural fertilizers.

It may be that the myth of poor French tap water started after the war, when allied troops confronted contaminated supply systems, or perhaps it is because the French prefer to drink bottled water, a practice that goes back centuries. Either way, French mains tap water is safe to drink and is supplied by a number of private companies that vary with the region. French water is metered and supposed to be some of the most expensive in Europe, yet most of our informants insisted they spent less than in the UK. A possible explanation for this is that, in a country as prone to water shortages as France is in the south, people become very sensitive to water consumption and, whether consciously or not, save water. Showers, for instance, are much more common than baths and most new lavatory cisterns have a half-flush option. Prices vary with each *commune* and with the services on offer. They are enormously variable, so, if you intend to carry on a business that involves a high consumption of water , it is vital to check the price.

Wood and Solar Power

Most central heating is electric and, although gas is common in the towns, you can't be in the French countryside long without noticing the number of wood-burning heating systems. Once again, the size of the country explains this, as making oil deliveries is tiresome and costly and there is still a sustainable supply of firewood. A hot-air domestic heating system run from an iron burner in the main fireplace (called an *insert*) is common. Wood is measured by the cubic metre (a *stère*, pronounced 'stair') and can be supplied cut into the 30cm lengths ideal for a woodburner or 1m lengths suitable for a wide, open fireplace. Wood is ordered by the *brasse*, which is four *stères*, so you will need a place in which to store four cubic metres of wood.

Ask your friendly neighbour or at the *mairie* for a recommended local supplier. If you buy a property with its own woodland and cut your own timber, you will obviously have a free supply, but don't forget that this 'wet' wood must be stacked in the open air for at least two years before it is usable.

Solar power is also on the increase in the parts of the country where there are sufficient hours of sunlight. To help you decide what power source is best for you, there is an agency called Agence Française pour la Maîtrise de L'Énergie that, for a fee, will advise on your heating and insulation problems of all kinds. It is to be found at 27 rue Louis Vicat, F-75737 Paris 15 Cedex (**t** 01 47 65 20 20). There are grants available for installing solar panels. For more information, visit **www.ademe.fr**, which is the national organization dealing with such things. It can supply lists of registered installers and, if you use one of these installers, you will qualify for a subsidy. Alternatively, visit the Infos Tecsol (**www.tecsol.fr/uk/accueil1-uk.htm**) site, which is in English, or ask at your *mairie*.

Post and Telecommunications

The eccentricities that once made French communications systems different from those of the UK – such as the Parisian compressed air message delivery service – have now disappeared and the service offered by all national postal organizations is tending towards uniformity. Apart from the colour scheme, the main difference between the French and UK services are the Minitel, some strange-looking phones and the places where you can buy stamps.

Postal Services

French post offices, with their distinctive livery of bright yellow and blue, not only sell stamps and process and deliver mail but, as in the UK, also act as a bank and offer savings accounts. They also have Minitel terminals (*see* below), public telephones and offer fax and telex services. They are indicated by the sign La Poste, but were formerly called PTT and so, in out-of-the-way places, may still be signposted as such. Postboxes are painted yellow and are plentiful. A letterbox for your home is often a separate unit rather than a slot in the door. They can be bought from the postman and must be positioned close to the road. If you don't put one up straight away, it does mean that you get to meet your postman or woman and practise your French. They'll enjoy finding out about what you are up to, too, so, if this doesn't appeal, put the letter box up as soon as you can. Postal services are quite quick, but this does depend on where you live. Post to and from the UK takes between two and five days. When sending anything important, such as legal documents, always ask that it be *recommandé avec accusé de réception* (registered with confirmation receipt). *Tabacs* sell stamps and there is usually a postbox (bright yellow) outside them. Post office opening times vary depending on how far out in the country you are and they may shut for lunch in the more bucolic environments but are otherwise open from at least 9am to 7pm, Monday to Friday. Saturday morning has variable opening times in the country districts, while, in Paris, there is Sunday morning opening until 11am in at least one post office per *arrondissement*.

Telephones

In the not too distant past, if you asked the *patron* of a country café if it were possible to telephone from his establishment, he would helpfully show you a museum piece of a handset and, over a crackling line, you would struggle to hear and make yourself heard and understood. Thirty years later, the proprietor pushes a contemporary handset across the counter. The charge, he indicates, is on the monitor, up behind the bar. The point is that, from having an obsolescent phone system a generation ago, France now has one of the most advanced and sophisticated in the world. The French telephone system is run by France Télécom, the actual workings of which have very little to distinguish them from those of British Telecom. France Télécom controls all phone lines, but, as in Britain, phone services have been deregulated and there is choice of provider, such as Onetel and 9 Télécom. There are others, but they are often transient, as in the UK, and it may be a good idea to check who is in the market by looking at **www.pagesjaunes.fr** under *télécommunications*. That way you can compare prices and services offered.

Most public telephones are phonecard-operated only (buy them in much the same places as you do in the UK – look for a blue bell sign), but BT says that surveys show the French to prefer the British card and cash system. It's certainly the case that being caught at midnight with an important call to make and no card is aggravating. A half-price rate applies to calls made between 10.30pm and 8am.

French telephone directories are listed by *commune*, with each village and town in alphabetical order, so, if you don't know where someone lives, you have to either phone **t** 12 for directory enquiries or look it up on Minitel at a post office (Minitel is also available as an installable program for computers). The disadvantage is largely for people who need to look up a dozen numbers countrywide at one go, as Minitel is slow and only gives you three numbers at a time. There are other services available from France Télécom that are similar to those in the UK. For example, you can have incoming calls only, for a *gîte* phone (*service téléséjour*), and you can have itemized billing (*facturation détaillée*). Staff in the France Télécom offices are helpful and there is an office in most towns of any size.

Mobile Phones

The main mobile phone companies are SFR, Bouygues and Itineris (which is now run by Orange). As a generalization, Itineris is supposed to cover the largest area of France, while SFR and Bouygues are more geared for town-dwellers where there are more *émetteurs* (transmitter masts), but this scenario is changing rapidly as more signal stations are installed. While, at the time of writing, it is not actually illegal to do so, you will be pulled over for dangerous driving if seen using a mobile at the wheel. If you want to use your French mobile phone in the UK, you must ask for Option Europe and will have to enter a PIN code in order to retrieve your messages – do this before you leave France. If you are taking your British mobile phone to France, check with your service provider to make sure that you can phone and text using their service – the company should be able to provide you with a leaflet outlining the costs of making and receiving calls from the UK and within France, numbers to dial, information on accessing voicemail and so forth, all of which varies with each provider.

If your French property is going to be a second home, you may not want to pay the substantial standing charges that a France Télécom land line will entail. You can take your mobile with you, but as you may have discovered, costs to mobiles abroad are high, even receiving calls. It is often possible to get over this by installing a French SIM card in your mobile.

Minitel

This was the system that epitomized the renaissance of the French telecommunications network. Dating from 1985, it is a phone-line-based videotext and teletext information system using monitors that can be bought or rented from France Télécom and are also situated in every post office. Most observers say that it is becoming redundant because of the internet, but, for things specifically French, it is still a useful tool, offering access to at least 25,000 public and professional services.

The Internet

France Télécom also dominates the French internet scene and has its own ISP – *wanadoo.fr*. Use of the internet has not spread as fast in France as in the UK, probably because Minitel made it less revolutionary. Minitel can be accessed on the Net, of course, from anywhere. The other main servers are Compuserve, AOL France and Vivendi, and the major search engine is called Voilà. It is often recommended that you use a French, rather than an Anglophone, server to help you improve your French and integrate, but many British people prefer to stay with their original ones for the logical reason that, if they are not computer-literate in English, it makes no sense to try to understand support in French. For the record, the French word for a server is a *fournisseur d'accès*, for a search engine it is *moteur de recherche* and to surf is *naviguer*.

Health and Emergencies

The good news is that France has one of the best health services in the world. The bad news is that you pay for it. Well, actually the French taxpayer pays for most of it, but that is probably what you are going to become. If you do, you will probably pay an insurance company to cover what the government doesn't. Complicated? Not really. It works like this. You get ill and go to the doctor. Assuming the practitioner is government-approved, you can seek 75 per cent of the fee back. If you are having a baby or need something vital, such as insulin, you will be refunded 100 per cent, but if it is a medicament for a common disorder, the refund can be as little as 35 per cent. For a term in hospital, it is 80 per cent, for a dentist 75 per cent, for spectacles 70 per cent,

Medical Care

Letter to The Daily Telegraph, January 2002

On holiday in France recently, I felt the need for medical care for chronic arterial fibrillation. A glance at the Yellow Pages showed some 30 cardiologists in Finistère. Which one? I phoned the local GP and he advised a cardiologist in the nearby town. I phoned the man's secretary at 9.45am on New Year's Eve. At 10.30am I was with the cardiologist in a private clinic. He took a case history, did an ECG and modified my medication. I was with him 30 minutes. Cost: £30. 'Come back on Thursday,' he said. On Thursday, feeling much better, I went again to the private clinic. More discussions and an echocardiogram carried out and analysed. Another 30 minutes. Cost: £60. Then medication for £14. Total cost: £104, all paid. The following morning I presented my E111 and paid invoices to the Caisse Primaire. After a 20-minute wait I left with a cheque for £94. Total cost for my treatment: £10. How do the French do it? When I expressed my admiration for the French system to the cardiologist, he laughed. 'It cost a lot,' he said.

MA, Cambridge

for a therapist 65 per cent, and so on. Be careful which doctor you choose as there are three categories and a mistake can be costly. The equivalent of the British GP is a *médecin conventionné secteur 1*, who charges the lowest, government-contracted fees, and you should confirm this before treatment.

France has just overhauled the mechanics of its free reclaimation system. The old way was as follows: you paid the doctor and got a receipt called a *feuille de soins*. This you then signed and dated and took to the Caisse Primaire d'Assurance Maladie, which would, in due course, reimburse you a percentage of the charge. If you had been given a prescription (*ordonnance*), you took it to the chemist (*pharmacie*) who attached the appropriate adhesive stamp (*vignette*) covering the relevant percentage of the cost of the medicine, usually 40–70 per cent. Then you returned to the Caisse to be reimbursed. To recoup the balance of their expenditure, most French citizens had insurance cover known as a *mutuelle* provided by a French-based insurance company. Note that foreign private insurance policies are no longer recognized and it is illegal to have complete private insurance to cover all medical costs outside the state system.

The new way is based on a 'smart card'. The *Carte Vitale* is credit card-sized and has a microchip that contains all your health service details, such as social security number and contribution data. This has to be updated every now and again using a small machine found either in a hospital foyer or in a social security office. Both the doctor and the chemist have machines that complete the whole transaction that was done with *feuille de soins* and *vignettes* under the old system. The relevant sums are electronically credited to your bank account. Very clever and French. The services of the French health system are available to you if you have a *carte de séjour* or an E111 form, so it is important not to get caught between the two!

In an emergency, Dial 15 (or 112 if you don't speak French for a multilingual service) to be connected to a SAMU (*Service d'Aide Médicale d'Urgence*) office that will take the details of the emergency or injury and where you are – be prepared for these questions – and will despatch an ambulance. In some big cities, there are designated phone boxes on major roads linked to the emergency services and marked *Services Médicaux*. SAMU should have ascertained that the hospital it takes you to be appropriate to your needs. It will probably be a local government one (*conventionné*), but if you prefer a private one they will take you there, too. There are also municipal and private ambulance services, listed in the Yellow Pages. Once in hospital, you are in the care of one of the world's most efficient healthcare systems. You will have to pay before you leave, with the charges regulated by the system described above. In an emergency, they are obliged to treat you, whether you can pay or not. If you call the police or fire brigade (*sapeurs-pompiers*, dial 18) and they give you medical treatment, they will also charge you and your expenses will be recouped in the same way.

Entitlements

- **EU/EEA Visitors up to 90 days**: To benefit from medical treatment as a tourist from an EU country you are best asking for a form E111 before you leave home. Although the form E111 is valid indefinitely it only provides cover for up to 90 days at a time. If you have a form E111 then upon presentation of the form you will be entitled to medical care and you will have to pay only the same contribution to charges as a French person would pay. If you do not have a form E111 you may be charged the full cost of your treatment. These will be reimbursed, to the extent permitted under UK law, upon presentation of the bills to the DSS on your return to UK.

  EU or EEA (European Economic Area) pensioners enjoy a special status as 'tourists'. They are entitled to any treatment that may become necessary during a stay in another EU country – whatever the cost and whether it is urgent or routine. Non-pensioners from EU or EEA countries (and their dependants) enjoy the slightly more restricted entitlement to 'immediately necessary benefits'. This covers accident and sudden illness.

  In principal for both groups this treatment includes, under EU regulations, medical and basic dental care, medicines and hospitalisation costs. Your entitlement is assessed by reference to the local French regulations – after all, you could not expect the local French doctor to understand the rules in every EU country when assessing what to allow or prescribe. Thus you will be treated exactly like a Frenchman. This is no bad thing as the health care system is excellent. You therefore need to understand what the rules are. Needless to say, they are different from the UK rules. For example, you will have to pay a percentage of the costs involved. See below. Both groups are only entitled in France if they would have been entitled to state medical care in their home EU country. Neither group can travel abroad for the purpose of obtaining medical treatment, for example to bypass NHS waiting lists. To do this requires the prior consent of the UK NHS. If you use your form E111 you will usually have to pay for your medical treatment – just like a French person would – and claim the money back later. Instructions as to how to do so are on the form. Bear in mind that you will be expected to pay for part of the cost of treatment. See 'What Do You Have to Pay?', p.240.

Despite your entitlement under the E111 provisions it is well worth considering taking out a multi-visit travel policy if you intend to go to France regularly for short visits of up to a month. The benefits go well beyond the emergency reciprocal entitlements and the cost is modest – often as little as £60 per year. Such policies rarely cover stays in excess of 1 month at a time. Check the wording.

- **EU/EEA citizens visiting for over 90 days at a time**: The form E111 will not, in theory, protect you. You need specialist long stay visitors health insurance. This is available from many sources. Read the policies very carefully to see what is covered and what is not. Shop around.

Many people who regularly spend more than 90 days in France do not take out special insurance and rely on the E111 arrangements. If you are caught and refused cover remember that the medical bills you will be incurring will be astronomical.

- **Non EU/EEA Visitors**: Visitors from non-EU countries have no such entitlements and need health insurance. There may, however, be bilateral agreements between your country and France that will give you at least some benefits.

- **Residents and people entitled to State medical assistance**: Those entitled to state medical care include qualifying workers (workers paying Social Security contributions and who have worked, generally, 100 hours per month), retired people from EU countries and their respective dependants. Workers may also be entitled to a daily sickness allowance, similar to UK incapacity benefits. Your contributions to the UK National Insurance scheme are taken into account when calculating your entitlements in France. Thus you may be entitled in France on the basis of your UK contributions for a few months after your arrival. Ask the DSS for a form E104 before you leave.

If you are a pensioner you should obtain form E121 from your pensions office before leaving the UK. This confirms your status as a pensioner and is your passport to the benefits enjoyed by pensioners.

All groups should register with a local doctor in France.

You may generally choose treatment from any doctor, dentist or authorised hospital. Certain types of treatment need prior consent from your local health service administrators or a prescription from your local doctor. These include contact lenses, physiotherapy and certain types of tests. If you are entitled to French medical treatment the general system is that you pay for the care received and are then reimbursed the cost of that care, less your contribution to it. In emergencies or cases of hardship there can be exceptions to this rule. Main hospitals forming part of the main state scheme (*hôpitals conventionnés*) invoice the state directly for their services. If you choose to be treated by a private hospital not part of the state care system you will have to pay all of the costs and then claim repayment. You will only be repaid the standard charge for that treatment, not the (much) higher charge raised by the institution.

- **People not entitled to State health care:** These include:
  - **the economically inactive – i.e. those 'retired' below retirement age**
  - **students no longer the dependants of an EU/EEA worker or pensioner (but they may be covered by special schemes in France)**
  - **non EU/EEA nationals**
  - **civil servants covered by special schemes. This will not apply to UK civil servants.**

They will need health care insurance in order to obtain their residence cards. Study the cover on offer carefully and shop around.

Who Do You Contact to Receive Medical Care?

You will usually access all medical care via your GP or dentist. Referrals are then made as necessary to more specialist services. In an emergency you can go direct to a hospital.

If you need a paramedic in an emergency call SAMU (*Service d'Aide Médicale d'Urgence*). The number is on the front page of your phone book. In case of difficulty contact the Fire/Rescue service (*Sapeurs Pompiers*). Dial 18. Or try the police. Dial 17. They will tell you who to contact. Ambulances are private and listed in the phone book. All will charge you and their fee will be recoverable (in part) by those entitled to State medical care.

What Do You Have to Pay?

If you qualify for State medical aid you will be reimbursed a part of your medical expenses by the state. The percentage depends on your circumstances, the nature of the treatment and who supplies it. For most people the scale is as follows:

Percentages of Medical Expenses Reimbursed

Maternity Expenses	100%
General Hospital Costs in a State Authorised hospital	80%
Hospital Expenses in a non regulated private hospital of the standard approved amount	80%
Doctors & Dentists bills	70%
Sundry expenses – ambulances, laboratories, spectacles	65%
Medical Auxiliaries (nurses, chiropodists etc)	60%
Essential daily medication – e.g. insulin or heart pills	100%
Most medicines	65%
Minor medicines ('blue label' or comfort medicines)	35%

Certain people are exempt from paying these charges. These include those entitled to disability benefit in France and the seriously ill. Many people will carry supplementary insurance to cover these expenses. These *mutuelle* policies are generally fairly inexpensive.

Burial and Cremation

Please remember that deaths in France must be registered within 24 hours. This, like everything else, is done at the town hall. If it is a British person, the death should also be recorded at the British consulate.

Burial is much more common in France than is cremation. Land is plentiful; crematoria are expensive to build. Crematoria are usually only found in larger towns and cities.

Funerals are as ridiculously expensive in France as they are in the UK – possibly more so.

Taking the body home to England is possible but complex and even more expensive.

All in all, it is hardly worth bothering. Far better to stay alive and have another glass of wine.

Social Services and Welfare Benefits

People can qualify for welfare benefits in one of three ways – by enforced reciprocal EU/EEA rules, under the rules of the country where they pay social security contributions or under the rules of the country where you are living.

The General EU Rules

The basic idea behind the EU/EEA rules is that a person exercising his right to move from one EU/EEA state to another should not lose out on his welfare benefit rights by doing so.

The people covered by the EU/EEA rules are:

- **employed and self-employed nationals of EU/EEA states**
- **pensioners who are nationals of EU/EEA states**
- **subject to certain restrictions, members of the families of the above, whatever their nationality**
- **civil servants of EU/EEA states and members of their families, provided they are not covered by an enhanced scheme for civil servants in their own country. This is generally not a problem for UK civil servants**

Note that the EU/EEA rules do not cover the economically inactive (people retired early, students, etc.).

The rules cover:

- **sickness and maternity benefits**
- **accidents at work**
- **occupational diseases**
- **invalidity benefits**
- **old-age pensions**
- **widows and other survivors benefits**
- **death grants**
- **unemployment benefits**
- **family benefits**

The rules do not replace the national benefits to which you might be entitled. They co-ordinate the national schemes. They decide in which of several possible countries a person should make a claim and which country should pay the cost.

Apart from the basic principle that you should not lose out by moving within the EU the other principle is that you should only be subject to the rules of one country at a time.

The law of a Member State cannot – except in the case of unemployment benefit – take away or reduce your entitlement to benefit just because you live in another Member State.

If you remain entitled to a, say, a UK benefit whilst living in France payment of benefit to which your were entitled in your original Member State can be paid in a number of different ways, depending on the State and benefit concerned:

- **it can be paid by the benefit authorities in the Member State in which you now live acting on behalf of the benefit authorities in your original country.**
- **It can be paid to you directly in your new country by the benefit authorities in your old country.**

How Do You Decide Which Rules Apply to You?

There are two main factors:

Which Country Insures You?

You are insured in the country where you carry out your work. If you work regularly in more than one Member State you are insured in the country where you live. Short term posting (less than one year) to another country is ignored.

Retired people who have only worked in one Member State will remain 'attached' to that State for pension and other purposes for the rest of their lives. People who have worked in several states will have built up pension entitlements in each Member State in which they worked for more than one year.

In Which Country Do You Live?

Some benefits flow from your presence in a country.

Each potential benefit, both in Britain and in France, has associated rules stipulating which categories of people are entitled to benefit from it.

Living in France – What French Benefits Can You Claim?

The French social security scheme is divided into a scheme for employed persons and an entirely separate scheme for self-employed people. The employed persons' scheme covers all of the categories of benefit listed below. The self-employed scheme covers only sickness and maternity benefits but provides for other benefits via a variety of other schemes relating to different professions. There is yet another scheme for farmers. The law is complex and so if you think you may have an entitlement to benefit seek specialist advice.

Sickness and maternity benefits

See 'Health and Emergencies', pp.235–40.

Accidents at Work

Unless you have worked in France at some time you are not likely to benefit from this benefit. It is outside the scope of this book.

Occupational Diseases

Unless you have worked in France at some time you are not likely to benefit from this benefit. It is outside the scope of this book.

Invalidity and Disability Benefits

Unless you have worked in France at some time you are not likely to benefit from these benefits. They are outside the scope of this book.

You should continue to receive any benefits your are entitled to in your former country, e.g. the UK. Unless you have been insured in several Member States the amount of the benefit you will receive will be calculated solely in accordance with your former country's (normally the UK's) rules. You will still have to comply with directions received from the UK authorities in respect of medical examinations, etc.

Old-age Pensions

Unless you have worked in France at some time you are not likely to benefit from either a French basic pension or a French means tested supplemental pension.

You will, of course, continue to receive your UK pension. See below.

Widows' and Other Survivors' Benefits

Unless you have worked in France at some time you are not likely to benefit from these benefits. These benefits are outside the scope of this book.

Death Grants

Unless your deceased partner worked in France at some time you are not likely to benefit from this benefit, but the rules are complex, so seek advice.

Unemployment Benefits

If you lose your job the French unemployment benefit authority must take into account any periods of employment or NI contributions paid in another EU country when calculating your entitlement to benefits in France.

You must, however, have paid at least some insurance payments in France prior to claiming unemployment benefit in France. That means you cannot go to France for the purpose of claiming benefit.

You should obtain form E301 from the UK benefit authorities (or from your home state if it is not the UK) before going to France.

If you travel to France to seek employment there are restrictions on your entitlement to benefit.

- **You must have been unemployed and available for work in your home country for at least four weeks before going to France**
- **You must contact your 'home' unemployment benefit authority and obtain a form E303 from them before leaving for France. If you do not have this payment of benefit in France can be delayed substantially.**
- **You must register for work in France within seven days of your arrival**
- **You must comply with all the French procedural requirements**
- **You will be entitled to benefit for a maximum of three months**
- **If you cannot find a job during that period you will only be entitled to continuing unemployment benefit in your home country if you return within the 3-month period. If you do not you can lose all entitlement to benefits.**
- **You are only entitled to one 3-month payment between two periods of employment.**

Family Benefits

If the members of your family live in the same country as you are insured in then that country pays the benefits. You are entitled to the same benefits as nationals of that state.

If your family do not live in the same country as you are insured in then, if you are entitled to benefits under the rules of more than one country, they will receive the highest amount to which they would have been entitled in any of the relevant states.

If you work in one State and your spouse works in another State the benefit is paid by the State in which the children live with, if necessary, a top up from the State in which the other parent works.

Pensioners normally receive family benefits from the State that pays their pension.

In practical terms these cases are complex and you should seek advice.

What UK Benefits Can You Claim?

Welfare benefits in the UK are divided into 'contributory' and 'non-contributory' benefits.

The former are benefits to which you only become entitled if you have paid (or been credited with) sufficient National Insurance contributions to qualify you for payment. The latter do not depend on paying any National Insurance contributions.

In the UK there are various classes of National Insurance contributions. Not all rank equally for benefits purposes and some types of National Insurance contributions cannot be used to qualify payments for certain benefits.

The categories are:

Class 1: Paid by employees and their employers and consisting of a percentage of income.

Class 2: A flat-rate payment paid by self-employed people.

Class 3: Voluntary payments made by people no longer paying Class 1 or Class 2 contributions. Their rights are protected for a limited range of benefits.

Class 4: Compulsory 'profit-related' additional contributions paid by self-employed people.

The differing types of NI payments qualify you for various benefits:

NI Contributions and Entitlement to UK Benefits

	Class 1	Class 2/4	Class 3
Maternity Allowances	Yes	Yes	No
Unemployment Benefit	Yes	No	No
Incapacity Benefit	Yes	Yes	No
Widow's Benefit	Yes	Yes	Yes
Basic Retirement Pension	Yes	Yes	Yes
Additional Retirement Pension	Yes	No	No

As well as being categorized as 'contributory' and 'non-contributory' benefits, benefits are also categorized into 'means tested' and 'non means tested' benefits. The former are paid only if you qualify under the eligibility criteria for the benefit in question and are poor enough to qualify on financial grounds – generally covering income and savings. The latter are paid to anyone who meets the eligibility criteria, irrespective of their wealth.

Means-tested UK benefits are likely to be of little interest to the resident in France.

Sickness and Maternity Benefits

See the 'Health and Emergencies', pp.235–40.

Accidents at Work

Any benefits you presently receive from the UK benefits system as a result of an accident at work should remain payable to you despite the fact you have moved to France.

Occupational Diseases

Any benefits you receive from the UK benefits system as a result of an occupational disease should remain payable to you despite the fact you have moved to France.

Invalidity Benefits

Any National Insurance benefits you receive from the UK benefits system as a result of invalidity should remain payable to you despite the fact you have moved to France.

Attendance Allowance, SDA and DLA are not usually payable if you go to live abroad permanently.

Old-age Pensions

If you are already retired and you only ever paid National Insurance contributions in the UK you will receive your UK retirement pension wherever you choose to live within the EU/EEA. You will be paid without deduction (except remittance charges) and your pension will be updated whenever the pensions in the UK are updated.

If you have established an entitlement to a retirement pension in several EU countries by virtue of working in them all of the pensions will be payable to you in France. Once again they will be paid without deduction (except remittance charges) and your pension will be updated whenever the pensions in those countries are updated.

If you have not yet retired and move to France (whether you intend to work in France or not) your entitlement to your UK pension will be frozen and the pension to which you are entitled will be paid to you at UK retirement age.

This freezing of your pension can be a disadvantage, especially if you are still relatively young when you move to France. This is because you need to have made a minimum number of NI contributions in order to qualify for a full UK State pension. If you have not yet done this but are close it may be worth making additional payments whilst you are resident overseas.

You may choose to pay either continuing Class 2 or Class 3 contributions.

You may pay Class 2 contributions if:

- **You are working abroad**
- **You have lived in the UK for a continuous period of at least three years during which you paid NI contributions and you have already paid a set minimum amount of NI contributions**
- **You were normally employed or self employed in the UK before going abroad**

You may pay Class 3 contributions if:

- **You have at any time lived in the UK for a continuous period of at least 3 years**
- **You have already paid a minimum amount in UK NI contributions**

Class 2 contributions are more expensive but, potentially, cover you for Maternity Allowance and Incapacity benefits. Class 3 contributions do not.

In both cases you apply in the UK on form CF83.

The decision as to whether to continue to make UK payments is an important one. Seek advice.

Widows' and Other Survivors' Benefits

Any benefits you receive from the UK benefits system as a result of your being a widow should remain payable to you despite the fact you have moved to France.

Death Grants

The position here is complex. Seek advice.

Unemployment Benefits

You may be able to get contribution-based Jobseeker's Allowance in the EEA for up to 13 weeks if you:

- **Are entitled to contribution-based Jobseeker's Allowance on the day you go abroad**
- **Have registered as a jobseeker for at least four weeks before you leave. This can be less in special circumstances**
- **Are available for work and actively seeking work in Great Britain up to the day you leave**
- **Are going abroad to look for work**
- **Register for work at the equivalent of a Jobcentre in the country you are going to within seven days of last claiming Jobseeker's Allowance in the UK. If you do not, you may lose benefit**
- **Follow the other country's system for claiming benefit**
- **Follow the other country's benefit rules, such as being available for and actively seeking work, that would have applied if you had stayed in the UK**

Family Benefits

See the section on French benefits above.

Security, Crime and the Police

In the cities of France, you should take all the precautions you would in British cities. The rise in urban crime and the perception that it is connected with immigrants, both legal and otherwise, has done much to advance the fortunes of the country's far right National Front party along the south coast and in some industrial centres. However, petty theft was not unknown in France before the recent wave of immigration and particular care should be taken in places such as Marseille, the Côte d'Azur, Lille and parts of Paris. Rural France has a much lower crime rate – some remote areas claim to be virtually crime-free. The reason for the difference in the two countries is the same one that makes so many things in France different: its size. While a large proportion of Britain is within easy striking distance of her inner cities, much of France is so distant from her population concentrations that the burglar, mugger and pickpocket face enormous logistical problems. Nevertheless, crime is on the increase and basic security measures are not uncommon, such as bars on windows (although the prevalence of shutters in much of France limits their popularity). But electric alarm systems, popular in much of rural Britain, are not widespread in rural France.

Another dramatic difference between the two countries is the organization of the police services. France has basically two – a national police force (*police nationale* – flat caps and silver buttons), who police urban areas, and the *gendarmes* (*gendarmerie nationale* – kepis and gold buttons), who police everything else. Because you see the latter on the roads and in small towns and villages you may have had the impression that they are the only police force. In fact, they come under the Ministry of Defence rather than the Ministry of the Interior and have all sorts of other paramilitary duties as well. There are two other types of police to look out for, too: the CRS, essentially a riot police, but often called on for other duties, and localized city police, who will normally be concentrating on urban traffic problems. The one time you don't want to practise your French is if you get arrested. Insist on an English-speaking lawyer and keep quiet. No French police force has won prizes for being gentle and caring. They are, however, reasonably efficient. Further to these, as there are no controls on land borders, customs officers (*douaniers*) have the right to stop and search anywhere and at any time. Foreign vehicles in particular may be stopped and checked over for hidden drugs, illegal immigrants and so forth – on certain main roads this is not uncommon, and caravanettes and lorries coming back from Spain are their prime target. If they are suspicious of you, they can phone ahead to the ferry port and you will be pulled over and your vehicle checked over minutely at your port of entry.

If you are going to live in the countryside, you will probably receive a visit from the *gendarmerie nationale* shortly after you have moved in. This will be presented as a courtesy call, although candour might suggest it is to look you over. There are some differences in law of which you should be aware. There is more latitude in the way a householder can forcibly protect his property. This doesn't mean you can shoot people at random, but if a burglar sustains injuries while visiting your home it will probably be reckoned to be his occupational hazard. Also, if you see a mugging or road accident in progress, you are compelled by law to assist the victim or, if you are unable, to call the police. People and police in France have not shared the traditional good relations enjoyed in Britain. The difference in attitudes towards policing illustrates perfectly the different attitudes towards government and society. The idea of unarmed local constabularies, beloved of parochial, tribal democracy, would not be understood by a tradition that has historically been centralized and rigid. However, modern policing, with its problems of crime, drugs and terrorism, has made a lot common to all forces. Like their British colleagues, French police have occasionally been accused of racism and, at least in the past, they have had a reputation for being rougher than required. However, watching a pair of immaculate, white-gloved gendarmes on a sunny village market day, formally kissing some ladies of their acquaintance, it is hard to feel intimidated.

To call the police, dial 17.

Food and Drink

Come in, you Anglo-Saxon swine,
And drink of my Algerian wine,
Twill turn your eye-balls black and blue
But is quite good enough for you.

Brendan Behan is supposed to have penned these lines for a non-English-speaking French café owner who innocently thought it might attract custom. It says something about what used to be the British perception of the French perception of the British as culinary barbarians. Happily, those days are almost gone. Apart from football hooligans and Francophobes, which, as a prospective French property-buyer, you are probably not, British appreciation of food and wine has undergone a revolution in the last couple of generations, while, ironically, junk food outlets in France multiply. More garlic is consumed in southern England than northern France. Modern techno-driven France can no longer accommodate those four-hour, wine-anointed luncheons that were once part of her social fabric. The ethos on both sides of the Channel has changed since Behan composed his mischievous lines.

Having said that, there is still a huge gulf in the status of food in the two countries. You can see it as you walk into the supermarket. While consumer durables are roughly similar in range and price, the food section is a culture shock for the British buyer. There is a much larger range of goods, especially fresh produce, than you would expect at home and you might be confronted with what appears to be a fishmonger in a provincial land-locked town's supermarket. The wine section, as you would expect, will have an excellent range of French wines, but precious few from elsewhere in Europe, let alone the rest of the world – a characteristic myopia as the new world makes huge inroads into France's traditional export markets. Still, they will be wider in range and price than anything the UK shopper is used to, not to mention in volume – there is nothing you can buy in units of 10 litres in the UK that doesn't come out of a pump!

However, the main difference between food shopping in Britain and France is not in the supermarket, but in the high street. The *boulangerie* (bread and associated products), *pâtisserie* (pastries, cakes, etc.), *épicerie* (grocer), *boucherie* (butcher), *charcuterie* (pork and other meat products), the *traiteur* selling ready-made meat dishes, the *poissonnerie* (fishmonger) and the *crèmerie* (dairy) are still alive and well in most communities. If there are local specialities – something that went out north of the Channel with the mail coach – you can still find them here, too. It is the existence of these outlets, and the society that supports them, that is one of the main attractions for people whose cities have been dehumanized. The village or town market is the other aspect of food shopping that is different in France. Some markets are huge, some ancient – all are interesting. Locals take their weekly market seriously and small producers, who might have no other way of selling their wares, can still be found. French shoppers tend to be conscious of what vegetables are in season and the market is an excellent place to select the freshest. They will not undercut the hypermarket in price or convenience, but they will knock spots off it for entertainment value and as a social event.

As with education, the status of food itself is different, with the average family spending a quarter of its disposable income on it. It is generally agreed that foodstuffs are cheaper in France than in Britain, although this may not always be true across the board. What is certain is that restaurants, quality for quality, are definitely so, and the French entertain in restaurants when the British would do so at home. The traditional values still flourish on the whole, despite the maledictions of some conservatives and the influx of exotic cuisines. The most dramatic changes to have occurred in the French restaurant trade are in marketing. This is particularly apparent where large numbers – whether shoppers or workers – are being catered for, and sometimes the sheer value is astonishing to British people used to the concept that convenience and quality are incompatible. That is not to say you can't eat badly in France – there are cowboys in the catering trade, too, but they normally go for the susceptible tourist. Personally, I would avoid anything that wants to look like an American steak house. If you are a potential house-buyer in France, you will probably know all about French restaurants, so there is no point wasting your time with advice about how to read a menu. You may also know that even motorway food in France embarrasses its British counterparts.

A thought that may not have occurred to you is the possibility of missing British food or, if not British food as such, some products that are quite difficult to obtain in parts of France. Marmite probably tops a list that might also

A Taste of the South

Eric and Madeleine Vedel, who run an establishment for the teaching and preservation of the traditions of southern cuisine (http://www.cuisine-provencale.com), say:

'Should you dine at the table of a friend in Provence, be prepared for a long, leisurely meal, rich in conversation and liberally sprinkled with anecdotes and local wines. For the first course, perhaps some anchovies marinated in lemon juice, olive oil and garlic or maybe some small toasts spread with rich black olive tapenade, accompanied by a chilled, sharp rosé wine. Next may come a dish of *moules marinière*, steamed open and covered in a light sauce of white wine, garlic, bay leaves and just one crushed tomato, accompanied by a white wine of Languedoc, the Picboul de Pinet, dry and crisp to marry well with seafood. Your main course might be roast lamb accompanied by rosemary jelly and puréed courgette with a touch of anchovy, accompanied by a rich red wine of Provence, be it a distinguished Châteauneuf-du-Pape – strong on the grenache grape – or a more humble, but often equally good, Côteaux d'Aix from the Alpilles mountains. A light salad comes next to cleanse the palate, followed by the cheese plate with a sampling of local goat cheeses (one creamy and fresh and one tangy and dry), sheep cheeses (perhaps the day-old Gardian and a Tomme that's aged two months) and even a cow cheese from the north, such as the wood-ashed Morbier, or a ripe and creamy Brie. For dessert, shall it be fresh strawberries sprinkled with a little sugar and a glug of red wine or a fruit tart? Maybe a cherry clafoutis... And in your glass? Why not a muscat from Beaumes-de-Venise, sweet but not cloying, dense in the flavour of the grape from which it's made...?'

include crumpets, Cheddar cheese and fruit cake, Heinz baked beans – especially if kids are involved – digestive biscuits, Christmas pudding in December and good Stilton for feast days. Forget draught bitter unless you are near one of the English or Irish theme bars occasionally found in bigger towns. There are, however, many good French beers if you are prepared to acquire the taste. The white sliced loaf, or something similar, is often difficult to find if you have had enough of baguettes. If you are a serious tea-drinker and don't like tea bags, you could be in trouble, too. However, things such as smoked salmon are plentiful in French supermarkets and Scotch whisky is cheaper than in Britain. If you can't control your craving there are a few shops specializing in British brands and friends and relations coming to visit can bring you supplies.

Regional specialities do survive, but you have to keep your eyes open and the casual traveller can traverse the 'hexagon' without being aware of them. You probably won't take it as a serious factor when selecting a place to buy a house unless, for example, you are a *champignons de Paris* freak, in which case you should select the Loire where most of them are grown. It's a bit of a waste, on the other hand, to live in Normandy if you have a weight problem or are watching your cholesterol. It's a good place, though, if you want an excuse to take slugs of *calvados* between courses (*le trou normand*) and can convince yourself it's doing you good. The entire north is great for those with a high metabolic rate because it loves its *crêpes*, both sweet and savoury. The Mediterranean always exaggerates the quality of its fish, but the cuisines of Provence and Languedoc have the inestimable advantage of being, in their proper form, dairy-free and therefore very healthy and much more digestible if you are unused to a high-fat diet. Southern cuisine is just another facet of a lost regional identity that has been absorbed by northern France since the Middle Ages. For more on regional cuisine, see Part Three.

One of the great experiences of living in a wine-producing country is the adventure of wine tasting and buying from the estates. This is not only interesting, but also economical and, in many vineyards, you will be able to buy in bulk. Watch for the sign saying that wine is for sale *en vrac*. Many French households in vine-growing areas are equipped with sets of receptacles of up to 10 litres' capacity, which you can bring with you and have filled up. You can also buy *en vrac* in the producer's containers – or bring your own tanker.

Shopping

Dior, Hermès and Chanel are perhaps names that spring quickly to mind, but they are probably not going to feature very large in your daily life in France. Everyday shopping is more mundane, although not without its fascination, but really what you want to know is how it differs from the UK? Certainly there is high fashion, but then there is that in Bond Street. It is true that clothes feature prominently in Paris and other French cities, but in the countryside food comes much higher on the list of priorities. These two commodities, clothes and food, dictate much of the difference between the nature of retail outlets in France and the UK. The other factor is our old friend geography. The size and demography of France means that costs and margins are very different. The thought that the nearest shop could be five miles away is inconceivable in the southeast of England. It isn't in parts of rural France, where it could even be a lot further than that.

On the face of it, French supermarkets resemble those in Britain. Anything over 2,500 square metres is designated a *hypermarché* (hypermarket) and offers a huge range of goods, from clothes and sports equipment to lawnmowers and fridges on top of the usual groceries. The dominant chains are Carrefour, Casino, Intermarché, Leclerc, Auchan and Mammouth. Some are truly vast and have been around since the early 1960s. As mentioned in the previous section, their range of fresh food dwarfs the usual British offering, as does their selection of wine. Otherwise, there are more similarities than differences. Where they do differ is in their distribution. While there are some real behemoths in the bigger towns, many country districts have to rely on small co-ops and concessions. This, again, is down to distances. To have a hypermarket for every town in the Cévennes or Auvergne would simply be an economic impossibility.

The ordinary market is a different matter. The open-air – and sometimes covered – weekly market actually created many towns in France (as it did in Britain) as the *bastides* of the southwest, with their arcaded squares, bear witness. A huge range of goods is sold in the markets – greater than in British ones and of higher quality. There are also many more of them. Fresh produce is the central commodity, but there is much more besides. If you are not shopping for Dior, Hermès or Chanel that day, clothes are often a good buy at markets, too. Household linens – and even mattresses – are also good value, as is hardware. However, market day is an important occasion in its own right in the French countryside, so it is worth attending just for the sights, sounds and smells alone. Very often located in the same spot, but not the same day, are the equivalent of the flea market, the *braderie, vide-grenier* and *foire à tout*.

It is in the high street, though, that the greatest difference to shopping in the UK is probably made manifest. While British streets are dominated by chain stores, French ones are still the domain of the independent shopkeeper. We had a look at several in the Food and Drink section earlier, but we missed the *quincaillerie* (hardware shop) and the *pharmacie* (chemist). The British chemist also stocks the goods sold in a French *parfumerie* (perfume, obviously, and beauty products), which often confuses first-time visitors, who can be found trying to buy cough medicine in the *parfumerie*. An unusual feature of a French *pharmacie* is that it will identify for you any type of wild fungus that you may have picked, telling you if it is toxic or safe to put in your next omelette. Then there is the *tabac*, which holds the government licence to sell tobacco and revenue stamps, which can also be used for the payment of some fines, such as minor traffic infringements. It often also stocks newspapers, magazines, sweets and postage stamps. On top of that, it can also be a bar and café. High-quality clothes shops can also be found – some British residents who live in the countryside remark that, while cheap clothes can be bought on market day, and there are plenty of expensive shops around, there is no equivalent to the British high street's medium-priced outlets without travelling a great distance.

In larger towns, where the department stores and mid-range clothes shops can be found, the scenario resembles Britain much more. The French invented the department store, according to David Hampshire's excellent *Living and Working in France*, with Le Bon Marché in 1852. The other big names are Au Printemps, Trois Quartiers, La Samaritaine and Galeries Lafayette. It is also here in these larger centres that you can find some familiar names, such as Habitat, Gap and WH Smith. Opening hours in France vary according to the size of town, type of shop and, in some cases, latitude as, in some isolated parts of the deep south, lunch hours reminiscent of a siesta can take place. Outside the main centres, shops usually open at 9am, shut at noon and then open from 2–6 or 7.30pm. Food shops can open as early as 6.30am, particularly *boulangeries*, but will then shut at noon and not reopen until 3pm, after which they might keep serving until 7 or 8pm. Beware Mondays, particularly out of season and in the countryside, when a huge number of shops remain shut. Many food shops are open on Sunday mornings. For shopping, and everything else in France, remember that people use a 24-hour clock, although if you book dinner at eight, they won't think you mean breakfast.

France is also a good spot for the antique and collectables enthusiast, principally because the French themselves are not. Their taste in furniture is inclined towards the mass-produced country style or contemporary, when they will pay a lot for good quality, but traditionally have been less enthusiastic about finding bargains in forgotten sales rooms. So, look out for *brocante* or second-hand shops where there is probably more chance of finding bargains than in the more upmarket and often tourist-orientated *antiquités*.

Pets

You can bring three pets at a time into France, of which only one may be a puppy under six months old. You will have to get an Export Health Certificate from DEFRA via your local vet, but most people who have done so report difficulties in France finding someone to show it to. The problems occur, of course, if you need to re-import them into Britain, for which you will need the famous Pets' Passport.

For this you can order a Pets Travel Scheme information pack from PETS Helpline (**t** 0870 241 1710) or visit **www.defra.gov.uk/animalh/quarantine** or e-mail at **pets.helpline@defra.gsi.gov.uk**. To qualify for this scheme, you will need to get your pet fitted with a microchip, vaccinated against rabies, issued with a PETS certificate and treated for ticks and tapeworm just before re-entering the UK. You have to return to the UK by certain approved routes, too, and most of the budget airline routes are not included.

France is a pretty animal-friendly country (edible ones excluded), the vets are plentiful and good, most hotels put pets up for a modest charge and SNCF charges dogs half the second-class fare (puppies in arms or boxes go free). Dogs are commonly allowed in shops, cafés and restaurants. Dog owners should be aware that heartworm, *Filairiose*, is present in France, but not common. Erlichosi – *Erlichiose*, a parasite of the blood – is also present but rare. Piroplasmosis or *babesia*, a tick-borne disease that attacks the red blood cells and can kill in 48 hours, is present in some areas but not common and can be vaccinated against. French law concerning pets has recently changed and is different from other European law anyway. Once an animal has been in the country three months, it is deemed to be a resident so requires an annual rabies vaccination and has to be entered on a national database. The details are too extensive to include here, so we strongly advise that you go to the DEFRA website mentioned above, on the site map click on 'What pet owners need to do', then scroll down to 'Different procedures for France and Denmark'. This will give you the up-to-date instructions. If you are not online, get your vet to have a look. Cat-owners living in popular hunting areas have reported frustrated huntsmen taking pot shots at their pets. This may not be commonplace, but, if you are considering bringing Fluffy to live in a property on the edge of a wood used for *la chasse*, you may wish to reconsider.

The French Language and Learning It

'I speak Spanish to God, Italian to women, French to men, and German to my horse,' said the Holy Roman Emperor Charles V, France's great rival, showing how French had become an international language by the 16th century. It is the most northerly of the Latin languages, but, unlike others of the same family, sounds nothing like its Roman ancestor. Perhaps this is because of the influence of the Celtic Gaulish (with loan-words such as *chemise*, or shirt) and Frankish (with loan-words such as *fauteuil*, meaning armchair). It developed in northern France with various dialect influences, one of which was in the Paris region. As the French kingdom expanded, its language consumed all those in its path. Breton became a casualty in the northwest and Basque in the southwest, while the tongues of Oc fought a rearguard action for centuries. Although English, Spanish and Portuguese were more successful colonial languages, French would come to be established in Canada, the USA and huge areas of Africa. It is also spoken, of course, in Switzerland and Belgium (where at least they call 70 *septante*, instead of *soixante-dix* or 60-10!)

It is all very well for books like this one to encourage you to learn French, and it is pretty obvious that not speaking the language of a land in which you are living or visiting long term complicates life. However, some people, especially those who have never studied it before, may take some time and still never be very successful. As far as fitting in is concerned, attitude, as mentioned right at the beginning of this part of the book, is more important. If you are going to have any serious sort of job, you will probably have to be fluent. If you are going to get true value out of the country, you should have a reasonable command. Some British people speak like the locals, most are adequate and only a few don't bother. As a holiday homeowner you can get away with basic French. If you hide in a British enclave you can probably get away with even less. Some people do muddle through without much. A lack of the language is no reason to be deterred from buying property, but the French think their language is the most beautiful on earth and nothing else comes near it, so you can't really expect to be taken seriously by them if you don't try. More to the point, to not even try is defeatist, pointless and ultimately humiliating.

The best way to learn any language is to have a local girl- or boyfriend, but if your present partner is a spoilsport, you will have to resort to more tedious methods. If you already have a grounding, a good dictionary and a grammar, plus a lot of social intercourse will probably get you there. Otherwise, there are dozens of options, broadly falling into three categories. First, you can hire a private tutor, which is obviously expensive but you can tailor your learning to suit your own timetable and ability. Then there are courses. If you live in an area with a big foreign population, there may be one in your local town and it may be free. If you are officially unemployed and have a *carte de séjour*, you can get free lessons anyway (check with your nearest ANPE office). Otherwise, there are private courses – teaching French is big business and there is bound to be a tutor or group near you. Some universities have courses for foreigners, which may be worth checking out, or contact Eurocentre (**t** 020-831 85633), a non-profit organization owned by the Swiss Migros company, for a brochure. There are very effective total immersion courses in Amboise, La Rochelle and Paris. For those who want a complete command of the language in a relatively short time and don't care about the cost, there are total immersion courses, which often involve living with a host family and studying full time,

The Tongue of Oc

All over the southern part of France, you will notice what looks like a misspelling of a town's name under the familiar one by the roadside as you arrive. This custom has its origins in regional government legislation of 1982, and that apparent spelling mistake derives from the old southern tongues of 1,000 years ago. As Latin became French, two distinct languages appeared in northern and southern France. Provençal, as the southern tongue was known, is first recorded in the 10th century and came to be the language of the troubadours, with their poetry of love, satire and war. Spoken over a wide area and with no standard form, it is now better known as Occitan, from the word Languedoc. Close to the Spanish border, it is indistinguishable from Catalan and called Roussillonais. In the rest of modern Languedoc it is called Languedocien. To the north it was called Limousin and spoken as far as Limoges. Then there is a dialect found towards the Swiss border called Franco-Provençal, which spreads into Italy. All these tongues lost their battles with French in the years since the troubadours. Frédéric Mistral (1830–1914) was the great champion of their revival and won the Nobel Prize in 1904 for his efforts. There is increasing interest in them today, but, on the whole, these languages – like those of the Celtic world – are encouraged more as a defence of regional heritage against central government and internationalization than as a means of communication.

from weeks to months. You can find these on the Internet, in French-interest magazines and by word of mouth.

Alternatively, you could learn your French before going. Once again, there are lots of options. You can start with the 'teach yourself'-type books, but easier and more fun are tapes and CDs, of which there is a wide range. Computer shops will have a range of CDs or look on the Internet at sites such as Amazon and Swotbooks. Your local centre for continuing education will almost certainly have French courses available, too – contact your local council for details. Apart from that, there should be private classes and tutors offering their services listed in the Yellow (or Golden) Pages or local paper. Alliance Française, the French equivalent of the British Council, is the world's biggest organizer of French courses and is always worth checking, especially if you are near Bath, Belfast, Bristol, Cambridge, Exeter, Glasgow, Jersey, London, Milton-Keynes, Manchester, Oxford, York or the East-Midlands. It also organizes cultural events and trips to France (**t** 020-7723 6439 or visit **www.alliancefrancaise.org**). Your local university may well have extra-mural language classes, too.

Etiquette

The paradox that strikes so many British people about French life applies also to manners and behaviour for, despite having a reputation for a relaxed lifestyle, France is in many ways very formal. *Monsieur* and *Madame* are used in everyday speech, calling people by their first names is not done without invitation and using the second person singular (*tu* and *toi*) is frowned on, except to children, family members, between the young and good friends. It is said that even some (very posh) husbands and wives use the formal *vous*. Friends and acquaintances of all ages always shake hands. Kissing among friends is usual in much the same circumstances as in Britain but much more common, though some British residents resist it altogether. Children expect to be kissed. How many kisses should be given is debated even among the French – southerners seem to be more generous.

Entertaining at home is done much less than in Britain, and business entertainment is done in restaurants. If you do go to someone's house for dinner, be careful what gift you bring: chrysanthemums are associated with graves, red flowers of any type mean true love and, if you bring wine, make sure it's good. Otherwise you could end up giving the message that your host is dead boring, has no taste or that you fancy his wife (or him). More likely, though, he'll put it down to you just being another ignorant foreigner.

New arrivals in a rural *commune* are expected, as a matter of politeness, to arrange a meeting to present themselves to the Mayor. They should be prepared to give all their personal information: dates of birth, marriage date,

Etiquette

Jeremy from the Cévennes comments:

'Despite their reputation for being rude and setting fire to lorryloads of our sheep, the French are, in fact, incredibly polite. They even speak to their neighbours, which may disconcert anyone moving from London or the Home Counties. They shake hands a lot (none of this hands-in-pockets, avoid eye-contact nonsense) and then, of course, there's the cheek-kissing. You don't actually kiss (lips never meet cheeks) and different parts of France have different numbers of kisses (two in Marseille, three in Montpellier, four in some places...). The only difficulty here is in knowing which side to start; there's no rule and you can easily find yourself in one of those 'corridor' situations. And then there's the *vous* and *tu* thing. In general, apparently the Brits carry on *vous*-ing too long. Listen carefully for your French friends adopting the *tu* form and you know you're 'in' so you can follow suit. On the other hand, people in authority and the elderly in general are vous. And be ready for some different road etiquette. A 'friendly' flash of your lights to let someone go first actually means 'get out of my way, I'm coming through'. And, of course, the French are at their rudest and most dangerous behind the wheels of their cars.'

children and dates of birth, etc. At the same time, they should ask for instructions on acquiring a *carte de séjour*, which is still a legal requirement.

Relationships between you and your neighbours, once you have moved in, should obviously be governed by good manners rather than legislation, but, in case you should be thrown into a range war, the following legal points are worth remembering. Neighbours' trees should not overhang your garden, but if the branches do and this annoys you, then you can ask the owner to cut them. Never cut them yourself, as this is illegal. If he refuses, then you should go to the Tribunal d'Instance (somewhere between a magistrate's court and a small claims court) and request that they instruct the neighbour to do the necessary work. You will need to provide proof of his negligence, such as photos or a bailiff's report (*constat d'huissier*). The rules regarding planting distances from the fence or edge of your land vary from area to area, so ask at the *mairie*. However, if there are no specific local conditions, then the following applies. Anything that will grow more than 2m high must be planted at least 2m from the boundary. Anything that will not grow more than 2m can be planted up to 50cm from the boundary. However, if a tree has been over 2m high for over 30 years, then it has the right to stay in its place – squatter's rights! In the Paris area, there are no such rules, but householders should respect their neighbours' rights to light and space and get their trees and bushes trimmed regularly to avoid conflict.

The Media

The two principal differences between the media in France and Britain are that TV does not have the same dominance in France and that the press is largely regional (yet another reflection of the country's size). Perhaps because it is dominated by the regional papers, the press is much less tabloid-infested. Whether television is slightly anodyne because it is less important or it is the other way round is hard to say, but the fact is that it is quite smart in France to say you don't have a TV set – a boast made mostly among middle-class intellectuals. Another geographical factor is that TV reception in parts of the country is not as good as it could be, which also inhibits it achieving the paramountcy it has in the UK. Remember that your British set will be no use for Continental broadcasts, but that most modern video machines are usually PAL and SECAM, so you can play French or English tapes.

Television

TF1, originally state-run but privatized in 1987, is the most popular channel and offers a mixture of news, features, documentaries, soaps and the standard French space-filler – the game show. France 2 (previously Antenne 2) is produced by government-run France Télévison and carries news programmes, although perhaps slightly tepid by British standards, cultural programmes and films, often dubbed. FR3 is also state-run and caters more for the regions. Canal Plus (Canal+) is a privately owned, and Europe's biggest, subscription channel for which you need a decoder. It thrives on a diet of sport, films, music and news and has many subscribers outside France. Arté is a Franco-German effort, which concentrates on cultural programmes. Channel 6 is light entertainment and porn. Living near one of the borders of France offers viewers foreign TV as well: Catalan-speakers in Languedoc can pick up Barcelona channels. If it is real international TV you want, a huge number of channels are available on both European and French satellite TV.

In France, at the time of writing, there are six ways of obtaining British TV and radio programmes – all systems needing a satellite dish. First, the French digital system CanalSatellite broadcasts films in their original language. It also has BBC World and Sky News. Second, the French TPS digital system broadcasts BBC World and BBC Prime in addition to the normal French channels and, occasionally, has films in English. Both of these are subscription systems, available from any French high street supplier. Third, BBC Prime can be obtained in digital with a card from the BBC, costing about £75 per annum, and it is strictly for addresses outside the UK. Receivers are available from specialized dealers. BBC radio, commercial radio, limited television channels, including news and information channels, one movie and one cartoon channel are available using a free-to-air digital receiver, no cards, no subscription. Receivers are obtained from specialized dealers and some large electrical stores. Fifth, all of the last options plus BBC digital channels (including BBC1 and 2), ITV, Channels 4 and 5 and Sky, are available using a digital receiver available from specialists only. This requires a card from the UK. European broadcasting copyright laws and UK licensing rules are such that the cards are officially issued for use only within UK. Finally, BBC World is available free in analogue form and the necessary equipment can be found very cheaply in most large DIY stores and TV shops.

All systems will work with any UK or French television that has a scart connector.

The websites to check out are:

www.bbc.co.uk/reception
www.BBCPrime.com
www.BBCWorld.com
www.bigdishsat.com

Many French towns have cable TV, offering French and some US and Spanish networks. There is a licence fee for the TV receiver and you have to pay it even if your set is locked in a trunk in the attic – unless, that is, you are a pensioner or earning less than the taxable minimum, as it is a tax rather than a licence.

Radio

In number terms, it is the regional stations that dominate, with over 50 to choose from, ranging from those of the government-run Radio France to the dozens of independent ones, although this is a rationalization of the 1,500 that blossomed after deregulation, jamming the airwaves. As for the Radio France national stations, these are France Inter, which is news and general interest, France Culture and France Musique, which roughly correspond with Radio 4 and Classic FM. There is a station for the elderly, too, called Radio Bleu. Dating from the days before deregulation are the foreign-based commercial stations of Europe 1 and Radio Monte-Carlo. UK stations can be picked up in the north of the country, otherwise you have the option of the BBC World Service on 12095, 9410, 7325, 6195, 3955, 648 and 198kHz. You can also get a range of UK stations on your radio via a TV satellite link.

The Press

France has no national daily newspapers in the sense that Britain does, although the main Paris dailies are read nationwide in provincial editions. You won't be surprised at that if you have been following the theme through much of this book – that it is the size of the country in relation to its population that accounts for many of the practical differences between France and Britain. As you would expect, it is the provincial French press that dominates the daily publications and, of these, one, *Ouest-France*, has a circulation to rival any in Paris. Yet it is the Paris papers that are known in the outside world: *Le Monde* (politically centre), *Le Figaro* (right) and most sportsmen will have noticed *L'Equipe* ('the team'), a newspaper dedicated entirely to sport. Others in the ring are *Libération* (leftist), *France-Soir* (evening) and *Le Canard Enchaîné* (satirical). Compared to other countries, the French probably enjoy their periodicals more than their newspapers. *Paris-Match* is perhaps the only one widely known outside the country, but there are many others, including *L'Express, Le Point, Le Nouvel Observateur*. There is also a crop of society weeklies and the usual celebrity gossip magazines.

British and US newspapers are easy to get hold of in the holiday areas, which now comprise a huge proportion of France. The US and several of the London papers have European editions. All of the British broadsheets have weekly overseas versions and daily ones by subscription or you could download them from their websites.

Insuring Your House and Car

Insurance is big business in France – so big that two of the largest groups, *Groupement d'Assurances Nationales* and *Assurances Générales de France*, are nationalized. There are over 500 companies regulated by a *Code des Assurances* and overseen by a *Commission de Contrôle des Assurances*. The main difference between insuring your house in France and in Britain is that, in France, you must have third-party cover by law. How likely it is that your house is going to damage somebody or something is debatable, but it is a legal requirement. In practice, house-buyers inherit the insurance of the previous owner and it is the *notaire*'s responsibility to check that basic buildings and liability insurance is in force on the day of sale, *see* **Making the Purchase**. Other than that, house insurance is much the same, with the house and contents being insured separately on a replacement value basis. If the property is to be used as a holiday home or rented out, be careful that the policy gives all the cover needed, see further 'Property Insurance', pp.168–9.

Car insurance is very expensive thanks (the British say) to the high number of accidents and because (the French say) it is taxed at 36 per cent. The result is that some people do not insure beyond the legal minimum of third-party cover. You may want to, though, and the combinations on offer are much the same as anywhere else, starting with third-party, called in French *responsabilité civile*, and ending with comprehensive – *tous risques*. A comprehensive policy will not cover you if you are illegally parked or driving illegally – for example, drunk – but then no policy will. The only policy that won't be cancelled is third-party, which has to run until it expires, by law. It is important to shop around because quotes will vary and there can be big differences in cost and cover. Also, read the fine print because the policies differ quite a bit from UK ones. When you get your cover you will also a get a sticker (*vignette d'assurance*) that you stick to your windscreen.

Personal third-party cover is popular in France and is obligatory for children going to school. If your erratic golf swing brains your partner or if your Rottweiler eats your neighbour's poodle, such a policy will be useful, too. They usually come in a family package and can be attached to your building policy.

Bringing, Buying and Selling Your Car

Obviously, if you are just visiting a second home, your car remains a tourist's car. If you become a French resident, though, you should register it in France (officially within three months of importation) and this is not always a painless procedure. It varies from region to region, but, at the very least, you will need your passport, car registration document, insurance certificate, MOT or *contrôle technique* (*see* below), if applicable, *carte de séjour* and a certificate from an official technical inspector (*Inspecteur des Mines*) who checks that the vehicle conforms to French safety specifications. You may also be asked to obtain a letter from the car manufacturer's French head office to confirm that your car conforms to the makers' norms – another example of overly exuberant French bureaucracy. Take all these documents to your local *préfecture* or *sous-préfecture* (or *mairie* if you live in Paris). You will then receive your registration document, or *carte grise*, and take it to a shop that makes number plates, usually an ironmonger. The only hazard in this procedure is if, for some reason, your car does not conform to the required standard and you have expensive repairs or adjustments to make.

At the time of writing, all cars, even British ones, are cheaper in France than in Britain so it makes sense to buy one locally. Also, although some people like to stick with right-hand drive in a right-side driving country, most people find it inconvenient in the long run. Having decided to buy in France it makes a sense to buy French, too – the range and quality is good and the service and spares infrastructure better than for imported cars. Buying new cars in France differs little from buying them in the UK, with the usual range of finance available. The main difference in buying a used car in France is that a seller should be able to supply you with a *lettre de non-gage*, issued by the *département* and confirming there are no hire-purchase debts outstanding. You can also ask for a written declaration that it hasn't been involved in an accident. Otherwise, most precautions have their British equivalent: check that it has a valid MOT (*contrôle technique*), has been serviced, the chassis number is correct and so forth.

Selling cars is usually done via a local newspaper or advertising board. The act of selling is registered by the completion of a document (*certificat de vente*) that can be obtained at dealers' showrooms, *préfectures* or *mairies* – one copy of which goes to the registrar and one to the buyer. As in the UK, the other car documents are also handed over and you are obliged to give the buyer a *lettre de non-gage* and a guarantee that it is accident-free if he or she requests it.

The MOT in France is called *contrôle technique* and is carried out in much the same way as in Britain. It earns you another little badge to put on your windscreen. Your British or Irish driving licence will suffice indefinitely in France under EU reciprocity agreements.

If you are not used to French roads, the thought of driving on the right may be alarming. In fact, you do get used to it quite quickly, although there will always be momentary lapses – lapses that a few hundred tons of truck approaching at a closing speed of 100mph should soon rectify. Some people find that it helps to write something on the dashboard. What is more difficult to remember is to look left first, instead of right, at junctions, and that can be dangerous, too. There is also a tendency for traffic approaching from the right to think it has right of way, a misapprehension from a time when it often did. Furthermore, a flash of the headlights in France means 'I have right of way' not, as in Britain, 'you have right of way' – such a signal would never be used in France! Much has been written about French drivers and much of it is true. Although they defend themselves with claims that they drive with a *panache* of which stolid Anglo-Saxons are not capable, the figures indicate that this just means *too fast*. Fatalities on French roads are twice those of the UK, despite their better quality and less traffic. They are more considerate to cyclists though!

Assistance Services

The huge volume of British people moving to France has prompted several entrepreneurs to set up help and information services to make life easier. Among them is Val Gascoyne's Purple Pages (**www.purplepages.info**) – custom-made directories that cover everything from refuse collection to sport in a specific area, the idea being that all the information for living is there, available for the new arrival. There are also Petites Pages – less detailed directories to the four departments of Poitou-Charentes, where the concept has been developed and is based. Both directories have lots of 'snippets' of information, such as a sample cheque and how to complete it, how to live with a septic tank, good woods for burning on the fire and so forth.

When someone commissions a directory, they start doing the research, which includes going to the *commune* and doing all the footwork so that the client doesn't have to. It is then presented as a hardback volume within

28 days of the order being received. It is best if the order is placed as soon as you have first signed for the property, as then the directory will be ready before you move in, giving you a chance to read up before you arrive. It also means that you have it to use from the day you move in and, without a doubt, it will be referred to greatly in the first three or four months at least. Owing to the high interest in Purple Pages for other parts of France, Val and her team now produce them for other areas at an increased cost (because if the distances that they have to travel and the potential requirement for overnight accommodation). Petites Pages – the general directories for departments in Poitou-Charentes – are £19 each and the hardback tailored directory Purple Pages is £95 for commissions in Poitou-Charentes, but prices vary for directories outside this area. For example, Brittany in the north and Carcassonne in the south are each £175.

Ouicanhelp (**www.ouicanhelp@wanadoo.fr**) is run on a membership basis and deals with all of your settling in requirements in France. Though not estate agents, the company can help you find property (with its free property search service, included in your membership). It also has independent specialist legal, insurance, planning and accountancy advisors and can organize your bank account, *carte de séjour*, insurance and registration requirements and will discuss schooling requirements and arrange school visits. Advice is also available on transporting your pets, it can liaise with the utility services before your arrival and is happy to advise on, and order, your building materials. It can arrange translations (written or verbal), find local tradespeople, help with French bureaucracy and generally make your transition into French life a little easier. It has a 24-hour helpline for emergencies and operates on a nationwide basis. There is an initial joining fee of £25 and a membership fee of £70 per year.

Politics

Ever since the French revolution of 1789, politics has been a tug of war between a left and right, stereotyped as Catholic, monarchist conservatives and atheistic, republican socialists. Nowadays, of course, this has metamorphosed into a gentle swaying between left- and right-of-centre republicans, but France's successful fine-tuning of the constitutional machine really only dates back to Charles de Gaulle and his Fifth Republic of 1958. For the previous century, French politics had served as a laboratory for every possible form of political thought that the creativity of her people could devise and, if this was a fine illustration of their genius, it did nothing to encourage stability from which a prosperity equal to her potential could develop. The period leading to the collapse of the Fourth Republic (1948–58) would have made modern Italy look stable.

There have, of course, been other dynamics. One has been centralization. Compared to, say, England, which had reached its present borders 1,000 years ago, France is a geographically new state – Franche-Comté only joining in 1674, Nice in 1860 and Alsace-Lorraine, albeit for the second time, in 1918. Her entire history has been one of expansion by war or dynastic marriage, which endeared her neither to her neighbours, nor to many of her new Breton, Provençal, Basque or other subjects. Not that secession has ever been a serious issue, but the battle against centralization has. The vicious war in the Vendée in 1792, when radical Republicans fought a Catholic peasantry, was at least partially caused by a general obsession with uniformity, as was the Protestant Camisard revolt against Louis XIV in 1702. Louis XIV and Napoleon both saw a centralized bureaucracy as the means to tackle the problems caused by huge distances and demographic diversity and de Gaulle said much the same, using the hundreds of France's different regional cheeses as a metaphor. The same problems remained well beyond de Gaulle's time, bringing about one of the most drastic ever reorganizations of French provincial government. In 1982, regional assemblies were created and the position of departmental prefect, which had been the local government-appointed administrator since 1800, was replaced by a chairman of an elected body.

Nationally, France is governed by an executive, directly elected president and a bicameral parliament elected by proportional representation. There are five main political parties that, on the face of it, seem to represent a wider political spectrum than in the UK, but this is a little misleading. By European standards, the two main UK parties are tremendously broad churches and many French National Front (nationalist) voters would be quite at home in the Conservative Party while some French communists would sleep easy in Old Labour. Today, the main political parties are the Rassemblement pour la République (RPR), the Gaullist party, but considerably mellowed since his day; the conservative Union pour la Démocratie Française (UDF), a coalition of smaller centre-right parties; the Socialists (PS); the Communist Party (PCF); and the far right National Front (FN). The present governing party is a newly created alliance called the Union pour la Majorité Presidentielle. Because France, like most European countries, has a system of proportional representation, coalitions are common, with power oscillating between the centrist parties (RPR, PS and UDF). Apart from the European integration, about which most French have extremely mixed feelings, the perennial political problem is the cost of France's social services, particularly the health system, which economists say can't be afforded but which the electorate doesn't want meddled with.

The ability of the truculent Breton, Jean-Marie Le Pen, leader of the FN, to push Lionel Jospin, the Socialist Prime Minister, into third place in the first round of the 2002 Presidential election was an idiosyncrasy caused by a low electoral turnout and a plethora of leftist candidates. However, it did represent a Continent-wide concern with rising immigration and crime, and the belief that the two were related. It was also symptomatic of the fear that a combination of globalization and the European Union were robbing individual countries of their national identity, and few people are as sensitive to that as the French.

Religion

Historically and traditionally, France is a Roman Catholic country, but, in reality, the Church hasn't got many more practising members than the Anglican Church does in Britain. However, the majority of French citizens call themselves Catholic. Unlike in England, a rigid separation of Church and state has been in place since 1905. As with so many things in France, there are ironies, contradictions and paradoxes. State schools are so strictly non-sectarian that religious emblems such as crucifixes are banned, yet the state subsidizes Catholic schools. Even if France today is constitutionally secular, her culture and ethos are historically Christian and she is the heir to a remarkable legacy of Christian art, architecture and history. There is a number of very active Catholic charity groups, (set up, according to Victoria Pybus's most useful *Live & Work in France*, after World War II to stop leftist priests meddling in politics) such as *Caritas France* and *Les Chiffonniers d'Emaüs*.

Despite their impact on French history, or perhaps because of it, there are not many Protestant churches in France. The south was always the most religiously free-thinking, producing the Albigensian and others heresies in the Middle Ages, and a swathe of Protestantism, from the Atlantic to Provence, during the Reformation. Today, they number less than a million, grouped around Paris, Alsace-Lorraine and their old haunts in the south. There are Anglican churches in cities that historically have had a large British population. France has the biggest Jewish population in Western Europe, which has maintained a continuous presence since the Roman Empire. France was also the first European country to emancipate the Jews, at the time of the Revolution, the crowds tearing down the gates of the ghetto with their bare hands. Muslims are the largest non-Catholic group with four million, most coming from North Africa, and mostly Sunni. Many other sects, including most Christian and Muslim ones, are represented in France.

Letting Your Property

08

Letting for Income

A large portion of British property-owners in France are second home-owners. The usual plan is to keep a pleasant French hideaway where you can spend the time that suits you and let it out when it doesn't. A growing number of people do this with a view to retiring to it. This often works well and many a ruined farm has had a new lease of life as a holiday and retirement home for foreigners. In theory, you should get a *carte de séjour* after three months, but, in practice, second homeowners don't bother. So long as you are not working in France and are still covered by UK national insurance – specifically the reciprocal health cover form E111 – there is no point. As you begin to spend more time in your second home, the next hurdle comes at six months, when you become liable for French tax.

If you are not spending all your time in your second home, who is? Naturally, most people try to offset their costs by letting their property out and, if you do this, you are liable for tax on that rent.

Very few people with jobs in Britain have three months a year spare to spend in a holiday home or anywhere else, so the three-month limit should be fine for most people anyway. However, when all is said and done, this is not a huge matter of debate where genuine, rate-paying (*taxe d'habitation* and *taxe foncière* – *see* p.182) householders are concerned. There have to be laws, but, on the whole, the ordinary people have no objections to well-behaved foreigners spending their time and money among them. What concerns them more is what happens when the new householder is not there. On the topic of the excellent relations between locals and newcomers, an English lawyer practising in France has observed, 'While they were doing up barns in the countryside there was no problem, but if they come into the villages, price out the locals, and then leave their houses empty for half the year, they won't be so welcome.' This does not apply, of course, if your second home is a studio in central Paris or a seaside flat in Cannes, but it is worth bearing in mind in the agricultural hinterland.

As to the taxes on rent, there is an important distinction between furnished and unfurnished letting. A second home – by its very nature – will be furnished and letting is judged as a commercial activity. By keeping proper French accounts, you can offset depreciation and loan interest against income, but, if that is too much of a hassle, you can opt for a flat rate deduction of 70 per cent of gross rents in lieu of all other deductions. *Taxe foncière* is a tax on property paid by the owner and *taxe d'habitation* is a tax paid by the resident. (New buildings are sometimes exempt from *taxe foncière* for a period, so check.) Both together do not usually approach the level of British council tax. Both British and French taxpayers are liable to these taxes, but also remember that it is easy to become a French taxpayer by default. There is not only the danger of inadvertently staying over your

183 days, but you can be deemed a French resident if your home is permanently in France – even if you don't spend 183 days in it – or if you are a tax resident of no other country but you have a place in France. You can find yourself in trouble at the other end, too, if, say, you have property in the UK that is being let. Be careful that you don't find yourself a resident for tax purposes in both countries. It's quite possible to be assessed for rental income on French property by both countries and, although there is a double taxation agreement between the two , it is you who will have to pay both accounts while they are sorting it out and we all know how long that can take. For most people, though, this is academic.

Rental Potential

As I have already said, there are two types of people who decide to rent out their home in France. There are those who see the property as mainly, or even exclusively, an investment proposition and there are those who are buying what is, predominantly, a holiday home but who wish to cover all or part of the cost of ownership from rental income. For the first group this is a business. Just as in any business, the decisions they take about where and what to buy, how to restore the property and what facilities to provide will be governed by the wish to maximise profit. The second group will have to bear in mind most of the same considerations, but will be prepared to compromise (and so reduce potential income) in order to maximise their enjoyment of the property as a holiday home.

Both groups will need to understand the rental potential of the property they are buying. The most important thing to understand is that there are thousands of properties in France which are, commercially speaking, impossible to let. A rustic house in a rural backwater may find one or two tenants during the year but they will not be anywhere near enough to generate a sensible commercial return on your investment. If you are interested in such a house you will probably have accepted this and view any rental income as a bonus that may help to defray some of the expenses of ownership.

If you can make it available for rental July, August and early September (particularly August) and also at Easter you will dramatically increase your rental income.

Assessing rental potential is a skill that takes time to acquire. There are, however some good indicators of property that is likely to let well, *see* 'The Right Area', pp.271–3 and 'The Right Property', p.274.

Are You Going to Use the Services of a Managing Agent?

This is someone who will look after the letting of the property, deal with the cleaning and handovers, pay the bills, look after repairs etc. They will typically charge about 20 per cent of rental income received as their fee. Management companies generally operate only in popular areas where there is enough demand to keep them in business (*see also* 'Management', p.281).

If you do not use a managing agent you will still (usually) need to employ a cleaner and someone to deal with handovers. This could be the same person and, in rural areas, would probably be a neighbour.

In our experience it is seldom sufficient to rely on a management company if you want to let the property to its full potential. Owners, through family, friends, work mates and other contacts, are usually better at filling the off season weeks than a management company is. The management company, however, will capture passing trade that you would not pick up and can redirect visitors from over booked property to yours.

In our experience the people who make most money from rental income are those who do not use a management company but deal with these things themselves. This does not mean you should not use a company! You may have neither the time nor the inclination to do this work yourself.

If your property is well located, attractive and clean you should expect about 30 per cent repeat visitors in most areas. Generally it takes four or five years for a rental property to reach its full potential.

Having said all of this, what can you expect to generate by way of rental income? In our experience a reasonably diligent person, doing their best to find tenants and not relying wholly on a management company but not totally obsessive about the property – can expect to produce roughly the following results:

Renting Out Your Property – Performance Targets

Area and Type of Property	Target Weeks	Percentage Return
Paris – apartment	35	7
Nice – apartment	30	7
Cote d'Azur villa	25	5
Normandy/Brittany – coastal house/apartment	20	6
Normandy/Brittany – inland	16	5
Atlantic Coast	20	6
Dordogne	16	5
Provence	16	5
Other Inland France	12	4

The Target Weeks is the number of weeks you could expect to let an average property provided you did not use it for July or August.

The Percentage Return is the amount you should expect to generate as a percentage of the value of the property, after payment of all agents fees, water, electricity, cleaning and other outgoings related to the rental period but before taking into account your own personal tax liability.

These are general guides only and will vary significantly from property to property, management company to management company and owner to owner.

The Right Area

The choice of the area in which to buy your rental property is far and away the most important decision that you will make. There are many parts of France where it is fairly easy to let your property sufficiently regularly to make it a commercially viable proposition. There are other areas where this is almost impossible. There is nowhere where it will be impossible to find a single tenant, but low occupancy levels are not going to be enough to make a profit on the investment you have made, or even to cover the costs of running the property.

The factors to take into consideration when deciding on the area are slightly different from the factors relevant when you're thinking about buying a home for your own personal use. They will also vary depending on your target clientele and your preferred way of administering the property.

Climate

Most people going on holiday hope for decent weather. Fortunately, not everybody has the same idea about what this means. The number of people taking summer holidays in Brittany shows that a higher than average rainfall is not fatal. Despite this, you are likely to have more success if you are in an area that is known to have decent weather.

It is particularly important that the area has good weather during the prime British holiday season – normally July, August and September. The most successful areas for rental purposes are those that are reliably warm and dry or hot and dry during this period. Apart from this main holiday season there are the months of May, June and October, which offer reasonable letting prospects if you are in an area with a mild climate. There is also a relatively small market for longer lets in areas with particularly mild climates or that are socially desirable. Study the climate charts for a comparison of the regional variations (*see* **References**). Information is also available from local tourist offices, in travel publications and on the Internet.

Access

Just as important as the climate is the ability of tenants to get access to your property. This is true at two levels. The area in which the property is located must offer convenient access from the places where the tenants live, and the property itself must be easy to find. For most British visitors, convenient access to the area means convenient access from the Channel ports or a major local airport. Convenient access is much more difficult to define if you are trying to attract French visitors.

It is worth repeating the results of research conducted by the travel industry. This that shows that 25 per cent of all potential visitors will not come if it involves travelling for more than one hour from a local airport at either end of their journey and that if that figure rises to an hour and a half, then the number that will choose not travel rises to 50 per cent. This research was undertaken in the context of package holidays, but the principles must also apply to people renting holiday homes. Of course, this does not mean that if your home is more than one hour's drive from a Channel port or airport you will not let it. There are many people who are much more adventurous and those wanting to rent property in rural France will often be in that category. Indeed, they will often view the journey as being part of the holiday. It is beyond doubt, however, that if you are within easy travelling distance of the ports or major airports, then the numbers of people renting from you will increase and so will your profit.

Do not underestimate the importance of being able to find your property. Navigation in the depths of rural France can be trying. There are few people to ask for directions (especially if you don't speak French) and there are few signposts of much help when it comes to locating a rural cottage. The situation is not much better if you are trying to locate a villa in Cannes. So, the closer it is to a main road, the better (within reason – ideally far enough away to escape traffic noise and fumes). Giving decent maps and guidance notes is also essential. Nothing is guaranteed to ruin the start of your holiday as much as cruising around for three hours to cover the last 500m of your journey.

Tourist Attractions

Governments are keen on tourist attractions because they attract tourists! The fact that they are prepared to invest billions of euros of taxpayers' money in encouraging these attractions should persuade you that having one near to you is a good thing when it comes to letting your property.

'Tourist attractions' is a term that covers a multitude of things. At one extreme it could be Disneyland Paris, attracting millions of visitors each year, all of whom have to find somewhere to sleep. Going slightly down in scale it could mean being near to a famous wine region or châteaux or a championship golf course or famous beach or sailing area. Remember too that something very local, such as falconry,or the lady in the village who runs pottery or cooking classes, could provide all the visitors you need, provided you strike a deal whereby she refers visitors to you. 20 per cent of the rent received should do the trick!The point is that there must be something to bring people to your area so that they will need to use your accommodation. The mere fact that the house is located in the middle of the countryside is not, of itself, enough to attract a significant number of tenants.

To find out the tourist attractions in the area you are thinking of buying contact the French Tourist Office and/or study the tourist guides to France available in libraries and bookshops.

The attractions near to you will not only determine the number of visitors but the type of visitor. Your property should be geared to deal with them. So, for example, if you are near an area famous for windsurfing your property should be furnished robustly enough to cater for the young enthusiasts, should have somewhere to store their gear and somewhere to dry off wet clothing. This will help attract people choosing between your property and that of your neighbour and will bring repeat visitors.

Other Facilities

Many people going on holiday want to eat out. Even those who will probably end up buying food in their local supermarket and cooking it at home think that they will want to eat out. It will be much easier to let your property if it is within easy walking distance of one or more restaurants. It should also be within walking distance, or a short drive, of shops and other facilities.

Different markets require different facilities. Think what, for you, would make the place special and do a bit of market research by asking people similar to those you want to attract what they would like.

The biggest issue is whether to have a pool. If you are catering to a family market in rural France a pool will dramatically increase bookings. They are expensive. It will cost £10,000 – £15,000 to construct a decent sized pool and, perhaps, £3,000 per year to maintain it.

Can You Let the Property?

There are some parts of France where there are restrictions on the right to let property as a commercial landlord. Make sure that there will be no restrictions in the area where you are buying. It is probable that your activities will not be classed as being a commercial landlord in any case, but it is worth making sure. Also, make sure that there is no restriction on your right to let the property itself. This will normally only be the case in a very small number of apartments or condominiums *copropriétés* (*see* pp.148–9) where the rules of the community impose restrictions.

The Right Property

The choice of property is almost as important as the choice of area. Not all properties let to the same extent. Our experience suggests that those properties the potential clients find attractive will let up to five times more frequently than properties that do not stand out for any reason. This is such a significant difference that you ignore it at your peril.

New property is generally cheaper to maintain than older property. It is, however, not nearly is likely to be attractive to potential tenants. Most people going on holiday – to rural France – are looking for a character property.

Pick an Attractive Home

Most people will decide whether or not to rent your property after they have seen only a brief description and a photograph. The photograph is by far the more important factor. Research that we carried out showed that 80 per cent of a group shown 32 potential rental properties picked the same three properties. The common factor in these properties was that they were all pretty. If the person was looking at properties in Normandy, then they went for a traditional Norman cottage (wood beams, wattle and daub construction, steeply angled slate or thatch roof) and not a modern, semi-detached house. If they were looking for somewhere by the sea, then they opted for a seaside cottage, preferably with either sand or water in view. If you are buying a house for rental purposes, therefore, make sure you buy one that 'takes a pretty picture'. Brittany Ferries (who run a property rental programme) tell me that some of their properties are so pretty they can find tenants 50 weeks of the year. A more usual figure for Brittany might be 16 weeks per year.

Make sure the external decoration and garden/pool area are kept in good order. These are what will show up in your photographs and will create the first impression for your guests.

Equipping the Property

If you advertise the property well you will get tenants. However, you will only get repeat tenants, and recommendations from existing tenants, if the property meets expectations in terms of the facilities it offers and its cleanliness. The facilities required will depend on the target market you are trying to attract. Think about that audience and think about what you would want if you were one of them. For example, if you are trying to attract a clientele of mountain walkers or sailors, they will appreciate somewhere to dry their clothes quickly so that they can be ready for the following day. The property must be spotlessly clean. This applies in particular to the kitchen and bathroom and your cleaner may require some training as our expectations when going into rented accommodation are possibly higher than our expectations of an ordinary home.

Documents

Make sure that all guests are sent a pre-visit pack. This should include notes about the area and local attractions (usually available free from the local tourist office), a map showing the immediate vicinity, notes explaining how to get to the property, emergency contact numbers and instructions as to what to do if they are delayed for any reason.

Welcome

It is much better if someone is present, either at the property or at a nearby house, to welcome your guests when they arrive. They can sort out any minor problems or any particular requirements of the guests. You should make sure that basic groceries, such as bread, milk, coffee, sugar and a bowl of fruit are left in the house to welcome your guests. A bottle of wine goes down well, too!

A house book should be available in the property. It should give more information about local attractions, restaurants, shops and so forth, and a comprehensive list of contact numbers for use in case of any conceivable emergency. It can also act as a visitors' book. This will be a useful vehicle for obtaining feedback and a means of making future contact direct with visitors who might have booked via an agency.

Kitchen

The kitchen must be modern, even if traditional in style. Everything should work. You should have a microwave. You should also make sure that there is sufficient cutlery, crockery, cups, glasses and cooking equipment and that it is all in good condition. A cookbook giving local recipes is a nice touch. A washing machine and tumble dryer are now commonplace and, for a large property, a dishwasher is becoming equally so.

Bathroom

An en suite bathroom for each bedroom is ideal, but is seldom possible. A bidet will be welcomed by French visitors and contribute a local feel for British visitors. Make sure that there is soap in the bathrooms. Guests will much prefer it if you provide towels as part of your service, too.

Bedrooms

The number of bedrooms you choose is very important. Generally, in seaside areas and cities, you will get a better return on your investment for properties with fewer (one or two) bedrooms – which will be cheaper to buy – than larger properties. In rural areas, where the majority of your guests may well be families, a three-bedroom property is probably your best compromise. Bedrooms should have adequate storage space. Most importantly, they should have clean and comfortable beds. The only beds that last well in a regularly used property and where the people sleeping in them will be all sorts of different sizes and weights are expensive beds, such as those used in the hotel industry.

Beds should be protected from obvious soiling by the use of removable mattress covers, which should be changed with each change of tenants. Uncomfortable beds are second only to dirt in producing complaints. Clients will much prefer it if you supply bedding as part of your service rather than expecting them to take their own.

Living Areas

Furniture and upholstery should be in good condition. The style is a matter of personal preference, something with a 'local' flavour is often attractive. The furniture must be comfortable, and there should be adequate means of cleaning, including a vacuum cleaner.

Heating

Heating is essential. It should be effective and cover the whole house.

Air-conditioning

Air-conditioning is probably best avoided, except in the most expensive lettings. It is not yet considered compulsory and can be expensive both to run and maintain.

Swimming Pool

If you are catering to a British audience, a swimming pool is highly desirable. In a rural area it will significantly increase your potential number of tenants. A pool should be of reasonable size, but need not be heated.

The Right Price

When buying a property as a business, you will be concerned to pay as little as possible for a property consistent with getting the right level of rental return. If you are only buying the property as a business proposition, then this price/rental balance (or return on investment) is the main criteria on which you should base your decision as to which property to buy.

If you are going to use the property not only as a rental but also as a holiday home, then there is an additional factor. This is the amount of time that you will be able to use the property yourself consistent with getting a certain level of rental return. For example, if you bought a one-bedroom property on the seafront in Nice for £150,000, that property might be let for 35 weeks per year and produce you a return, after deducting all expenses, of, say, 7.5 per cent. If you bought a two-bedroom apartment in the old town of Nice for, say, £100,000 and let that for 25 weeks per year, you might also generate 7.5 per cent on your investment. Both would be performing equally well, but the apartment in the old town would allow you and your family to use the property for 25 weeks per year whereas the seafront apartment would only allow you to use it for 15 weeks per year. This, and the fact that it had one more bedroom, could make the old town property the more attractive proposition. I hasten to say that the figures I'm quoting are simply examples to illustrate the point rather than indications as to what is actually obtainable at any particular moment. Whatever way you look at it, paying the minimum necessary to buy the property is the key to maximizing performance.

In some parts of France, there are many estate agents competing for your business and it is very easy to compare the prices of the various properties on offer from these sources. In other parts of France, there may only be one estate agent covering your area. He may not operate from shopfront prices and it may be very difficult to get any meaningful comparison of prices. In the circumstances, it might be sensible to get someone experienced in renting property to give you a second opinion as to the viability of the project and seek projections from a managing agent.

As a general proposition, cheaper properties will produce a better rate of return than more expensive properties. This is because it does not cost 25 times as much to rent a £1 million house as it does to rent a £40,000 house. There are also usually more vacant weeks with a more expensive property because there is a smaller pool of possible tenants.

Marketing Your Property

Properties do not let themselves – you will have to do some marketing. In the early years, you will have to do more marketing than in later years because you will have no existing client base. As in any other businesses, the cheapest type of marketing is catching repeat clients or via client recommendations and so money spent on making sure that the property lives up to or exceeds their expectations (and thus secures their return) is probably the best spend that you will make. There seems to be no correlation between the amount spent on marketing and the results achieved. Much money spent appears to be money wasted.

The key points are to choose the method of marketing most appropriate to your property and circumstances and to follow up all leads generated at once. Contact them again after a couple of weeks to see if they have made the minds up. Send them your details again next year at about the same time, as they are likely to be taking another holiday. Remember that your marketing is only as good as the quality of the response you give to people making enquiries. You will probably do better spending less money on advertising and paying more attention to following up the leads that you have actually generated than anything else.

Directories

If your property is pretty, then you are likely to get good results from the various directories and magazines focusing on properties to let in France. They only work if they are inexpensive because, for most private owners with only one property to let, if you only have one opportunity of letting each week and a directory produces, say, 50 enquiries for the first week in September, it is not particularly helpful. We have had good reports of results from Brittany Ferries' directory (for property in northern France) and Private Villas magazine (for upmarket properties).

Advertising

The problems with advertising are its scattergun effect and, in many cases, its cost. You only need a very small number of responses. You cannot afford to pay a large amount in advertising fees for each week let. Except for very expensive properties, traditional advertising is too expensive. We have had good reports of results from the specialist French property press and Dalton's Weekly – and even better reports from advertising on the local supermarket's noticeboard!

Your Own Contacts

Your own contacts are, without doubt, the best opportunity you have for marketing your property in France. Remember how few people you need to rent it out for, say, 25 weeks per year. Given that many people will take it for two weeks or more, you will probably only be looking for 10 to 15 lettings per year.

The people who find this easiest are those who work for large organizations. If you work for a major hospital or manufacturing or service industry, you will almost certainly be able to find enough people to keep your property fully occupied from within your working environment. You will have the additional advantage of knowing the people who are going to rent the property and reducing substantially the risk that they will cause it damage or fail to pay you.

Even without people from work, most owners will be able to find enough friends, neighbours and relatives to rent a nice property in France for ten weeks per year. This will leave only a relatively small number of tenants to be found by advertising or other marketing means.

When renting to family and friends or, indeed, close working colleagues, you will have to learn how to raise the delicate issue of payment. Given that you are not going to be incurring any marketing costs and, probably, very little in the way of property management costs, you should be able to offer them an attractive price and still generate as much income as you would have done by letting through an agency. Make sure that you address the issue when you accept the booking, as doing so later can be very embarrassing.

The French Market

Most British people do not speak French well enough to offer their property on the French market in any other way than through a letting agency.

Other Markets

There are significant English-speaking markets in Scandinavia, Germany, the United States and elsewhere. The specialist French property press will address these, but they are most successfully addressed via the internet.

The internet offers tremendous opportunities for bringing a specialist niche product to the attention of a vast audience at very little cost. It also offers the possibility of showing lots of pictures and other information about your property and the area in which it is to be found. As such, it is ideal for the person wanting to rent out property.

It is worth having your own small website designed especially for this purpose. Not only can it be your brochure, but it can also act as a way of taking bookings. It is much cheaper to have someone print off a copy of your brochure from his or her own computer than it is for you to send it by post! You may have the expertise to create your own website. If you do not, it's quite fun learning how. If you have neither the time nor inclination, a simple but very effective site can be put together for you for as little as £250.

You will have to decide whether you want to use the site only as a brochure or you are prepared to take electronic bookings as well. You will also have to decide whether to price your product only in sterling, only in euros or, perhaps, in multiple currencies, including US dollars. You will be able to take payment only by cheque unless you are lucky enough to be a merchant with a credit card account or prepared to incur the expense of setting up the facility.

As well as having your own website, you should consider listing your property on one of the many French property websites currently to be found on the internet. These listings are either free or low-cost. You will soon find the ones that work and the ones that don't.

Management

Letting Agencies?

Strangely, the decision as to how you are the going to let your property is one of the first that you are going to have to take. This is because if you decide to use a professional management or letting agencies it will alter your target market and therefore the area in which you ought to be buying.

If you are going to let your property through a professional management agency then it is worth contacting such agencies before you make a final selection of area to see what they believe they can offer in the way of rental returns. They will also be able to tell you what type of property is likely to be most successful as a letting property in that area.

If you are thinking of finding the tenants yourself then you will have to decide upon your primary market. Most British people letting property themselves let it primarily to the British. There are a number of reasons for this. Lack of language skills is probably the most common. The rest of this section is targeted mainly at the person wishing to let to a British market

Letting agencies – or at least good letting agencies – will have the opportunity to capture clients from the domestic French market as well as from various international markets. They will argue that the fee that you will pay them (typically 17.5 to 20 per cent of your letting income + VAT) will be recovered by extra lettings that they make during the season. This may or may not be true. In our experience the people who are most successful at letting their property are those who attract the clients themselves. This, however, assumes a level of commitment that many people simply cannot afford. It is simpler to use a letting agency.

If you decide to use a letting agency the choice of agency is critical. There are some excellent agencies both in France and operating from Britain. There are also some crooks. The difference in performance between the two will make the difference between making a profit and a substantial loss. The temptation is clear. If somebody comes into their office on a Friday in August and wants to rent an apartment yours may be available. Will the agent put the rent – perhaps £1,000 – in your bank account or in his own pocket? Will the agent rent your apartment or the apartment belonging to one of his 'special friends'—? In the past too many have thought that you would never find out that they had let the property because you were 1000 miles away and so have succumbed to temptation.

Selecting an Agency

When selecting which letting agency to appoint there are various checks that you should make. Remember these people hold the financial success of your venture in their hands.

- **If the agency is a French agency, are they professionally qualified? In France you need to be qualified to offer property management services. Most such services are offered as an adjunct to estate agencies.**
- **Check their premises. Do they seem welcoming and efficient? Is there evidence of significant letting activity?**
- **What marketing do they do? If they are reliant upon passing trade then, except in the most exceptional areas, they will not get you good results.**
- **Ask to see a sample information pack sent to a potential client. You will be able to judge a lot from this. Is it the image you want to give of your property?**
- **Inspect two or three properties that they are presently managing. If they are dirty or ill cared for then so will yours be. Then it will not let.**
- **Ask the references. Preferably they should be from other overseas clients. Take the references up. Preferably speak to the people on the telephone. Ask whether there are happy with the performance and whether the financial projections given to them have been met.**
- **What contract are they offering you? Unless you are familiar with French law it is sensible to get this checked before you sign it as some give you far more rights than others. Make sure that the contract gives you an entitlement to full reports showing when the property was let and for what money. Do not accept an analysis by period. Insist on a breakdown the week by week. Also insist on a full breakdown of all expenses incurred in connection with the property. Make sure the contract gives you the right to dismiss them on fairly short notice.**
- **How many weeks rental do they think you will be able to obtain in this area? How much do they think they would generate for you after deduction of all expenses including the charges?**
- **What type of property do they think would be the best for letting purposes in this area?**

Controlling the Agency

Once you have appointed a letting agency you must control it.

- **Check the report you receive from the agency and check that the money you receive corresponds to the amounts shown in the reports.**
- **Let the agency know, in the nicest possible way, that you and all of your friends in the area check each other's properties every time you are there and compare notes about which are occupied and the performance of your letting agencies. If they believe you then this is a deterrent to unauthorised lettings.**
- **Telephone the property every week. If someone answers the phone make a note and make sure that there is income shown for the week of the phone call.**
- **From time to time, have a friend pose as a prospective customer and send for an inquiry pack.**
- **If you get the opportunity, calling to see the property without warning to see what state it is in.**

All this may sound like hard work. It is not. It will significantly increase the income you receive from your rental property.

Furnished or Unfurnished?

From the point of view of the landlord the safest type of letting is a short holiday letting of furnished property.

To be classified as furnished the property must be properly or fully furnished. In other words, it must have all of the key items required to live successfully in the home. A property let without, for example, a bed or a cooker or a table or a refrigerator or chairs would in each case the likely to be treated as an unfurnished property. The result could be that the tenant could acquire the right to stay on at the end of the tenancy.

A holiday letting is a letting that takes place during the recognised holiday season. That season is obviously different in an Alpine resort than in Nice. It will generally cover at least the period from June to September.

If a furnished property is let as a holiday letting for a period of less than three months the tenant's rights to stay on at the end of the period of the tenancy are extremely limited. You will be entitled to recover possession of the property if the tenant has another home to go to (or had one at the time they took possession of the property).

The Letting Agreement

A suitability drafted tenancy agreement will take into account all these factors and protect you in the event of a dispute with your tenant and, in particular, in the event that he wishes to stay on at the end of the tenancy.

If your property forms part of a *copropriété* your tenants will have to agree to abide by the rules of the community and should be supplied with a copy of the rules or at least of the part of the rules that govern their conduct.

In the rental contract you should stipulate what things are going to be covered by your insurance and what are not. Typically the tenants personal possessions would not be covered under your policy.

Taxation of Rental Income

See **Financial Implications**, 'Taxation', pp.176–206 and also p.268.

'Leasebacks'

The Leaseback is an interesting variant on the normal way to own an investment property.

The French have more tourists than any other country in the world. 20 years or so ago the government was receiving lots of complaints that there was an inadequate amount of tourist accommodation and that what there was was too often of poor quality. In response to these criticisms they introduced a scheme to grant incentives to encourage the private investor to invest in high quality tourist accommodation. The individual schemes or programmes vary from each other in detail but the main points apply to them all.

The investor must buy a property – usually an apartment but sometimes a chalet in a ski resort or a house in a development – in a complex approved for this purpose.

The properties must either be brand new or completely renovated, such as where an old building in Paris is rebuilt behind the original façade. You cannot buy an old house in the countryside and put it into such a scheme.

You buy an apartment and furnishings in one of these complexes and enter into a contract with the company running the scheme whereby you grant a lease of the apartment to the company for a minimum period of nine years. That period is fixed by law. This is the basis of the name 'leaseback' applied to these schemes. They then rent the property to tourists.

These are complexes where at least a large part of the properties are being managed under a hotel type arrangement. There is a central administration for the scheme from which the tourist rents your apartment rather than a hotel room.

You will receive a rent for letting the company use your property. This is usually fixed, at the outset, as a percentage of the price you have paid for the property. It is typically 5.5 or six per cent of the price you paid. It is normally index linked so that, as the years go by, your rent will rise in line with inflation.

That rent is payable to you however successful or unsuccessful the company is in letting the property to tourists. You take comfort from the fact that the company with which you have the contract is usually a substantial company which will be 'good for the money', even if they have a bad year.

They will also usually be responsible for paying all of the outgoings in relation to the property – water, electricity, community fees, repairs, etc. Even if someone comes in drunk and wrecks the place this is the company's problem, not yours. You will only be responsible for your own personal taxation.

These two factors make this an attractive option for the person who is cautious and who likes the certainty of a fixed return on their investment and the person who has neither the time or the inclination to manage the property themselves.

In addition to the fixed return you will usually be allowed to use the property yourself, free of charge, for two, three or four weeks per year. This makes this attractive to the person – perhaps in his 40s or 50s who does not have much holiday entitlement at present but who will have a lot more freedom in 10 years time.

As an incentive to go into these schemes the government usually allows you to buy the property free of VAT. As VAT on a new property in France is 19.6 per cent this is a substantial saving which, if added back to the rental income received, makes the rental return on these investments competitive with even the best performing buy to let property in France.

You also, of course, benefit from the capital gain on the property whilst you own it. As these are effectively four and five star hotels they are generally in superb locations with better than average growth potential. As I have said earlier, capital growth in places like Cannes and central Paris has been very strong indeed over many, many years.

At the end of the nine years you can either keep the property to use as a holiday home, continue to rent it out (possibly through the same agency), sell it or – in most cases – live in it.

Mortgages are available to buy these properties. Because of the discount on the price resulting from not having to pay the VAT you can often borrow 95 per cent of the price paid. If you borrow this much the rental income will not be enough to pay off both capital and interest on the amount borrowed. It will go a long way towards doing so but you will need to make additional payments to fund the difference. If, on the other hand, you borrow only, say, 65 per cent of the price paid then the rental income should be enough to pay off the capital and interest in full. For the cautious fixed rate mortgages (for the whole duration of the mortgage) are usually available.

These can be a very interesting introduction to investing in European property and can also be interesting for someone who has retired and who wants a property portfolio. Instead of having all the property near where he lives he can have fully managed property in, for example, Paris, Nice and a ski area. They will probably generates a decent income and capital growth and, as a bonus, they will allow him free use of the properties for his holidays for, say, a total of 12 weeks per year.

References

09

Dictionary of Useful and Technical Terms

abîmer	deteriorate
abonnement	standing charge
abri	shelter
acajou	mahogany
accueil	reception
acompte	deposit
acquérir	to buy
acte authentique	legal paper drawn up (with all due formalities), by a public officer empowered by law (e.g. a *notaire*) in the place where he officiates
acte de commerce	commercial act
acte de vente	a conveyance or transfer of land (sometimes referred to as *acte d'achat*)
acte sous seing privé	private agreement in writing with no witnesses (the pre-sale agreement)
actuellement	currently
affaire	bargain/business
agence immobilière	estate agent
Agence Nationale Pour l'Emploi (ANPE)	French National Employment Office
agence	agency
agrandissement	extension
agréé	registered
alimentation	supply (water, electricity, etc.)
aménagé	converted
amiante	asbestos
ancien	old
antenne	aerial
antenne parabolique	satellite dish
ardoise	slate
arrhes	sum paid in advance by the purchaser, forfeited if purchaser withdraws or double the amount refunded if the vendor withdraws
arrière-pays	back country
artisan maçon	expert builder
assurance complémentaire maladie	independent health insurance
attestation d'acquisition	a notarial certificate that the property purchase has been completed
atelier	workshop
attestation	certificate
avocat	solicitor
baguette	beading
bail	lease to tenant
balcon	balcony
banque	bank
bâtiment	building

béton	concrete
bois	wood
bon état	good condition
bord de mer/rivière	beside the sea/river
bouche d'aération	air vent
bouchon	stopper
boulon	bolt
bureau	office
cabinet	small room
cadastre	local town planning register
cadenas	padlock
cadre	frame
caisse des dépôts et consignations	deposits and consignment office
Caisse d'Epargne	savings bank
Caisse des Allocations Familiales	child benefit office
Caisse Nationale d'Assurance Vieillesse ou de Retraite	pensions office
Caisse Primaire d'Assurance Maladie	medical expenses office
cale	wedge
campagne	country
caoutchouc	rubber
carillon	doorbell
carrelage	ceramic tiles
carreleur	tiler
carte de santé	medical record book
carte de paiement	payment card
carte de résident	resident's card
carte de séjour	government permit to reside in France (also called *permis de séjour*)
carte grise	car registration
carte professionnelle	granted by the Préfecture to estate agents to carry out business
carte verte	car insurance
carte vitale	health card
cause réelle et sérieuse	legitimate cause
caution solidaire	guarantor
cave	cellar
centre commercial	shopping centre
centre des impôts	tax office
certificat de ramonage	certificate of chimney sweeping
certificat d'urbanisme	zoning certificate (equivalent to a local authority search)
cession	sale
chambre	bedroom
chambre des métiers	chamber of trades
charges comprises	service charges included
charges sociales	social charges

charnière	hinge
charpentièr	carpenter
chasse	hunting
chaudière	water heater/boiler
chauffage	heating
chauffe eau	hot water tank
chaumière	thatched cottage
charges	maintenance charges on a property
chaux	carbonate of lime
chèque de banque	banker's draft
cheminée	chimney/fire-place
chêne	oak
cheville	expanding wall lug
chiffre d'affaire	turnover
clause d'accroissement	(*also see tontine*) agreement that purchase is made for the benefit of the last surviving purchaser
clause pénale	penalty clause governing performance of an agreement
climatisation	air-conditioning
cloison	partition
clôture	fence
clou	nail
code du travail	labour code
commerçant	commercial trader
commissariat de police	police station
comptabilité	accounting, book-keeping
compensable	the clearing of a cheque
comprenant	including
compromis de vente	contract for sale and purchase of land
compte à terme	deposit account
compte courant	current account
Compte d'Epargne Logement	home-buyers saving scheme
compte titre	shares account
concessionnaire	distributor
concours	selective entrance exam
condition suspensive	conditional terms stated in the pre-sale agreement (e.g. the acquiring of a loan, the gaining of a positive zoning certificate)
constructible	land which is designated for building under local planning scheme
Conseil de Prud'homme	labour court
conservation des hypothèques	mortgage/land registry
constat amiable	accident report form
constat de dégat des eaux	water damage form
contrôle technique	MOT
contrat de réservation	the purchase contract used for purchase 'on plan' (sometimes called *contract préliminaire*)
contrat multirisques habitation	all risks household policy
contrat à durée déterminée	fixed-term contract
conventionné (médecin)	doctor working in the health service

conventions collectives	collective agreements
copie exécutoire	enforceable copy
copropriété	co-ownership
couloir	corridor
courtier	broker
cuisine	kitchen
cuivre	copper
dallage	paving
dalle	flagstone
débarras	box room
déclaration de sincérité	compulsory formula providing that the purchase price has not been increased by a counter-deed
dépendance	outbuilding
dépôt de vente	sale room
détendeur	gas pressure regulator
devis	estimate
disjoncteur	electric trip switch
distributeur automatique de billets	cash machine, ATM
domicile fiscal	tax address
droit au bail	right to a lease
droit de préemption	pre-emptive right to acquire the property instead of purchaser
droit de succession/donation	inheritance/gift tax
ébéniste	cabinet maker
échafaudage	scaffolding
échelle	ladder
éclairage	lighting
écurie	stable
EDF/GDF	the state utilities: Electricité de France, Gaz de France
émoluments	the scale of charges of the *notaire*
emplacement	site
emprunt	loan
encadrement	framing
enduit	filler
enregistrement (droits d')	registration of the title of ownership (following which are the payment of transfer duties).
entreprise individuelle	one-person business
entreprise unipersonnelle	one person limited company
entretien	maintenance
épaisseur	thickness
équipé	equipped
escabeau	step ladder
escalier	stair
espace	space
espèces	cash
espagnolette	shutter/window fastening

établi	work bench
Etablissement Public de Coopération Intercommunale	planning agency for a group of *communes*
étagère	shelf
étage	storey, floor
étanche	watertight
états des lieux	schedule of condition or schedule of dilapidation depending on whether it applies to the beginning or end of a lease
expédition	the certified copy of a notarial document showing the date of its registration and the registration duty paid
expert comptable	chartered accountant
expert foncier	professional to check on the state and value of the property (usually an architect)
expertiser	to value a property
facture	invoice/bill
faillite	bankruptcy
faute grave	serious fault
fer	iron
ferme	farm
ferraillage	ironwork
fibre dure	hardboard
finitions	finishings
FNAIM – Fédération Nationale des Agents Immobiliers	national association of estate agents, providing a compensation fund for defaulting agents
Fonds Commun de Placement	unit trusts
fonds de commerce	business plus goodwill
fonds de roulement	capital supplied by all flat-owners, in an apartment block, on top of service charges to meet unexpected liabilities
forfait	fixed amount
fosse septique	septic tank
foyer	fireplace
frais de dossier	arrangement fee
frais de notaire	notary's fee
franchisé	franchisee
franchiseur	franchisor
garantie d'achèvement	guarantee of completion
garde-corps	railings
gardien	caretaker
gazon	turf
géomètre	surveyor appointed by the *notaire* to certify the dimensions of the property according to the *cadastre*.
Gendarmerie Nationale	police
gérant	legal manager
gond	shutter hinge pin

gouttière	gutter
grange	barn
gravier	gravel
Greffe du Tribunal de Commerce	clerk of the commercial court
grenier	attic
guichet	counter, ticket office
haie	hedge
honoraires libres	any amount above the recommended social security fee
HT – hors-taxe	not including sales tax
huissier	has many official duties, including bailiff and process server; is used to record evidence (for example on the state of property) where legal proceedings are considered
hypothèque	mortgage – where the property is used as security for the loan
indemnité d'éviction	compensation for eviction
indivision	joint-ownership
interrupteur	switch
impôt foncier	land tax
isolation	insulation
jardin	garden
joint	grouting
jouissance	right of possession which must occur simultaneously with the transfer of ownership
laiton	brass
lambris	grooved wood panelling
lavabo	wash basin
laverie	laundry
lettre de change	bill of exchange
lettre de non-gage	letter showing there are no outstanding debts attached.
liège	cork
lime	file
lingerie	washing room/airing cupboard
linteau	lintel
lisse	smooth
livraison	delivery
livret A, B jeune or CODEVI	savings accounts
location	renting (tenancy)
logement	accommodation
loi Carrez	law by which property measurement are certified
loi Scrivener	the law protecting borrowers from French lenders and sellers on French property purchases in all cases other than a purchase on plan
longueur	length

loquet/loqueteau	door catch
lotissement	housing estate
lots	land registry plots applied in appartment blocks
maçon	builder
mairie	town hall
maison de campagne	country house
maison de maître	gentleman's house
maison mère	parent company
mandat	power of attorney, proxy
mandat de recherche	private agreement giving power to estate agent to look for property
manoir	manor house
marchand de biens	real estate dealer
marquise	porch
mas	farmhouse
mazout	heating oil (domestic use)
médecines douces	alternative medicine
médecin généraliste	GP
médecin spécialiste	specialist
menuiserie	woodwork factory
meubles	furniture
meuleuse	angle grindstone, millstone
minuteur	time switch
monuments historiques	listed buildings
moquette	fitted carpet
mortier	mortar
moulure	moulding
mur	wall
mutuelle (complémentaire santé)	top-up health cover
niveau	level
notaire	notary
notaire public	notary public
nue-propriété	reversionary interest where the purchaser has no occupational rights over the property until the death or prior surrender of the life tenant
occupation	occupant of the premises (either tenant or occupant without good title)
offre d'achat/de vente	an offer to buy or sell property which is not itself a binding contract
ordonnance	prescription
Organismes de Placement de Capital en Valeurs Mobilières	unit trusts
pacte civil de solidarité (PACS)	tax application to non-marital relationships
paillasson	door mat
paiement comptant	cash payment
paiement de notes de frais	benefit in kind

papier peint	wall paper
parc	park
parquet	wood floor
parties communes	common parts of buildings
participation aux résultants	profit sharing
parties privatives	parts of the building restricted to the private use of the owner
peinture	paint
pelle	shovel
pelouse	lawn
permis de construire	planning permission
pépinière	garden centre
perceuse	drill
pharmacie de garde	chemist on duty
pièce	room
pierre	stone
pilier	pillar
pin	pine
pinceau	paint brush
pince universelle	pliers
piquet de terre	earthing pin
piscine	swimming pool
placard	cabinet
plafond	ceiling
plain pied	single storey
planche	plank
plan de financement	financing scheme
plan d'occupation des sols	zoning document
plâtre	plaster
plomberie	plumbing
plus-value	capital gain realized on the sale of the property
poignée	handle
portail	garden gate
porte coulissante	sliding door
potager	kitchen garden
poteau	post
poussière	dust
poutre	wooden beam
poutre apparente	exposed beam
poutrelle	girder, RSJ
Préfecture de Police	police headquarters
prélèvement	direct debit
prieuré	priory
prime à l'aménagement du territoire	regional selective assistance
prime de frais d'installation	settling in funds
prise	electric socket
prise de terre	earthing socket
privilège de prêteur de deniers	mortgage
prolongateur	extension lead

propriétaire	owner
propriété	property
promesse de vente	unilateral agreement to sell
promoteur immobilier	property developer
quincaillerie	hardware shop
quotient familial	family quota (insurance)
rage	rabies
ramoneur	chimney sweep
rangements	storage space
refait	restored
redevance TV	TV licence
registre du commerce et des sociétés	registrar of companies
rejeter	to bounce a cheque
règlement national d'urbanisme	national town planning rules
rénové	renovated
relevé d'identité bancaire (RIB)	bank account details
répertoire des métiers	register of trade
réservation	the deposit paid in a *contrat de réservation*
réservation, contrat de	type of contract for the purchase of property *état de achèvement futur*
réservoir	cistern
résiliation	cancellation of a contract
responsabilité civile	public liability cover
restauré	renovated
retraite	retirement
revenu minimum d'insertion	income support
revêtement	surface
rez-de-chaussée	ground floor
robinet	tap
roche	rock
sable	sand
SAFER	local government organization supposed to ensure the proper use of agricultural land, sometimes they will hold pre-emptive rights to buy land
salle de bains	bathroom
salle de séjour	living room
salon	drawing room
Sapeurs-Pompiers	fire brigade
SAMU (Service d'Aide Medicale d'Urgence)	emergency medical service
scie	saw
seau	bucket
sécurité sociale	social security
séjour	living room
serre joint	clamp

Service Mobile d'Urgence et de Réanimation	emergency medical unit
société	legally registered company
société à responsabilité limitée (SARL)	limited liability company
société anonyme (SA)	company with limited shares
société civile (SC)	non-trading company
société civile immobilière	non-trading property company
société commerciale	commercial company
Société d'Investissement à Capital Variable	unit trust
société de fait	de facto company
société en commandite (SEC)	joint stock company
société en nom collectif (SNC)	general partnership company
sol	ground
sous couche	under-coat
sous seing privé	non registered deed
sous-sol	underground, basement
store	roller blind
store vénitien	Venetian blinds
surface commerciale	commercial premises
syndicat de copropriétaires	assembly of co-owners
tacite reconduction	automatic renewal (of a contract)
tantième	proportion of of the common parts of a *copropriété* owned jointly with other *appartement* owners
tartre	lime deposit
taxe d'habitation	rate levied on the occupation of property
taxe foncière	local tax on the ownership of property
taxe nationale	state tax
taxe professionnelle	business licence fee
teck	teak
terrain	grounds
terre cuite	terracotta
testament	will
timbre fiscal	Revenue stamp
toit	roof
toiture	roofing
tontine	joint ownership
titre de propriété	title deeds
tournevis	screwdriver
tout à l'égout	main drainage system
tribunal de commerce	commercial court
tribunal administratif	civil service court
troisième âge	senior citizens (old age pensioners)
tronçonneuse	chain saw
truelle	trowel
TTC – toutes taxes comprises	including sales tax
tuile	roof tile

tuile à canal	roman tile (curved)
tuile de rive	edge tile
TVA – taxe sur la valeur ajoutée	value added tax (VAT)
urgences	emergency units
usufruit	usufruct (right to use an asset)
vanne	heavy duty tap
variateur	dimmer switch
vente en l'état futur d'achèvement	purchase of an un-built property
verger	orchard
vernis	varnish
vestibule	entrance hall
vignette	fiscal stamp
volet	shutter
vue	view
vitre	window pane
virement bancaire	credit transfer

Internet Vocabulary

adresse électronique	e-mail address
annexe	attachment
arobas	at (@)
deux points	colon (:)
groupe de discussion	newsgroup/discussion group
lien/hyperlien	link
messagerie/courrier électronique	e-mail
mot de passe	password
moteur de recherche	search engine
naviguer/fureter	browse, navigate
navigateur/explorateur	browser
page d'accueil	home page
page web	web page
point (point-com)	dot (dotcom)
rafraîchir	refresh, reload
se loguer	to log on
signet	bookmark
site web/site internet	website
slash	/
télécharger	download
tiret	hyphen
tout en petites lettres/ tout en minuscules	all in lower case
tout attaché/en un seul mot	all in one word
www (trois double-vé)/le web	the World Wide Web

Directory of Contacts

French Consular Services in Britain and Ireland

Consulate General, London

21, Cromwell Road, London SW7 2EN
t 020 7073 1200
f 020 7073 1201
www.ambafrance-uk.org

Consulate General, Edinburgh

21, Randolph Crescent, Edinburgh, EH 3 7TT
t 0131 225 7954
f 0131 225 8975
www.consulfrance-edimbourg.org/

Consular Office of the French Embassy, Dublin

Chancellerie Diplomatique, Consulat, 36 Ailesbury Road, Ballsbridge, Dublin 4
t (00 353) 1 260 1666
f (00 353) 1 283 0178
www.ambafrance-ei.org

British and Irish Consular Services in France

The UK consular service is represented in France by five Consul-Generals with offices at Paris, Lille, Bordeaux, Lyon and Marseilles.

Paris Office

18bis rue d'Anjou, 75008 Paris
t 01 44 51 31 00
f 01 44 51 31 27
Consularemail@pavis.mail.fco.gov.uk
(Postal address: British Embassy, BP111-08, 75363 Paris Cedex 08)

Open to the public Monday, Wednesday, Thursday, Friday 9.30–12.30 and 2.30–5. On Tuesday the Consulate is open 9.30–4.30. (Outside normal working hours a consular emergency service is in operation and a Duty Officer can be contacted on **t** 01 44 51 31 00.)

The British Consulate-General in Paris covers the following *départements:* Aube, Calvados, Cher, Côtes-Du-Nord, Eure, Eure-et-Loir, Finistère, Ille-et-Vilaine, Indre, Indre-et-Loire, Loir-et-Cher, Loire, Loire-Atlantique, Loiret, Maine-et-Loire, Manche (St-Lô), Marne, Haute-Marne, Mayenne, Meurthe-et-Moselle, Meuse, Morbihan, Moselle, Nièvre, Oise, Orne, Bas-Rhin, Haut-Rhin, Sarthe, Paris (Seine), Seine-Maritime, Seine-et-Marne, Yvelines, Vendée, Vosges, Yonne, Essonne, Hauts-de-Seine, Seine-St-Denis, Val de Marne and Val d'Oise.

Lille Office

11 square Dutilleul, 59800 Lille
t 03 20 12 82 72
f 03 20 54 88 16
consular.lille@fco.gov.uk

Open to the public Monday–Friday 9.30–12.30 and 2–5. (Outside normal working hours a consular emergency service is in operation and a Duty Officer can be contacted by telephoning **t** 03 20 54 79 82.)

The British Consulate-General in Lille covers the five northernmost *départements:* Nord, Pas-de-Calais, Somme, Aisne and Ardennes.

Bordeaux Office

353 boulevard du President Wilson, 33073 Bordeaux cedex
t 05 57 22 21 10
f 05 56 08 33 12
postmaster.bordeaux@fco.gov.uk

Open to the public Monday–Friday 9–12 and 2–5. (Outside normal working hours a consular emergency service is in operation and a Duty Officer can be contacted by telephoning **t** 06 85 06 38 32.)

The British Consulate-General in Bordeaux covers the 20 southwest *départements*: Ariège, Aveyron, Charente, Charente-Maritime, Corrèze, Creuse, Dordogne, Haute-Garonne, Gers, Gironde, Landes, Lot, Lot-et-Garonne, Pyrénées-Atlantiques, Hautes-Pyrénées, Deux-Sèvres, Tarn, Tarn-et-Garonne, Vienne and Haute-Vienne.

Lyon Office

24 rue Childebert, 69002 Lyon
t 04 72 77 81 70
f 04 72 77 81 79
britishconsulate.mail@ordilyon.fr

Open to the public Monday–Friday 9–12.30 and 2–5.30. (Outside normal working hours a consular emergency service is in operation and a Duty Officer can be contacted by telephoning **t** 04 72 77 81 78.)

The British Consulate-General in Lyon covers the Auvergne, Bourgogne, Franche-Comté and Rhône-Alpes regions.

Marseille Office

24 avenue du Prado, 13006 Marseille
t 04 91 15 72 10
f 04 91 37 47 06
MarseilleConsular.marseille@fco.gov.uk

Open to the public Monday–Friday 9–12 and 2–5. (Outside normal working hours a consular emergency service is in operation and a Duty Officer can be contacted by telephoning **t** 04 91 15 72 10.)

The British Consulate-General in Marseille covers the following *départements* in the southern part of FrancePyrenées-Orientales, Aude, Hérault, Lozère, Gard, Vaucluse, Bouches-du-Rhône, Var, Alpes-Maritimes, Hautes-Alpes, Alpes-de-Haut-Provence, Corsica and Monaco.

Irish Embassy

Embassy of Ireland, 12 Avenue Foch, 75116 Paris
t 01 44 17 67 00
f 01 44 17 67 60

Other Useful Addresses

Estate Agents

Accord Immobilier, specializing in Languedoc-Roussillon;
www.accord-immobilier.com; **t** (00 33) 4 68 11 96 96.

Agence Hamilton, specialists in Languedoc and Midi-Pyrenees;
www.agence-hamilton.com; **t** (00 33) 4 68 72 48 38.

Agence Immobilier Guy Laffitte, concentrating on the southwest;
www.glaffit@club-internet.fr; **t** (00 33) 5 62 09 83 88.

Agneau Immobilier, for Normandy and Brittany;
www.agneau-immobilier.com; **t** (00 33) 2 33 05 55 25.

Alpine Apartment Agency, for the French Alps and lakesides;
www.alpsapartmentagency.com; **t** 01544 388234.

A Place in France, consultants specializing in new building;
www.aplaceinfrance.co.uk; **t** 023 9283 2949.

Azur Assistance, specialist agents in Provence-Côte-d'Azur;
uk@azurassistance.com; **t** 020 8671 9293.

Beaches International Property, specializing in the French Alps;
www.beaches.int.co.uk; **t** 01562 885181.

Bouichou *notaire* offering properties in the southwest;
Bouchiou-rey@notaires.fr; **t** (00 33) 5 59 68 10 16.

Burgundy 4 u, agents offering properties in south Burgundy;
www.burgundy4u.com; **t** (00 33) 385 98 96 24.

Cabinet Jammes, specializing in Aude;
www.cabinet-jammes.com; **t** (00 33) 6 75 64 24 67.

Century 21, featuring properties in the southwest;
www.century21france.fr; **t** (00 33) 5 53 35 67 67.

Charente Homes, centred on Charente;
www.french-property-news.com/charentehomes/htm; **t** (00 33) 5 45 89 12 09.

Charente Property Services, specializing in Poitou-Charentes; **www.charenteproperty.co.uk**; **t** (00 33) 5 45 85 49 93.

Christopher Kay, for southern and central Charente-Maritime; **www.kaydreamhomes.com.fr**; **t** (00 33) 6 81 74 98 46.

Coastal and Country Properties, concentrating on Brittany; **www.movetofrance.co.uk**; **t** 01273 606828.

Dordogne & Lot Properties, featuring the Dordogne and Lot in the southwest; **www.dorlotproperties.net**; **t** 01865 558659.

Duval Immobilier, specialists in Provence; **www.duvalagents.com**; **t** (00 33) 4 90 65 03 07.

EJC French Properties solicitor and estate agent in Provence; **www.ejcfrenchproperty.com**; **t** (00 33) 4 94 99 72 00.

Fourways French Properties, properties all over France; **t** 01297 489366.

France Limousin Immobilier, a network of agents in Limousin; **www.franceimo.com**

Francofiles Ltd., wide-ranging agents; **www.francofiles.co.uk**; **t** 01622 688165.

French Discoveries, for Normandy, Brittany and Charente; **www.french-discoveries.com**; **t** 0121 449 1155.

French Property Pages, database of properties; **www.frenchpropertypages.com**

Guegan Immobilier, French-registered agent specializing in the northwest; **www.brittany-property.com**; **t** (00 33) 2 96 33 29 30.

Hexagone France Ltd., specialists in northern France; **www.hexagonefrance.com**; **t** 01303 221077.

Homefinder for Limousin, Indre and Paris; **www.homefinderfrance.com**; **t** (00 33) 5 55 71 07 91.

Immorama Aquitaine, experts in the southwest, based near Bergerac; **www.green-acre.com/immorama**; **t** (00 33) 5 53 61 91 89.

Jacwood Estate, centred on the southwest; jacwood@compuserve.com; **t** 01926 883714

L'Affaire Francaise, French-registered English estate agent for the southwest; **www.French-Property-Net.com**; **t** 020 8570 9844.

La Foncière Charantaise, property throughout Poitou-Charentes; **www.french-property-news.com/lfcprofile.htm**; **t** (00 33) 54521 78 38.

La Forêt Immobilier, two coastal agencies in Brittany, and over 350 throughout France; **www.laforet.com**; **t** (00 33) 2 96 46 29 29.

La Maison de Bonheur, property consultants in Gers; **www.maisondebonheur-gers.com**; **t** (00 33) 5 62 62 54 06.

Lamalou Immobilier specialist around Bezier; **www.lamalou-immobiler.fr**; **t** (00 33) 4 67 95 62 89.

La Manche Immobilier, English consultancy based in Normandy; **www.lamanche-immobilier@wanadoo.fr**; **t** (00 33) 2 33 72 05 01.

Latitudes French property agents; **www.latitudes.co.uk**; **t** 020 8951 5155.

Lavender Homes, specialist in the South of France; **www.lavenderfrance.com**; **t** 020 8287 2459.

Leggett Immobilier, specialists in Charente; **www.frenchestateagents.com**; **t** (00 33) 5 53 56 62 57.

Loire Property Services, for property in the Loire Valley; **www.LPSfrance.com**; **t** (00 33) 2 41 40 50 00.

Michéle Paganin, *notaire* offering properties in Brittany; **www.michele-paganin.com**; **t** (00 33) 2 97 51 50 14.

Normandy Immobilier, offering a full range of properties in Normandy; **t** (00 33) 2 32 45 43 83.

North and West France Properties, complete property package offered over a wide area; **www.all-france-properties.com**; **t** 020 8891 1750

Nowac Immobilier, specialists in Poitou-Charentes; **www.nowakimmobilier.fr**; **t** (00 33) 5 49 87 39 85.

Papillon Properties, based in Poitou-Charentes; **www.papillon-properties.com**; **t** (00 33) 5 49 87 45 47

Paris Property Options, permanent and temporary apartments in Paris; **t** 01424 717281.

Paul Clifford & Partners, for the southwest; **www.frenchconnections.co.uk/realestate/trui-seys**; **t** 01874 636969.

Powell & Partner, for Normandy and Mayenne; **t** 01883 730159.

Properties in France, concentrating on the Loire Valley; **www.propertiesinfrance.com**; **t** 0121 744 0820.

Propriétés Roussillon, specializing in the southwest; **www.proprietes-roussillon.com**; **t** 0121 459 9058.

Ricq & Doby Immobilier, for Quercy and Périgord; **www.123immo.com/ricquetdoby46**; **t** (00 33) 5 65 41 02 02.

Sarl Agence Globe Immo, properties in southwest France; **www.tcproperties.com**; **t** (00 33) 5 63 76 48 19.

Select Properties, concentrating on the southwest; sp@french-houses.demon.co.uk; **t** 01296 707045.

Sifex, specializing in the south; **www.sifex.co.uk**; **t** 020 7384 1200.

Sinclair Overseas Property Network, associate agencies in most western regions; **www.sinclair-frenchprops.com**; **t** 01525 375319.

SINB, Normandy and Brittany specialists; sinb@wanadoo.fr; **t** (00 33) 2 33 58 04 77.

Sovimo Immobilier, specializing in Poitou-Charente; **www.immobiliersovimo.com**; **t** (00 33) 5 45 85 45 65.

Tarn Properties, featuring Languedoc, sale or rent; **www.tarnproperties.co.uk**; **t** (00 33) 6 12 33 32 37.

The French Property Shop centred on southwest France; **www.frenchpropertyshop.com**; **t** 01233 66902.

Vialex International, specializing in the southwest; **www.vialex.com**; **t** (00 33) 5 53 95 46 24.

Waterside Properties International specialists in waterside properties; **www.watersideproperties-int.co.uk**; **t** 01892 750011.

Removal Firms

Anglo French Removals, Maidstone, Kent; **www.anglofrench.co.uk**; **t** 01622 729911.

Armishaws; **t** 01963 34065.

Bishop's Move Group, branches nationwide; **www.bishopsmove.co**; **t** 0800 616425.

Britannia, Wolverhampton; **t** 01902 454141.

Burke Brothers, Wolverhampton; **www.burkebros.co.uk**; **t** 0800 413256.

Cotswold Carriers, Chipping Norton, Oxon; **www.cotswoldcarriers.co.uk**; **t** 01608 730500.

David Dale Removals, Harrogate; **t** 01423 324948.

French Moves, France and UK; **t** 01932 881634.

Greens of East Anglia, Stowmarket; **cp.greensremovals@virgin.net**; **t** 01473 215532.

Handle With Care, Walton-on-Thames; **t** 0800 132 146.

H. Appleyard & Sons, Rotherham, Yorkshire; **t** 01709 549718.

Metro Removals, Kettering, Northants; **t** 01536 519450.

Reflex Move, Old Sarum, Salisbury; **www.reflexmove.com**; **t** 01722 414350.

Richman-Ring Ltd., Sittingbourne, Kent; **www.richman-ring.com**; **t** 01795 427151.

Simpson's of Sussex; **t** 0800 027 1958.

The Old House; **www.amsmoving.co.uk**; **t** 0800 243941.

Tooth Removals, Bedfont, Middlesex; **t** 01784 251252.

White & Co., branches nationwide; **t** 01252 541674

Other Services

Building/Advice

Adrian Barrett; **www.adrian-barrett.co.uk**; **t** 01722 333583

Maisons SIC; **www.thefrenchdream.co.uk**; **t** 01248 689066.

Financial

Anthony & Cie; **www.antco.com**; **t** 00 33 4 93 65 32 23.

Charles Hamer; **www.charleshamer.com**; **t** 01844 261886.

Credit Agricole Britline; **www.britline.com**; **t** 00 33 2 31 55 67 89.

Currencies4less.com; **www.currencies4less.com**; **t** 020 7228 7667.

French Mortgage Advice; **www.french-mortgage-connection.co.uk**; **t** 0800 0745388.

Michael Hackney; nh@hackneym.fsnet.co.uk; **t** 01869 277314.

Moneycorp; **www.moneycorp.co.uk**; **t** 020 7823 7800.

Siddalls; **investment@johnsiddalls.co.uk**; **t** 01329 288641.

Help and Support

Abbott Management; **www.ampmfrance.com**; **t** 020 7225 1995.

Auvergne sur Mésure; **www.auvergnesurmesure@yahoo.co.uk**; **t** 01962 864318.

Live France Group; **www.livefrancegroup.com**; **t** (00 33) 4 68 45 69 19.

Purple Pages; **www.purplepages.info**; **t** (00 33) 5 45 29 59 74.

The Owner Groups Company Ltd.; **www.ownergroups.com**; **t** 01628 486360.

Insurance

Thierry Marcq; marcqt@agents.agf.fr; **t** 00 33 321 96 77 77.

Continent Assurances; **t** 00 33 297 47 31 97.

Legal

Anthony Wilkin; twilkinfrenchproperty@btopenworld.com; **t** 01373 824979.

Bennett & Co.; **www.Bennett-and-co.com**; **t** 01625 586937.

Blake Lapthorn; **www.blakelapthorn.co.uk**; **t** 020 7430 1709.

Fox Hayse; **grahamplatt@foxhayse.co.uk**; **t** 0113 209 8922.

Fralex; **t** 020 7323 0103.

Pannone & Partners; **www.pannone.com**; **t** 0161 909 300.

Riddell Croft & Co.; **sue.busby@riddellcroft.com**; **t** 01473 784870.

Sean O'Connor & Co.; seanoconnor@aol.com; **t** 01732 365378.

Public Holidays and Festivals

There are thousands of festivals each year in France, celebrating every conceivable sort of sport, art and food. To list then would take a book of its own but happily technology has come to our aid in the form of the French Tourist Office website (**www.franceguide.com**) where you can find details of everything from truffle fairs to film festivals. Here is a selection to give you a taste of what's on offer. Public holidays are shown at the start of each month, in italics.

January

New Year's Day (nouvel an/Jour de l'An)
1 January

Monte-Carlo Car Rally
This classic winter race takes place in January.
t 01 42 96 12 23
f 01 42 61 31 52
www.monaco-congres.com
dtcparis@monaco-congres.com

25th Monte-Carlo International Circus Festival
The largest circus festival in the world.
End of January, Monaco.
t 01 42 96 12 23
f 01 42 61 31 52
www.monaco-congres.com
dtcparis@monaco-congres.com

International Snow Sculpture Competition
January, Valloire (Savoie)
t 04 79 59 03 96
f 04 79 59 09 66
www.valloire.net
valloire@laposte.fr

February

International Festival of Short Films
End January/start February, Clermont-Ferrand (Puy-de-Dôme)
t 04 73 91 65 73
f 04 73 92 11 93
www.clermont-filmfest.com
info@clermont-filmfest.com

Fête de la Saint-Blaise, du raisin et des produits du terroir
Festival of Saint Blaise, of the grape, local products and traditional arts and crafts.
End January/start February, Valbonne/Sophia-Antipolis (Alpes-Maritimes)
t 04 93 12 34 50
f 04 93 12 34 57
www.alpes-azur.com/vsa
vsa@alpes-azur.com

Traversée du Vercors à ski de fond
The oldest cross country ski event, in the largest natural reserve in France.
Villard de Lans (Isère)
t 04 76 95 50 10
f 04 76 94 91 90
www.ot-villard-de-lans.fr
info@ot-villard-de-lans.fr

March

Easter Sunday and Monday (Pacques)
March–April

International Carnival
One of the biggest carnivals in France.
Mulhouse (Haut-Rhin)
t 03 89 35 48 48
f 03 89 45 66 16
www.ot.ville-mulhouse.fr
ot@ville-mulhouse.fr

Transalpine Dog Team Racing Championship
International dog sled race with over 50 entries.
Mid-March, Bessans (Savoie)
t 04 79 05 91 57
f 04 79 05 80 96
www.hautemaurienne.com
info@hautemaurienne.com

Pierramenta-Tivoly
International Downhill ski race and show.
Arèches-Beaufort (Savoie)
t 04 79 38 15 33
f 04 79 38 16 70
www.areches-beaufort.com
otareches-beaufort@wanadoo.fr

Grenoble Jazz Festival
More than 50 concerts in Grenoble and Isère, almost 30 of them free of charge.
Grenoble (Isère)
t 04 76 51 65 32
f 04 76 44 81 83
www.jazzgrenoble.com
contact@jazzgrenoble.com

International Festival of Sacred Music
In the basilica of Rosaire, the Romanesque abbey of Saint-Savin and in Tarbes cathedral.
Lourdes (Hautes-Pyrénées)
t 05 62 42 77 40
f 05 62 94 60 95

Paris–Nice Cycle Rally
A classic cycle race.
Ends at Nice (Alpes-Maritimes)
t 04 92 14 48 00
f 04 93 92 82 98
www.nicetourism.com
info@nicetourism.com

April

Easter Sunday and Monday (Pacques)
March–April

La Sanch Procession
Religious festival with procession of the *caperutxes* on Good Friday night.
Perpignan (Pyrénées-Orientales)
t 04 68 66 30 30
f 04 68 66 30 26
www.little-france.com/perpignan
contact-office@little-france.com

Daffodil Fair
An annual event draws 70,000 people to see floats made up of three million daffodils.
Gérardmer (Vosges)
t 03 29 27 27 27
f 03 29 27 23 25
www.societe-des-fetes-gerardmer.org
contact@societe-des-fetes-gerardmer.org

Laughing Spring
Established names and young hopefuls, café-theatre pros and magicians – Toulouse transforms itself into the comedy capital.
End March/early April, Toulouse (Haute-Garonne)
t 05 62 21 23 24
f 05 61 59 63 66
www.printemps-du-rire.com
printempsdurire@libertysurf.fr

Monte-Carlo Spring Arts Festival
Ballet, outstanding concerts and recitals by some of the greatest international soloists.
April–May, Monaco (Alpes-Maritimes)
t 01 42 96 12 23
f 01 42 61 31 52
www.monaco-congres.com
dtcparis@monaco-congres.com

Grand Music Show
International classical music show.
Paris-Grande Halle de la Villette (Seine)
t 01 49 53 27 00
f 01 49 53 27 04
www.salondelamusique.com
musiques@secession.fr

May

Labour Day (Fête du Travail)
1 May

Liberation/Victory Day 1945 (Libération /Victoire)
8 May

Ascension Day (Ascension)
Sixth Thursday after Easter

Pentecost (Pentecôte)
Second Monday after Ascension (so sometimes June)

Chocolate Days
Tradition has it that Jews fleeing Spain took refuge in Bayonne, bringing their expertise in chocolate-making with them.
End May/early June, Bayonne (Pyrénées-Atlantiques)
t 05 59 46 01 46
f 05 59 59 37 55
bayonne.tourisme@wanadoo.fr

International Film Festival
The Cannes Film Festival calls itself the biggest film festival in the world and the largest media event after the Olympic games.
Cannes (Alpes-Maritimes)
t 01 45 61 66 00
f 01 45 61 97 60
www.festival-cannes.fr
festival@festival-cannes.fr

Formula 1 Grand Prix
End May/early June, Monaco (Alpes-Maritimes)
t 01 42 96 12 23
f 01 42 61 31 52
www.monaco-congres.com
dtcparis@monaco-congres.com

French Tennis International
End May/early June 2002, Paris-Stade Roland Garros (Seine)
t 01 47 43 48 00
f 01 47 43 41 55
www.fft.fr

Wine and Fine Food Festival
Local produce from all over France; admission free.
Plombières (Vosges)
t 03 29 66 00 22
f03 29 66 09 09

June

One Summer in Bourges
Classical music, jazz and world music in various venues and historic buildings in the town, every evening.
Mid-June–mid-September, Bourges (Cher)
t 02 48 23 02 60
f 02 48 23 02 69
www.ville-bourges.fr
tourisme@ville-bourges.fr

International Show-Jumping
Cannes (Alpes-Maritimes)
t 04 93 39 24 53
f 04 92 99 84 23
www.cannes-on-line.com
semoftou@palais-festivals-cannes.fr

International Gardens Festival
30 extraordinary gardens created by landscape gardeners from all over the world
Mid-June–mid-October, Chaumont-sur-Loire (Loir- et -Cher)
t 02 54 20 99 22
f 02 54 20 99 24

International Aeronautics and Space Show
Le Bourget-Parc des Expositions (Seine-Saint-Denis)
t 01 53 23 33 33
www.salon.du.bourget.fr
siae@salon.du.bourget.fr

July

Bastille Day (Fête National)
14 July

International Song Festival – European Academy of Music
A thousand years of music from every land and culture, from sacred Tibetan chants to Bach's St Matthew Passion.
Aix-en-Provence (Bouches-du-Rhône)
t 04 42 17 34 34
f 04 42 63 13 74
www.festival-aix.com

Operetta Festival
Weekends, Aix-les-Bains (Savoie)
t 04 79 88 68 00
f 04 79 88 68 01
www.aixlesbains.com
accueil@aixlesbains.com

International Folk Festival
Mid-July, Alençon (Orne)
t 02 33 80 66 33
f 02 33 80 66 32
www.ville-alencon.fr
alencon.tourisme@wanadoo.fr

Arles Festival
End June/early July, Arles (Bouches-du-Rhône)
t 04 90 18 41 20
f 04 90 93 17 17
www.arles.org
ot.accueil@arles.org

Avignon Festival
Dance, music and drama
Avignon (Vaucluse)
t 04 90 27 66 50
f 04 90 27 66 83
www.festival-avignon.com

August

Assumption (Fête de l'Assomption)
15 August

Garden Fever
In the streets and at the foot of the château, modern jazz, drama and visual arts.
Early August, Assier (Lot)
t 05 65 40 50 60
f 05 65 40 41 99

Classical Music at the Heart of Tapestry
The marriage of live music and heritage.
End July/early August, Aubusson (Creuse)
t 05 55 66 32 12
f 05 55 66 12 20

September

Round the Ramparts
Vintage car parade and race.
Mid-September, Angoulême (Charente)
t 05 45 94 95 67
f 05 45 94 95 66
www.psb-organisation.com
psbo@psb-organisation.com

Besançon – Franche-Comté International Music Festival
Classical music in Besançon and throughout the area.
Two weekends in September, Besançon (Doubs)
t 03 81 25 05 85
f 03 81 81 52 15
www.festival-besancon.com
contact@festival-besancon.com

Great Vintages of Burgundy Festival
Festival split between five locations – Noyers-sur-Serein, Meursault, Chablis, Cluny, Gevrey-Chambertin.
June–September, Burgundy (Côte-d'Or)

World Puppet Theatre Festival
The biggest of its kind in the world.
Charleville-Mézières (Ardennes)
t 03 24 59 94 94
f 03 24 33 72 50
www.marionnette.com
festival@marionnette.com

October

Les Oralies de Haut Provence
A storytellers' convention in 20 *communes*.
(Alpes-de-Haut-Provence)
t 04 92 74 85 55

Bastia Concert Season
From baroque to world music.
Mid-October, Bastia (Haute-Corse)
t 04 95 32 75 91

Witches' Festival
Hallowe'en market at Cognelot fort.
Chalindrey (Haute-Marne)
t 03 25 88 82 03

Tour de Corse Car Rally – Rallye de France
French leg of the Rally World Championship.
Northern Corsica (Haute-Corse)
t 04 95 23 62 60
f 04 95 20 47 85

November

All Saints' Day (Toussaint)
1 November

Armistice Day (Fête de L'Armistice)
11 November

International and Fine Food Fair
Dijon (Côte-d'Or)
t 03 80 77 39 00
f 03 80 77 39 39
www.dijon-expocongres.com
contact@dijon-expocongres.com

Book Fair
The leading literary event of the provinces. Many literary prizes are awarded here.
Brive-la-Gaillarde (Corrèze)
t 05 55 92 39 39
f 05 55 24 57 22

D'jazz
International festival.
Mid-November, Nevers (Nièvre)
t 03 86 57 88 51
f 03 86 57 93 05
www.neversdjazz.com
djazz@wanadoo.fr

December

Christmas Day (Noël)
25 December

Christmas Lights and Market
Craft markets, street theatre, exhibitions and fairy lights with more than 65,000 bulbs in this town with a strong German tradition.
To 24th December, Montbéliard (Doubs)
t 03 81 94 45 60
f 03 81 94 14 04
www.agglo-montbeliard.fr/tourisme
office.de.tourisme.montbeliard@wanadoo.fr

Christmas Crib Figure-makers' Show
Apt (Vaucluse)
t 04 90 74 03 18
f 04 90 04 64 30

Festival of Snow, Ice and Adventure Film
Early December, Autrans (Isère)
t 04 76 95 30 70
f 04 76 95 38 63
www.ot-autrans.fr
info@ot-autrans.fr

Christmas Carol Festival
Carols and Christmas market at Brissac château.
Brissac (Maine-et-Loire)
t 04 76 95 30 70
f 04 76 95 38 63
www.ot-autrans.fr
info@ot-autrans.fr

Saint-Nicolas Festival
Procession of floats in the old town, handing over of the keys of the town to Saint Nicholas by the mayor in Place Stanislas, fireworks.
1 December, Nancy (Meurthe-et-Moselle)
t 03 83 35 22 41
f 03 83 95 90 10
www.ot-nancy.fr
tourisme@ot-nancy.fr

Old Lyon Music Festival
Lyon (Rhône)
t 04 78 38 09 09
f 04 78 38 72 62
la.chapelle@wanadoo.fr

Mass and Nativity Play
24 December, Châteauneuf-en-Auxois (Côte-d'Or)
t 03 80 49 21 59
f 03 80 49 21 64

Further Reading

Make Yourself at Home in France (Chambre de Commerce Française de Grande-Bretagne)
Live & Work in France (Vacation Work)
Alistair Sawday's French Bed & Breakfast, Ann Cooke-Yarborough and Emma Carey (Alistair Sawday Publishing)
Alistair Sawday's French Holiday Homes, Clare Hargreaves (Alistair Sawday Publishing)
Buying and Restoring Old Property in France, David Everett (Robert Hale)
Buying and Renovating Property in France, J Kater Pollock
Letting French Property Successfully, Stephen Smith and Charles Parkinson (Pannell Kerr Forster)
Savoir Flair! Polly Platt (Culture Crossings Limited)
French or Foe? Polly Platt (Culture Crossings Limited)
Selling French Dreams, Alan Biggins (Kirkdale Books)

Buying a Home in France, David Hampshire (Survival Books)
French Law for Property Buyers, Kerry Schrader (French Property News Limited)
Taxation in France, Charles Parkinson (Pannell Kerr Forster, published annually)
The Alien's Guide to France, Jim Watson (Survival Books)
French Letters, George East (La Puce Publications)
René & Me, George East (La Puce Publications)

Climate Chart

Average Monthly Temperatures, °Centigrade (daily maximum and minimum), and Rainfall (monthly mm)

(*Source: USA Today/US Met Office*)

	Jan	Feb	Mar	Apr	May	June	July	Aug	Sept	Oct	Nov	Dec
Le Havre												
max	6	6	8	10	13	16	18	19	17	14	9	7
min	4	3	6	7	11	13	16	16	14	11	7	5
rainfall	14	10	12	11	11	9	9	9	11	12	12	13
Carcassonne												
Max	9	11	14	16	19	24	28	28	24	18	13	10
Min	2	3	4	6	10	13	15	15	12	9	5	3
rainfall	76	64	66	66	71	66	53	58	71	86	89	86
Lyon												
max	6	8	12	14	19	23	27	26	22	16	10	7
min	1	1	3	6	10	14	16	16	12	8	4	2
rainfall	43	41	51	61	76	79	66	79	76	86	69	51
Corsica												
max	13	13	14	17	21	24	27	28	26	22	17	14
min	4	4	6	7	11	14	17	17	15	12	8	5
rainfall	74	64	61	53	41	23	8	15	43	91	102	84
Nice												
max	13	13	14	16	19	23	26	27	24	20	16	13
min	6	6	8	9	13	17	19	20	17	13	9	6
rainfall	76	74	74	64	48	38	18	30	66	112	117	89
Paris												
max	6	7	11	14	18	21	24	24	21	15	9	7
min	1	1	3	6	9	12	14	14	11	8	4	2
rainfall	20	16	18	17	16	14	13	12	14	17	17	19
Strasbourg												
max	4	6	11	14	19	22	24	24	21	14	8	5
min	-1	-1	2	4	9	12	14	13	11	7	2	0
rainfall	36	33	36	46	66	74	76	71	61	51	48	3

Appendices

10

Appendix 1

Checklist – Do-it-yourself Inspection of Property

Task ✓

Title – Check that the property corresponds with its description:
Number of rooms
Plot size

Plot
Identify the physical boundaries of the plot:
Is there any dispute with anyone over these boundaries?
Are there any obvious foreign elements on your plot such as pipes, cables, drainage ditches, water tanks, etc.?
Are there any signs of anyone else having rights over the property – footpaths, access ways, cartridges from hunting, etc.?

Garden/Terrace
Are any plants, ornaments, etc. on site not being sold with the property?

Pool – is there a pool? If so:
What size is it?
Is it clean and algae-free?
Do the pumps work?
How old is the machinery?
Who maintains it?
What is the annual cost of maintenance?
Does it appear to be in good condition?

Walls – stand back from property and inspect from outside
Any signs of subsidence?
Walls vertical?
Any obvious cracks in walls?
Are walls well pointed?
Any obvious damp patches?
Any new repairs to walls or repointing?

Roof – inspect from outside property:
Does roof sag?
Are there missing/slipped tiles?
Do all faces of roof join squarely?
Lead present and in good order?

Guttering and Downpipes – inspect from outside property:
All present?
Securely attached?
Fall of guttering constant?
Any obvious leaks?
Any recent repairs?

Checklist – Do-it-yourself Inspection of Property (*cont.*)

Task ✓

Enter Property

Does it smell of damp?
Does it smell musty?
Does it smell of dry rot?
Any other strange smells?

Doors

Signs of rot?
Close properly – without catching?
Provide proper seal?
Locks work?

Windows

Signs of rot?
Close properly – without catching?
Provide proper seal?
Locks work?
Excessive condensation?

Floor

Can you see it all?
Does it appear in good condition?
Any sign of cracked or rotten boards?

Under floor

Can you get access under the floor?
If so, is it ventilated?
Is there any sign of rot?
How close are joists?
Are joist ends in good condition where they go into walls?
What is maximum unsupported length of joist run?
Is there any sign of damp or standing water?

Roof Void

Is it accessible?
Is there sign of water entry?
Can you see daylight through the roof?
Is there an underlining between the tiles and the void?
Is there any sign of rot in timbers?
Horizontal distance between roof timbers
Size of roof timbers (section)?
Maximum unsupported length of roof timbers
Is roof insulated – if so, what depth and type of insulation?

Checklist – Do-it-yourself Inspection of Property (*cont.*)

Task	✓
Woodwork	
Any sign of rot?	
Any sign of wood-boring insects?	
Is it dry?	
Interior walls	
Any significant cracks?	
Any obvious damp problems?	
Any sign of recent repair/redecoration?	
Electricity	
Check electricity meter:	
How old is it?	
What is its rated capacity?	
Check all visible wiring:	
What type is it?	
Does it appear in good physical condition?	
Check all plugs:	
Is there power to plug?	
Does plug tester show good earth and show 'OK'?	
Are there enough plugs?	
Lighting:	
Do all lights work?	
Which light fittings are included in sale?	
Water	
Do all hot and cold taps work?	
Is flow adequate?	
Do taps drip?	
Is there a security cut-off on all taps between mains and tap?	
Do they seem in good condition?	
Hot water:	
Is hot water 'on'? If so, does it work at all taps, showers, etc.?	
What type of hot water system is fitted?	
Age?	
Gas	
Is the property fitted with city (piped) gas? If so:	
Age of meter?	
Does installation appear in good order?	
Is there any smell of gas?	
Is the property fitted with bottled gas? If so:	
Where are bottles stored?	
Is it ventilated to outside of premises?	

Checklist – Do-it-yourself Inspection of Property (*cont.*)

Task ✓

Central Heating

Is the property fitted with central heating? If so:
- Is it on?
- Will it turn on?
- What type is it?
- Is there heat at all radiators/outlets?
- Do any thermostats appear to work?
- Are there any signs of leaks?

Fireplaces

Is the property fitted with any solid fuel heaters? If so:
- Any sign of blow-back from chimneys?
- Do chimneys (outside) show stains from leakage?
- Do chimneys seem in good order?

Air-conditioning

Which rooms are air-conditioned?
Are units included in the sale?
Do the units work (deliver cold air)?
What type of air-conditioning is it?
How old is it?

Phone

Does it work?
Number?

Satellite TV

Does it work?
Is it included in the sale?

Drainage

What type of drainage does property have?
If septic tank, how old?
Who maintains it?
When was it last maintained?
Any smell of drainage problems in bathrooms and toilets?
Does water drain away rapidly from all sinks, showers and toilets?
Is there any inspection access through which you can see drainage taking place?
Is there any sign of plant ingress to drains?
Do drains appear to be in good condition and well pointed?

Checklist – Do-it-yourself Inspection of Property (*cont.*)

Task ✓

Kitchen

Do all cupboards open/close properly?
Any sign of rot?
Tiling secure and in good order?
Enough plugs?
What appliances are included in sale?
Do they work?
Age of appliances included?

Bathroom

Security and condition of tiling?
Ventilation?

Appliances

What appliances generally are included in sale?
What is *not* included in sale?

Furniture

What furniture is included in sale?
What is *not* included in sale?

Repairs/Improvements/Additions

What repairs have been carried out in last two years?
What improvements have been carried out in last two years/ten years?
What additions have been made to the property in last two years/ten years?
Are there builders' receipts'/guarantees?
Is there building consent/planning permission for any additions or alterations?

Defects

Is seller aware of any defects in the property?

Appendix 2

Checklist – What Are You Worth?

Asset	Value (Local Currency)	Value (£s)
Current Assets		
Main home		
Holiday home		
Contents of main home		
Contents of holiday home		
Car		
Boat		
Bank accounts		
Other cash-type investments		
Bonds, etc.		
Stocks and shares		
PEPs		
Tessas		
ISAs		
SIPS		
Other		
Value of your business		
Value of share options		
Future Assets		
Value of share options		
Personal/company pension – likely lump sum		
Potential inheritances or other accretions		
Value of endowment mortgages on maturity		
Other		

Index

France touring atlas

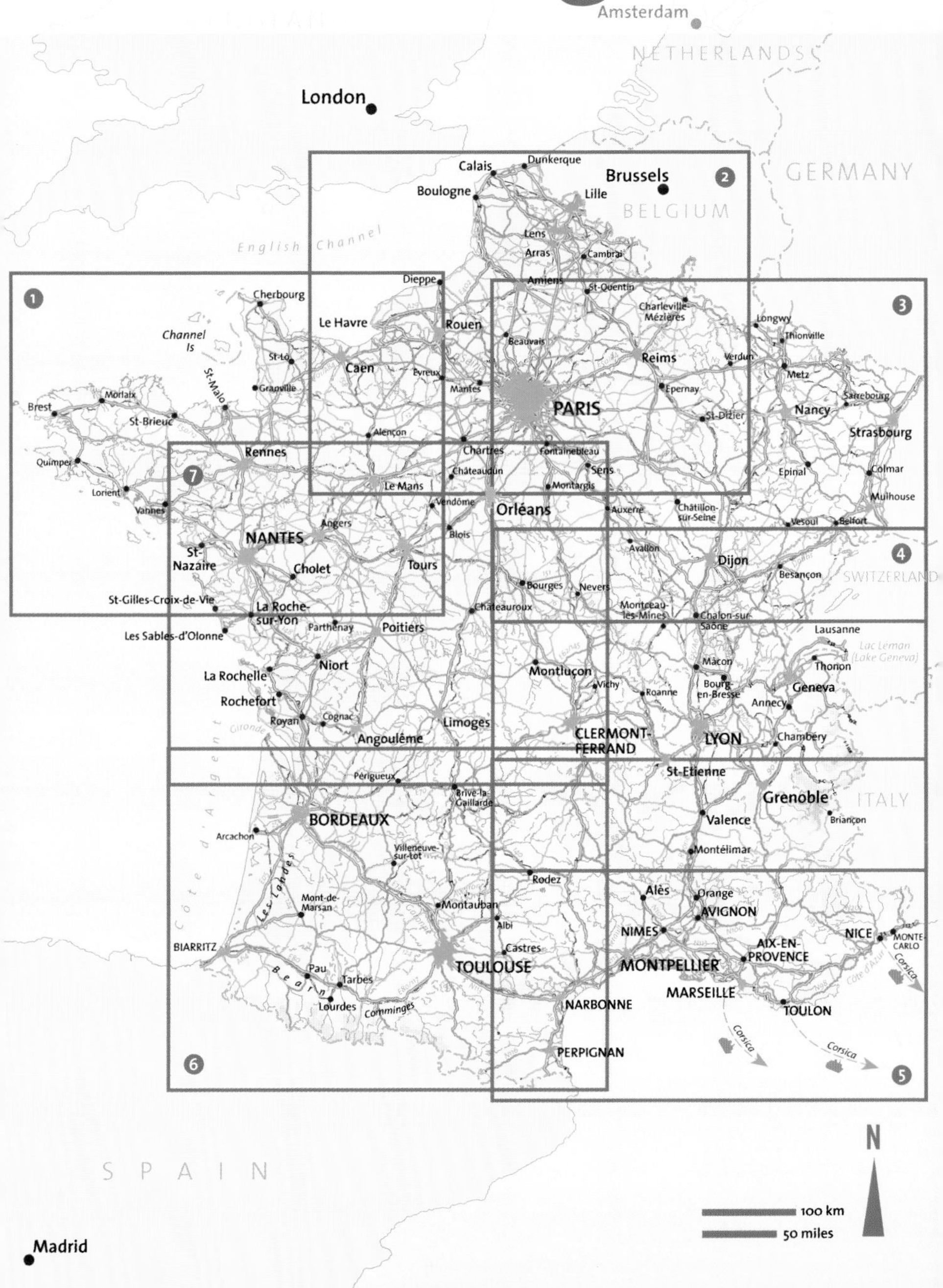

20 km
10 miles
N
Alderney
Guernsey
Sark
Channel Islands
Jersey
Trégastel
Ploumanach
Ile de Bréhat
Perros-Guirec
Pleumeur-Bodou
Pointe de l'Arcouest
Brignogan-Plages
Roscoff
Trébeurden
Lézardrieux
Tréguier
Paimpol
St-Pol-de-Léon
Lannion
Locquirec
l'Aber-Wrach
Plouescat
Carantec
St-Michel-en-G
Pontrieux
Plouha
Lesneven
Morlaix
St-Quay-Portrieux
Le Folgoët
Cap Fréhel
Dinard
St-Malo
Lampoul
St-Thégonnec
Guingamp
Binic
Le Val-André
Erquy
St-Cast
Brest
Landerneau
Guimiliau
Les Rosaires
Pléneuf
Lancieux
St-Briac
Le Conquet
Châtelaudren
St-Jacut
St-Laurent-de-la-Mer
Plancoët
Plougastel-Daoulas
Monts d'Arrée
Callac
Bulat-Pestivien
St-Brieuc
Lamballe
Huelgoat
Quintin
Dinan
Camaret
Le Faou
Brennilis
St-Herbot
Pointe de Penhir
Landévennec
Lannédern
CÔTES-D'ARMOR
Léhon
Morgat
Crozon
FINISTÈRE
Carhaix-Plouguer
Ménez-Hom
Moncontour
Cap de la Chèvre
Pleyben
Châteaulin
Châteauneuf-du-Faou
Mur-de-Bretagne
Douarnenez
Montagnes Noires
Locronan
St-Aignan
Tréboul
Loudéac
Pointe du Raz
Audierne
Quimper
Le Faouët
Kernascléden
Pontivy
Comper
Forêt de Paimpont
Penhors
Plonéour-Lanvern
Fouesnant
Tréhorenteuc
Paimpont
Pont-l'Abbé
Bénodet
Concarneau
Quimperlé
Plélan-le-Grand
St-Guénolé
Loctudy
Pont-Aven
Riec
Quistinic
Josselin
Ploërmel
Pointe de Penmarch
Guilvinec
Moëlan
Blavet
Scorff
MORBIHAN
Hennebont
Pipriac
Lorient
Port-Louis
Ste-Anne-d'Auray
Rochefort-en-Terre
Groix
Ile de Groix
Etel
Erdeven
Auray
Vannes
Redon
Carnac
Locmariaquer
Vilaine
St-Pierre
Quiberon
La Roche-Bernard
Pénestin
Pontchâteau
Houat
Brière
St-Joachim
Guérande
Bréca
Marsh
Ile-de-Fédrun
Hœdic
Le Croisic
St-André-des-Eaux
Belle-Ile
Batz-sur-Mer
St-Nazaire
La Baule
St-Brévin
St-Michel-Chef-Chef
Pornic
Ile de Noirmoutier
Noirmoutier
Fromentine
La Barre-de-Monts
Notre-Dame-de-Mont
Challans
Soullans
St-Jean-de-Monts
Port-Joinville
Ile d'Yeu
St-Hilaire-de-Riez
St-Gilles-Croix-de-Vie
E50
E60/165
E50/12
E401/176
164
787
785
764
769
24
776
775
166
177
772
758
38

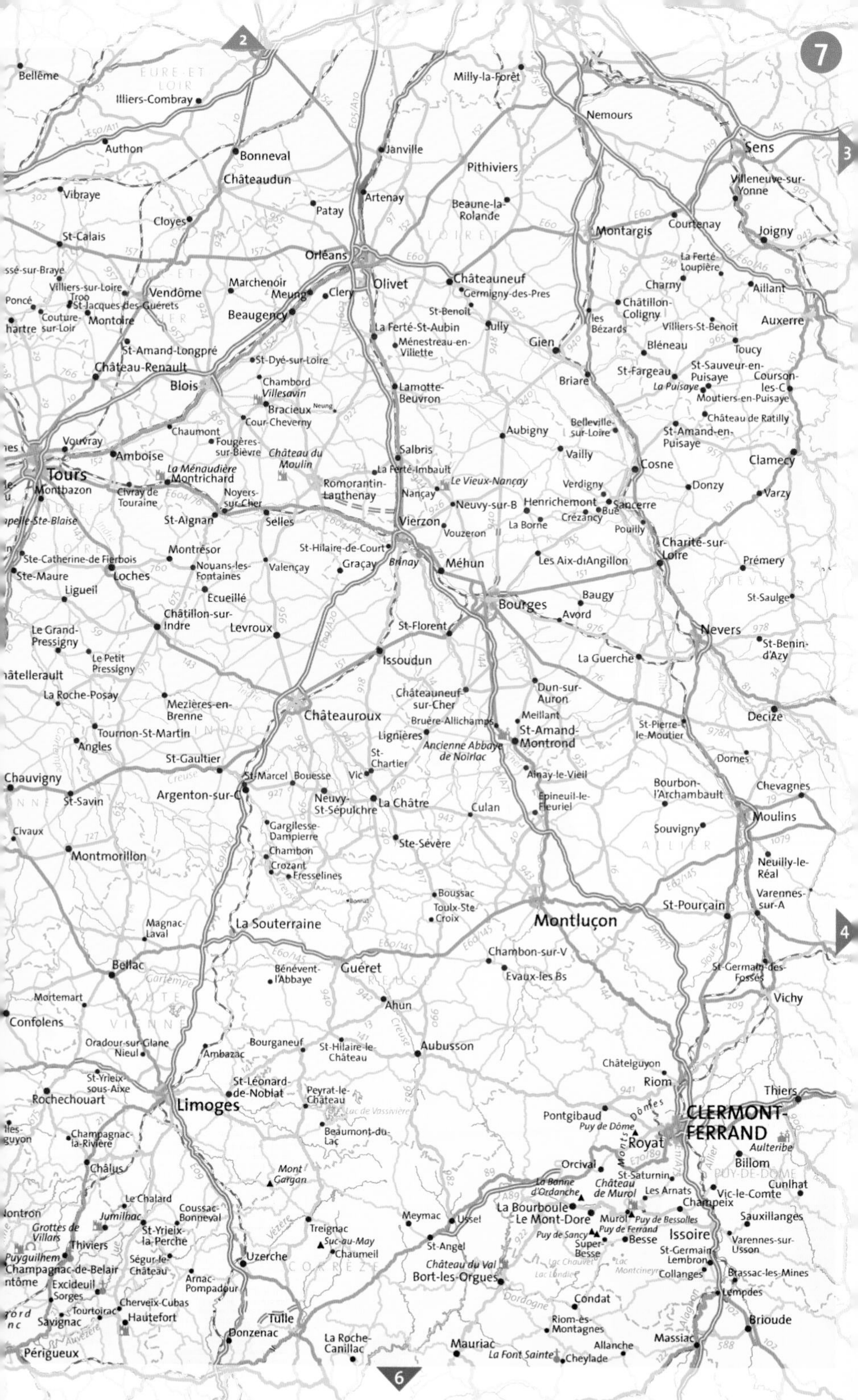
7
2
3
4
6
Bellême
EURE-ET-LOIR
Illiers-Combray
Milly-la-Forêt
Nemours
Sens
Authon
Bonneval
Janville
Pithiviers
Villeneuve-sur-Yonne
Vibraye
Châteaudun
Artenay
Patay
Beaune-la-Rolande
Cloyes
Courtenay
Montargis
Joigny
St-Calais
LOIRET
Orléans
La Ferté-Loupière
Villiers-sur-Loire
Vendôme
Marchenoir
Meung
Cléry
Olivet
Châteauneuf
Germigny-des-Pres
Charny
Aillant
Troo
St-Jacques-des-Guérets
Montoire
Couture-sur-Loir
Beaugency
St-Benoît
Châtillon-Coligny
Auxerre
Sully
La Ferté-St-Aubin
Ménestreau-en-Villette
les Bézards
Villiers-St-Benoît
St-Amand-Longpré
Gien
Bléneau
Toucy
Château-Renault
St-Dyé-sur-Loire
St-Fargeau
La Puisaye
St-Sauveur-en-Puisaye
Courson-les-C
Moutiers-en-Puisaye
Blois
Chambord
Villesavin
Lamotte-Beuvron
Briare
Bracieux
Neung
Cour-Cheverny
Château de Ratilly
Chaumont
Aubigny
Belleville-sur-Loire
St-Amand-en-Puisaye
Vouvray
Fougères-sur-Bièvre
Château du Moulin
Salbris
Vailly
Amboise
La Ménaudière
Montrichard
La Ferté-Imbault
Cosne
Clamecy
Tours
Montbazon
Civray de Touraine
Romorantin-Lanthenay
Le Vieux-Nançay
Nançay
Verdigny
Donzy
Noyers-sur-Cher
Neuvy-sur-B
Henrichemont
Sancerre
Varzy
St-Aignan
Selles
Vierzon
Vouzeron
La Borne
Crézancy
Bué
Pouilly
St-Hilaire-de-Court
Charité-sur-Loire
Montrésor
Les Aix-d'Angillon
Ste-Catherine-de-Fierbois
Nouans-les-Fontaines
Valençay
Graçay
Brinay
Méhun
Prémery
Ste-Maure
Loches
NIÈVRE
Ligueil
Écueillé
St-Saulge
Châtillon-sur-Indre
Baugy
Bourges
Avord
Le Grand-Pressigny
Levroux
St-Florent
Nevers
St-Benin-d'Azy
Le Petit Pressigny
Issoudun
La Guerche
Châtellerault
La Roche-Posay
Mezières-en-Brenne
Châteauneuf-sur-Cher
Dun-sur-Auron
Châteauroux
Meillant
Bruère-Allichamps
St-Pierre-le-Moutier
Decize
Tournon-St-Martin
Lignières
St-Amand-Montrond
Angles
Ancienne Abbaye de Noirlac
St-Gaultier
St-Chartier
Dornes
Chauvigny
St-Marcel
Bouesse
Vic
Ainay-le-Vieil
Bourbon-l'Archambault
Chevagnes
St-Savin
Argenton-sur-C
Neuvy-St-Sépulchre
La Châtre
Culan
Épineuil-le-Fleuriel
Moulins
Civaux
Gargilesse-Dampierre
Souvigny
ALLIER
Chambon
Ste-Sévère
Neuilly-le-Réal
Montmorillon
Crozant
Fresselines
Varennes-sur-A
Boussac
Toulx-Ste-Croix
St-Pourçain
Magnac-Laval
La Souterraine
Montluçon
Chambon-sur-V
Bellac
Bénévent-l'Abbaye
Guéret
Evaux-les Bs
St-Germain-des-Fossés
CREUSE
Mortemart
Ahun
Vichy
Confolens
HAUTE-VIENNE
Oradour-sur-Glane
Nieul
Bourganeuf
St-Hilaire-le-Château
Aubusson
Ambazac
Châtelguyon
Riom
St-Yrieix-sous-Aixe
Thiers
Rochechouart
St-Léonard-de-Noblat
Limoges
Peyrat-le-Château
Lac de Vassivière
Pontgibaud
Puy de Dôme
Monts Dômes
CLERMONT-FERRAND
Royat
Aulteribe
Champagnac-la-Rivière
Beaumont-du-Lac
Billom
Châlus
Mont Gargan
Orcival
St-Saturnin
PUY-DE-DÔME
La Banne d'Ordanche
Château de Murol
Les Arnats
Cunlhat
Le Chalard
Vic-le-Comte
Champeix
Jumilhac
Coussac-Bonneval
Meymac
Ussel
La Bourboule
Le Mont-Dore
Murol
Puy de Bessolles
Sauxillanges
Nontron
Grottes de Villars
St-Yrieix-la-Perche
Treignac
Suc-au-May
Puy de Ferrand
Puy de Sancy
Super-Besse
Besse
Issoire
Thiviers
St-Angel
Varennes-sur-Usson
Puyguilhem
Ségur-le-Château
Uzerche
Chaumeil
Château du Val
Lac Chauvet
Lac Pavin
Montcineyre
St-Germain-Lembron
Champagnac-de-Belair
CORRÈZE
Bort-les-Orgues
Collanges
Brassac-les-Mines
Brantôme
Excideuil
Arnac-Pompadour
Lempdes
Sorges
Tourtoirac
Cherveix-Cubas
Dordogne
Condat
Savignac
Hautefort
Tulle
Riom-ès-Montagnes
Brioude
Périgueux
Donzenac
La Roche-Canillac
Mauriac
La Font Sainte
Allanche
Cheylade
Massiac

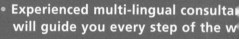